The John Nix

Farm Management Pocketbook

THIRTY-NINTH EDITION
(2009)

SEPTEMBER 2008

Copies of this book may be obtained from:

The Pocketbook, 2 Nottingham Street,
Melton Mowbray, Leicestershire LE13 1NW.
(Tel: 01664 564 508 Fax: 01664 503 201)

PRICE £19.00 + **£1.50 p&p**

5 to 19 copies: £18.00

20 to 99 copies: £16.00

100 to 999 copies: £14.50

Postage & Packaging free for 5 or more copies

ISBN 978-0-9541201-7-7

FOREWORD TO THE FIRST EDITION

This booklet is intended for farmers, advisers, students and everyone else who, frequently or infrequently, find themselves hunting for data relating to farm management - whether it is for blunt pencil calculations on the back of an envelope or for feeding into a computer. The material contained is based upon the sort of information which the author finds himself frequently having to look up in his twin roles as adviser and teacher in farm management. There are several excellent handbooks already in existence, but this pocketbook endeavours to cover a wider field and thus to be substantially more comprehensive. It is intended that most of the data herein contained will have a national application, although there is inevitably some bias towards conditions in the south-eastern half of the country.

The development of farm planning techniques in recent years has outstripped the quality and quantity of data available. It is hoped that this booklet will go a little further in supplying the type of information required. It cannot, however, claim to be the ultimate in this respect. For example, there are many variations in labour requirements according to farm conditions and sizes and types of machine used and there are many more variations in sheep and beef systems than are dealt with here. More detailed data on these lines are gradually becoming available from various sources. It is hoped further to refine the material in this booklet and to keep it up to date in subsequent editions, as the information becomes available. As a help towards this end, any comments or criticisms will be gratefully received.

The author wishes to thank his many friends and colleagues who have given him so much time and help in compiling this information.

John Nix

John Nix
October, 1966

First published October 1966

Thirty-ninth Edition   September 2008

FOREWORD TO THE THIRTY-NINTH EDITION

The price changes we have seen over the last year have astounded most of us in the agricultural industry. Last summer, the foreword to the 38th edition of the Pocketbook identified how quickly prices were changing and setting new boundaries. For example, it noted how the oil price was 'pushing towards $80 per barrel'. It since doubled. It noted how the oilseed rape price was heading for £200/tonne. It reached £350. A year ago, fertiliser was less than half the price it is now and even then raised some eyebrows. Livestock prices have been taking a welcome upward shift in recent months too.

The economics of farming in the UK and overseas has therefore changed dramatically in 12 months, by more than anybody can remember and by more than anybody honestly expected only last summer. Managing a business in volatile conditions requires focus, and a continued rational discipline. Therefore whilst some figures in last year's budgets now look quite wrong, the ongoing need for budgeting and enterprise costing has actually risen in importance. We are all learning on the job and this book is one of several tools that can help us to accommodate the changes.

Most of the figures in this book are predicted forward one year, i.e. to 2009. *Thus the crops data relate to the 2009 harvest. The livestock data relate either to the 2009 calendar year (e.g. for milk production) or to 2009/2010 (e.g. for winter finished beef), as appropriate.* In a few cases current (i.e. mid-2008) figures are given, where it seemed particularly difficult to try to forecast ahead. The year to which the figures relate is normally stated.

The figures for yields and prices assume a 'normal', or average, season, based on trends, e.g. for potatoes, looking 18-24 months ahead to 2009/2010, no one can predict what the actual average yield and price for that particular year will be.

The data in this book should always be used with caution. *The figures should be adjusted as appropriate according to circumstances and price and cost differences.* As far as possible the assumptions in the tables are set out so as to enable this to be done fairly readily.

As ever, all the enterprises have been reviewed and revised for this edition. The author would like to thank the Andersons Business Research team, who have assisted greatly in the production of this edition.

John Nix
August, 2008

CONTENTS

I GENERAL

1. THE USE OF GROSS MARGINS

DEFINITION

The data on the crop and livestock enterprises in the Pocketbook is based on gross margins. The gross margin of an enterprise is its output less its variable costs. Enterprise output includes the market value of production retained on the farm. The variable costs must (a) be specific to the enterprise and (b) vary in proportion to the size of the enterprise, i.e. number of hectares or head of stock. The main items of variable costs are: Crops: fertiliser, seed, sprays, casual labour and contract work specific to the crop. Non-Grazing Livestock: concentrate feed, vet. and med., marketing expenses. Grazing Livestock: as for non-grazing livestock, plus forage crop variable costs.

POINTS TO NOTE

1. The gross margin is in no sense a profit figure. The so-called 'fixed costs' (rent, labour, machinery, general overheads) have to be covered by the total farm gross margin before arriving at a profit.

2. The gross margin of an enterprise will differ from season to season, partly because of yield and price differences affecting output and partly because variable costs may vary, e.g. the number and type of sprays required. Different soils and other natural factors, as well as level of management, will also cause differences between farms.

3. Items of variable cost may vary from farm to farm, e.g. some farmers use casual labour (a variable cost) to plant and pick their potatoes, others use only regular labour (a fixed cost); some farmers employ a contractor to combine their cereals (a variable cost), others employ their own equipment (a fixed cost); some employ a contractor to cart their sugar beet to the factory (a variable cost), others have their own lorry (a fixed cost). These differences must be borne in mind in making inter-farm comparisons.

4. Provided points 2 and 3 are borne in mind, comparison of gross margins (particularly averages over several seasons) with standards can be a useful check on technical efficiency.

5. The other main usefulness of gross margins lies in farm planning. This is not simply a matter of substituting high gross margin enterprises for low gross margin enterprises. The gross margin is only one relevant feature of an enterprise, although an important one. It says nothing about the call the enterprise makes on the basic farm resources - labour at different times of the year, machinery, buildings, working capital requirements, etc. All these factors and more have to be taken into account in the planning process.

6. This is not to argue that these other costs should be allocated. Complete allocation of many farm expenses is only possible on an arbitrary basis, since they are shared by two or more, possibly all, farm enterprises. Allocation can therefore be completely misleading when making planning decisions. The same is true even when regular labour and machinery are employed specifically on certain enterprises, if such costs are calculated on a per hectare or per head basis. This is because when enterprises are substituted, expanded, contracted or deleted the variable costs for each enterprise will vary roughly in proportion to the size of that enterprise, but other costs will not, except possibly for fuel and some repair costs. Most 'fixed' costs may stay the same, others will change - but not smoothly in small amounts at a time. Either the same regular labour force will cope with a revised plan or a smaller or larger number of men will be needed. The same is true of tractors, other machines and buildings. Such cost changes must of course be taken into account, but allocating these costs on a per hectare or per

1

head basis will not aid, and may positively confuse, planning decisions. The only point of making such calculations is for efficiency comparisons, e.g. labour costs per cow.

7. Allocating fixed costs at a flat rate (e.g. per hectare) for all enterprises, deducting this from the gross margin and hence calculating a 'net profit' from each enterprise can also be misleading. It ignores the whole problem of enterprise inter-relationships, differences between enterprises in total and seasonal requirements for labour, machinery and capital, and other factors such as different quality land on the same farm.

8. Changes in the scale of an enterprise may well affect its gross margin per unit, e.g. increasing the area of winter wheat from 30% to 50% on a farm will mean more second and third crop wheats being grown and a smaller proportion of the crop being drilled under the best conditions; hence yields will in all probability fall. Even if yields remain the same, variable costs (e.g. fertiliser use) will probably increase.

9. Gross margins used for planning future changes should also take account of possible changes in price, and the effect of changes in production techniques.

LOW, AVERAGE AND HIGH LEVELS

The three performance and production levels given for most crop and livestock enterprises are meant for the most part to indicate differences in natural factors, soil productivity, and/or managerial skill, *given the level of variable cost inputs*. They refer, at each level, to *an average over several years* taking *trends* into account. The evidence on the effect of significantly higher or lower levels of variable inputs on gross margins is conflicting and highly uncertain, depending on many factors, including soil type, and will vary from season to season.

2. COMPLETE ENTERPRISE COSTINGS

Requests are occasionally made for this book to include 'complete' enterprise costings, by which is meant the allocation of all costs to each individual enterprise, not only the variable costs as in the calculation of gross margins.

In the early days of farm business management teaching and research this was the preoccupation of most of those specialising in the subject. The system was, however, abandoned by nearly all practising farm economists in the 1950s. The main reasons are given in item 6 of the previous section explaining gross margins. Much meaningless and arbitrary allocation of 'joint costs' is required, (attempting 'to allocate the unallocatable'), and the results are often misleading in making farm decisions. Furthermore, it requires a considerable amount of record-keeping - in allocating labour on a mixed farm, tractor and machinery costs, telephone bills and so on. Few farmers are prepared to spend the required time and money to do this, nor do they need to.

Another problem in 'complete enterprise costing' is where to stop. Should interest on capital be included, whether borrowed or not? Further problems of asset valuation and allocation are involved if so. What of management and marketing supplied by the farmer? Should these be for free, as is usually assumed in such cases?

Variations between farms in their financial situations are considerable as, for instance, between the farmer who owns all his land without any mortgage and has no other borrowings and the one with both a rent to pay for all his land and heavy borrowings in addition.

In some situations, e.g. in some company-owned farms, farm managers are obliged to supply such data to their employers, whether they want to or not. Also, if enterprise costs are used for price fixing purposes governments, or price negotiators, usually require some such attempt to be made, whatever the difficulties and shortcomings of the methodology employed.

The above problems arise when 'costs per tonne' or 'costs per litre' are calculated. Wheat can be calculated to cost anything between £70 and £170 a tonne according to just what costs are included, how they are calculated (allocated) and the yield level assumed.

This is not to decry the efforts that are sometimes made in this direction. Particularly when product prices are falling it seems a natural thing to want to do - to calculate 'unit costs' to compare with prices received. Sometimes they do make clearer particular costs that need investigating and by that means economies that might be made, and they always attract interest. For these reasons costs per litre of milk are included, although the calculation of some of the 'fixed cost' items is difficult. If a farm has only one enterprise such calculations on that farm are obviously straightforward. However, even on solely dairy farms followers are usually reared, which is a second enterprise to milk production.

If required a cost per tonne of wheat (and other combinable crops) can be calculated by adding the fixed costs per hectare of mainly cereals farms (according to size range, given on page 186) to the variable costs per hectare given in the enterprise gross margin data and dividing by the selected yield. Such calculations need to be interpreted with caution because the allocation of fixed costs per hectare is inevitably fairly crude.

The allocation of specific labour (e.g. a full-time cowman), machinery (e.g. a potato harvester) and buildings (e.g. a grain store) is relatively simple and can provide useful information both for purposes of efficiency comparisons and partial budgeting. For some enterprises on many mixed farms, however, there are few, if any, such specific items and the question of the other so-called fixed cost items remains if a full costing is attempted.

3. TOTAL FARM GROSS MARGIN

No attempt is made in this book to compile total gross margins for the whole farm, based on the forecasts made for individual enterprises for 2008, since the possible permutations in terms of enterprise combinations and performance levels are endless. Nor has it ever been the intention in the Pocketbook to include 'historical data', except for some of the material in the Agristats section. Hence total farm survey results, which are inevitably a year or two old by the time they are collated, analysed and published, are not included. Their usefulness for any particular farm is bound to be limited, particularly if the farm systems are broadly defined and cover much of the United Kingdom.

Furthermore, such data is readily available from surveys of farm businesses. These are undertaken on a regional basis by UK agricultural departments;

ENGLAND

The Farm Business Survey (FBS) is the main source of business-level data in England. It is carried out on behalf of DEFRA by a consortium of Universities and Colleges. There has recently been a reorganisation of the FBS which has meant that each individual University/College no longer publishes a booklet for its own region covering all farm types. Instead, the data is collected regionally, and then fed into a national database. This can be found at - www.farmbusinesssurvey.co.uk . This site gives access to a number of sets of FBS data:

- By Government Office Region, customised by farm type etc.

- Farm Business Benchmarking, allows comparison of farm results with the average and top performing farms of the same type.

- Data Builder, a specialist interactive system for professionals and researchers.

As part of the restructuring every University/College will specialise in a particular enterprise (or enterprises). Each of the centres will produce reports giving more detail on their individual enterprises. Some of these Reports are already available on arable, horticulture, dairy, pig and poultry enterprises.

The following institutions are invloved in the FBS;

- Askham Bryan College, York– www.askham-bryan.ac.uk/for_business/rural_business_research_unit (Pigs)
- University of Cambridge – www.landecon.cam.ac.uk/research/eeprg/rbu/index.htm (cereals)
- Duchy College - http://www.cornwall.ac.uk/rbs/
- Imperial College, London – www.imperial.ac.uk/wyecampus/research/aebm/themes/fbm/survey.htm
- University of Newcastle – http://www.ncl.ac.uk/afrd/business/farmbusinessinfo (oilseed rape)
- University of Nottingham – www.nottingham.ac.uk/rbru/
- University of Reading – www.apd.rdg.ac.uk/AgEcon/ (horticulture)

WALES

The Farm Business Survey in Wales is undertaken on behalf of the Welsh Assembly Government by the University of Aberystwyth. The results are published at - www.irs.aber.ac.uk/fbs/

SCOTLAND

In Scotland the data for the Farm Accounts Survey is collected by the Scottish Agricultural College. It is available in the publication 'Farm Incomes in Scotland'. See www.scotland.gov.uk/Topics/Statistics/15631/8884

NORTHERN IRELAND

The Department of Agriculture and Rural Development for Northern Ireland undertakes the Farm Business Survey in the province. Results can be found at www.dardni.gov.uk/index/dard-statistics/statistical-reports/agricultural-statistics-farm-business-survey.htm

4. MAIN ASSUMPTIONS

Budgeting future prices, by necessity requires making several assumptions about how they are likely to move in the future from current levels (July 2008). This 39th Edition of the Pocketbook uses the following key assumptions:

- The pound: euro exchange rate throughout the book is 78p/€, equivalent to €1.282 per pound.

- Fertiliser prices for nitrogen (N), phosphate (P) and potash (K) are the same throughout. A full schedule of fertiliser valuations can be found on page 235. For calculating the gross margins, the following are used:

  - N: 107 p/kg (£368/t 34.5% N) (UK Ammonium Nitrate)

  - $P_2 O_5$: 150 p/kg (£690/t 46% P_2O_5) (Triple Super Phosphate)

  - K_2O: 97 p/kg (£580/t 60% K_2O) (Muriate of Potash)

- Farm machinery fuel price (red diesel) is taken to be 65ppl.

- Feed wheat price (from which so many other commodity prices are benchmarked), is £135/tonne. This is an ex-farm price for November /December 2009 delivery.

II ENTERPRISE DATA

1. CROPS

WINTER WHEAT

Feed Wheat

Production level..........................	Low	Average	High
Yield: tonnes per ha (tons per acre)	6.75 (2.7)	8.25 (3.3)	9.75 (3.9)
	£	£	£
Output:...................................	911 (369)	1114 (451)	1316 (533)
Variable Costs:			
Seed....................................		49 (20)	
Fertiliser...............................		323 (131)	
Sprays..................................		139 (56)	
Total Variable Costs...................		511 (207)	
Gross Margin per ha (acre).............	**400** (162)	**602** (244)	**805** (326)

Milling Wheat

Production level..........................	Low	Average	High
Yield: tonnes per ha (tons per acre)	6.15 (2.5)	7.55 (3.1)	9.00 (3.6)
	£	£	£
Output:...................................	904 (366)	1110 (449)	1323 (536)
Variable Costs:			
Seed....................................		54 (22)	
Fertiliser...............................		354 (143)	
Sprays..................................		143 (58)	
Total Variable Costs...................		551 (223)	
Gross Margin per ha (acre).............	**353** (143)	**559** (226)	**772** (313)

1. *Prices*. The average feed wheat price for the 2009 harvest crop (i.e. 2009/10 marketing year) is taken to be £135 tonne. The average milling price is taken to be £147/tonne. This is based on a 'full specification' premium of £20 over feed wheat, a 'biscuit' grade milling specification of £10 and a 20% failure rate of achieving the specification. The average premium achieved varies widely according to quality and season: see further comments below (note 3). Full Specification is defined as NABIM Group 1 wheat with Hagberg of 250 or more, 13% Protein or more and a bushel weight of at least 76Kg/hl.

   Intervention. For the 2009 harvest the intervention price is €101.77/tonne delivered to centre (£79.38 at 78p/euro) in November, rising by €0.46 (35.9p) each month to €104.53 (£81.53) in May, but this excludes most feed wheat on specification issues. Transport and merchant charges are likely to total at least £6.50/tonne.

2. *Yields*. The overall average yield, for all winter wheat, i.e. all varieties, is taken as 8.0 tonnes per hectare, the trend yield (3.2 tons (64 cwt.)/acre).

3. *Milling v. Feed*. The yield of bread and biscuit wheat (generically known as milling) averages 8.5% below that of feed wheat (the difference could be greater on high-yielding land and less on moderate quality land and also tends to be greater on second than on first wheats). Slightly higher costs for seed, fertiliser and sprays might be expected for milling wheats. The actual price premium in any one season varies according to quality and scarcity. The average premium for full specification

breadmaking quality exceeds the £12/tonne (9%) used. However, that for other (biscuit) milling wheat is generally below. Furthermore, not all deliveries achieve full specification. Grade 2 varieties normally achieve a premium of only a few pounds a tonne but their average yields are higher than grade 1 varieties. Overall, the full specification breadmaking premium averaged approximately £16.50/tonne for the five harvest years 2003-2007 with a range of almost nothing to £53.00 per tonne. The premium in 2007/2008 averaged over £30 per tonne, higher than any year since 1997/98. Nabim wheat group 1 varieties have accounted for about 15% of wheat area in 2006, 2007 and 2008, with group 2's falling from 27% to 19% then 16% respectively.

4. *First v. Second (Feed) Wheats.* The evidence concerning the effect of different types and lengths of rotational breaks on subsequent cereal yields is inevitably variable given the differences between seasons (weather effects), soils, varieties etc. The table below (for feed wheat) assumes a yield reduction of approximately 10% for second wheats compared with first and higher fertiliser and seed costs as shown; (the later the sowing date the less the yield gap tends to be). The same price is assumed as in the initial table. Only average and high levels are shown. Third wheats could yield 10-15% below second wheats; variable costs are likely to be similar. Large scale NIAB trials from 1996 to 2000 showed second wheats yielding an average of just under 1 tonne/ha less than first wheats; the yield difference varied between varieties. Heavy, well-structured, well-drained clay soils appear to be best suited to second wheats; lighter, silty soils usually have a greater risk of Take-all; a firm seedbed is needed. A seven year Arable Research Centre project gave the average yield of first wheats as being approximately 20% above continuous wheats.

Comparison between First and Second Wheat Crops

Production level	Average		High	
Year (after break)..................	First	Second	First	Second
Yield: tonnes per ha (tons/acre)	8.75 (3.5)	7.9 (3.15)	10.0 (4.0)	9.0 (3.6)
	£	£	£	£
Output.....................................	1,181 (478)	1067 (432)	1,350 (547)	1,215 (492)
Variable Costs	511 (207)	527 (210)	511 (207)	527 (210)
Gross Margin per ha (acre) ...	670 (271)	539 (222)	839 (340)	688 (282)

5. *Straw* is costed as being incorporated. Average yield is approx. 3·5 tonnes per hectare (range 2·5 to 5); value £30 to £50 per tonne according to region and season but mainly £30 to £40 baled ex-field (£5 less in big bales); (average sale value approx. £85/ha); variable costs (string) approx. £2.70 per tonne. Standing straw (sold for baling): anything from no value to £150/ha (£60/acre), according to type of crop, season and area of the country/local demand: national average around £30/ha (£12/acre), double this in the west, at least treble in a season when straw is in short supply.

6. *Seed.* Seed rates vary according to soil, season, variety, farm policy, etc. Seed: main range £300-425 per tonne (C2) with a single purpose dressing (£330 used); 175kg/ha in good conditions, but more is often applied; 30% farm-saved including grain value, cleaning, dressing, testing and BSPB levy of £34.06/tonne (£5.42 per hectare) for autumn 2008 and spring 2009.

7. *Fertiliser* costs are based on P and K replacement cost for an average yield crop, with straw incorporated. Nitrogen is 170kg/ha for feed wheat and 210kg/ha for milling.

8. *Sprays.* Amounts variable according to season, variety, policy, etc. Typical breakdown: herbicides 43%, fungicides 45%, insecticides 5%, growth regulators 5%, slug pellets 2%.

9. If a *Contractor* is employed, extra variable costs will be approximately as follows:

      Spraying: £13-£16/ha (LV-HV; material included above)

      Drilling: £30/ha

	Combining:	£80/ha (excluding carting)
		£109/ha (including carting)
	Drying:	£16.50 for 6% moisture per tonne.
	Baling Straw:	£30-50/ha (including string) depending on bale type.

10. *Fuel and Repairs* (per hectare). Grain £125, straw £45.

11. *Specialised Equipment Prices*. see p.163.

12. *Labour*: see p. 148.

SPRING WHEAT

Production level............................	Low	Average	High
Yield: tonnes per ha (tons per acre)	4.75 (1.9)	5.75 (2.3)	6.75 (2.7)
	£	£	£
Output:...................................	689 (279)	835 (338)	980 (397)
Variable Costs:			
Seed..		62 (25)	
Fertiliser......................................		259 (105)	
Sprays..		87 (35)	
Total Variable Costs....................		408 (165)	
Gross Margin per ha (acre).............	**281** (114)	**427** (173)	**572** (232)

1. *Price*: In general, see Winter Wheat (previous pages). A far higher proportion of spring wheat is sold for milling compared with winter wheat. Here we assume 85% making the average price £145.2/tonne for the 2009 harvest.

2. *Straw:* See Winter Wheat but yields are considerably lower.

3. If a *contractor* is employed, extra variable costs (£/ha) will be shown as for Winter Wheat above.

4. *Fuel and repairs* (per hectare): grain £120, straw £45.

5. *Specialised Equipment Prices*: see P.163.

6. *Labour:* see p. 148.

N.B. Normally, only about 1% of the UK wheat area is spring sown although survey data is hard to come by. It is popular after root crops. The percentage is naturally higher after a particularly wet autumn. The percentage is even lower in Scotland (1% or less) than in England or Wales.

WINTER BARLEY

Feed Barley

Production level.............................	Low	Average	High
Yield: tonnes per ha (tons per acre)	5.4 (2.2)	6.6 (2.7)	7.8 (3.2)
	£	£	£
Output:..	702 (284)	858 (347)	1014 (411)
Variable Costs:			
Seed...		53 (21)	
Fertiliser..................................		284 (115)	
Sprays......................................		100 (41)	
Total Variable Costs.....................		437 (177)	
Gross Margin per ha (acre).............	**265** (107)	**421** (171)	**577** (234)

Malting Barley

Production level.............................	Low	Average	High
Yield: tonnes per ha (tons per acre)	4.7 (1.9)	5.75 (2.3)	6.8 (2.8)
	£	£	£
Output:..	682 (276)	834 (338)	986 (399)
Variable Costs:			
Seed...		56 (23)	
Fertiliser..................................		206 (83)	
Sprays......................................		109 (44)	
Total Variable Costs.....................		370 (150)	
Gross Margin per ha (acre).............	**311** (126)	**463** (188)	**616** (249)

1. *Prices.* The average feed barley price for the 2009 harvest crop (i.e. 2009/10 marketing year) is taken to be £130/tonne, a £5 discount to feed wheat (the average over 5 and 20 years is about £4.60). The winter malting price (£145/tonne) assumes an average premium over feed of £15/tonne. This accounts for malting varieties cropped that do not reach malting standards. The actual premium obtained over feed barley varies according to season and quality: For the best malting barleys the premium in the past has often been £25 and in some years higher.

2. *Straw* is not included. Average yield is approx. 2·75 tonnes per hectare, value £45 to £55 per tonne baled ex-field according to region and season (£5 less in big bales); (average sale value approx. £100/ha), variable cost (string) approximately £2.70 per tonne. Standing straw (sold for baling): anything to £150/ha (£60/acre) according to crop, season and area of the country (local demand): average around £55/ha (£22/acre), double this or more in the west.

3. *Seed.* Seed includes 25% farm-saved; amounts average 175-180kg/ha, varying according to soil, conditions etc. and BSPB levy of £33.06/tonne (£5.55 per hectare) for autumn.

4. Fertiliser costs are based on P and K replacement cost for a 6.6t/ha crop, with straw incorporated. Nitrogen is 160kg/ha for feed varieties and 100kg/ha for winter malting crops. Fertiliser costs on continuous barley will be approximately £30/ha higher.

5. *Sprays.* Amounts variable according to season, variety, policy, etc. Typical breakdown: herbicides 47%, fungicides 44%, growth regulators 6%, other 3%.

6. If *Contractor* employed, extra variable costs as shown for Winter Wheat (note 8).

7. *Fuel and Repairs* (per hectare): grain £125, straw £45.

8. *Specialised Equipment Prices*: see p.163.

9. *Labour:* see p. 148.

SPRING (MALTING) BARLEY

Production level........................	Low	Average	High
Yield: tonnes per ha (tons per acre)	4.4 (1.8)	5.25 (2.1)	6.1 (2.5)
	£	£	£
Output:...................................	660 (267)	788 (319)	915 (371)
Variable Costs:			
Seed......................................		59 (24)	
Fertiliser................................		176 (71)	
Sprays....................................		79 (32)	
Total Variable Costs....................		314 (127)	
Gross Margin per ha (acre).............	**346** (140)	**474** (192)	**601** (244)

1. *Prices.* Virtually all spring barley grown is a malting variety, most of it is grown with a premium in mind. Malting premiums for spring barleys are normally significantly higher than for winter varieties. In this schedule, the premium over feed barely is £20/tonne. Again, this allows for failed samples.

2. *Seed.* Spring barley seed averages £400/tonne. This gross margin uses a seed rate of 175Kg/ha, 25% is home saved with BSPB royalty rates of £37.00/tonne (£6.59 per hectare) for spring 2009 included.

3. The notes for *variable costs, straw etc.* are as for Winter Barley above except sprays, which consist typically of: herbicides 54%, fungicides 41%, other 5%.

4. *Areas and Use of Winter and Spring Barley.* Since 2001, spring barley has commanded the majority of the UK barley area (57% in 2007, 56% in 2006). In the 1970's, spring barely accounted for over 90% of the combined crop. This fell to around 40% in the 1990's. Overall barley hectarage has slipped to less than 900 thousand hectares, a halving since the late 1980's.

5. Approximately 56% of the UK 2007 barley crop was used for animal feed in the UK and a third for domestic malting. Some 7% of the total barley crop was exported. However, net exports of around 278 thousand tonnes represents the smallest over the last 2 decades (net exports in 2006/7 at 440 thousand tonnes, were the second smallest by a considerable margin). Net exports for that period averaged over 1.1 million tonnes per year peaking in 1996/7 at just over two million tonnes.

WINTER OATS

Production level..........................	Low	Average	High
Yield: tonnes per ha (tons per acre)	5.3 (2.1)	6.5 (2.6)	7.8 (3.1)
	£	£	£
Output..............................	656 (266)	813 (329)	969 (392)
Variable Costs:			
Seed.....................................		52 (21)	
Fertiliser................................		218 (88)	
Sprays..................................		70 (28)	
Total Variable Costs..................		341 (138)	
Gross Margin per ha (acre).............	316 (128)	472 (191)	628 (254)

1. Prices are the assumed average for the 2009 harvest crop, i.e. the whole 2009/10 marketing year, at £125 per tonne for milling oats. Milling specification required a minimum bushel weight of 50Kg/Hl. Conservation grade milling oats may obtain a premium of £10/tonne.

2. Seed: Margin uses 175kg/ha seed at £380/tonne, with 40% home saved including the BSPB levy of £30.97/tonne (£4.46 per hectare) for autumn 2008 and spring 2009.

3. Straw is not included above. Average yield is 3.5 tonnes per hectare; value £40 to £60 per tonne according to region and season; variable costs (string) approximately £2.70 per tonne.

4. If a contractor is employed, extra variable costs will be as shown for Winter Wheat (note 8).

5. For Naked Oats refer to page 21

6. *Fuel and Repairs* (per hectare): grain £125, straw £45.

7. *Specialised Equipment Prices*: see p. 163.

8. *Labour:* see p 148.

SPRING OATS

Production level..........................	Low	Average	High
Yield: tonnes per ha (tons per acre)	4.5 (1.8)	5.5 (2.2)	6.5 (2.6)
	£	£	£
Output Feed	563 (228)	688 (278)	813 (329)
Variable Costs:			
Seed.....................................		60 (24)	
Fertiliser................................		180 (73)	
Sprays..................................		59 (24)	
Total Variable Costs..................		299 (121)	
Gross Margin per ha (acre).............	263 (107)	388 (157)	513 (208)

1. The notes re. *prices, straw etc.* are as for winter oats above.

2. Around 75% of the oats in Great Britain are winter crops; the proportion increases from north to south; it is normally 90% or more in England and Wales but only 25% to 35% in Scotland. Oats only account for about 3.5% of the total UK cereals area; however, the area has increased in recent years: 121,000ha in 2006 was 40% more than the 1999 area. The risk of lodging and thus difficult harvesting remains a drawback despite the lower costs of production.

OILSEED RAPE

Winter Rape

Production level..........................	Low	Average	High
Yield: tonnes per ha (tons per acre)	2.25 (0.9)	3.25 (1.3)	4.25 (1.7)
	£	£	£
Output:................................	675 (273)	975 (395)	1275 (516)
Variable Costs:			
Seed.....................................		41 (16)	
Fertiliser...........		306 (124)	
Sprays.........		118 (48)	
Total Variable Costs....................		465 (188)	
Gross Margin per ha (acre).............	210 (85)	510 (207)	810 (328)

Spring Rape

Production level..........................	Low	Average	High
Yield: tonnes per ha (tons per acre)	1.5 (0.6)	2.00 (0.8)	2.75 (1.1)
	£	£	£
Output:................................	450 (182)	600 (243)	825 (334)
Variable Costs:			
Seed.....................................		44 (18)	
Fertiliser...........		149 (60)	
Sprays.........		72 (29)	
Total Variable Costs....................		265 (107)	
Gross Margin per ha (acre).............	185 (75)	335 (136)	560 (227)

1. *Prices*. The price assumed for the 2009 crop is £300/tonne, including oil bonuses.

2. *Varieties.:* Winter crops are mainly sown between 10th August and 10th September (before the end of August if possible). Spring-sown crops are best sown between late March and mid-April. Winter crops normally are harvested between late-July and mid-August, spring-sown crops in the first half of September. Inputs are lower with spring-sown crops, pigeons are less trouble and the late summer/autumn workload is eased. However, later harvesting tends to clash with the winter wheat harvest, there is less time for ground preparation and drilling the following winter cereal crop, and spring droughts are a potential hazard to establishment. Above all, yields average only 60% of those of winter rape; hence normally less than 10% of the total oilseed rape crop is spring-sown (less than 5% for the last 3 years). The proportion of the total area sown with hybrid winter rape is increasing rapidly (now about a quarter); an average increase in yield of 0·5 tonnes/ha is claimed by its plant breeders.

3. *Seed.* The price quoted is for standard merchants OSR. However, hybrid rapeseed is used on approximately 25% of the UK land area. This seed is dearer, costing in the region of £60 per hectare. Also, £20/ha or so can be saved from the gross margin by home saving although other costs appear elsewhere. BSPB levy of £1702.35/tonne (£8.51 per hectare) for autumn 2008 and spring 2009.

4. *Sprays*. Variable with season, etc. Typically: herbicides 65%, fungicides 25%, insecticides 10%.

5. *Labour:* see p148.

LINSEED

Production level........................	Low	Average	High
Yield: tonnes per ha (tons per acre)	1.25 (0.5)	1.75 (0.7)	2.75 (1.1)
	£	£	£
Output:.................................	500 (203)	700 (284)	1 100 (446)
Variable Costs:			
Seed.....................................		85 (34)	
Fertiliser................................		152 (61)	
Sprays..................................		48 (19)	
Total Variable Costs...................		285 (115)	
Gross Margin per ha (acre).............	**215** (87)	**415** (168)	**815** (330)

The price assumed for the 2009 crop is £400/tonne. Contract prices are normally tied to a standard 38% oil content and 9% moisture content. Some contracts are now also linked to wheat price (despite the 2 markets not correlating). Open market prices are usually lower. Some specialist contracts for specific varieties such as Yellow Linseed can be worth more.

The vast majority of linseed is spring-sown, drilling mid-March to mid-April (best mid-March to end March). It is susceptible to frost. It should not be grown more than 1 year in 5. Care is needed regarding the level of nitrogen used: too much (over 90 kg/ha) can cause severe lodging, delayed maturity and excessive weed growth – and hence difficult harvesting, poor quality and lower yields; it should be applied early.

Harvesting: normally not before September and can even be after mid-October in a late season as it does not shed. Moisture content most likely 12-16%: must be dried to 9% for storage.

Inputs: seed, 50kg/ha (sold in hectare bags), Fertiliser N/P/K of 50/14/11.

Winter Linseed

There was a surge in plantings of winter linseed for the 1997 harvest: around 30,000 ha, but this fell to about 20,000 the following year, when crops were again disappointing; there has been little sustained interest since – which has been true of all linseed since 2001. The main attractions are easier establishment and earlier harvesting (about a month before the spring varieties). Higher yields than the spring-sown crop were expected but trials indicated little difference. Yield affected by frost heave, disease and thrips (thunder-bugs), with most varieties susceptible to lodging; pigeons and rabbits can also be troublesome. Early sowing (early to mid-September) appears best, with higher seed rates; otherwise variable costs are similar to spring.

Linola

Edible linseed: the oil contains more linoleic and less linolenic acid than conventional linseed, like sunflower oil. It is difficult to see much future for the crop, because its gross margin is very low. It is grown on contract, with the price based on the oilseed rape price. Spring-sown: agronomy and yield similar to conventional linseed; good weed control is essential.

FIELD BEANS

Winter Beans

Production level............................	Low	Average	High
Yield: tonnes per ha (tons per acre)	3.0 (1.2)	4.0 (1.6)	5.0 (2.0)
	£	£	£
Output:..	530 (215)	695 (281)	860 (348)
Variable Costs:			
Seed...		60 (24)	
Fertiliser...		93 (38)	
Sprays..		102 (41)	
Total Variable Costs......................		255.3 (103)	
Gross Margin per ha (acre).............	275 (111)	440 (178)	605 (245)

Spring Beans

Production level............................	Low	Average	High
Yield: tonnes per ha (tons per acre)	2.8 (1.1)	3.7 (1.5)	4.6 (1.9)
	£	£	£
Output:..	525 (213)	683 (276)	840 (340)
Variable Costs:			
Seed...		74 (30)	
Fertiliser...		86 (35)	
Sprays..		76 (31)	
Total Variable Costs......................		236 (96)	
Gross Margin per ha (acre).............	289 (117)	447 (181)	604 (245)

1. *Price.* The 2009 harvest price for feed winter beans is budgeted at £165 per tonne. White hylum varieties can fetch another £15/tonne with no yield penalty. This therefore accounts for the majority of winter beans. The higher price is achievable subject to meeting minimum quality criteria.

2. *EU Protein Supplement.* Under the Single Payment there is a supplement of €55.57/ha for beans, peas and lupins harvested dry. The output figure above includes the value of this supplement, worth around £35/ha (€1 = 78p) after deducting modulation (19%). This assumes a stipulated maximum EU-wide guaranteed area of 1.648 million hectares is not exceeded. It hasn't been yet.

3. *Physical inputs.* Seed: 185-220 kg per hectare @ £400/tonne. About 60% is farm-saved including BSPB levy of £8.85/ha or £44.05/tonne (winter and spring). Fertiliser: based on 9kg phosphate and 10kg potash per tonne of bean harvested per hectare. No nitrogen is applied.

4. *Labour:* see p 148.

Spring Bean Notes

5. *Price.* Spring beans are all grown for the human consumption market. It is only the poor quality beans (predominantly Bruchid beetle damaged) that are rejected and redirected to feed compounders. Even in some years when supply is particularly tight, these are also exported (North Africa). Hence the spring bean price is budgeted higher than winter at £175/tonne. In a 'normal' year, about 30% of spring beans will not make the export (human consumption) grade. This is accounted for in the price.

6. *Physical inputs.* Seed: 185-220 kg per hectare @ £475/tonne. About 40% is farm-saved. Fertiliser and sprays: as for winter beans.

7. *Winter versus Spring Beans.* The key determinant between which to crop is soil type. Winter beans are more suited to heavy soils and springs on lighter land. As the schedules illustrate, there is little real difference between the gross margins.

FIELD PEAS

Blue Peas

Production level...........................	Low	Average	High
Yield: tonnes per ha (tons per acre)	3.0 (1.2)	3.75 (1.5)	5.0 (2.0)
	£	£	£
Output:....................................	608 (246)	751 (304)	990 (401)
Variable Costs:			
Seed.....................................		91 (37)	
Fertiliser.................................		87 (35)	
Sprays...................................		121 (49)	
Total Variable Costs....................		298.7 (121)	
Gross Margin per ha (acre)............	309 (125)	453 (183)	691 (280)

Marofats

Production level...........................	Low	Average	High
Yield: tonnes per ha (tons per acre)	2.7 (1.1)	3.40 (1.4)	4.5 (1.8)
	£	£	£
Output:....................................	615.5 (249)	766 (310)	1003 (406)
Variable Costs:			
Seed.....................................		108 (44)	
Fertiliser.................................		79 (32)	
Sprays...................................		131 (53)	
Total Variable Costs....................		317.9 (129)	
Gross Margin per ha (acre)............	298 (121)	448 (181)	685 (277)

1. *Price.* All peas are now grown for a premium market. Only a small proportion (5%) end up being sent to compounders as second grade peas will go for pet food. Feed value is therefore no longer relevant as a base price. The price forecast for the Blue Peas here is £191/tonne, taking account of some very high premiums (achieving up to £230/tonne) and a failure rate (which can be high). Most peas are Blues, used for micronising and exports.

   Marofats, the other main group of peas, and illustrated in the second half of the table can achieve considerable premiums over wheat. They are used for canning, packets and export trade. About a third is grown on a forward contract. They control a higher price premium than blue peas but yield about 10% less. Being used for human consumption their quality requirements are greater. The average price in this gross margin is £215/tonne.

   EU Protein Supplement. (See Winter Beans), is included in the above.

2. *Physical Inputs.* Seed: 210 to 250 kg, about 50% farm-saved including BSPB levy of £8.85/ha or £44.05/tonne. Fertiliser: based on 9kg phosphate and 10kg potash per tonne of pea harvested per hectare. No nitrogen is applied. Sometimes the crop is desiccated before direct combining.

3. *Labour:* see p. 148.

14

4. In 1998 the area of field beans was 20% above that of dried peas but the difference has widened substantially since then: the area of field beans was more than double that of peas for harvesting dry in 2001 and 2002. By 2006 beans outstripped pea area more than 4 fold.

LUPINS

The following table refers to spring sown *white lupins*. Differences in yield and price for yellow and blue lupins are given in the accompanying notes:

Production level............................	Low	Average	High
Yield: tonnes per ha (tons per acre)	2.25 (0.9)	3.00 (1.2)	3.75 (1.5)
	£	£	£
Output:......................................	429 (174)	560 (227)	691 (280)
Variable Costs:			
Seed...		120 (49)	
Fertiliser.....................................		95 (39)	
Sprays..		102 (41)	
Total Variable Costs....................		317 (128)	
Gross Margin per ha (acre).............	112 (45)	243 (98)	374 (152)

The price used here is £175 per tonne plus estimated £35/ha protein supplement, net of modulation.

A leguminous crop traditionally associated with light land. Their protein content is about 40 to 50% higher than peas and beans, making lupins a good substitute for soya bean meal in livestock feed compounds.

The area grown in the UK has increased from about 2,500 hectares in 2001 to approximately 5,000 hectares. The area is now static. They are virtually all spring lupins. They are a non-GM source of high quality digestible protein. The crop can be cut whole for silage, crimped or milled and fed directly to stock or the grain traded as a cash crop. Determinate varieties (single stem, uniformed ripening) can be harvested easily, non determinate varieties (with multiple heads at various stages of ripening) are more difficult.

Lupins can be grown on all but the heaviest land but are not tolerant of alkaline soils. They need a good cereal seedbed and pre-emergence weed control. Sowing is from mid-March to early April and harvest from mid-August onwards (and can be late September). If the crop is for silage, sowing can be as late as mid-May using an appropriate variety. No nitrogen fertiliser is necessary although 10kg/ha is often used to accelerate early stage growth. P and K at 50-55kg/ha should be replaced later. There are no serious crop pests. Anthracnose is a potentially serious threat but plant health measures have so far kept it under control. Other diseases are not a problem. Determinant varieties don't generally need pre-harvest desiccants if weed-free, indeterminant ones do.

Appropriate species and variety choice is important depending on area of the country, soil pH, intended end use and growth habit required. There are three distinct species of spring lupins, white (lupinus albus), blue (lupinus angustifolus) and yellow (lupinus luteus). All are suitable for grain or livestock feed. White lupins have higher protein and potentially greater yield than blue lupins but require a longer growing season. Yellow lupins fall between blue and white on both counts.

About 67% of the national lupin area is white and 33% blue. There is minimal yellow lupin remaining. In the South-East and East Anglia 90% of lupins are white. In Scotland 60% are blue 30% white and 10% yellow, with blue and yellow grown for combining or crimping and white for whole crop.

Lupin characteristics

	White *Lupinus Albus*	**Blue** *lupinus angustifolius*
Flower Colour	white or blue	white or blue
Growth habit	semi-determinate	fully or semi-determinate
pH tolerance	5 to 7.6	5 to 6.8
Protein	36-40%	31-35%
Oil content	10%	6%
Main use	Combining in Southern England on acidic land Forage in all areas	Combining in the North (determinate) Forage in the very North (semi-determinate)
Yield	3-3.5 t/ha	3-3.5 t/ha

Acknowledgement: Thanks to Premium Crops 02392 632 883

HERBAGE SEEDS

	Italian Ryegrass		Early Perennial Ryegrass	
	Average	High	Average	High
	£	£	£	£
Yield (tonnes per ha)	1.3	1.7	1.25	1.60
Price per 50 kg (£)	38		45	
Output	988	1292	1125	1440
Variable Costs:				
Seed	60		50	
Fertiliser	314		314	
Sprays	75		75	
Cleaning	208	264	201	250
Total Variable Costs	657	713	640	689
Gross Margin per ha	**332**	**580**	**486**	**752**
Gross Margin per acre	134	235	196	304

	Intermediate Perennial Ryegrass		Late Perennial Ryegrass	
	Average	High	Average	High
	£	£	£	£
Yield (tonnes per ha)	1.3	1.6	1.25	1.60
Price per 50 kg (£)	50		55	
Output	1250	1600	1375	1760
Variable Costs:				
Seed	60		50	
Fertiliser	314		314	
Sprays	75		75	
Cleaning	201	250	201	250
Total Variable Costs	650	699	640	689
Gross Margin per ha	**601**	**902**	**736**	**1072**
Gross Margin per acre	243	365	298	434

	Hybrid Ryegrass		Kent Wild White Clover & Kent Indig. Peren. R'grass	
	Average	High	Average	High
	£	£	£	£
Yield (tonnes per ha)	1.2	1.6	0.09 (Clover)	0.11 (C)
			0.6 (R'grass)	0.8 (R)
Price per 50 kg (£)	45		300 (C)	45 (C)
Output	1080	1395	1080	1380
Variable Costs:				
Seed	60		50	
Fertiliser	298		141	
Sprays	75		75	
Cleaning	194	243	135	169
Total Variable Costs	627	676	401	435
Gross Margin per ha	**453**	**719**	**679**	**945**
Gross Margin per acre	183	291	275	382

Notes

1. The following were the number of hectares entered for certified seed production for the main grasses and clovers in the UK for the 2007 harvest;

Italian / Westerwold Ryegrass....	148	Cocksfoot................................	325
Early Perennial Ryegrass............	190	Timothy	65
Inter. Perennial Ryegrass............	1,491	Red Fescue...............................	411
Late Perennial Ryegrass	1,826	White Clover	46
Amenity Perennial Ryegrass	1,061	Red Clover...............................	57
Hybrid Ryegrass	397	Common Vetch........................	83

The ryegrasses total 5,113 ha (12,634 acres).

All herbage seeds total 6,100 ha (15,073 acres).

2. Average *yields* are approximate NIAB recorded averages for cleaned certified seed. The crop is very risky, i.e. yields are highly variable, depending especially on the weather at, and precise timeliness of, harvesting. A considerable amount of skill is necessary to average the 'high' levels over a number of years. Most grasses give their highest yield in their first harvest year, assuming good establishment. Yields can be increased by up to 30% with a combination of higher Nitrogen applications along with a growth regulator (e.g. Moddus). The cost of the growth regulator is likely to add £25 per ha (£10 per acre) to the chemical figure in the margins above, with a similar cost increase for the extra Nitrogen.

3. Prices in the table are estimated prices for certified seed for the 2009 year. The figures relate to Diploid varieties. Tetraploid prices are lower (intermediate and late varieties achieving around £40-£45 per 50kg). However, tetraploid yields should be higher (1,500-2,000 kg per ha). High sugar varieties should command a small premium over the values seen in the tables.

4. No allowance has been made above for by-products. Some crops produce 4 to 5 tonnes of threshed hay, which is, however, of low feeding value. This could be worth £150 or more per hectare. Some grasses, especially spring-sown ryegrass, also provide substantial quantities of autumn and winter grazing. Clovers can be either grazed or cut for hay or silage and do not have to be 'shut up' until mid or late May, or, in some cases and seasons, even early June. More grazing (until end of May) and better quality threshed hay is provided with a combination of ryegrass and white clover than with the specialist herbage seed grasses.

5. If the seed crop is to be undersown, specialist growers often reduce the seed rate for the cover crop by up to half and restrict nitrogen dressing: the cereal yield may thus be reduced by up to 0.6 tonnes per hectare. If this is not done the grass seed yield is usually lower in the first year compared with direct drilling, except for ryegrass.

6. Labour: see page 148.

RYE

Production level.............................	Low	Average	High
Yield: tonnes per ha (tons per acre) ..	4.75 (1.9)	6.00 (2.4)	7.25 (2.9)
	£	£	£
Output:..	736 (298)	930 (377)	1124 (455)
Variable Costs:			
Seed		80 (32)	
Fertiliser...............................		300 (121)	
Sprays		95 (38)	
Total Variable Costs	475 (192)	475 (192)	475 (192)
Gross Margin per ha (acre)............	**262** (106)	**455** (184)	**649** (263)

Largely grown on light, infertile, sandy or stony soils, where yields are poor for other cereals. Yields would clearly be higher on better soils, but then rye has difficulty in competing with wheat and barley; it could never do so on good wheat land. The average yield in the UK in the five years 2003 to 2007 was 6.01 tonnes/ha.

The area grown in the UK has been in the range 5,000-6,000 ha for a number of years. Rye crispbread is the major outlet. It is also milled into flour, used in mixed-grain bread and muesli. About two-thirds of UK requirements are imported, mainly from Canada (which produces the highest quality), Denmark, Germany and Spain. The demand for UK-grown rye has been falling in recent years, owing to increased competition in the crispbread market.

The price assumed above (£155 per tonne) is an estimated 2009 price at harvest. There are two main contracts on offer – this fixed price, or a £20 per tonne premium to the prevailing feed wheat price at the point of movement. Both prices assume the milling specification is achieved. Deductions are made for low quality, particularly if it is only of feed grade (price then between feed wheat and feed barley price). Only a small percentage of the crop is grown for the free market, which is risky.

Rye, which is autumn-sown, is drought tolerant and very hardy, can withstand low temperatures and starts growing early in the spring. It has all-round resistance to wheat and barley diseases, e.g. eyespot, and suffers less from take-all than wheat – hence it is a possible replacement for third or fourth wheat. Its vigour keeps weeds down. Its herbicide, fungicide and fertiliser requirements are lower than for other cereals, except for growth regulators. Harvested earlier than winter wheat (useful for following with oilseed rape).

Drawbacks: it sprouts in a wet harvest: must therefore harvest early, at relatively high moisture content. It grows very tall and lodges easily: hence high levels of nitrogen are not possible; but growth regulators help. Its heavy straw crop means very slow combining (takes about twice as long per hectare as wheat and barley), and difficult straw incorporation. New hybrid varieties, with shorter, stiffer straw, are being developed; these would improve the comparative profitability of rye on better soils.

Drilling: 2nd and 3rd weeks September.

Harvesting: by mid-August at relatively high moisture content, then dry to 14-15% (no drying costs included in margin).

TRITICALE

Production level	Low	Average	High
Yield: tonnes per ha (tons per acre) ..	4.00 (1.6)	5.00 (2.0)	7.20 (2.9)
	£	£	£
Output:	520 (211)	650 (263)	936 (379)
Variable Costs:			
Seed		50 (20)	
Fertiliser		263 (107)	
Sprays		60 (24)	
Total Variable Costs	373 (151)	373 (151)	373 (151)
Gross Margin per ha (acre)	**147** (60)	**277** (112)	**563** (228)

A 'man-made' cross between rye and hard wheat. Combines the hardiness of rye and the marketability of feed wheat. It is favoured in livestock feed, particularly pig and poultry rations, due to its high levels of lysine. However, due to the relatively low quantities available it is not widely used by feed compounders. The area grown in the UK has risen over recent years from 15,000 ha to 18,000 ha. A large proportion of this rise may well be in the newer spring varieties (see below).

The price is usually £3 or £4 per tonne below the price for feed wheat, but this tends to vary from season to season; £130 per tonne is assumed above for the 2009 harvest crop.

The average yield in the UK in the five years 2003 to 2007 was only 4.12 tonnes/ha, but in the previous five years it had been 5.47 tonnes per ha – showing that the potential of the crop is not always fully realised. The low yields are a result of it mainly being grown on light land, especially thin, drought-prone, poorish, marginal cereal-growing soils. In these circumstances, it can frequently out-yield wheat or barley, especially the former, and it has lower input requirements. Its yields tend to be more consistent on such soil than those of barley. Triticale tends to do well compared with second and subsequent wheats owing to its resistance to drought and fungal diseases.

Lower levels of fungicide are needed because of its good disease resistance, except for ergot, but including take-all (making it a possible replacement for a third or fourth wheat, as indicated above). It is a tall crop, which helps to suppress weeds, but it is susceptible to lodging; growth regulators are beneficial. New semi-dwarf varieties are being developed, to overcome straw strength weakness and susceptibility to rust infections.

The crop is best drilled early (September) on very light, drought-prone soils; otherwise October is satisfactory. Harvesting is at approximately the same time as wheat. There is more straw, which slows combining, and incorporation is difficult; this is less of a problem on poor soils as there is less straw.

Spring Triticale

New spring varieties of this crop have been introduced in the last few years. These have been taken up strongly in livestock areas – the north and west of England, as well as western Scotland, Wales and N. Ireland. Being a spring crop means that winter water logging is not an issue, and it can be grown on a wider range of soils. In total over 5,000 ha of spring triticale may well now be grown in the UK.

It has lower yields than winter triticale if it is harvested for grain in the conventional way. However, most is whole-cropped to produce an 'arable forage'. Often it is grown in a mixture with a proteins crop – peas or lupins for example. Inputs for spring triticale will be lower than those for winter varieties.

NAKED OATS

Production level..............................	Low	Average	High
Yield: tonnes per ha (tons per acre) ..	4.50 (1.8)	5.50 (2.2)	6.50 (2.6)
	£	£	£
Output:..	810 (328)	990 (401)	1170 (474)
Variable Costs:			
Seed		60 (24)	
Fertiliser..............................		230 (93)	
Sprays		85 (34)	
Total Variable Costs	375 (152)	375 (152)	375 (152)
Gross Margin per ha (acre)...........	**435** (176)	**615** (249)	**795** (322)

Naked oats have a higher protein, energy and oil content than 'traditional' oats, but the fibre content is lower – as the husk is removed during harvesting. Contracts require a maximum moisture content of 14%, which is also recommended for long-term storage.

The area being grown has increased steadily over the last few years, and naked oats now account for in excess of 10% of the traded tonnage of UK oats (i.e. excluding those grown for on-farm use). The traditional markets such as racehorse feed, dog food, and bird feed markets are all increasing. Over recent years the human consumption market has developed so that at least half the crop is now sold for health foods, fancy breads and breakfast cereals. In future, a further growth area is likely to be from demand for inclusion of the crop in monogastric animal feeds. The poultry industry in particular is setting up supply chains.

The 2009 harvest crop price assumed is £180 per tonne, based on contracts offering premiums 35% above the average feed wheat price. The premium can be reduced according to husk content.

Over 90% of the crop is winter sown, which is assumed above. NIAB survey results have suggested that yields average 20%-25% less than conventional oats. New spring varieties have become available that offer yields much closer to winter crops. The actual difference in yield will depend on the particular season, but are likely to be in the range 15-20%.

The agronomy of naked oats is similar to that of husked oat varieties. Variable inputs are lower than for wheat or barley. Traditionally, high nitrogen use has not been possible due to the risk of lodging, however, new semi-dwarf varieties with stiff straw have been introduced. As well as increasing the scope for higher fertiliser applications, this means the crop is also suited to more fertile soils, and growth regulators may be avoided. Oats provide a break in the take-all cycle.

Harvest is early (coming just after winter barley). New varieties are less susceptible to shedding than in the past, however care needs to be taken with both the timing of harvest, and the set-up of the combine, to ensure a clean, saleable, sample.

Naked Barley

Naked barley, suitable for roasting, flaking or milling as pearl barley, is now rarely heard of. It is grown like normal barley, but yields are reckoned to be some 15% lower. It could be either autumn or spring sown.

DURUM WHEAT

Production level	**Low**	**Average**	**High**
Yield: tonnes per ha (tons per acre) ..	5.20 (2.1)	6.20 (2.5)	7.50 (3.0)
	£	**£**	**£**
Output:	936 (379)	1116 (452)	1350 (547)
Variable Costs:			
Seed		90 (36)	
Fertiliser		284 (115)	
Sprays		100 (41)	
Total Variable Costs	474 (192)	474 (192)	474 (192)
Gross Margin per ha (acre)	**462** (187)	**642** (260)	**876** (355)

N.B. Extra drying costs estimated at £10 per tonne not shown in the margin.

A Mediterranean crop. As well as pasta, it is used to produce ethnic foods, semolina, biscuits, etc. Must be grown under contract as there is a very limited number of end users. Domestic demand is relatively small, but expanding; UK consumption per head is approx. 4% that of Italy and 10% that of France but total UK use nevertheless amounts to about 60,000 tonnes a year.

The crop started to be grown in England in the late 1970s and built up to 11,000 ha (27,000 acres) in 1984. A series of years of poor yields reduced this to a few hundred hectares by the mid-1990s. It has now recovered, with around 2,000 ha (5,000 acres) grown in most years.

On average the crop should yield 75%-80% of conventional feed wheat in the same situation. These levels are assumed in the margins above.

Contracts are based on a premium over the feed wheat price. For the 2009 harvest this will be £45 per tonne ex-farm for 'Grade A' durum, giving an estimated price of £180 per tonne. However this will be reduced if the crop does not fully meet quality specifications.

As with milling wheat, there is a risk of rejection if contaminated with excess foreign seeds, especially self-set cereals from previous crop; thus safer as a first cereal crop. A poor price is obtained if quality is too poor for pasta and thus has to go for feed.

The crop is likely to be grown only in the driest parts of the east/south east, where it can best compete with second and third wheats. It may be either autumn or spring sown; around two-thirds is currently autumn sown and this is assumed in the table above. The crop is very sensitive to stress and frost-kill in severe winters; the spring-sown crop is more reliable, and cheaper to grow, but the yield is usually 15-20% lower. Spring crops also allow more opportunities for black grass control. The crop has a higher disease resistance than other wheats, except for eyespot and ergot.

Harvesting is a critical operation; it needs to be done as soon as the crop reaches 20% moisture content, or at most 18%: it is very prone to sprouting and the quality for semolina is reduced if harvest is delayed. Must be dried (slowly) to 15%. It is easier and quicker to dry than normal wheat. The straw is of poorer quality and lesser quantity than conventional wheat straw and is therefore rarely baled.

MINORITY CROPS

Borage

Borage is indigenous to Britain (or at least here since Roman times); it has both been grown in the wild, and been cultivated for centuries. It is produced principally for use as a dietary supplement, but it may also be used in cosmetics and pharmaceuticals. The oil has a high gamma linolenic acid (GLA) content. It was first grown as a field crop in the UK in the early 1980's. The area planted for harvest 2009 is likely to be somewhat less than 5,000 hectares. It is essential for a grower to have a buy-back contract with a reputable company, and the crop should not be grown speculatively.

The crop is spring sown (March-April) into a good seedbed. Its aggressive growth gives good weed control with a high plant density. There are no significant pests and diseases, except for powdery mildew. Low rainfall areas are preferred owing to harvesting difficulties in wet conditions. It is combined in late July/early August, after swathing and drying, which takes a minimum of two weeks. Harvesting can be difficult and seed shedding at maturity is a problem. Seed should be promptly dried to 10% for safe storage. Cleaning may be necessary. Contract prices for 2009 are around £2,500/tonne.

Borage should only be considered by those prepared to invest sufficient time in the crop's husbandry, harvest and storage. Borage is a low yield / high risk crop – yields are from virtually nothing to 0.75 tonnes/ha (6 cwt./acre); average 0.4 (3.2).

Yield 0.4t/ha (0.2t/acre), Price £2500/t ex-farm	£/ha	(£/ac)
Output	1000	(405)
Variable Costs:		
Seed	140	(57)
Fertiliser	147	(60)
Sprays	25	(10)
Total Variable Costs	312	(126)
Gross Margin per ha (acre)	**688**	(279)

Camelina Sativa

Camelina, or Gold of Pleasure, or False Flax is a fast growing spring (or occasionally winter) sown crop. It is easily grown and harvested and is drought tolerant. The oil contains a range of essential fatty acids. It can be used as a food supplement or in industry as a drying oil. A few hundred hectares are being grown at present including 100 ha of organic production. It is thought that current requirements could support around 1,000 ha of the crop. Yields are in the 2.5tonne/ha range. Price is variable depending on the end use but the minimum for 2009 is likely to be £250/tonne.

Crambe - Abyssinian Mustard

Crambe is an industrial oilseed that contains high levels of erucic acid. Converted into erucamide it is used as a slip agent in plastics and is a constituent of heat sensitive dyes. The area of crambe in the UK had grown to around 5,000 ha. However, the major promoter/buyer of the crop went into receivership and little is being currently grown.

Crambe is a cruciferous spring crop managed in a similar way to spring oilseed rape. It has a short growing season, requiring only 100-120 days to reach maturity after emergence. As with oilseed rape, timely harvesting is important. Crambe can be combined direct, desiccated and combined or swathed. The crop should be stored and marketed at a moisture content of 9% or less. Yields are in the 2.5tonne/ha range. Contract prices offered in the past were £180/tonne. Growing costs are likely to be in the range £300-£350/ ha.

Echium

Echium is a relatively new commercial plant to the UK. It has been cultivated on contract for less than a decade. Currently there are fewer than 1,000 ha or so grown in the UK but the area is steadily increasing. It is a member of the Boraginacea family and is rich in stearidonic acid, which is used in cosmetic creams to reduce skin wrinkling and the effects of sunburn. It is essential for a grower to have a buy-back contract with a reputable company, and the crop should not be grown speculatively. In the past prices have collapsed to almost nothing due to over-supply in the market.

The crop can be grown as far north as Yorkshire. It has a husbandry programme similar to that of borage but does not shed its seed as readily as borage. The seed is relatively small in size. Echium is suitable for light to medium land whereas borage performs better on a wider range of soil types.

The crop is sown in April and should come to harvest in July/August. There appear to be no significant pests of the crop. Harvesting is carried out with the use of a swather. Yields are approximately 250kg/ha (100kg/acre). Contract prices for harvest 2009 are likely to be around £3,500/tonne of clean seed.

Evening Primrose

This crop is still an important source of gamma linolenic acid (GLA), but it is no longer grown in the UK and very little is cultivated elsewhere in Western Europe – it has been largely superseded by borage, which is easier to grow. The crop is still widely grown in China where the climate is more suitable, and labour costs are lower. Previous editions have given details of the crop and possible gross margin data.

Flax (cut flax for industrial fibre)

Flax was re-introduced into the UK during the 1990s, not as the traditional, pulled, long fibre variety used for linen textiles but as a cut, combinable crop producing shorter fibres for industrial uses – 'short-fibre flax'. As a natural, biodegradable fibre and a renewable resource it was promoted as a 'green' alternative to synthetic fibres and plastics. New markets were developed and several processing plants set up - the area of flax expanded to 20,200 ha in 1996. Following low prices and reform of the subsidy regime, the area fell to less than 2,000 ha by 2003, and the one remaining processing facility in Wales was closed. Little, if any, is currently grown.

The agronomy of flax is similar to that of linseed but it is harvested earlier. It is spring sown, suitable for most soil types although lighter soil is preferred. It is a low input crop but weed control is essential. It grows best in areas of high rainfall such as Wales and the South-west. There are several harvesting options (described in earlier editions). Currently the preferred option is desiccation followed by combining. The straw is left to rett in the field and then baled. Retting takes 10-21 days, depending on weather conditions. The price paid for straw will reflect quality. The fibre content of a reasonable crop is 20-30%.

Hemp

Production is co-ordinated by Hemcore of Essex under licence from the Home Office - growers no longer need individual licences. A new factory in Suffolk opened for the 2008 crop. This has the capacity to process the crop from 4,000 ha. Due to the bulkiness of the crop, the majority of it is still grown in the eastern counties, near to the processing facility.

It is drilled in late April/May and the fibre crop grows 3 to 3.5m (10-12 feet) tall. Hemcore suggests a minimum area of 10 ha. A well-grown crop should have no weed or pest problems. Improved technology in the new factory means fibres do not have to be left to rett in the field for as long. Instead of a retting period of 4-6 weeks, the crop is mowed, and then baled after 2 weeks. This increases saleable yields as the crop is allowed to grow for longer (cutting mid to late August), and there is less field-losses from the rows. Average yields should be around 7 tonnes/ha (2.8t/acre), with target yields at 8.5t/ha (3.4t/acre). The margin below assumes that the grower will undertake the cutting and baling operations. If contractors are used then the variable costs will obviously be higher.

The crop must be stored under cover. It is delivered to the factory throughout the year. The price of the delivered crop will be a minimum £130/tonne in October. This increases by an increment of £1.50/tonne/month (giving a price of £145 in August). An average delivered price of £135/tonne is assumed in the table below. Transport costs need to taken into consideration. A figure of £15/tonne is used in the table below. This should be applicable up to 50 miles from the factory (less if closer).

The outlook for hemp is good, as new markets have opened up. The main markets are in building insulation, and producing insulating panels for the automotive trade. Some hemp is also goes for the trading use in clothing. In the past, the core or pith of the plant has mainly been used for horse or poultry bedding. There is still a strong demand from this market, but it is also now been used as a binding fibre in plasterboard-type products for the building trade.

Yield 7.0t/ha (2.8t/acre), Price £135/t ex-farm	£/ha	(£/ac)
Output	945	(383)
Variable Costs:		
Seed	120	(49)
Fertiliser	284	(115)
Sprays	0	(0)
Haulage to factory (£15/tonne)	105	(43)
Total Variable Costs	509	(206)
Gross Margin per ha (acre)...	**436**	(177)

Dual Hemp

Hemp may also be grown as a dual-purpose crop. At present around 10-15% of the national hemp crop is of this type. The crop is left to mature longer, and then the top can be combined for the seed before the straw is mown and retted. A yield of 1.0-1.2 tonne/ha (0.4-0.5 t/ac) of seed is possible, with a contract price of up to £500/tonne. However, the yield of straw is lower at 5-6 tonnes/ha (2.0-2.4 t/ac), with the price being the same as 'conventional' hemp. The seed is cold-pressed to produce a high-value cooking oil, and is also used for bird feed, fishing bait and in nutritional supplements and cosmetics. Agronomy and costs are likely to be similar to a fibre crop. Because of the time needed to let the seed heads mature, an earlier-maturing variety (e.g. Finola) is often used. The later harvest also means that this crop is more suitable for early land in the East and South.

Grain Maize

Maize is one of the major global grains – with world output being higher than that for wheat. However, the climate of the UK has made it difficult to ripen the crop and most maize is grown for forage rather than grain. A combination of earlier varieties, the development of machinery that copes with wet conditions, and even possibly the effects of warmer summers has improved the prospects of this crop.

There is market potential, as over a million tonnes of grain maize are imported annually. It is used in animal rations, human foods, and in industrial processes. Marketing the UK crop is a problem at present as consignments are generally not big enough to interest the major buyers. The animal feed market is the likeliest outlet for domestic production - a specialised or local market can be developed, for example feed for pigeons or corn-fed chickens. The basis of pricing in the margin as a £20-£30/tonne premium over feed wheat. A further price premium of £10-20/tonne may be available for GM-free crops.

There is no fundamental difference between forage and grain maize – the same varieties are simply left in the field for 3-6 weeks longer to let the cobs mature. It is difficult to know how much of the total UK maize area is taken for grain but it could be around 3,000 ha. The crop can be grown south of a line from Bristol to East Anglia, excluding the far south-west. Fields should be below 500ft in elevation and south-facing. To maximise heat units, the crop should be drilled as soon as soil temperatures are above 8°c – usually late April/May. Harvest by conventional combine with an adapted header in

October/November. In UK conditions grain maize seldom drops below 30% moisture. The crop needs to be dried to 15% for storage which can be expensive and time-consuming. On good land the crop can yield 8-10 t/ha but the average is not likely to be so high.

Yield 7.0t/ha (2.8t/acre), Price £150/t ex-farm	£/ha	(£/ac)
Output	1050	(425)
Variable Costs:		
Seed	100	(41)
Fertiliser	300	(121)
Sprays	35	(14)
Total Variable Costs	435	(176)
Gross Margin per ha (acre)......................................	**615**	(249)
But note high drying costs:		
£15-20/t on-farm; £20-25/t off-farm	105-175	(42-71)

The majority of grain maize is currently stored as a crimped product. This sees the crop cut at 30-35% moisture from mid October to early November with the 'wet' grain being processed, and an additive added (usually an organic acid). The overall cost of crimping and preservative is around £12/tonne. The grain is clamped or put into large bales or bags. It provides a very digestible dairy feed of high nutrition content. Yields can be 11-13t/ha and it sells of £100-£125/tonne ex-farm.

Contact: Maize Growers Association: Town Barton Farm, Sandford, Crediton, Devon. EX17 4LS. www.maizegrowersassociation.co.uk

Millet

Millet is grown to contract and harvested exclusively for bird seed. The UK currently imports approximately 20,000 tonnes per year. It grows well in the South of England requiring warm temperatures.

Agronomically, it is a good break crop for tackling Blackgrass, being late drilled (late May or June), and is harvested in mid to late September. It does not grow well in heavy or very chalky soils.

Yield 3.5t/ha (1.4t/acre), Price £250/t ex-farm	£/ha	(£/ac)
Output	875	(354)
Variable Costs:		
Seed	100	(41)
Fertiliser	190	(77)
Sprays	40	(16)
Total Variable Costs	330	(134)
Gross Margin per ha (acre)......................................	**545**	(221)

Acknowledgement: Particular thanks to Premium Crops 02392 632 883

Navy Beans

Navy beans are the basis for the familiar canned 'baked beans'. Over 100,000t of these are consumed annually in the UK – with the vast majority of these being imported from North America. A few years ago there was some interest in the crop, as varieties adapted to the soil types and climate of the UK were introduced. However, disappointing prices, and the lack of area aid discouraged growers. Under the Single Payment navy beans are no longer at a disadvantage and growing contracts are available along the south coast, Kent, and some areas of East Anglia. The crop requires good fertile land and some care in growing. Sowing is in mid-May when there is no further frost risk. Harvesting is late August/early September.

The target yield is 3.0t/ha but the average is likely to be substantially less. When budgeting an average of around 2.0t/ha (0.8t/acre) could be assumed. There is very little market information available on price, but it is likely to be in the region of £250-£300/tonne. Variable costs are likely to be in the range £300-£350/ha.

Poppies

The growing of this crop in the UK is a relatively recent development. The poppy heads are processed to produce morphine for pharmaceutical purposes. A bit less than 3,000 ha of the crop are currently grown – all on contract to the sole UK processor.

The crop needs free-draining alkaline soils, it is planted in the second half of March, and is harvested in early to mid August. The processor undertakes the harvesting operation with a specialised machine. Seed is included as part of the contract, as is agronomy advice (the processor specifies the pesticides to be used). The grower needs to be able to offer on-floor drying facilities.

Yields are expressed in terms of the alkaloid that is derived from the poppy heads. For an average crop this should be in the region of 12kg/ha. The current (2008) contract pays a basic 'fee' of £350/ha plus £35/kg of alkaloid resulting in an average output of £770/ha. Prices for harvest 2009 were not available at the time of writing but are likely to feature a lower basic fee and higher alkaloid payments. Growing costs should be in the region of £300/ha (excluding the seed).

Contact: Johnson Matthey Macfarlan Smith, Unit 3, Shurnhold Farm Business Park, Bath Road, Melksham, Wiltshire SN12 8DF. 01225 793 679.

Soya Beans

Soya is a sub-tropical crop in origin, grown mainly in North and South America, but also to a small extent in southern Europe. The UK imports three quarters of a million tonnes each year as beans and almost a further 2 million tonnes as meal, all for animal feed, so there would appear to be a ready market for the home grown product.

Various attempts have been made to commercialise the crop in the UK. In the late 1990's new varieties were introduced and by the early 2000's the area expanded to 1,700 ha. But after several difficult years the planted area has declined. Currently, less than 100 ha are being grown. No significant expansion is expected until more reliable varieties are available to growers. However, the plant breeding process continues and the introduction of types more suited to the UK climate could see the viability of the crop improve. As a legume, soya is a good alternative break crop.

Sown from mid-April, depending on soil temperature, altitude should not exceed 70m above sea level. The crop is combine harvested in September. The crop should be cleaned and dried to 14% moisture and 2% admixture. Fertiliser and spray costs are low.

Target yield is 3.0t/ha but the average is likely to be less; an average of 2.5t/ha (1.0t/acre) could be assumed particularly in early years as producers become familiar with the crop. The price is largely determined by the price of imported crop. The UK crop is GM free, for which a premium is paid. A further premium may be paid for Identity Preserved UK crop which goes into human consumption or for organically grown soya. For 2009 the price is assumed to be £300/tonne. Variable costs are in the range £300-£350/tonne.

Sunflower

The UK imports the equivalent of about 400,000 tonnes of sunflower seed each year, mainly as sunflower oil. Currently none is commercially crushed in the UK. There has been continued interest in sunflower, but late harvests and low yields have restricted the development of the crop. Currently only about 500 to 600 ha are grown, producing some 1,000 tonnes of seed. Almost all UK production goes into the pet-food or bird seed market; with good demand, but only in localised areas. Producers should satisfy themselves of the end-market before planting the crop. The birdseed market takes 20,000 tonnes of sunflower seed annually, so there is scope for import substitution. Some attempts have been made to cold-press sunflowers to produce a UK-sunflower oil, but this market is still in its infancy.

Extra-early maturing semi-dwarf hybrid varieties are the most suitable to conditions in the UK. This should allow harvesting by mid-September without significant yield reduction. Yields of up to 2.5t/ha with oil content of 44% are possible. However, the crop still needs a relatively mild climate and is best grown south-east of a line from the Wash to east Dorset. Although sunflower will grow on a broad range of soil types its capacity to do well in dry and sandy soils and areas of low rainfall is a recommendation. Sowing is from April to early May when the soil temperature is 7-8°C. Pre-emergence weed control may be necessary; at the right plant density weeds should not subsequently be a problem. As it is a broad row crop, chemical or mechanical weed control is possible. Sclerotina and botrytis, in a wet season, may affect the crop; on areas of less than 6 ha bird damage can be serious. The crop is dried to 8 or 9% for safe storage (costs average £75/ha). Sunflower has a low nitrogen requirement, which may offer benefits in areas of restricted nitrogen use and in organic production.

The price is usually based on a premium over the price of oilseed rape, but other pricing mechanisms may be used in specialist markets.

	£/ha	(£/ac)
Yield 2.0t/ha (0.8t/acre), Price £350/t ex-farm		
Output	700	(284)
Variable Costs:		
Seed	110	(45)
Fertiliser	155	(63)
Sprays*	40	(16)
Total Variable Costs	305	(124)
Gross Margin per ha (acre)..	**395**	(160)

*   Note: drying costs can be very high.

Contact: United Kingdom Sunflower Association (UKSA) c/o HGCA

Others

Other crops that have been in the news in recent years as possible new crops for the future (or present crops capable of substantial development) include the following: chickpeas and lentils, fenugreek, meadowfoam, cuphea, peppermint, quinoa, buckwheat, honesty and herbs for their essential oils. At present there are no reliable data for these crops on average yield expectations and little on prices or variable costs, when grown on a commercial scale in this country. A number of them are either for the health food market or are sources of oil for industry as replacements for whale oil and light mineral oil. Research continues on many of them. More details may be available from the contact listed below;

Contact: National Non-Food Crops Centre (NNFCC): www.nnfcc.co.uk

VINING PEAS

Production level	Low £	Average £	High £
Output:	1000 (405)	1300 (527)	1 600 (648)
Variable Costs:			
Seed		180 (73)	
Fertiliser		87 (35)	
Sprays		116 (47)	
Total Variable Costs		383 (155)	
Gross Margin per ha (acre)	**617** (250)	**917** (371)	**1217** (493)

1. The table above relates to vining peas grown on contract where harvesting (approx. £65/tonne) and haulage (approx. £35/tonne) are paid for separately; the average price in this situation ranges from £220 to £350/tonne depending primarily on quality. The average yield is taken as 4.75 tonnes/ha; the national average (fresh weight) for the last five years has ranged between 4.3 and 5.4 although growers are paid on frozen weight. Top quality ('150 minute') peas have to be grown within 40 miles of the factory. More distant 'long haul' peas will be in the lower price range. A pea viner costs £280,000 - £320,000.

   The average yield of petit pois is lower but the price averages 12 to 15% more.

2. *Fertiliser.* many growers use no fertiliser; but refer to combining peas for details.

3. *Sprays.* both herbicide and aphicide are commonly used with fungicides being used dependant on seasonal requirements.

4. *Labour:* see p. 148.

5. Around 36,000 ha are grown in the UK annually with a view to vining a 150,000-tonne crop.

MAINCROP POTATOES

Production level..........................	Low	Average	High
Yield: tonnes per ha (tons per acre)	37.0 (15)	45.0 (18.2)	53.0 (21.5)
	£	£	£
Output:..	4477 (1,813)	5445 (2,205)	6413 (2,597)
Variable Costs:			
Seed..		690 (279)	
Fertiliser....................................		661 (268)	
Sprays..		502 (203)	
grading......................................	609 (247)	743 (301)	884 (358)
Sundries (levy, sacks, etc.).........	365 (148)	415 (168)	470 (190)
Total Variable Costs....................	2827 (1,145)	3010 (1219)	3207 (1,299)
Gross Margin per ha (acre).............	**1650** (668)	**2435** (986)	**3206** (1298)

1. *Prices.* The price assumed above is £130 per tonne for ware and £10 for stockfeed (assumed to be 7½ per cent), which is £121 per tonne for the whole crop. The actual price in any one season depends largely on the national average yield but also increasingly international trade. Variations according to quality and market (as well as season) are now considerable. The six-year average GB price for wares between 2002 and 2007 was £112/t but the average annual price varied from £69.30 in 2002 to £138 in 2007.

2. *Physical Inputs.* Seed: 60% planted with certified seed: 2.8 tonnes per hectare at £200-270 per tonne (the price varies widely from season to season); 40% with once-grown seed: 2.6 tonnes per hectare at £180 per tonne. Sprays: herbicide, blight control, and haulm destruction.

3. *Casual Labour.* The figure in the table above is for assistance during (machine) harvesting and for grading/riddling (approx. £17.00/tonne); it is assumed that most of the labour for the latter is supplied by casuals.

4. Contract mechanical harvesting: approximately £300/hectare (excl. pickers, carting, etc.). Other contract work see page 169.

5. British Potato Council levy: £39/ha (£15.78/acre) for growers in 2008, £44/ha for late payers; exempt from levy if less than 3ha grown. No decision is due for 2009 until December 2008 at the earliest.

6. Potato Land Rentals range depending on the year, location, soil and water from over £750/ha (£300/acre) to around £500/ha (£200/acre).

7. Sacks. Approx. £7.70 per tonne.

8. Fuel and Repairs (per hectare): £270.

9. Specialised Equipment Prices: see page 163.

10. Potato Store Costs: see page 195.

11. *Labour:* see p. 148.

EARLY POTATOES

Production level.........................	Low	Average	High
Yield: tonnes per ha (tons per acre)	17.0 (7)	22.0 (8.9)	27.0 (10.9)
	£	£	£
Output:..................................	2975 (1,205)	3850 (1,559)	4725 (1,914)
Variable Costs:			
Seed.....................................		805 (326)	
Fertiliser................................		650 (263)	
Sprays..................................		252 (102)	
Casual labour.........................		349 (142)	
Sundries (levy, sacks, etc.).........		265 (107)	
Total Variable Costs...................		2321 (940)	
Gross Margin per ha (acre)............	**654** (265)	**1529** (619)	**2404** (974)

Notes

1. Prices and Yields. The price assumed above is an average of £175 per tonne for a 22 tonne/ha yield. However, yields increase and prices fall as the season progresses. Thus both depend on the date of lifting, e.g. late May to early June, 7 to 12 tonnes per hectare; July, 20 to 30 tonnes per hectare. Prices in late May to mid June are typically three times those in July; the very earliest crops (early May) can even fetch more than £1,000 per tonne, but the price could be down to £500 by mid May and to £250 or even £200 by the end of May. Thus the average output of £3,850 given above could be obtained from 10 tonnes at £385 per tonne, 15 at £257, 20 at £192 or 30 at £128.

2. Casual labour for planting: £127 per hectare, plus help with harvesting/grading.

3. Fuel and Repairs (£ per hectare): £250.

4. *Labour:* see p. 148.

In 2007, the percentages of the total potato area in Great Britain planted in early, second early and main crop, respectively were 5, 31 and 63 in England, 20, 52 and 28 in Wales, 3, 38 and 59 in Scotland and 5, 33 and 62 of the total GB potato area.

SUGAR BEET

Production level..........................	Low	Average	High
Yield: tonnes per ha (tons per acre)*	48.0 (19)	62.0 (25.1)	72.0 (29.2)
	£	£	£
Output:..	1450 (587)	1873 (759)	2175 (881)
Variable Costs:			
Seed.......................................		159 (64)	
Fertiliser...................................		277 (112)	
Sprays......................................		152 (62)	
Transport (Contract)...............	216 (87)	279 (113)	324 (131)
Total Variable Costs...................	804 (326)	867 (351)	912 (369)
Gross Margin per ha (acre)............	**646** (262)	**1006** (407)	**1263** (512)

* 'Adjusted tonnes' at standard 16% sugar content

1. *Prices.* The 'all-in' delivered price for the entire 2009 crop is expected to be £31.21 per adjusted tonne. This is based on 95% sold 'in contract' and 5% over contract tonnage. For contracted tonnage, two marketing options are available; one is a minimum price of £24 plus upside (based on exchange rate and wheat price) or a fixed guaranteed price of £26 per tonne. These are before transport allowances and late delivery allowance, expected to average £4.75 per adjusted tonne (at 78p/€). For tonnage over contract, a delivered price of 20/tonne is used. This margin uses the fixed price option.

   This is not a reflection of what has happened in the past, but the change in contract and lower prices encourages growers to achieve closer to their contractual tonnage. All the above prices are per adjusted (contract) tonne.

   Late delivery bonus. 26th December — 7th January: 0.8% of UK minimum price; thereafter, the rate rises by 0.2% per day.

2. *Effect of Harvesting Date.* As the season progresses, changes occur in the crop before lifting, approximately as follows, on average:

	early Sept to early Oct.	early Oct. to early Nov.	early Nov. to early Dec.	early Dec to early Jan.
Yield (tons of washed beet /ha)	up 3.75	up 1.9	up 1.25	up 1.25
Sugar Content (%)	up 1%	up ¼%	down ¼%	down ¾%
Yield of Sugar (kg / ha)	up 1000	up 375	up 190	down 60

3. *Sprays.* Herbicides normally comprise between 85% and 92.5% of the total cost of spray materials.

4. *Contract.* Contract mechanical harvesting costs approx. £272 per hectare excluding carting or £303 per hectare including carting.

5. *Transport.* Contract haulage charges vary according to distance to factory. The figure assumed above is approximately £4.50 per (unadjusted) tonne of unwashed beet including loading and cleaning (dirt and top tare assumed at 14% in total).

6. *Fuel and Repairs* (per hectare): £270

7. *Specialised Equipment Prices*: see page 163

8. *Labour*: see page 153

TOP FRUIT

Established crops: per hectare

Note: This section was completely updated last year. This was to reflect the changes in production systems. The figures indicate a range within which the performance of many, but not all orchards, is likely to fall. The gross margin is calculated as lower yields less lower costs/higher yields less higher costs. In practice, of course, this does not necessarily follow.

	Dessert Apples	Culinary Apples	Pears
Yield: tonnes/ha	15–50	25-45	15-30
Price (£/tonne)	450-750	200-400	450-600
	£	£	£
Output	7500-35000	5000-18000	6750-18000
Variable Costs*			
Orchard Depreciation	250-1200	150-300	100-300
Fertilisers/Sprays	875-1300	650-1100	650-100
Crop Sundries	50-200	50-100	50-100
Picking	555-1850	925-1665	555-1110
Grading/Packing	1875-6250	1625-5625	1875-3750
Packaging	600-4000	375-2250	525-1800
Transport	825-2750	375-2475	570-1650
Commission/Levies	500-3000	300-1500	300-1000
Total Variable Costs*	5530-20550	4450-15015	4625-10710
Gross Margin	1970-14450	550-2985	2125-7290

* Excludes Storage

1. **Price:** Average of all grades. Varies significantly with grade-out.

2. **Orchard Depreciation:** Establishment costs written off over lifetime of orchard. Establishment includes trees, stakes (at approximately £5-7 per tree) and, in newer plantings, support structures and irrigation. Total establishment costs of £4000 - £20,000 per hectare at planting densities of 750 – 3500 tress per hectare.

3. **Orchard Duration:** Traditional apples around 20 years, pears 30 years plus. Denser apple systems likely to be nearer 15 years, with full cropping in years 3-5 (c.f. 6-9 for traditional systems).

4. **Crop Sundries:** Including tree ties, stake replacement, bee hire, picking hods, etc.

5. **Picking:** Based on £37 per tonne average (to include supervision). In practice can vary significantly with yield, apple size and quality, etc.

6. **Grading and Packing:** Based on £125 per tonne. Can vary considerably, particularly with crop quality.

7. **Packaging:** Average of between £30-60 per tonne. Considerable variations arise from both crop quality (i.e. grade-out) and customer.

8. **Transport:** Includes allowance for farm to packer cost, as well as delivery to final customer.

9. **Commission/Levies:** Including both marketeer's and retailer's commission, as well as promotional levies (e.g. English Apples and Pears).

Acknowledgements (Top & Soft Fruit): Andersons Midlands and Farm Advisory Services Team Ltd.

SOFT FRUIT

Established crops per hectare

Note: This section has been completely updated for this edition to reflect the changes in production systems. The figures indicate a range within which the performance of many, but not all crops is likely to fall. The gross margin is calculated as lower yields less lower costs/higher yields less higher costs. In fruit, of course, this does not necessarily follow.

	Strawberries Raised Bed June Bearers	Strawberries Everbearers	Raspberries
Yield: tonnes/ha	18-23	20-28	8-15
Price (£/tonne)	2400-2800	2300-2700	4500-5500
	£	**£**	**£**
Output	43200-64400	46000-75600	36000-82500
Variable Costs			
Plants/planting/Sterilisation (w/o over 3yrs)	2750-3500	9000-11000	1200-1500
Structures (average annual cost).	5000-8000	5000-8000	5000-8000
Fertilisers/Sprays/Predators	900-1300	950-1500	750-1100
Fieldwork	1260-2625	1575-3150	2625-4200
Picking	13000-17000	10500-15750	11600-21750
Grading/Packing	6300-8400	6300-8400	7600-14250
Packaging	2900-4200	2100-3700	3040-5700
Transport/Commission	5200-7800	6300-9500	4800-11250
Total Variable Costs	37310-52825	41725-61000	36615-67750
Gross Margin	5890-11575	4275-14600	(615)-14750

1. **Strawberries – June bearers:** Plants – assumes 35,000 per hectare. Assume 60 day cropping in year 1 followed by 2 further years. Plants/planting/sterilisation written off over crop life of 3 years. Bed making not included as a variable cost.

    Structures – annual cost of poly-tunnels including both metalwork (w/o 10 years) and plastic (w/o 3 years). Costs also included for erection, dismantling and venting.

    Fieldwork – weeding, removing runners, leaf thinning etc.

    Picking- including supervision. Variations with crop yield, quality.

2. **Strawberries – Everbearers:** Plants – assumes 25,000 per hectare. Plants/planting written off over crop life of one year. Sterilisation cost w/o over 3 years. Bed making not included as a variable cost.

    Structures – annual cost of poly-tunnels including both metalwork (w/o 10 years) and plastic (w/o 3 years). Costs also included for erection, dismantling and venting.

    Fieldwork – weeding, removing runners, leaf thinning, etc.

3. **Raspberries:** Plants – 8000 per hectare at 35 pence per plant. Planting at 10 pence per plant.

    Wirework – to include material and labour.

    Plants/planting/wirework written off over crop life of 5 years.

    Picking – at £1450 per tonne (£1.45 per kilo). Packing – at £950 per tonne (95 pence per kilo). Packaging – at £380 per tonne (38 pence per kilo).

Blackcurrants: Although a soft fruit this crop is much more of a field crop grown on arable farms with machine harvesting. The vast majority of the UK blackcurrant crop is grown for processing into cordial drink. Typical output would be 6-7 tonnes/ha sold at £650-£700 per tonne = £3,900-£4,900/ha, with annual variable costs at £1,370/ha leaving a gross margin of £2,530-£3,530/ha (fertiliser £300, sprays £470, and casual labour £600). Establishment costs approximately £7,000/ha for bushes with full production in year 2 followed by up to 10 years cropping.

FIELD-SCALE VEGETABLES

Per hectare (per acre in brackets)

Note: This section has been greatly reduced this year because it has become so difficult to source reliable figures for these types of crops. The changes in the fresh produce supply sector in recent years are commented on further in the notes below. The enterprises shown below are still grown by non specialist farmers with suitable land, and the figures shown are on the basis that these output levels and variable costs represent 'typical' levels for the farmer with other major costs such as harvesting, packing and marketing expenses born by the produce company taking the crop.

	Dry Bulb Onions	*Cauliflower*	*Calabrese*
Yield: tonnes/ha (tons/acre)........	41 (16.6)		
Net Price (£/tonne)......................	100		
	£	£	£
Output...	4,100 (1659)	2,100 (850)	1,900 (768)
Variable Costs:			
Seed..	470 (190)	820 (332)	725 (293)
Fertiliser....................................	345 (140)	260 (105)	285 (115)
Sprays...	510 (206)	155 (63)	200 (81)
Total Variable Costs.................	1,325 (536)	1,235 (500)	1,210 (489)
Gross Margin.............................	2,775 (1123)	865 (350)	690 (279)

Notes on the fresh produce market: most of the crops included in past editions are now grown predominantly by a few highly specialised growers or produce companies – crops such as carrots, parsnips, leeks, lettuce, rhubarb, and many of the brassicas. These growers supply the multiple retailers with high volumes and working to high specification. The other key market for fresh produce is the local market with growers usually on a small scale and often tied into a local food chain such as a farm shop. These crops tend to have a high entry cost relative to other cropping alternatives, and bear significant risk, and it is therefore necessary to research carefully the potential end market in terms of its expectations and cost structure.

HORTICULTURE – WHOLE FARM DATA

Comparative whole farm data is less generally available for horticultural holdings than for various types of farm in different regions of the country (see sources of reports listed on page 4). Data from across a wide area of England is presented below. Because the results vary so much from year to year two-year averages are presented: for 2005 and 2006 harvest/cropping years. The data is collected by seven College/University centres: Askham Bryan, Cambridge, Duchy College, Newcastle, Nottingham, Reading and Wye.

All financial figures are per hectare. The averages cover a wide range.

Type of Holding	Specialist Glass		Specialist Outdoor	
	Mainly edible crops	Flowers & nursery stock	Fruit	Hortic.
No. of Farms in Sample	31	58	40	30
Average Size (ha [acres])	1.59 (3.92)	0.63(1.6)	32 (79.1)	50 (123)
	£	£	£	£
Gross Output	197,345	514,182	5,735	8,476
Less:				
Bought Seed and Plants	9,486	132,767	66	909
Market Charges	16,252	13,004	741	283
Packing Materials	11,298	23,182	634	324
Other Variable Costs	2,398	206	25	10
Net Output	157,911	345,023	4,269	6,950
Other Costs:				
Labour (inc. Unpaid Manual)	71,632	175,482	2,052	2,768
Glasshouse Fuel	23,022	18,305	3	44
Manures	4,776	15,579	54	267
Sprays and Fumigants	2,239	2,882	280	216
Horticultural Sundries	8,813	17,635	302	684
Power and Machinery	14,706	40,710	696	1,167
Land Rent, Glass Deprecn.	12,085	24,282	438	568
Other Fixed Costs	13,494	37,716	549	553
Total Other Costs	150,767	332,591	4,374	6,267
Management and Inv. Inc.	7,144	12,432	-105	683
Grower and Spouse Labour (+)	13,310	33,309	412	362
Net Income	20,454	45,741	307	1,045
Tenant's Valuation	126,410	331,950	5,148	4,601

Source: Horticultural Business Data, compiled by R. L. Vaughan and R. T. Crane, Department of Agricultural and Food Economics, The University of Reading, 2007.

Glasshouse Crop Outputs (at 5-year average yields (2002-2006) and 5-year average prices (same period); all figures rounded): Source, Defra.

	Yield t/ha (t/acre)	Price £/tonne	Output £/ha (acre)
Tomatoes, heated	424 (172)	888	376,512 (152,372)
Tomatoes, cold	128 (52)	1,077	137,856 (55,888)
Cucumbers	484 (196)	552	267,168 (108,121)
Lettuce	35 (14)	1,317	46,095 (18,654)

HOPS

1. *Output data*

Average Yield: per ha, 2002-2007: 27.61 zentners (1 zentner = 50 kg); range 26.0 (2006) to 31.6 (2004).

Average Price (£ per zentner)	Contract	Spot	Overall
2000.	204	140	193
2001.	191	131	178
2002.	177	114	142
2003.	160	104	155
2004.	164	67	134
2005.	191	136	186
2006	199	-	198
2007	241	419	254

Main Varieties*	ha 2007	av. yield 2001-2007 (z. per ha)	prices (£ per zentner)					
			2007			2006		
			contract	spot	overall	contract	spot	overall
Target..........	121	31.5	126	340	151	121	-	121
Challenger...	81	30.8	230	-	230	214	-	214
Goldings......	275	32.4	250	500	288	235	-	235
Fuggles........	40	31.7	260	500	307	238	-	238
First Gold	166	20.1	178	500	185	170	-	170
Phoenix	11	31.1	170	350	200	103	-	103
Admiral.......	47	37.4	150	324	165	119	-	119
Others..........	204	24.5		-	300			200
Organic........	13	20.0	560	-	560	560	-	560

* over 85% of the total area grown.

Total area of hops (ha): 2007; 1,062: 2006: 1,042; 2005: 1,071: 1997: 3,067; 1984: 5,091. Early last century over 28,000 ha (70,000 acres) were grown.

2. *Variable Costs* per mature hectare (acre) (materials only)

	£/ha	(£/ac)
Fertilisers and Manure...	214	(87)
Insecticide / Fungicide...	589	(239)
Herbicide..	127	(51)
String...	188	(76)
Pockets / Bales..	60	(24)
Drying Fuel..	452	(183)
Total...	1,630	(660)

3. *Average Direct Labour Costs* per mature hectare (acre)

	£/ha	(£/ac)
Growing...	1,074	(435)
Picking...	1,926	(780)
Drying..	452	(183)
Total...	3,452	(1398)

A new hop garden (erecting the poles, wiring and planting) could cost in the order of £20,000 per hectare (£8,000 per acre).

Acknowledgement: Chris Daws, Sales Director, English Hops and Herbs.

VINEYARDS

As at August 2007 the total area under vines in England and Wales was 992 hectares, although the actual area in production was 697 hectares. There were 383 registered vineyards; any vineyard over 0.1 hectare must be registered with the Wine Standards Branch of the Food Standards Agency (FSA), though many of the smaller vineyards are run purely as a hobby. Although the average size of vineyards in the UK is only 2.59 ha, there are several vineyards of over 100 ha and around 60 vineyards account for 70% of the planted area. There has been a fall in the number of vineyards and the area planted since the mid-1990s (479 vineyards, 1,065 ha in 1993), although numbers have recovered in more recent years. Industry observers estimate that FSA figures underestimate the area planted and that today (2008) the area under vines is nearer 1,250 ha.

In 2007 (a low cropping year owing to poor flowering conditions) 994,800 litres (1,427 litres per productive hectare) were produced. Around 80% of production is white wine and 20% red. Since the very warm year of 2003, the plantings of Champagne varieties (Chardonnay, Pinot Noir and Meunier) have increased significantly, and almost all plantings in the last five years (2004-2008) have been for the production of sparkling wine. Pinot Noir is now the most widely planted variety (121 ha), followed by Chardonnay (120 ha). Although these varieties now account for around 50% of the total vine area, the amount of sparkling wine on the market is still small as bottle-fermented sparkling wines take between 2 and 5 years to mature after bottling.

There is no EU ban on planting vines in the UK and in 2008 it was confirmed that there will not be one in the future, whatever level production reaches. A Quality Wine Scheme for England and Wales was introduced in 1991 and a Regional Wine Scheme in 1997. Hybrid varieties may be planted in the UK but may not currently be made into Quality Wine. They may be used for Quality Sparkling Wine and Regional Wine. All wines sold in the UK bear the same VAT and duty, irrespective of origin (although the duty on sparkling wines is higher than that for still wines). A significant proportion of home-produced wine is sold at the farm gate but supermarkets and off-licences are increasingly stocking it. It supplies only 0.3% of the home market. UKVA has set up a marketing arm, English Wine Producers, to promote all English wine. From 2003, to conform with EU legislation, English table wine has been called United Kingdom table wine unless it qualifies for a description of regional origin. From the 2003 vintage, regional wines have been allowed to carry details of vintage, vineyard and varieties on their labels. Since then there has been a marked increase in successful applications for Quality and Regional wine labelling and overall, quality levels have risen. Sparkling wines are not covered by the Quality or Regional Wine Schemes.

The quality of any wine is dependent on the quality of the site, and vineyards ideally need south facing, well-drained and sheltered land, less than 100 metres (330 ft.) above sea level, in the southern half of England and Wales. A high level of management and marketing is essential, as is expert advice. There is no minimum area for profitable production. A small enterprise selling wine at the farm gate and to local hotels and restaurants may be more profitable than one with 10 hectares selling only grapes. Some vineyards have associated gift shops and restaurants and are involved with corporate entertaining, which provide extra income. It is now possible to grow grapes under contract for several successful vineyards that have run out of suitable land of their own. Contracts vary, but prices can be up to £1,000/tonne for grapes for still wine and £1,500/tonne for sparkling.

There are various growing systems: the intensive Double Guyot, the most common in France and Germany, and now 75% of British vineyards, and the more extensive Geneva Double Curtain. Other systems such as the divided canopy Scott Henry system are being tried. The Double Guyot system will yield little until year 3 and be in full production in year 4. Geneva Double Curtain will not have a full yield until year 5 or 6 but crops more heavily. The Scott-Henry system crops fully in year 4 or 5.

Investment capital (to include materials and labour for planting and the first two years establishment but not the cost of the land) of £18,000 to £24,000/ha is typically required for the vineyard. Equipment for a winery costs a minimum of £50,000-£60,000 and a suitable building is needed. Contract winemaking is, however, generally considered better for smaller vineyards of less than 4 ha as it gives them access to state of the art equipment and techniques. Growers who produce their own wine will also have to budget for the picking, processing and bottling of at least two vintages (still wine) or three to five vintages (sparkling wine) before income from selling their wines starts making a meaningful contribution to the enterprise.

Yields and quality are very variable, according to the variety of grape, the year and the quality of management, in particular the quality of pest and disease control. In a reasonable year a well-sited, well-managed vineyard should yield 7.5-10.0 tonnes/hectare (3-4 tonnes/acre), but higher annual yields are possible. An average yield over ten years could be around 8.65 tonnes/ha (3.5 tonnes/acre). For still wine production, around 950 75cl bottles will be produced from 1 tonne of grapes; for sparkling wine the production will be nearer 750-800 75cl bottles

The following costs refer to a commercial enterprise on a suitable site with a broad variety range. Establishment costs could be double if the site has to be drained and provided with windbreaks and rabbit fencing. Annual growing costs can also be significantly greater, depending on planting density, variety, yield and management.

	Double Guyot		Geneva Double Curtain	
	per ha	(per acre)	per ha	(per acre)
Number of Vines..............	2,600-5,000	(1,050-2,025)	1,120-1,800*	(450-725)
	£ per ha	£ per ac	£per ha	£ per ac
Establishment Costs:	over 2 years		over 3 years	
Materials	12,350	(5,000)	8,500	(3,450)
Labour.......................	11,000	(4,450)	7,000	(2,835)
Total Establishment Costs	23,350	(9,450)	15,500	(6,270)
Subsequent Annual Costs:				
Materials	975	(395)	975	(395)
Labour (growing)......	3,850	(1,560)	3,850	(1,560)
Harvesting**.............	450	(180)	450	(180)
Total Annual Costs	5,275	(2,135)	5,275	(2,135)

* The Scott-Henry System uses a lower planting density, but the extra trellis work means that establishment costs are typically some 5-10% higher.

** Harvesting costs are very yield dependent. Growers without wineries will also have transport costs.

Prices: Grape prices will vary according to the variety and the vintage. They range from £600 to £1,000 per tonne delivered to a winery. Pinot Noir or Chardonnay for sparkling wine may be £1,200 to £1,500 per tonne. Wine prices vary widely but are likely to be in the range £5 to £6.50 per bottle for typical still white wines, and up to £10 for red wine at retail. English sparkling wine may retail at £15 to £20 a bottle but is more costly to produce. A retail price for still wine of at least £5.50 per bottle is necessary to break even for most enterprises.

e.g.　£5.50 less 17.5% VAT and £1.46① duty = £3.22②

Less own winery costs (materials and labour) £1.75 per bottle③ = £1.47.

At 8.75 tonnes per ha and 950 bottles per tonne = £12,220 per ha (£4,950/acre).

① Sparkling wine of 8.5% or more has a duty rate of £1.87 per 75cl bottle; other wines £1.46 per 75cl bottle

② If wines are sold via a wholesaler and/or retailer, gross profit margin of at least 10% (wholesaler) and 30% (retailer) must be allowed for.

③ Having still wine made under contract costs about £2.50 a bottle. Sparkling wine will be £5.00 per bottle.

Acknowledgements:

Stepehn Skelton MW, Viticultural Consultant, 1B Lettice Street, London, SW6 4EH. Tel: 07768 583 700. www.englishwine.com *United Kingdom Vineyards Association*, Mrs Sian Liwicki, General Secretary, PO Box 534, Abingdon, OX14 9BZ. Tel: 01865 390 188.

2. GRAZING LIVESTOCK

DAIRY COWS

Holstein Friesians (per cow per year)

	Low	Average	High	Very High
Yield Group (1)..	Low	Average	High	High
Milk Yield per Cow (litres) (2)........................	5,500	7,000	8,000	9,000
	£	£	£	£
Milk Value per Cow (3)...................................	1430	1820	2080	2340
Plus Value of Calves (4).................................	50	45	40	40
Plus Value of Cull Cows (5)............................	100	100	100	100
Less Cost or Market Value of Replacements (6, 7)	£375	375	375	375
Output...	1205	1590	1845	2105
Concentrate Costs (8)....................................	285	380	494	618
Miscellaneous Variable Costs (10)....................	184	189	197	208
Gross Margin before deducting Forage Variable Costs (inc. Bought Fodder).................	736	1021	1154	1280
Margin of Milk over Concentrates (MOC) (9).......	1145	1440	1586	1723

Gross Margins per Cow and per Hectare (acre) at 4 different stocking rates (11)

Performance Level	Low	Average	High	Very High
1. At 1·75 cows per forage hectare (low):				
(0·57 forage hectares (1·4 acres) per cow)				
Forage Var. Costs & Bulk Feeds per Cow (11)	165	165	165	165
Gross Margin per Cow	571	856	989	1114
Gross Margin per Forage Hectare	998	1497	1730	1950
Gross Margin per Forage Acre	404	605	700	788
2. At 2 cows per forage hectare (average):				
(0·5 forage hectares (1·25 acres) per cow)				
Forage Var. Costs & Bulk Feeds per Cow (11)	**198**	**198**	**198**	**198**
Gross Margin per Cow	**538**	**823**	**956**	**1081**
Gross Margin per Forage Hectare	**1075**	**1645**	**1911**	**2162**
Gross Margin per Forage Acre	**435**	**665**	**773**	**874**
3. At 2·25 cows per forage hectare (high):				
(0·45 forage hectares (1·1 acres) per cow)				
Forage Var. Costs & Bulk Feeds per Cow (11)	222	222	222	222
Gross Margin per Cow	514	799	932	1058
Gross Margin per Forage Hectare	1157	1798	2097	2380
Gross Margin per Forage Acre	468	727	848	962
4. At 2·5 cows per forage hectare (very high):				
(0·4 forage hectares (1 acre) per cow)				
Forage Var. Costs & Bulk Feeds per Cow (11)	258	258	258	258
Gross Margin per Cow	478	763	896	1021
Gross Margin per Forage Hectare	1194	1906	2239	2553
Gross Margin per Forage Acre	483	771	905	1032

1. This is yield group per cow. Increases in this are usually (though not necessarily) associated with more intensive farming operations. Intensification focuses on higher gross margins per hectare, whilst extensification on higher gross margins of other resources. Increase in concentrate feeding (kg/litre) and other inputs have been assumed as yields rise: see note 8.

2. *Yield.* The yield referred to is litres produced during a year divided by the average number of cows and calved heifers in the herd. The average yield given (7,000 litres) is an estimated national figure for sizeable herds of black and white cows in 2009. Note average yields for *costed* herds are usually above national averages; they exceeded 7,500 litres in 2008, with the highest yielding 10% exceeding 9,000. The same is true of 'recorded herds', i.e. those in milk recording schemes, where the average yield is well over 1,000 litres above the national average. The average yield for organic milk producers is around 6,000 litres.

3. *Milk Price.* This is assumed (as an average for the 2009 calendar year) to be 26.00p per litre, after deducting transport costs. It incorporates all adjustments: for milk composition, hygiene and seasonality. This is an average for all milk marketing groups, after bonuses etc., assuming an average-sized herd. Variable transport charges according to the amount collected mean that smaller herds will achieve a lower average price.

The average price received by individual producers depends on seasonality of production and compositional quality. Output and Gross Margin per cow are changed as follows by each 0·25p per litre difference in price at each performance level:

Low	Average	High	Very High
±£13.75	±£17.50	±£20.00	±£22.50

Seasonality Price Adjustments. These are diverse between the various dairy companies. An increasing number of companies no longer operate conventional seasonal adjustments but instead have payment systems that encourage a level monthly production, with a range of deductions and bonuses related to the individual producer's spring and autumn deliveries. The average adjustments for a selection of companies operating conventional adjustments were as follows in 2008/09:

April	May	June	July	Aug	Sept	Oct	Nov	Dec	Jan–Mar
–2	–3	–2	0	+1.5	+2	+2	+1.5	+0	0.00

Some companies also offer a premium for a level delivery option if supplies in a calendar month are within 10% of an agreed daily volume; the premium is typically 0·2 ppl. The trend towards new production profile payments is continuing, with more and more co-ops and companies introducing them, along with more individual pricing mechanisms.

Compositional Quality Payments

Constituent values vary widely between buyers and months. As an example, the average values for the major dairies were, in June 2007:

Butterfat: between 1.50p and 3.69p per litre per 1 per cent; average 2.33p.

Protein: between 2.00p and 3.73p per litre per 1 per cent; average 2.85p.

The *standard litre* price is typically 4·1% butterfat and 3·3% protein.

Average milk composition by breed is as follows (England and Wales, MMB recorded herds, 2-year averages, 1999/00 and 2000/01):

Proportional Split of Dairy Breeds and milk Compositions

	Cows %*	Butterfat %	Protein %
Holstein Friesian.......................	94·1	3·905	3·26
Ayrshire................................	1·9	4·005	3·33
Dairy Shorthorn........................	0·6	3·86	3·29
Jersey....................................	1·7	5·365	3·86
Guernsey................................	1·4	4·68	3·56
All Breeds.................................		3·93	3·27

*1988/9; no later data known. Holstein Friesians probably around 96% in 2008/09, within that, the number of Friesians in on the increase. More recent (partial) data suggests the butterfat is increasing over 4% and proteins over 3.3%

Within Breed Quality Variation. For Holstein Friesians the range can easily be as follows, without going to extremes: between 3.5 and 4.1 for butterfat and from 3.1 to 3.4 for protein. The difference in value between these two levels combined is about 2.25p per litre. This is being achieved by both breeding and feeding for different milk quality to meet varying contractual requirements.

Hygiene Price Adjustments. These vary widely between the different dairy companies. A mid-2008 example is as follows:

A. *Bactoscan (bacteria measure)*

Bactoscan Reading	Price Adjustment (ppl)
0- 50,000	+0.5
51-100,000	nil
101-250,000	− 1
Over 250,000*	− 7
Over 250,000**	−10

*1st month. **2nd and any subsequent months.

B. *Somatic Cell Count (Mastitis)*

Count	Price Adjustment (ppl)
0-200,000	+ 0.3
201-250,000	nil
251-300,000	− 0.5
301-400,000	− 2
Over 400,000*	− 6
Over 400,000**	−10

*1st month. **2nd and any subsequent months.

Several milk buyers have no premium for the top hygiene bands – they expect their suppliers to deliver top quality milk in order to receive the standard litre price.

C. *Antibiotics.* The price of all milk in a consignment that fails an antibiotics test ranges from l-5p/litre.

Organic milk. Organic milk price tends to fluctuate over a large range depending on supply and demand. Farmgate organic milk price averaged about 10ppl more than conventional farmgate milk price in recent years although this margin is closing. Organic milk price for 2009 is forecast at 33ppl, 7ppl more than conventional. The average conventional feed cost per litre of milk is 5.43ppl at £190/tonne (see point 8). With organic dairy feed at £400/tonne, this is 6ppl more expensive suggesting the high feed organic system would struggle.

4. *Value of Calves.* Average annual value per cow of purebred and beef cross heifer and bull calves, at 10-20 days old, allowing for mortality and an average calving index of

385 days. Calves from lower yield herds will normally have more beef genetics so be more valuable.

5. *Value of Cull Cows.* £400 allowing for casualties and a 25% per year replacement rate.

6. *Cost of Replacements* (N.B. average in 2009). £375 is £1,500 per down-calving heifer (purchase price or market value (mainly home-reared)) and a 25% per year replacement rate.

7. *Herd Depreciation* thus averages £275 per cow per year, i.e., 25 per cent of £1,100 (i.e., £1,500-£400).

   Net Replacement Cost = £225 to £235 per cow per year, i.e., herd depreciation (£275) less value of calves (£40 to £50).

   Bull. AI is assumed in the tables; bull depreciation would be approx. £150 a year (£1,500 purchase price less £750 cull value, 5-year herd life); tight calving pattern: 60 cows per bull, well spread calving pattern: 100; 10 to 20 tonnes silage, 0·75 tonnes concentrates a year. Very high yield herds may use more expensive (dairy) bulls reaching £2,500 purchase price).

8. *Concentrate Costs.*

Amounts:	Yield group	Low	Average	High	Very High
	kg/litre (approx.)	0.273	0.286	0.325	0.361
	tonnes/cow	1.50	2.00	2.60	3.25
	pence / litre (ppl)	5.18	5.43	6.18	6.86
	pence/ marginal litre*		6.33	11.4	12.35

* This is the additional cost of feed between yield groups, and the cost of the additional feed divided by the additional litres production.

Concentrate Price: taken (for 2009) as £190 per tonne, which is an average of home-mixed rations and purchased compounds of varying nutritive value, averaged throughout the year. Use of blends and straights are currently about 10% cheaper at £180/tonne average and compounds £200/tonne.

A difference of £5 per tonne has approximately the following effect on margin over concentrates and gross margin per cow, on the assumptions made regarding the quantity fed at each performance level:

Low	Average	High	Very High
±£7.50	±£10.00	±£13.00	±£16.25

Seasonality: Typically, specialist spring calving herds (60% or more calvings between January and May) use 0.09 kg per litre / 550 kg (£104.50) per cow per year less concentrates compared with autumn calving herds (60% or more calvings between August and December). See further note 12 below.

Typical Monthly Variation in Concentrate Feeding (kg per litre, 7,000 litre herd)

Winter		Summer	
October	0.30	April	0.27
November	0.33	May	0.16
December	0.33	June	0.16
January	0.33	July	0.22
February	0.33	August	0.24
March	0.30	September	0.27
Average winter:	0.32	Average summer:	0.22
	Average whole year:	0.28	

The actual distribution on any farm will obviously vary according to such factors as seasonality of calving, level of milk yield, grazing productivity during the summer, the quantity and quality of bulk feeds in the winter, and turnout and housing dates. The March figure in particular will be affected by type of soil and seasonal rainfall.

Yield with no concentrates and good quality silage: approximately 4000 litres for spring calvers.

9. Margin over Concentrates and Concentrates per litre

The emphasis in the initial tables should be laid on the differences between the margin of milk value over concentrates per cow; the same large variation can occur with widely differing combinations of milk yield and quantity of concentrates fed.

In the following table, at each yield level figures are given for *(a) margin of milk value over concentrates* per cow (£) and (b) *concentrates per litre* (kg) at seven levels of concentrate feeding.

Margin Over Concentrates (£) and Concentrates per Litre (kg)

Yield Level	Low		Average		High		Very High	
Milk yield per cow (litres)	5,500		7,000		8,000		9,000	
	(a)	(b)	(a)	(b)	(a)	(b)	(a)	(b)
	£	kg	£	kg	£	kg	£	kg
1.0 tonne (£190) concs. per cow	1,240	0.18	1,630	0.14	-	-	-	-
1.5 tonne (£285) concs. per cow	1,145	0.27	1,535	0.21	1,795	0.19	-	-
2.0 tonne (£380) concs. per cow	1,050	0.36	1,440	0.29	1,700	0.25	1,960	0.22
2.5 tonne (£475) concs. per cow	-	-	1,345	0.36	1,605	0.31	1,865	0.28
3.0 tonne (£570) concs. per cow	-	-	-	-	1,510	0.38	1,770	0.33
3.5 tonne (£665) concs. per cow	-	-	-	-	-	-	1,675	0.39
4.0 tonne (£760) concs. per cow	-	-	-	-	-	-	1,580	0.44

At £190/tonne, 1kg feed costs 19p. This means that using 0.44kg feed per litre would cost 8.36p for every litre of milk.

10. *Miscellaneous Variable Costs (average)*

	£
Bedding*...	40
Vet. and Med**...	63
A.I. and Bull Hire**..	30
Recording, Consultancy, Consumables, Dairy Stores.................	56
Total...	189

* Straw can vary from 0.4 to 1.5 tonne per cow and from £15 to £65 per tonne (or even more in some areas in exceptional years).

** Both Vet and Med and A.I. and Bull Hire tend to increase with higher milk yield. This explains the higher variable costs in the higher milk yield data.

11. *Stocking Rate and Forage Costs.* The stocking rates given assume that nearly all requirements of bulk foods – both winter and summer – are obtained from the forage area, i.e. little is bought in. On average about 55 per cent of the forage area (or production) is grazed and 45 per cent conserved. Note that as the stocking density increases, gross margin per cow falls, but gross margin per hectare rises.

The levels of nitrogen on forage area are assumed to be as follows:

Stocking rate Cows per Ha (acre)	Kg N/Ha	*units/acre*
1.75 *(0.7)*......................................	180	*143*
2.00 *(0.8)*......................................	220	*175*
2.25 *(0.9)*......................................	275	*220*
2.50 *(1.0)*......................................	360	*287*

An increase in potash application is also assumed. Seed costs clearly depend on the percentage of permanent pasture, if any, the length of leys, etc. The following total variable costs per hectare (fertiliser, seed and sprays) have been assumed for grassland:

Inputs per hectare of forage area depending on stocking rate

Stocking rate Cows per Ha (acre)	£/Ha	£/acre
1.75 *(0.7)*	255	*103*
2.00 *(0.8)*	343	*139*
2.25 (0.9)	423	171
2.50 (1.0)	544	220
Forage Maize	440	178

Refer to the Forage Variable Cost section for more information on this. A small amount of purchased bulk fodder is normal, and is included in these costings increasing with the stocking rate as follows (per cow): low £20, average £27, high £34, very high £41.

An increase in stocking density can be obtained not only by intensifying grassland production, as above, but also by buying in winter bulk fodder (assuming the same level of concentrate feeding in both cases). Theoretically, a zero-grazed farm buying in forage needs no land. In this situation, the gross margin could be extreme.

Overheads such as labour and depreciation on buildings are likely to increase per hectare and fall per cow as stocking density rises. Management challenges occur with higher stocking rates such as poaching which can be alleviated with good cow tracks. In addition the Nitrate Vulnerable Zone regulations must still be met.

12 Seasonality. Price and concentrate feeding differences according to the seasonality of production have already been outlined in notes 3 and 8.

Under similar levels of management mainly autumn calving herds average up to 1,000 litres more milk/cow/year than mainly spring calving herds but feed around a tonne more concentrates per cow/year; spring calving herds should normally only be feeding about 0.15 kg/litre. The average milk price would be expected to be higher for autumn calving herds, but the difference is less than might be supposed and has been steadily reduced with better prices being paid for summer milk.

13. *Quota.* Values are particularly dependent on the levels of farmgate milk prices and national milk production v. quota. For seven out of the eight years since 2000, the UK has been under quota, and the trend has been downward for the last decade. Throughout the 2008/09 season, milk quota values have been around 0.75 to 1 pence per litre to buy (clean) and 0.1 pence per litre to lease. These prices are all-time lows. If production rises beyond the present falling trend in 2008/09, the price of quota may rise with it. It is fairly certain that milk quota will end on 31 March 2015. To make gentle transition to this date, more quota is proposed to be given to all producers (see chapter III Section 1 for details).

14. *Labour*: see page 159.

15. *Building Costs*: see page 195.

16. *Costs per litre* (Holstein Friesians)

	Average (pence)		Premium (pence)	
Concentrates	5.43		4.61	
Forage and Bought Bulk Feed...	2.83		3.17	
Vet. & Med.	0.90		0.60	
Other Variable Costs	1.80		1.26	
Total Variable Costs		10.96		9.65
Labour: direct (milking etc.)	4.48		3.23	
: field/farm work	1.10		0.75	
Power and Machinery	3.77		2.964	
Rent/Rental Value	1.50		1.15	
General Overheads	1.21		1.034	
Total Fixed Costs		12.06		9.13
Net Replacement Cost *(Herd Dep'n)*		3.93		3.06
Total (excl. Quota Leasing/Purchase)		**26.95**		**21.85**

Notes on the above

With regard to the average costs the variable costs per litre are derived from the data (and therefore the assumptions made) in the main per cow cost table using the 7,000l per cow data. The labour cost is as on page 159. The average fixed costs are as for the medium-sized farm data on page 186, with adjustments made to allow for the greater use of resources by dairy cows compared with followers (and possibly cereals). The 'Premium' figures are as estimated for the average of the most profitable 10% of herds, with lower than average costs per cow (except for forage costs).

Labour includes farmer and any unpaid family labour.

Power and machinery cover all machinery and equipment costs, including the use of farm vehicles, etc.

General overheads similarly relate to the whole farm, including property repairs.

Where the dairy is part of a farm with other enterprises on a significant scale most of the fixed costs per cow and therefore per litre are difficult to determine.

The net replacement cost is herd depreciation less the value of calves.

As said in the table, the cost of additional quota, whether leasing charges or the annual cost of purchased quota, is not included.

Note too that neither interest on capital nor any management charge have been included.

If leasing or buying extra quota is being considered it is of course not the average but the marginal cost of producing the extra milk that needs to be considered. This will depend largely on whether the extra milk is being obtained through increasing yield per cow or by keeping more cows (or a combination of the two). For example refer to the extra cost of concentrate per additional litre (point 8).

Channel Island Breeds

Performance level (yield)............................	Low	Average	High	Very High
Milk Yield per Cow (litres) (1).....................	4,150	4,850	5,550	6,250
	£	£	£	£
Milk Value per Cow (2)..............................	1287	1504	1721	1938
Concentrate Costs (3)................................	253	341	432	534
Margin of Milk over Concentrates (MOC).......	1034	1162	1288	1404
Herd Depreciation less calf value (4)	110	110	110	110
Miscellaneous Variable Costs (5)..................	184	189	197	208
Gross Margin per cow before deducting Forage Variable Costs	740	863	981	1086
Forage Variable Costs (inc. Bought Fodder)......	163	170	177	184
Gross Margin per Cow...............................	577	694	804	902
Gross Margin per Forage Hectare (6) (2.4 cows per ha: 0.42ha/cow)	1385	1665	1931	2164
Gross Margin per Forage Acre (1.05 cows per acre: 0.97acre/cow)	561	674	782	877

Notes

1. *Yield.* Average of Jerseys and Guernseys. See Note 2 for Holstein Friesians (page 42). Guernseys average some 300 litres more than Jerseys (i.e. giving an average of approximately 4,700 for Jerseys, 5,000 for Guernseys) but Jerseys achieve a higher average price of above 2.5p per litre. Note that the average for Channel Island costed herds should not be compared with the average national (Pocketbook) figure for Holstein Friesians; costed herd yield averages are normally well above national averages; (i.e. they will well exceed 5,250 litres for Guernseys and 5,000 for Jerseys in 2009).

2. *Milk Price.* This has been assumed to be 31.00p per litre (average of Jerseys and Guernseys), i.e. 5p above Holstein Friesian milk; (32.25p Jersey milk, 29.75p Guernsey). In addition to the higher price obtained through the higher compositional quality for Channel Island milk some companies pay a premium for Channel Island milk.

3. *Concentrate Costs.* The price taken (for 2009) is £190 per tonne.

Amounts:	*Yield Group*	*Low*	*Average*	*High*	*Very High*
	kg/litre	0.32	0.37	0.41	0.45
	tonnes/cow	1.33	1.795	2.275	2.81
	pence / litre (ppl)	4.81	5.55	6.15	6.74
	pence/ marginal litre*		9.96	10.29	11.46

* This is the additional cost of feed between yield groups, and the cost of the additional feed divided by the additional litres production.

4. *Net Annual Replacement Value*: (i.e. Value of Calves less Herd Depreciation) were calculated as follows:

	£ per cow in herd
Cost of replacements: 25 per cent of herd per year @ £800	200
LESS Value of culls: 25 per cent of herd per year @ £260 (allowing for casualties)*	65
Herd Depreciation	135
Annual Value of Calves**	25
Net Annual Replacement Cost	110

* Cull cow prices for Guernseys are about £40 higher than for Jerseys.

** Allowing for calving index of 390 days and calf mortality; mixture of pure bred calves and beef crosses. Guernsey calves, especially crosses, fetch more than Jersey calves, averaging perhaps £10 more per head — but substantially more for some Guernsey beef crosses.

5. *Miscellaneous Variable Costs*. See Note 10 for Holstein Friesians (page 45).

6. *Stocking Rate*. See, in general, Note 11 for Holstein Friesians (page 45). The effect of varying the stocking rate on gross margin per forage hectare is as follows:

Gross Margin per Cow before deducting Forage V.C.s

Cows per Forage Hectare	Forage Hectares (acres) per cow	Gross Margin per cow before deducting forage V.Cs				Forage V.C. £ per cow*
		Low £740	Average £863	High £981	Very High £1,086	
		Gross Margin £ per Forage Ha (acre)				
2.1	0.48 (1.18)	1396 (565)	1656 (671)	1903 (771)	2122 (860)	75
2.4	**0.42 (1.03)**	**1385 (561)**	**1682 (681)**	**1964 (796)**	**2215 (897)**	**163**
2.7	0.37 (0.91)	1534 (621)	1867 (756)	2186 (885)	2467 (999)	172
3.0	0.33 (0.82)	1665 (674)	2036 (825)	2389 (968)	2702 (1094)	185

* A small amount of purchased bulk fodder is assumed, increasing with the stocking rate as follows (per cow): low £20, average £27, high £34 very high £41.

At the average stocking rate given above for combined Channel Island breeds (2.4 cows per forage hectare) the average figure for Jerseys would be approximately 2.55 and that for Guernseys 2.25.

Ayrshires

Performance level (yield)	Low	Average	High	Very High
Milk Yield per Cow (litres) (1)	4,900	5,725	6,550	7,375
	£	£	£	£
Milk Value per Cow (2)	1323	1546	1769	1991
Concentrate Costs (3)	233	299	373	455
Margin of Milk over Concentrates (MOC)	1090	1247	1395	1536
Herd Depreciation less calf value (4)	100	100	100	100
Miscellaneous Variable Costs (5)	184	189	197	208
Gross Margin per cow before deducting Forage Variable Costs	806	958	1098	1228
Forage Variable Costs (inc. Bought Fodder)	163	170	177	184
Gross Margin per Cow	643	788	921	1044
Gross Margin per Forage Hectare (6) (2.4cows per ha: 0.42ha/cow)	1544	1890	2211	2506
Gross Margin per Forage Acre (1.05cows per acre: 0.97acre/cow)	625	766	896	1015

Notes

1. *Yield*. See Note 2 for Holstein Friesians (page 42).

2. *Milk Price*. See in general, note 3 for Holstein Friesians (page 43). The price assumed in the above table is 27p per litre. The compositional quality of milk from Ayrshires is higher than for the black and white breeds.

3. *Concentrate Costs*. See notes 8 and 9 for Holstein Friesians. In the above table, the levels of feeding kg/litre (and tonnes per cow) are as follows: low 0.25kg/l (1.225

tonne/cow), average 0.275kg (1.575t), high 0.30kg (1.965t), very high 0.325 (2.397t); price £190 per tonne.

4. Net Annual Replacement Value. (i.e. Value of Calves less Herd Depreciation) were calculated as follows:

	£ per cow in herd
Cost of replacements: 25 per cent of herd per year @ £800	200
Less Value of culls: 25 per cent of herd per year @ £260	
(allowing for casualties and slaughter premium)............	65
Herd Depreciation	135
Annual Value of Calves*......................................	35
Net Annual Replacement Cost..................................	100

*Allowing for calving index of 385 days and calf mortality; mixture of pure bred calves and beef crosses.

5. *Miscellaneous Variable Costs.* See Note 10 for Holstein Friesians (page 46).

6. *Stocking Rate.* See, in general, Note 11 for Holstein Friesians (page 46).

Shorthorns. The above data could be used for Shorthorns, although one would expect their average yield to be about 5% lower, their cull and calf prices to be higher and their stocking rate to be slightly lower – similar to Holstein Friesians.

DAIRY FOLLOWERS
(per Heifer reared)

A. Holstein Fresians

Performance Level	Low	Average	High
	£	£	£
Value of heifer (allowing for culls) (1).....	1350	1350	1350
Less Value of calf (allowing for mortality)	200	200	200
Output...	1150	1150	1150
Variable Costs:			
Concentrate Costs (2)	220	200	180
Miscellaneous Variable Costs (3)	136	124	112
Total Variable Costs (excluding Forage)...........................	357	324	292
Gross Margin per Heifer, before deducting Forage Variable Costs...........	793	826	858
Forage Variable Costs (4)...................	149	150	152
Gross Margin per Heifer...................	644	676	707
Forage Hectares (Acres) per Heifer reared (5).......................................	0.95 (2.3)	0.73 (1.8)	0.58 (1.4)
Gross Margin per Forage Hectare (6)...	678	933	1229
Gross Margin per Forage Acre...........	275	378	498

B. Channel Island Breeds

Performance Level	Low	Average	High
	£	£	£
Value of heifer (allowing for culls) (1).....	720	720	720
Less Value of calf (allowing for mortality)	25	25	25
Output...	695	695	695
Variable Costs:			
Concentrate Costs	187	170	153
Miscellaneous Variable Costs	123	112	100
Total Variable Costs (excluding Forage)...........................	310	282	254
Gross Margin per Heifer, before deducting Forage Variable Costs...........	385	413	441
Forage Variable Costs (4)...................	134	135	136
Gross Margin per Heifer...................	251	279	305
Forage Hectares (Acres) per Heifer reared (5).......................................	0.68 (1.7)	0.58 (1.4)	0.50 (1.2)
Gross Margin per Forage Hectare (6)...	372	485	610
Gross Margin per Forage Acre...........	151	196	247

N.B. on average Channel Island heifers calve about three months younger than Holstein Fresian Heifers

C. Ayrshires

Performance Level	Low	Average	High
	£	£	£
Value of heifer (allowing for culls) (1).....	640	640	640
Less Value of calf (allowing for mortality)	45	45	45
Output...	595	595	595
Variable Costs:			
Concentrate Costs	198	180	162
Miscellaneous Variable Costs	125	114	103
Total Variable Costs			
(excluding Forage)............................	324	294	265
Gross Margin per Heifer, before			
deducting Forage Variable Costs...........	271	301	330
Forage Variable Costs (4)...................	107	108	109
Gross Margin per Heifer...................	164	193	221
Forage Hectares (Acres) per Heifer			
reared (5)......................................	0.68 (1.7)	0.58 (1.4)	0.50 (1.2)
Gross Margin per Forage Hectare (6)...	243	336	442
Gross Margin per Forage Acre...........	98	136	179

Notes

1. The heifer values are based on the purchase price of down-calving heifers, allowing for culls. Most heifers are home-reared. If heifers are reared for sale, the price of whole batches is likely to be lower than the values given in the tables, by perhaps 10 or 15 per cent. On the other hand the purchaser will often take the batch a few months before the average expected calving date, thus reducing feed and area requirements for the rearer.

2. The lower levels of concentrate costs are the combined result of more economical feeding, lower cost per tonne and a lower average calving age. (Other things being equal, however, including the overall level of management, a lower calving age requires higher levels of feeding.) Average (Holstein Friesians) = £58 to 3 months (see Calf Rearing on page 90) plus 250 kg calf concentrates @ £210/tonne and 500 kg @ £180/tonne.

3. Miscellaneous variable costs include bedding (£30): straw requirements average approx. 1 tonne per heifer reared, but are variable, depending on time of year and age when calved, as well as system of housing and extent of outwintering. Vet. and med. approximately £42 per heifer reared.

4. Forage variable costs. Grass for both grazing and conservation, at £147, £188 and £233/ha respectively (low, average and high) plus a small amount of bought and bulk food (£5, £10, £15 a head).

5. With an average calving age of 2 years 4 months, a "replacement unit" (i.e. calf + yearling + heifer) equals about 1·25 livestock units. The three stocking rates used above are equivalent to approximately 0·1.2, 0·9 and 0·7 forage hectares (0.48, 0.37, 0.31 acres) respectively per Holstein Friesian cow (Livestock Unit).

6. Much higher gross margin figures per hectare can be combined by intensive grazing methods, particularly if combined with winter feeding systems which involve little dependence on home-produced hay or silage (cf. Note 11, last three paragraphs, page 46).

7. Contract Rearing: see page 68.

8. Labour: see page 159.

Self-Contained Dairy Herd: Cows and Followers

At average annual replacement rates (25 per cent of the milking herd), nearly one-third of a replacement unit is required for each cow in the herd, i.e. roughly one calf, yearling and heifer for every three cows (including calved heifers), allowing for mortality and culling. At average stocking rates for both, this means more than 1 hectare devoted to followers for every 3 hectares for cows. Since surplus youngstock are often reared and frequently the stocking rate is less intensive the ratio often exceeds 1:2 in practice. 1: 2·75 is about the minimum where all replacement heifers are reared, unless their winter feeding is based largely on straw and purchased supplements, or unless there is a combination of long average herd life and early calving, i.e. at 2 years old or just over.

Gross Margin per Forage Hectare (Acre) (£) for the Whole Herd (i.e., Cows and Followers Combined); (at four levels of performance, including four commensurate levels of stocking rate, for the dairy cows; and three levels of performance, including different stocking rates, for the followers) are as follows, assuming a 2:1 land use ratio (dairy cow area: followers area); (Holstein Friesians only):

Gross Margin per Forage Hectare for Cows and Followers Combined

			G.M per Forage Hectare (acre) Dairy Cows							
			Low		Average		High		Very High	
			£		£		£		£	
G.M. per			998	(404)	1645	(666)	2097	(849)	2553	(1034)
Forage	Low	678 (275)	892	(361)	1323	(536)	1624	(658)	1928	(781)
Hectare	Ave.	933 (378)	977	(395)	**1408**	(570)	1709	(692)	2013	(815)
(acre)	High	1229 (498)	1075	(435)	1507	(610)	1808	(732)	2111	(855)

As an example, the above table indicates that at the average level of performance and stocking rate for both cows and followers, the whole dairy gross margin per hectare (acre) figure falls to £1,408 (570) compared with £1,645 (666) for the dairy cows alone, a reduction of 15 per cent. If more than the assumed (minimum) number of dairy followers are kept and the ratio is 1·5:1 (i.e. 40% of the dairy herd forage area is devoted to followers rather than a third) the gross margin for the whole forage area figure (on the assumption again of average performance) falls to £1,134 (459), which is a reduction of 31 per cent compared with cows.

BEEF

Outlook for 2009

The 2008 year has seen more rapid change in the UK beef market than all involved in the industry could have anticipated. Declining national dairy and beef herds, together with more favourable export conditions finally tightened beef supplies to a point where prices of finished cattle have risen by over 40% compared with a year earlier.

Breeding cow numbers in the dairy herd are still declining, which together with a swing to dairy inseminations will continue to tighten supply from the dairy herd in 2009. This will be exaggerated further by continued export to Europe of black and white bull calves. A weakened Sterling to Euro exchange rate has created an increased export demand from Europe, which has also lead to improved cow beef prices.

Conditions of tight supply and favourable export conditions look set to continue in 2009 and maintain beef prices. The only factor to potentially pull back prices is customer resistance to higher prices at a retail level. This could affect buying patterns with a switch to cheaper cuts or away from beef.

Improving beef prices have also coincided with rapidly rising input costs for fertiliser, feed and fuel. So instead of the sector gaining substantially from the rising beef prices, gross margins have increased by only modest amounts. Forage costs for most systems have doubled due to the fertiliser and fuel price rises. This alone has eroded most of the price rise gains. Producers will therefore need to review their production systems to operate with lower forage costs, by use of legumes and grass/clover or more extensive systems where land is available at modest rentals in some parts of the UK. Suckler margins look set to actually decline in 2009, which will further result in reducing the national suckler herd.

Finished Cattle Prices

Finished cattle prices in 2008 have risen week on week to peak in June at 275p/kg deadweight (156p/kg liveweight) for steers and 273p/kg dwt for heifers (158p/kg lwt). These peak prices were 44% higher than the same period in 2007. Since June 2008 prices have eased back to around 145p/kg lwt following falls of retail demand. Budget prices for 2009 of around 140 to 145p/kg liveweight have been used depending on the system and type of animal.

Cull cow beef prices have shown similar increases to prime beef with beef cows achieving 120p/kg liveweight and well fleshed dairy types averaging around 100p/kg liveweight.

Calf Prices

Calf prices have increased along with finished beef prices. Demand for dairy bull calves has now made them worthwhile to market, rather than being disposed of on farm. European export demand has pushed prices up for dairy bull calves, plus margins for cereal beef have improved stimulating a return to the system for some. Increasing herd movement restrictions because of bovine tuberculosis has also meant some dairy holdings being forced to start up beef enterprises, and tightening the supply of young calves onto the market for specialised beef rearers and finishers.

Bluetongue restrictions may also continue to have an impact on local prices for calves which may continue into 2009 until the whole of the UK is classed as one zone. Control measures for Bluetongue if continued into 2009 will also have an impact on the marketing of store cattle and access of stores by specialised finishing units, which could result in price variations between regions.

The values in the table below are assumed for 2009 and relate to Black and White bulls or beef cross calves of all qualities, less than three weeks old. These values have been used in the budgets for the various systems.

Calf Values of various Beef Cattle £

	Bulls	Heifers
Holstein Friesians	40 (export)	-
Holstein Friesians	20 (home market)	-
Hereford Cross	115	80
Continental Cross	180	140

A. Calf Rearing

Early Weaning - Bucker Rearing (per calf)

	3 months	6 months
	£	£
Value of Calf.	290	380
Less Calf Purchase (1)	166	166
Output	**124**	**214**
Variable Costs:		
Milk Substitute (2)	32	32
Concentrates (2)	37	102
Hay (3)	1	8
Miscellaneous Variable Costs (4)	20	30
Total Variable Costs	**90**	**172**
Gross Margin per Calf Reared.	**34**	**41**

Notes

1. Assumes equal number of male and female calves (Holstein Friesian/Continental beef cross, 1-2 weeks old). £160 average price, plus 4% mortality assumed, mainly in first 3 weeks. Value of pure Holstein Friesian bull calf £120 less; sale value at 3 or 6 months old correspondingly less).

2. Milk substitute: 20 kg @ £1,600/tonne = £32.00. Calf concentrates: to 3 months, 160 kg @ £230/tonne = £36.80; to 6 months, additional 290kg @ £225/tonne = £65.25. Calves fed on machine or lib milk systems will use more milk powder.

3. Hay: 10 kg to 3 months, 200 kg to 6 months. Variable costs assume made on farm; double the cost if purchased.

4. Misc. Variable Costs include vet. and med.: 8 (3 months), 11 (6 months); bedding: 3 (3 months), 7 (6 months); plus ear tags etc.

5. Weights: at start, 45 to 50 kg; at 3 months, 115 kg; at 6 months, 210 kg. Contract rearing charge (both 0 to 3 months and 0 to 6 months): £9 per week. Direct labour cost: approximately £19 per head to 3 months, £32 per head to 6 months.

   Labour requirements (all beef systems): see page 159.

B. Suckler Cows

Single Suckling (per Cow): Lowland

System	Spring Calving		Autumn Calving	
Performance Level	Average	High	Average	High
	£	£	£	£
Value of Calf (2)	392	443	469	548
Calf Sales / Valuation per Cow (3)	353	407	422	504
Less Cow and Bull Depreciation and				
Calf Purchases (4)	56	56	64	64
Output	**297**	**351**	**358**	**439**
Variable Costs:				
Concentrate Costs (Cow and Calf) ...	36	29	80	72
Misc Variable Costs (5)	57	52	77	72
Total Variable Costs (excl. forage)	**93**	**81**	**157**	**144**
Gross Margin per Cow, before				
deducting Forage Variable Costs ...	204	270	201	295
Forage Variable Costs	140	150	140	150
Purchased Bulk Feeds	20	15	20	15
Gross Margin per Cow	**44**	**105**	**41**	**130**
Cows per Hectare	1.80	2.20	1.65	2.00
Forage Hectares (Acres) per Cow	0.56	0.45	0.61	0.50
	(1.37)	(1.12)	(1.50)	(1.24)
Gross Margin per Forage Hectare	**79**	**232**	**67**	**261**
	(32)	(94)	(27)	(105)

Notes

1. Performance level relates to variations in two factors: weaned calf weight and stocking rate. 'High' refers to the average levels likely to be achieved by the better fifty per cent of producers. It is clearly possible to set still higher 'targets'.

2. Weight of calves (kg) at sale/transfer: spring calving: average 280 (at approximately 7.25 months old), high 295 (slightly older); autumn calving: average 335 (at approximately 10.25 months old), high 365 (11 months old). Price (per live kg): spring calving: average 140p, high 150p; autumn calving: 140p, 150p. These prices are averages for steers and heifers.

3. Calves reared per 100 cows mated: average 90, high 92.

4. *Assumptions.* Herd life: spring calving, 7 years; autumn calving, 6 years. Purchase price £800, average cull value £500. Calves purchased: average per 100 cows mated: spring calving 2, autumn calving 3; at £160. Bull: purchase price £2,100, cull value £750; (one bull per 35 cows on average; 4-year herd life). Dairy cross beef cows have better fertility performance than continental pure bred cows, but lower cull sale prices.

5. *Vet. and med.:* spring calving £20, autumn £25; bedding: spring calving £22, autumn £34; miscellaneous: spring calving £15, autumn £18. *Straw:* where yarded in winter, straw requirements average 0.5-0.75 tonne per cow for spring calvers and around 0.75 tonne for autumn calvers.

6. The forage area includes both grazing and conserved grass (silage and hay) plus any other forage crops, such as kale. The higher stocking density implies better use of grassland. Higher stocking rates can also be achieved by buying in more of the winter bulk fodder requirements, or by winter feeding largely on arable by-products, including straw. Purchased bulk fodder and/or straw balancer concentrates will reduce gross margin per cow but increase gross margin per hectare.

Single Payment: all headage payments have been decoupled under the Single Payment. However, a payment is made in Scotland on three-quarter breed beef calves from Suckler Cows. Headage payments under the Scottish Beef Calf Scheme are around £40/head (or £80/head for the first 10 calves claimed).

In lowland conditions rearing two or more calves per cow is an option, but needs substantially greater labour input. Output is raised by fostering a second purchased calf onto a cow soon after calving, with little impact on costs of keeping the cow. The cow breed needs to be of a quiet temperament and have enough milk to rear two calves.

Single Suckling (per Cow): Upland/Hill

System	Spring Calving		Autumn Calving	
Performance Level	Average	High	Average	High
	£	£	£	£
Value of Calf (2)	371	420	469	548
Calf Sales / Valuation per Cow (3)	338	391	427	509
Less Cow and Bull Depreciation and				
Calf Purchases (4)	59	58	67	65
Output	**278**	**333**	**360**	**444**
Variable Costs:				
Concentrate Costs (Cow and Calf) . . .	36	29	80	72
Misc Variable Costs (5)	57	52	77	72
Total Variable Costs (excl. forage)	**93**	**81**	**157**	**144**
Gross Margin per Cow, before				
deducting Forage Variable Costs . . .	185	252	203	300
Forage Variable Costs	125	140	125	140
Purchased Bulk Feeds	20	15	20	15
Gross Margin per Cow	**40**	**97**	**58**	**145**
Cows per Hectare	1.60	1.90	1.25	1.50
Forage Hectares (Acres) per Cow	0.63	0.53	0.80	0.67
	(1.54)	(1.30)	(1.98)	(1.65)
Gross Margin per Forage Hectare	**65**	**184**	**73**	**218**
	(26)	(75)	(29)	(88)

Notes

1. Performance level relates to variations in two factors: weaned calf weight and stocking rate. 'High' refers to the average levels likely to be achieved by the better fifty per cent of producers. It is clearly possible to set still higher 'targets'.

2. Weight of calves (kg) at sale/transfer: upland spring calving: average 265 (at approximately 7 months old), high 280 (7.25 months); upland autumn calving: average 335 (at approximately 10.25 months old), high 365 (11 months); Price (per live kg); upland spring calving: average 140p, high 150p; upland autumn calving: average 140p, high 150p. These prices are averages for bull and heifer calves.

3. Calves reared per 100 cows mated: upland average 91, high 93.

4. *Assumptions.* Herd life: spring calving, 7 years; autumn calving and hill, 6 years. Purchase price £775, average cull value £460. Calves purchased: upland average, 3 per 100 cows mated, premium 2, at £150. Bull: purchase price £2,100, cull value £750.

5. *Vet and Med.* Spring calving £20, autumn £25; bedding: spring calving £22, autumn £34; miscellaneous: spring calving £15, autumn £18. *Straw:* when yarded in winter, requirements average 0.5-0.75 tonne per cow for spring calvers and around 0.75 tonne for autumn calvers.

6. The forage area includes both grazing and conserved grass (silage and hay) plus any other forage crops, such as kale. The higher stocking density implies better use of grassland. Higher stocking rates can also be achieved by buying in more of the winter bulk fodder requirements, or by winter feeding largely on arable by-products, including straw. Purchased bulk fodder and/or straw balancer concentrates reduce gross margin per cow but increase gross margin per hectare.

Support: all headage payments have been decoupled under the Single Payment, apart from the Scottish Beef Calf Scheme (see above margin). Hill payments - Hill Farm Allowance in England, Tir Mynydd in Wales, LFASS in Scotland - are not included in the gross margins. These payments are available in disadvantaged and severely disadvantaged acres and are paid on an area basis (but have a minimum stocking density). See Page 137. Additional payments for keeping native beef suckler cows are available from environmental schemes such as ELS in England and Tir Gofal in Wales. These payments are not included in the margins.

C. Rearing / Finishing Stores

Traditional Finishing of Strong Store Cattle (per head) (1)

	Summer Finishing	*Winter Finishing*
	£	£
Finished Sales	754 (2)	770 (3)
Less Purchased Store (incl. mortality)	606 (4)	594 (5)
Output	**148**	**176**
Variable Costs:		
Concentrates	7	80 (6)
Miscellaneous Variable Costs (4)	25	45 (7)
Total Variable Costs (excluding Forage)	**32**	**125**
Gross Margin per Head, before		
deducting Forage Variable Costs	116	51
Forage Variable Costs	64	32
Gross Margin per Head	**52**	**19**
Animals per Hectare (Acre)	4 (1.6)	10 (4.0)
Forage Hectares (Acres) per Head	0.25 (0.62)	0.10 (0.2)
Gross Margin per Forage Hectare	**208**	**187**
Gross Margin per Forage Acre	(84)	(76)

Notes

1. The financial results of this enterprise are highly dependent on the market margin, i.e. the difference between the price per kg paid for the store and the price per kg obtained for the finished animal. Other important factors are the stocking rate and the degree of dependence on cash-crop by-products and the quality of conserved grass (and hence the quantity of concentrates required in relation to the liveweight gain) in the case of winter finishing.

   There is a large price range for store cattle based on quality, which will be reflected in carcase classification results. Heifers tend to finish better off grass with less concentrate requirements and therefore are more appropriate than steers for summer finishing at grass.

2. 520 kg @ 145p.

3. 520 kg @ 148p.

4. 400 kg @ 150p. Includes mortality at 1%.

5. 420 kg @ 140p. Includes mortality at 1%.

6. 400 kg @ £200/tonne.

7. Including straw: average 0.75 tonne per head

BEEF

Finishing/Rearing on Suckler-Bred Stores (per head):

	Winter Finishing Average (£)	High (£)	Grass Finishing Average (£)	High (£)	Overwintering and Grass Finishing Average (£)	High (£)	Grazing and Yard Finishing Average (£)	High (£)
Sales	783	814	636	649	701	774	725	799
Less Store (1)	438	438	490	469	424	424	417	395
Output	**345**	**376**	**146**	**180**	**277**	**350**	**308**	**404**
Variable Costs:								
Concentrates (2)	132	113	6	4	78	67	90	70
Miscellaneous (3)	48	43	25	23	43	40	42	38
Total Variable Costs (excl. Forage)	180	156	31	27	121	107	132	108
Gross Margin per head before Forage Var. Costs	165	220	115	153	156	243	176	296
Forage Variable Costs	68	56	58	58	80	72	90	90
Purchased Bulk Feed	6	6	-	-	10	8	7	4
Gross Margin per head	**91**	**158**	**57**	**95**	**66**	**163**	**79**	**202**
No. per ha (acre)	9 (3.6)	10 (4)	4 (1.6)	5 (2)	3.75 (1.5)	4.50 (1.8)	4 (1.6)	5 (2)
Gross Margin per Forage Ha	**819**	**1580**	**244**	**475**	**248**	**733**	**316**	**1010**
Gross Margin per Forage Acre	**331**	**639**	**99**	**192**	**100**	**297**	**128**	**409**
Weight at start (kg)	310	310	335	320	300	300	285	270
Weight at end (kg)	540	550	445	445	490	530	500	540
Purchase Price (p per kg LW)	140	140	145	145	140	140	145	145
Sale Price (p per kg LW)	145	148	143	146	143	146	145	148
Concentrates per head (kg)	625	600	40	25	390	350	450	350
Silage per head (tonnes)	3.25	3.25	-	-	3.6	3.6	2.1	2.3

All-System Assumptions:

(1) Allowing for mortality at 1%. (2) Concentrate costs per tonne: winter: average £200, high £190; summer: average £150, high £140. (3) Including vet. & med. and bedding.

Additional Note: The gross margin per ha figures must be treated with considerable caution, especially with regard to winter fattening/rearing systems: small variations in land requirements and margins per head cause wide variations in the per ha figures, and capital requirements are considerable. Differences in buying and selling prices per kg can be critical. Very little recent survey data is available on several of these systems.

BEEF

Finishing/Rearing on Dairy-Bred Stores (per head):	Winter Finishing		Grass Finishing		Overwintering and Grass Finishing		Grazing and Yard Finishing	
	Average £	High £	Average £	High £	Average £	High £	Average £	High £
Sales	789	820	660	703	681	717	705	792
Less Store (1)	529	515	498	498	412	412	327	341
Output	260	305	162	205	269	305	378	451
Variable Costs:								
Concentrates (2)	102	97	8	6	78	67	120	85
Miscellaneous (3)	48	42	24	23	49	45	43	39
Total Variable Costs (excl. Forage)	150	139	32	29	127	112	163	124
Gross Margin per head before Forage Var. Costs	110	166	130	176	142	193	215	327
Forage Variable Costs	58	58	58	58	94	88	92	94
Purchased Bulk Feed	4	2	-	-	7	5	7	4
Gross Margin per head	**48**	**106**	**72**	**118**	**41**	**100**	**116**	**226**
No. per ha (acre)	7.5 (3)	9 (3.6)	4 (1.6)	5 (2)	3.5 (1.4)	4.25 (1.7)	3.5 (1.4)	4.5 (1.8)
Gross Margin per Forage Ha	360	954	288	590	143	425	406	1017
Gross Margin per Forage Acre	145	386	116	238	58	172	164	411
Weight at start (kg)	385	375	350	350	300	300	230	240
Weight at end (kg)	560	570	475	495	490	505	500	550
Purchase Price (p per kg LW)	136	136	141	141	136	136	141	141
Sale Price (p per kg LW)	141	144	139	142	139	142	141	144
Concentrates per head (kg)	510	510	50	40	390	350	600	450
Silage per head (tonnes)	3.4	3.4	-	-	3.6	3.6	3.5	4.5

All-System Assumptions:
(1) Allowing for mortality at 1%. (2) Concentrate costs per tonne: winter: average £200, high £190; summer: average £150, high £140. (3) Including vet. & med. and bedding.

Additional Note: The gross margin per ha figures must be treated with considerable caution, especially with regard to winter fattening/rearing systems: small variations in land requirements and margins per head cause wide variations in the per ha figures, and capital requirements are considerable. Differences in buying and selling prices per kg can be critical. Very little recent survey data is available on several of these systems.

D. Intensive Beef

Cereal Beef (per Head)

System	Continental Cross Holstein/Friesian Bulls		Holstein Friesian Bulls	
Performance Level	Average	High	Average	High
	£	£	£	£
Finished Sales (1)	784	812	673	699
Less Calf Purchase (2)	185	183	41	41
Output	**599**	**629**	**632**	**658**
Variable Costs:				
Concentrates (3)	470	456	470	456
Other Feed	4	4	4	4
Misc Variable Costs (4)	66	61	66	61
Total Variable Costs	**540**	**521**	**540**	**521**
Gross Margin per Head	**58**	**109**	**92**	**137**

Notes

1. Weight at slaughter (kg): Cont cross bulls, average 560kg, high 580kg; Dairy bulls, average 530kg, high 550 kg. Prices: Cont cross bulls, average 140p/kg, high 140p/kg; Dairy bulls, average 127p/kg, high 127p/kg. All year round production is assumed. Average slaughter age is 14 months, with killing out percentages ranging from 54% to 60%, with the better conformation continental cross bulls achieving higher percentages.

2. Calf prices of £185 for continental cross male calves at 3 weeks of age including mortality; £41 for dairy bulls including mortality. Mortality, average 3%, high 1.5%.

3. £90 calf rearing (to 12 weeks: see page 55) + finishing ration. Finishing ration: 17 parts barley @ £140 per tonne, 3 parts concentrate supplement @ £280 per tonne; plus £10 per tonne milling and mixing. Total, £171 per tonne.

   Feed quantity (kg from 12 weeks (115 kg) liveweight to slaughter; FCR average 5·0, high 4·6): average 2225kg, high 2140kg. (FCR = Feed Conversion Ratio)

4. Vet. and med. £16, bedding £25, misc. £25.

   Margins are very sensitive to calf price and feed price movements. A £10 per tonne feed price movement equates to a margin change of £22 per head.

Note: Interest on Capital

Beef systems require large capital outlay on livestock and variable costs alone. For cereal beef with an interest rate at 7% on the calf price, and half the variable costs, interest charges amount to £32 per head.

18 Month Beef and Silage Beef (per Head Produced*)

System	18 Month Beef		Silage Beef	
Performance Level	Average	High	Average	High
	£	£	£	£
Finished Sales	776	821	761	806
Less Calf Purchase	187	184	187	184
Output	**588**	**637**	**574**	**623**
Variable Costs:				
Concentrates (incl. milk substitute) . . .	243	225	309	279
Other Feed	4	4	5	5
Misc Variable Costs	73	70	68	62
Total Variable Costs (excl. forage)	**320**	**299**	**382**	**346**
Gross Margin per Cow, before				
deducting Forage Variable Costs . . .	268	338	192	277
Forage Variable Costs	115	115	80	80
Gross Margin per Cow	**153**	**223**	**112**	**197**
Animals per Hectare	3.4	3.8	8.0	10.0
Forage Hectares (Acres) per Cow	0.29	0.26	0.13	0.10
	(0.73)	(0.65)	(0.31)	(0.25)
Gross Margin per Forage Hectare	**520**	**847**	**900**	**1,971**
	(211)	(343)	(364)	(797)

* *N.B. The variable costs, including feed and forage, the forage area and gross margin per head all relate to the full production period - 18 months or less for silage beef. Nevertheless, the gross margins per forage ha or acre* are *per year. During the winter there will be both the 0-6 month old calves and 12-18 month old cattle on the farm.*

Notes: 18 Month Beef

General: Autumn-born dairy-bred calves, beef crosses.

Slaughter weights (kg): average 550kg, high 570. Sale price per live kg: average 141p, high 144p.

Calf price/value: £180 (2 week old beef cross male calves, e.g. Limousin cross); mortality: average 4%, high 2%.

Feed: Concentrates (kg; average with high performance in brackets): Calf rearing to 12 weeks £69 incl. milk substitute. Other: first winter 220kg @ £200 (200kg), at grass 90kg @ £200 (80kg), second winter 560kg at £200 (500kg). Silage: 4.5 tonnes/head total, 0.75 tonne first winter, 3.75 tonnes second. Intensive grazing of fresh leys and good quality silage are needed - especially to achieve the high performance levels.

Other Costs: Miscellaneous (average): vet. and med. £21, bedding £27, other £25.

Notes: Silage Beef

General: Dairy-bred calves (beef crosses) fed indoors on grass silage and concentrates, for slaughter at 14 to 17 months old. Good quality silage is the key to high performance per head (otherwise concentrates per head rise and/or daily liveweight gain falls). High yields of silage per ha raise gross margins per ha.

Slaughter weights (kg): average 540, high 560. Sale price per live kg: average 141p, high 144p.

Calf price: £180. Concentrates per head (kg) (from 3 months (£69 to rear including milk powder)): average 1,200kg at £200/tonne, high 1,050kg at £190. Silage required: approximately 5.5 tonnes per head.

Other Costs: Miscellaneous (average): vet. and med. £16, bedding £28, other £24.

Note that the gross margin per ha figures must be interpreted with considerable caution: small differences in silage yields can have a large effect and, more important, the working capital and building requirements per ha are extremely high: well above even the high needs of 18 month beef.

E. Veal

General points: Veal consumption is very low in the UK: only a small fraction of the per capita consumption in France for example. Continental demand is mainly for white veal, produced in individual veal crates, a system that is illegal in the UK, where the less economic 'welfare system' of groups kept in straw pens is required, producing 'pink veal' at heavier weights. Imported 'white veal' is considerably cheaper.

As very little white veal is now produced in the UK validated economic data is rarely seen. This also applies to 'rose veal' produced at heavier weights, but again mainly on the Continent. Now that calf exports have resumed and, given that some continental countries have retained a headage subsidy payment, it is very unlikely that UK veal systems can make a comeback. *For these reasons the provision of gross margin data has been discontinued.*

SHEEP

A. *Lowland Spring Lambing per Ewe* (selling lambs off grass)

Performance Level	Low	Average	High
Lambs Reared per Ewe put to Ram (1) . . .	1.3	1.45	1.6
Finished Lamb Liveweight (kg)		37.5	
Finished Lamb Liveweight Price (£/kg)		1.30	
Store Lamb Price (£/head)		38.0	
Average Price per Lamb (£) (2)	44.9	46.6	48.4
Sales:	£	£	£
Lamb sales	58.3	67.6	77.4
Wool (3).	0.9	0.9	0.9
Cull Ewes and Rams (4)	7.5	7.5	7.5
Sub Total	66.7	76.0	85.8
Less Ewe and Ram Replacements (4)	20.5	20.5	20.5
Output per Ewe	**46.2**	**55.5**	**65.3**
Variable Costs:			
Concentrates (53kg ewes, 12kg lambs) (5)		10.7	
Vet and Med		4.9	
Miscellaneous and transport (6)		6.5	
Total Variable Costs (excluding Forage)		**22.1**	
Gross Margin per Ewe, before			
deducting Forage Variable Costs . . .	**24.1**	**33.4**	**43.2**
Forage Variable Costs (inc bought-in			
Forage and Keep	8.0	8.0	8.0
Gross Margin per Ewe	**16.1**	**25.4**	**35.2**
Stocking Rate (Ewes with Lambs per forage			
Hectare (acre)) (7)	8 (3.2)	11 (4.5)	14 (5.7)
Gross Margin per Forage Hectare	129	279	493
Gross Margin per Forage Acre	52	113	199

Notes

1. *Target Rearing Performance.* Lambs reared per ewe put to ram are based on: -
   Ewes lambing: 92% (2.5% deaths, 5.5% barren)
   Lambs born: per 100 ewes lambing = 168
   Live lambs: born per ewe lambing = 156
   Lamb mortality: 14% (7% at birth, 7% post birth)
   Lambs reared: per 100 ewes put to ram = 145

   These performance figures are assumed for flocks of mature ewes, i.e. shearlings and older. Where ewe lambs are included in flock performance adjustment needs to be made. The *Breed* will obviously have a large effect on lambing percentage, liveweight gains and carcase grades.

2. *Lamb Prices.* The UK breeding flock is expected to decline further by around 3% in 2008 to 14.4 million. This combined with increasing exports to Europe (+6% for the first half of 2008) facilitated by a favourable exchange rate indicates a further tightening of supply to the UK domestic market in 2009. Prices therefore look set to at least maintain the much improved 2008 levels and even rise further into 2009. By mid summer of 2008 lamb prices were 20% higher than a year earlier. The only negatives are signs of a downturn in domestic consumption following a rise in retail prices, resulting in switches away from joints to lower value cuts and mince.

Prices assumed for lambs sold for slaughter for the 2009 season assumes a strong export market without restrictions.

An average market price of 130p/kg liveweight (equivalent to 282p/kg deadweight) has been assumed giving £48.75 per finished lamb at an average liveweight of 37.5 kg. A reduction of lamb carcass weights have also been assumed in line with a trend set in 2008, due to seasonal factors plus less concentrate feeding of lambs as feed prices have risen.

The average budget price in the table above allows for 20% sold as stores. Store price is assumed at £38 per head. Low performance is £1.75 a lamb less, high £1.75 per lamb more for variations caused by differences in weights, time of marketing and proportion sold finished or retained as stores. Although lamb prices have risen substantially, gross margins are expected to decline in 2009 because of higher feed and forage costs.

3. *Wool.* Some recovery of wool price has been achieved but some caution has been exercised assessing returns for 2009. Budget price assumed for lowland flocks is 90p per ewe, based on a price of 45p/kg at 2 kg/ewe. Variations between flocks are because of ewe breed affecting wool quality and ewe size affecting weight of wool produced.

4. *Flock Depreciation.* (i.e. Market price of replacements less value of culls). It is assumed above that 20 per cent of the ewe flock is culled each year @ £36 each and that, allowing for 4 per cent mortality, 24 per cent are purchased or home-reared at £75 each. Rams: 1 per 40 ewes, 3-year life, purchased @ £300, sold @ £40. The net cost (flock depreciation) is £13.0 per ewe per year. N.B. Cull ewe prices are approximately £4 per head higher for heavy breeds and £4 lower for light breeds. Cull values tend to be highly variable but have been high of late, partly at least through a strong, consistent demand from the ethnic sector. No other changes in flock valuation are assumed.

5. *Concentrate Feeding.* Feed costs in 2009 will continue to rise and have a substantial impact on margins for most systems and even question the viability of some systems for individual producers. Concentrate finishing of late season lambs has been common, but there has been a swing to sell as stores rather than finish on high cost concentrates. Producers will as a result start to look at alternative methods of finishing lambs and utilize lower cost forage.

6. *Miscellaneous Costs* include contract shearing @ 75p/ewe, scanning 50p/ewe and lamb tags 25p/ewe, carcase disposal £1.00/ewe, straw £1.00/ewe, marketing, levy and transport £3.75/ewe.

7. *Stocking Density.* The stocking rates assumed are based on land requirements for the main grazing season (April to October) including land for conservation of winter forage.

Land quality and location will also have an effect on potential stocking density. However higher stocking rates can be achieved by catch crop roots for autumn/winter grazing or away wintering on grass keep which carry higher costs on a per ewe basis. Away grazing costs can range from 40p to 60p/ewe per week depending upon location.

On farms with grazing livestock other than sheep, the ewe flock is able to utilize land in the winter utilized by cattle in the normal grazing season. Alternatively ewes can be winter housed pre lambing to rest the land, but this does carry additional costs e.g. £6/ewe per year for building depreciation and interest over 10 years, plus straw and hay costs.

Ensuring good lamb growth rates and early finishing off grass also eases stocking pressures late in the season. Late lamb finishing into autumn and winter in most cases necessitates additional land available for lamb finishing lambs on catch crops or away grazing for ewes.

Other Costs

1. *Prices of Specialised Equipment*

Troughs (2.75 m)..........................	£50 to £60
Racks (2 to 3 m)...........................	£200 to £225
Foot Baths (3 m)..........................	£100 to £125
Shearing machines	£650 to £1050
Lamb Creep Feeders	£350 to £650

2. *Fencing:* Approximately £1.70 per metre +85p labour.

3. *Labour:* see page 159.

Home-reared tegs (shearlings)

Output: value £74 (allowing for culling and mortality) less £48 for the lamb, plus wool at £1, gives an output of £27/head. Variable costs (including forage) = £17. Gross margin per head = £10, per forage hectare £200 (£80 per acre).

Rearing replacements can be treated as a separate enterprise and margins compared on a per hectare basis. Where ewe lambs replacements are lambed in their first year they can be combined with the breeding flock which will reduce lambing percentage and output (£) per ewe but benefit from a reduction of replacement cost.

B. Other Sheep Systems (average performance level only)

	Early Lambing	Winter Finishing of Stores	Upland Flocks	Hill Flocks
	per ewe	per head	per ewe	per ewe
Lambs Sold per Ewe (put to ram)	1.375	-	1.325	0.75
Finished Lamb Liveweight (kg)	37.5	40.0	35.0	30.0
Finished Liveweight Price (£/kg)	160	140	130	120
Average Price per Lamb Sold (£)	60.0	56.0	45.5	36.0
	£	£	£	£
Lamb Sales	82.5	54.9	60.3	27.0
Wool	0.9	-	0.8	0.7
Sub Total	83.4	54.9	61.1	27.7
Less Purchases (net of Culls)	14.6	40.5	14.3	(+) 3.2
Output	**68.8**	**14.4**	**46.8**	**30.9**
Variable Costs:				
Concentrates	33.0	2.8	11.0	6.6
	(150)	(12.5)	(50)	(30)
Vet and Med	5.1	0.4	4.6	3.8
Miscellaneous	7.0	2.5	5.8	3.5
Total Variable Costs (excl. Forage) .	**45.1**	**5.7**	**21.4**	**13.9**
Gross Margin per Ewe, before Forage Variable Costs . . .	**23.7**	**8.7**	**25.4**	**17.0**
Forage Variable Costs (inc bought-in Forage and Keep	13.0	2.5	15.0	9.0
Gross Margin per Ewe/Head	**10.7**	**6.2**	**10.4**	**8.0**
Stocking Rate (Animals per forage Hectare (acre))	14 (5.7)	40 (16.2)	10 (3.8)	-
Gross Margin per Forage Hectare . . .	150	249	99	-
Gross Margin per Forage Acre	61	101	40	-

Notes:

Early Lambing. This system assumes January/early February lambing with all lambs sold by the end of August. Recent years have seen lamb prices peak later in the season, i.e. May rather than the traditional Easter market peaks. This has been due to the large retailers contracting to New Zealand lamb in the first part of the year and switching to UK new season lamb when large enough supplies are available i.e. in May. Hence early marketing of substantial numbers in April has not been beneficial.

This system is also very dependent upon concentrate feed inputs to ewe and lambs which will reduce margins per ewe to a level where they are now below the margins for Spring Lambing Flocks.

Winter Finishing of Store Lambs. The gross margin per head is particularly variable, being very dependent on the difference between purchase and sale price of the lambs. Some of the forage variable costs consist of bulk feed and agistment. It is risky to assume any great uplift in prices per kg from purchase to sale. Marketing costs and levy are a significant part of total costs so longer keep lambs gaining 8kg to 10kg liveweight on low cost forage are most likely to be worthwhile. Margin assumes 2% mortality from purchase to sale.

Upland Sheep. Due to the breeds used, the finished lamb weights from these flocks are likely to be lower than for lowland ewes. The margins assumes that all progeny are sold finished, but in practice many of these flocks will be selling breeding stock to lowland producers. Male lambs are often sold as stores in the autumn.

Hill Sheep. These flocks are self-maintained and a high proportion of the ewes bred pure. The overall lambing percentage is likely to be around 110%, but 0.35 lambs per ewe will be as flock replacements. Only rams are purchased to maintain the flock. Wool income includes yearling ewes carried on the farm. Results vary according to the quality of the hill grazing and stocking density.

Many flocks have historically away wintered ewes for up to six months to maximise ewe premium claims and latterly to be eligible for environmental schemes. Where ewes are away for 6 months £10 per ewe needs to be added to the forage costs set out in the table above.

Support: all sheep headage payments have been decoupled under the Single Payment. Hill payments - Hill Farm Allowance in England, Tir Mynydd in Wales, LFASS in Scotland - are not included in the gross margins above. These payments are available on disadvantaged and severely disadvantaged acres and are paid on an area basis (but have a minimum stocking density). See page 129.

GRAZING AND REARING CHARGES:
CATTLE AND SHEEP

Grazing charges vary widely according to the quality of the pasture and local supply and demand. The following figures are typical (estimated for 2009):

Summer Grazing (per head per week)

Store Cattle and in-calf heifers over 21 months, dry cows, and fattening bullocks over 18 months	£3.50-£4.50
Heifers and Steers, 12-21 months	£2.50-£3.50
6-12 months Cattle	£2.00-£2.75
Cattle of mixed ages	£2.50-£3.50
Ewes	40p-50p

Winter Grazing (per head per week)

'Strong' Cattle	£2.25-£3.50
Heifers	£2.00-£3.00
Sheep..	50p-60p

Note: the above figures assume the farmer whose land the livestock are on does all the fencing and 'looking after'. Where the owner of the, say, sheep does the fencing, shepherding, etc., the figures may be halved, or be even less depending on local demand.

Grass Keep (per hectare, per acre in brackets)

Most typically around £150-200 (£60-80), with the best £250-300 (£100-120) and poorer quality £75-£100 (£30-40).

These figures are highly variable, especially between one part of the country and another, and between one season and another. The charge can be very high where the pasture is good, the supply scarce and the demand strong. In an average price year poor quality keep may fetch only £75 (30), top quality (fenced and with mains water) more than £300 (120). For top quality grassland, fertilised, well-fenced and watered, with stock seen daily, prices can be even higher for some lots in the west and north-west in years of grass shortage; a top figure as high as £400 (160) is sometimes reported. The average price can exceed £300 (120) in some years in parts of the west and west midlands but can fall below £100 (40) or even at no charge in some eastern and south-eastern counties.

A lowering of these levels following the introduction of the Single Payment Scheme had been expected but experience of 2005, to 2008 has seen only minor reductions in averages let at auction in most parts of the country. On the other hand there is increasing evidence in some localities that grassland subject to environmental schemes is fetching very low or negative rents where the landowner is taking the payment. A new factor affecting future grass rents is very high fertiliser prices which will mean some producers taking on extra land in place of purchasing nitrogen fertiliser at £350/ tonne.

Winter Keep (Cattle) (per head per week)

Grazing + 9 kg hay and some straw	£8.00
Full winter keep in yards	£7.00-£10.00
Calf rearing for beef (0 to 12 weeks or 0 to 6 months)..........	£9.00

A typical rental for labour, buildings and maintenance diet would be £6 per head per week. These rates apply where feed to achieve maintenance plus some growth is supplied plus labour and buildings and bedding where applicable.

Heifer Rearing Charges

Points to clarify in any arrangement are: who pays for transport, who pays the vet. and med. expenses, who bears the losses or pays for replacements, how often are payments made (monthly payments save the rearer interest compared with lump sum payments when the heifer is returned)?

Two possible arrangements are:

1. Farmer X sells calf to Rearer at agreed price; the calf is then Rearer's responsibility and he pays for all expenses and bears any losses. Farmer X has first option on heifers, which he buys back two months before calving. Approximate price: £775above cost of calf for Holstein Friesians. Rearer fetches calf; Farmer X supplies transport for heifer.

2. Farmer X retains ownership of calf. Approximate charges: £35 per month from 10 to 14 days old (£38 if two-year old calving), or £33 per month from 6 months old (£37 if two-year old calving), (£40 per month from 10 to 14 days to 6 months). As Rearer has no interest on capital to bear, he supplies transport and pays for vet. and medical expenses. In the case of losses by accident/chance, the rearer either refunds payments or replaces calf (this means Farmer X and Rearer share a loss averaging approximately £35 each per heifer reared, assuming 10 per cent losses at average 6 months old). In the case of losses by negligence, the rearer both refunds payments and replaces calf. (The NFU can supply model agreements).

As livestock and beef margins decline, contract rearing availability may increase as farmers with spare land and buildings look for alternatives with agreed returns and less capital outlay in livestock.

Calf and Heifer Rearing for Shorter Periods

Costs are likely to rise to the levels outlined in line with rising feed and milk powder prices.

Calf, 10 days to 3 months, £125 (for food, labour and housing) to £135 (all costs, and rearer bearing losses). Heifers, average from 3 months old to steaming up: approximately £16 per month in summer, £45 in winter.

RED DEER

A. Breeding and Finishing	Per 100 Hinds
Sales:	£
42 Stags (15-18 months) : 55kg dw @ £3.25/kg	7,508
33 Hinds (15-18 months) : 42.5kg dw @ £3.25/kg	4,558
8 Cull Hinds @ £75	600
Average Annual Value of Cull Stags	70
Less Average Annual Cost of Replacement Stags	500
Output	**12,236**
Variable Costs:	
Concentrates @ 10.5 tonnes @ £150/tonne	1,575
Vet and Med	850
Miscellaneous	1,250
Total Variable Costs	**3,675**
Gross Margin before deducting Forage Costs	**8,561**
Forage Variable Costs (5.5 Hinds per hectare @ £120/ha)	2,182
Gross Margin per 100 Hinds	**6,379**
Gross Margin per Forage hectare (18.2 ha)	351
Gross Margin per Forage acre (44.9 acres)	142

B. Selling Calves	Per 100 Hinds
Sales:	£
43 Stag Calves @ £80/head (45 kg liveweight)	3,440
34 Hind Calves @ £62.50/head (40 kg liveweight)	2,125
8 Cull Hinds @ £75	600
Average Annual Value of Cull Stags	70
Less Average Annual Cost of Replacement Stags	500
Output	**5,735**
Variable Costs:	
Concentrates @ 7.0 tonnes @ £170/tonne	1,190
Vet and Med	550
Miscellaneous	700
Total Variable Costs	**2,440**
Gross Margin before deducting Forage Costs	**3,295**
Forage Variable Costs (6.5 Hinds per hectare @ £110/ha)	1,692
Gross Margin per 100 Hinds	**1,603**
Gross Margin per Forage hectare (15.4 ha)	104
Gross Margin per Forage acre (38.0 acres)	42

Additional Notes

Lowland systems assumed. Hind replacements home-reared in systems A and B.

Herd Life: hinds, 12 years; stags, 7 years. 25 hinds per stag. Calves reared per 100 hinds: 85.

Purchase price of breeding stock (good quality): hinds £275 plus, yearling hinds £225 plus, stags £500 plus.

C. Finishing Stag Calves

	Per 200 Stags
Sales:	£
195 Stags (15-18 months) : 55kg dw @ £3.20/kg	34,320
Less Purchases : 200 @ £75 per head	15,000
Output	**19,320**
Variable Costs:	
Concentrates @ 15.0 tonnes @ £125/tonne	1,875
Vet and Med	900
Miscellaneous	2,000
Total Variable Costs	**4,775**
Gross Margin before deducting Forage Costs	**14,545**
Forage Variable Costs (11.0 Stags per hectare @ £115/ha)	2,091
Gross Margin per 200 Stags	**12,454**
Gross Margin per Forage hectare (18.2 ha)	685
Gross Margin per Forage acre (44.9 acres)	277

The venison prices reflect projected sales for 2008/09 to wholesale buyers. Higher prices will be obtained for direct sales to consumers (e.g. farm shops and farmers' markets) and caterers, but extra costs will normally be incurred.

Capital costs: perimeter fencing, £5/metre; internal fencing, £2/metre; handling yard, pens, scales, crush: £10,000—in existing buildings. Total cost of establishing a 100-hind breeding flock is typically in the order of £50,000, including breeding stock and £12,500 for fencing, housing and handling facilities. Labour: with an experienced stockman: 400 plus head with additional help when yarding.

Sources of further information: *'Introduction to Deer Farming'* (Barony College, Dumfries. Tel: 01387 860251. *British Deer Farmers Association*, The Counting House ,Mill Road, Cromford, Derbyshire, DE4 3RQ. Tel. 01629 827037.

Acknowledgement: Russell Marchant, Principal and Chief Executive, Barony College.

HORSES: LIVERY

The horse industry is now reported to be the second biggest employer in the rural economy and is also one of the fastest growing. Although there are other equine enterprises that farm business can operate, by far the most common is providing accommodation for horses; i.e. livery. There are many different forms of livery and the charges, therefore, vary widely also. This is apart from the effects of local supply and demand. However, three fairly standard forms are offered on farms:

Grass Livery. Keep at grass, preferably with shelter, water supply and secure area to keep tack and store feed. Some grass livery will provide an exercise arena and off-road riding. Charges average £25 per week; range £20-£40.

DIY Livery. The owner still has full care of the horse but has the facilities of a stable, grazing, and in some cases an all-weather exercise arena. The owner is responsible for mucking out, turning out, grooming, exercising and all vet./med. care and the cost of all feed and bedding. Charges average £30 per week; range £20-£50.

DIY Plus Livery. As the above, except that the yard manager is responsible for certain tasks, such as turning out and feeding. Charges average £40 per week; range £30-£60.

In addition there is *Full Livery*. The Yard supplies a complete service to the horse owner including tasks such as grooming and exercise. Services provided by the yard the charges may be fitted to the needs of a particular horse. Few farm-based liveries would offer such a high level of management. Full livery charges average £100 per week; with a range between £75-£150.

The above are only guidelines. There is a wide variation both within, and between regions.

Other Costs:

Grazing. Variable costs will average some £50 per horse per year. Average stocking rates are 0·8 ha (2 acres) for the first horse and 0·4 ha (1 acre) for each horse after.

Hay. Average price £3 per conventional bale (approximately 20kg) (range £2-£4.50). It has to be of good quality. Average consumption is one to two bales per horse per week; less in the summer depending on the grass quality/quantity and the work of the horse. Some horses now have haylage; more expensive, dust free and higher fibre and energy/protein levels; less required per head.

Concentrate Feed. Can range from almost nil to 3.0-4.0 kg per day depending, amongst other factors, on breed, size and intensity of work. Compound feed 30 to 45p per kg.

Bedding. Averages around £5 per stabled horse per week for half the year, i.e. £110-£130 per year. Straw might cost only half as much; however, more expensive, but preferable, alternatives (such as wood shavings, shredded paper and hemp fibre) are now increasingly being used.

Vet. and Med. Averages approximately £150 per horse per year. Some yards include worming of the horse in the livery cost.

Rates. Livery is a non-agricultural use, and therefore any buildings being used for the enterprise are liable to business rates.

Further Notes:

The supply of livery yards appears to be increasing, from both farms diversifying and other yards setting up. Filling a yard is, consequently, getting more difficult. The level of service and facilities expected by customers has increased. There is a trend towards greater professionalism in the running and management of livery yards. Livery contracts should be exchanged showing clearly the responsibilities of each party. Comprehensive third party insurance is also important.

To be successful, a livery enterprise needs higher quality facilities than farm livestock. To the owner the horse can be anything from a highly trained athlete to a family pet. Horses are expensive: even modest quality horses cost between £1,500 and £3,000. Good customer relations and an effective security system (including burglar and fire alarms) are crucial to success, as is good market research and effective advertising.

A full livery yard will require stables, a secure room to store tack, a vermin-proof hard feed store, storage for hay and bedding, a muck heap and parking provision with room for horse boxes. Planning permission is required for the conversion of an existing building to stabling or the erection of new, purpose-built stables. Permission is also required for construction of an all weather arena used for training horses and exercising them in bad weather. Hay and straw should be stored away from the stables and down wind of them to minimise the fire risk. A hard standing area with a water supply and good drainage should be provided for grooming and washing down the horses.

Good ventilation in the stables is crucial as horses are prone to respiratory diseases caused by spores and dust. Provision should be made for owners to soak hay in clean water before feeding it, to reduce respiratory problems.

Fences must be sound and must be free of protruding nails, wire etc. Ideally fields should be fenced using post and rail, but this is expensive. Barbed wire should be avoided wherever possible or should be 'protected' with an offset electrified fence. Fields should be divided into smaller paddocks to reduce the possibility of fighting between incompatible horses and to separate mares and geldings. Paddocks may be divided using two or more strands of electrified tape or rope but wire is not advisable as it is not easily visible to the horse.

Off-road riding opportunities on the farm are a real asset. The farmer may provide riding trails, a jumping paddock, or a cross country course. An all-weather ménage for exercising horses, possibly with floodlighting, is highly desirable, and some livery yards have horse walkers too. Good facilities can be rented out to individuals or organisations such as pony clubs. It is sometimes possible to link up with nearby farms to increase the length of riding tracks available.

Construction Costs. The cost of conversion of existing buildings will depend on their quality; prefabricated hardwood and steel internal stable partitions can be purchased from upwards of £750 per stable, depending on size and specification. Free standing timber stables cost between £800 and £2,000 (plus base), depending on size and quality. As horses are fairly destructive animals (they both kick and chew) better quality stables will often prove more economic in the long run. All weather arenas (20 metres by 40 metres) cost between £10,000 and £25,000; construction is a specialist job as good drainage is essential; a badly constructed arena is worthless.

Contact: Further financial information on horse enterprises, including riding schools and equestrian centres, is available in 'Equine Business Guide', 5th Edition, 2005, edited by Richard Bacon, Warwickshire College; Tel. 01926 318 338.

OSTRICHES

Ostrich production was introduced to the United Kingdom during the early 1990s with breeding stock of very mixed genetics and no production history. Today production is limited to a handful of small farmers, working individually selling most meat production through local farmers' markets and into the catering industry. These farmers have their own breeding stock, incubate and raise their own chicks. Slaughter is carried out under contract in small, dedicated ostrich plants and red meat slaughter plants with a ratite license. Currently the farmers are responsible for all their own marketing. There is no production carried out under contracts to supply wholesalers or retailers. Ostrich are not sold through livestock auction markets.

Working in low volume presents significant challenges to both maximising revenue and controlling production costs; as it is not possible to achieve economies of scale. Ostrich are produced primarily for their meat, with their skins, fat and feathers providing additional revenue potential. Skins are generally sold to dealers, but minimum numbers of 200 skins are required, so it can require long-term storage to build up sufficient volume of skins. With the low production levels in the United Kingdom, the only market for the feathers and fat are those the farmers can generate from their own value adding.

It is difficult, due to the lack of processing infrastructure currently available to make farming ostrich a viable activity in the UK. It undoubtedly can be done but any prospective farmer needs to thoroughly research the slaughter / processing facilities in their chosen area and also be prepared to undertake direct marketing of the meat. This situation will continue until a substantial investment in production and provision of associated infrastructure is undertaken.

Breeding Stock

Current breeding stock is in limited supply with little or no records available to assist a prospective buyer to calculate a fair value based on revenue potential. Although there is almost no demand, it is unlikely a producer of birds would accept less for breeding stock that the birds would fetch for meat. A good meat bird can be worth £400 or more providing the meat is sold at retail and the hide is of good quality. No serious genetic improvement programs have been undertaken. There has been some preliminary work carried out on the use of AI, but it will be a decade or more before this technology can be incorporated into mainstream production.

Breeders are generally kept in Pairs - one male, one female; or Trios - one male, two hens. A trio will require about 0.2 ha (0.5 acre) for grazing and room in which to exercise: they must be able to run. (More land will be required if it is not free draining). A stout hedge or smooth wire fence of a minimum of 1.7 metres (5.5 ft) high should surround the enclosure. Adult birds need shelter from wind and rain, and a dry floor on which to sleep. Domesticated ostrich are generally docile and easily handled. But they are subject to the Dangerous Wild Animals Act, requiring licensing (£45-£360) and inspection by the Local Authority, though there are proposals where the operation of the licence may be relaxed in some situations.

Birds reared on high production rations generally start breeding from 15 months; the lower the production characteristics of the rations, the later breeding commences. There are many reports of breeders starting production as late as 3 years, adding to the rearing costs of breeders. A female from 2-3 years of age lays 30-60 eggs a year (March to October); on average, 75% will be fertile (settable). A female may have a productive life of 20 to 30 years. An experienced producer will aim to hatch and rear at least half the eggs set, but there can be significant losses. Incubation lasts 42-45 days. A 10% replacement rate is anticipated for breeding stock.

Ostrich are browsers and not grazers. The forage portion (usually lucerne) of an ostrich ration should be included in the rations. Dependency on grazing for a proportion of the nutrient requirements will result in reduced production. When the dry rations fed are adequate and fully balanced, grass consumption will be minimal even when kept in grass paddocks. The main ingredients suitable for ostrich are lucerne, maize and soyameal. Some wheat and/or barley in small proportions can replace some of the maize, but maize is required for optimum production. The birds must be provided with grit when young and small stones (up to 12 to 15mm) for adults, oyster shells, and perhaps vitamin supplement. A breeding ration is fed at 2.1kgs for 252 days and a maintenance ration at 2.1kgs for 113 days. For a trio of birds this equates to 2.3 tonnes per annum. A specialist feed can cost between £220 and £340 per tonne.

Rearing and Meat Production

Chicks are reared indoors with access to heat for two to three months and then allowed outside. A high level of care and expertise is required. Meat birds are grouped according to size rather than age from 12 weeks and kept at 25-35 per hectare (10-14 per acre) up to 6 months and 18 per ha (7.5 per acre) when older.

Performance Level	Low	Average	High
Days to Slaughter	500	800	1,200
Sales:	£	£	£
Meat: 40kg @ £8.00/kg (1)	320	320	320
Value of Skin (2)	50	50	50
Less Day Old Chick (3)	16	14	11
Output per Bird	**354**	**356**	**359**
Variable Costs:			
Concentrates (4)	181	174	98
Other Rearing Costs (5)	78	70	50
Slaughter, Processing etc. (6)	75	75	75
Marketing (7)	5	5	5
Total Variable Costs	**339**	**324**	**228**
Gross Margin per Bird	**15**	**32**	**131**

Notes

1. Birds are slaughtered at 7-14 months at a live weight of 90-120kg, giving 40kg of de-boned meat. On-farm slaughtering is permitted under poultry regulations but meat can only be sold locally and the producer will have the added cost of packaging and marketing, which could amount to £1 per kg. The meat price assumes all meat is marketed by the producer.

2. Ostrich skins can be just as valuable as the meat, but British producers have found it difficult to produce a bird with a highly saleable skin, and quality is all important. A top quality skin can fetch over £100, but in the absence of UK tanning facilities skins are generally exported in a batch at £40-£60 each. Feathers are potentially valuable but no market has been established yet. Skin Revenue is included at £50 – but this figure must be viewed with caution. The figures illustrate that when early slaughter is achieved with the correct meat yield, commercial viability is no longer dependent on skin revenue.

3. Fertile eggs are worth £10-£15 each (infertile eggs can be sold for cooking or crafts for about £10 each.).

4. Birds are fed starter crumb and then small pellets costing in the region of £300 per tonne. Feed consumption on low production rations can result in increased feed intake of 25%. Feed costs based on small quantities being purchased. Prices will be less for bulk buying.

5. Other production costs include a depreciation charge for capital invested in infrastructure. Costs will vary from farm to farm depending on existing infrastructure and size of operation.

6. The majority of ostriches are processed at one of the very few specialist slaughter facilities, which must have veterinary and meat hygiene inspections. The new EU-wide Slaughter Licence that came into effect on January 2006 means that red meat plants can slaughter ostriches providing they have appropriate de-feathering and chilling facilities. For slaughter, butchering and returning the meat vacuum packed to the producer the charge is £75/bird. Transport to the abattoir and return carriage for the meat may add significantly to this sum.

7. The margin assumes direct marketing of all produce as this is the current norm in the UK.

Fixed Costs

Housing £6; fencing £4; labour: adult birds require about 25 hours a year and chicks and young birds about 4 hours a year. One stockperson might look after 500 meat birds. Two people are needed at times to handle adult stock.

Contact: *British Domesticated Ostrich Association (BDOA)*, 33 Eden Grange, Little Corby, Carlisle, CA4 8QU. (Tel.: 01228 562946); www.ostrich.org.uk

WILD BOAR

Wild Boar are now being farmed in the UK on more than 60 farms, with a population probably exceeding 2,000 sows. They produce a firm dark meat with a characteristically 'gamey' flavour which is in demand particularly from the hotel and restaurant trade.

Wild Boar come under the Dangerous Wild Animals Act and wild boar farms must be licensed by the Local Authority. There is no uniformity of fee or conditions that have to be met, but typically licences cost £100-£150 and are renewed annually following an inspection of the farm. Enclosures must be secure with strong fencing: a minimum height of at least 1.8m is usually specified and most authorities require 30-80cm below ground plus an additional strand of electric fence inside the main fence. The estimated minimum cost of fencing using approved contractors is from £8 per metre erected plus the hire of a digger. All gates and access areas must be padlocked at all times. However, the Act is under review and there is a recommendation that farmed boar will be exempt, giving them the same legal status as the domestic pig.

Wild Boars are kept in groups of up to 10 sows per boar. They are nearly always kept outdoors, often on arable land (as outdoor domestic pigs), although rough land with some natural vegetation, such as scrub, or best of all, woodland, is ideal. Good husbandry requires some basic housing, such as arcs. Large arcs are suitable for a group of gestating sows, or sows running with maturing boarlets. Sows should have access to an individual shelter for farrowing and the first few days of lactation. If good vegetation is available sows may make their own farrowing nest away from the main group with satisfactory results.

Stocking rates vary according to the type of land but about a hectare would be needed for a group of 5 sows and a boar. They will forage actively on suitable terrain but this is unlikely to provide a significant part of their diet. They need to be fed a balanced ration (additive free pig concentrate is suitable but specially formulated feeds are available) with supplementary vegetable material. If a good supply of root crops is available this may replace some concentrate. Wild boar mate and farrow naturally and have few health problems, so little if any intervention is needed. Gilts mature at 18 months. In the wild breeding occurs in the autumn and early winter and the sows farrow from February to March after 4 months gestation. One litter per year is the norm. However, most farmed sows maintained at a good nutritional level will give two litters in most years. Young sows produce 2 to 3 boarlets and mature sows 6 to 8. A well-run enterprise should average 7 boarlets per sow per year raised to maturity. Wild boar can live from 12 to 15 years, perhaps more, but in a commercial herd the sows are usually culled at 7 to 8 years old.

The boarlets remain in the family group until they are all weaned together at 8 to 12 weeks (16 at the outside). Although some (usually smaller) producers leave growers to mature in family groups, they are generally separated into grower/finisher groups on rough grass or in open barns. Wild boar will take between 9 and 18 months to reach a slaughter weight of 75-85 kg. This produces a 45-50 kg carcase. They are slaughtered in the same way as pigs. The carcase has more shoulder and less on the hind-quarters than a domestic pig. It can be butchered like a domestic pig or without the skin like venison. The meat from male animals 2 years old or over is too strong, except for sausages, but sows up to 8 years old still have an acceptable carcase and a good cull value. A real problem for some producers is arranging slaughter: abattoirs are currently required to have wild boar specified on their licence and many expect them to be difficult to handle.

Labour requirements are low, owing to the 'hands off' nature of wild boar management. One person might manage a herd of 30-40 sows and fatteners.

In spite of the large and apparently unsatisfied demand for wild boar meat, as with other alternative enterprises, there is no organised marketing system and producers have to develop their own outlets. There are some wholesale butchers and game dealers who will take whole carcase in significant numbers, but many producers organise their own processing into a variety of pre-packed products and arrange their own retailing. Sold at retail the meat commands a considerable margin over the wholesale price, but butchering, packaging and marketing costs have to be considered. Wild boar production can be successful both as a secondary enterprise on a farm or as a stand-alone operation.

Performance:

Finished Boarlets per Sow per Year	7 (6 - 9)
Finished Carcase Weight (over 15 months)	45 - 50 kg
Price per kg deadweight	£3.50 (£3.00-£4.50)

Sales:	£
Meat sales per Sow per Year	1,164
Less Depreciation per Sow per Year (1)	30
Output per Sow	**1,134**
Variable Costs:	
Concentrates sow (2)	200
fatteners (@ £70 each)	490
Bedding	10
Vet, Med and Licence.	30
Miscellaneous (inc. Water and Electricity)	10
Total Variable Costs per Sow	**740**
Gross Margin per Sow	**394**

Notes

1. Cost of sow £400, cull value £200, herd life 7 years, plus share of boar

2. Including share of boar

Capital Costs Housing and fencing - £4,000 per hectare (£1,620 per acre); pure-bred boar - £300-£600; pure-bred sow - £250-£500.

SHEEP DAIRYING

Performance Level	Low	Average	High
Milk Yield (litres) per Ewe per Year	175	275	350
Sales:	£	£	£
Milk Value (1)	157.5	247.5	315.0
Value of Lambs (2)	56.6	56.6	56.6
Wool	1.5	1.5	1.5
Cull Ewes and Rams (3)	3.6	3.6	3.6
Output per Ewe	**219.2**	**309.2**	**376.7**
Variable Costs:			
Concentrates (4)		151.7	
Miscellaneous (inc. Vet and Med)		17.5	
Forage Variable Costs (5)		25.0	
Total Variable Costs		**194.2**	
Gross Margin per Ewe	**25.0**	**115.0**	**182.5**
Stocking Rate (Ewes with Lambs per forage			
Hectare (acre))		11 (4.5)	
Gross Margin per Forage Hectare	275	1,265	2,008
Gross Margin per Forage Acre	111	512	813

Notes

1. *Price:* 90p per litre at farmgate (range from 80p-105p per litre).

2. *Lambing %:* 175%. Assume a 300 Friesland ewe flock. Retain 60 ewe lambs for flock replacements. Sell 390 finished lambs reared from 2 days old (inc. 15% mortality) at £38. If meat-type terminal sires used then cross-bred lamb values per ewe increase to £63.

3. *Cull ewes:* Assumed 18% culled at £20.00 per head (average, including mortality).

4. *Concentrates:* Milking ewes: 200 days at 1.5 kg/head/day, 100 days at 0.5 kg/head/day; cost £250/tonne. Ewe lamb replacements and artificially reared finished lambs at £62/head.

5. *Forage costs:* Quality silage: 1 tonne per milking ewe (or hay equivalent). Grazing: early grass in March/April; good grazing on leys or pasture; similar for dry stock and lambs.

Additional Points

Fixed Costs per Ewe: Labour (paid) £73; Power and Machinery £22; Property Costs £12; Other £13; Total, excluding Finance and Rent, £120.

Capital Costs of Equipment: Complete milking unit for 300 ewes (including yokes, bulk tank, dairy equipment, installation): £12,000-£25,000. A small 50 ewe unit can be put together for under £10,000. Any building works would be additional to the above costs.

Acknowledgement: Anthony Hyde, FRICS, FBIAC.

GOAT DAIRYING

Performance Level	Low	Average	High
Milk Yield (litres) per Goat (1)	500	800	1,200
Sales:	£	£	£
Milk Value (2)	200.0	320.0	480.0
Value of Kids (3)	2.8	3.6	3.6
Less Livestock Depreciation (4)	27.7	27.7	27.7
Output per doe	**175.1**	**295.9**	**455.9**
Variable Costs:			
Concentrates (5)	57.8	92.4	138.6
Miscellaneous (inc. Vet and Med) . . .	55.0	55.0	55.0
Forage Variable Costs (6)	45.0	72.0	108.0
Total Variable Costs	**157.8**	**219.4**	**301.6**
Gross Margin per Doe	**17.4**	**76.5**	**154.3**
Stocking Rate (Goats per Forage Hectare (acre) - zero-grazed system)	6.5 (2.6)	8.0 (3.2)	9.5 (3.8)
Gross Margin per Forage Hectare	113	612	1,466
Gross Margin per Forage Acre	46	248	593

Notes

1. *Yield:* Per 300 day lactation, kidding each year. Autumn kidders tend to yield less.

2. *Price:* 40p per litre; seasonal variation from 33p in June to 53p in November. 12.5% solids delivered.

3. *Kid(s):* Prolificacy relates to age, breed, seasonality and feed level. Assumptions: low 140%; average and high 180%. There is very little trade in kids for meat (£2 per kid assumed).

4. *Culls and Replacements:* Replacements at £180/head; culls £17.50, average life 6 years. Bucks: 1 per 40-50 does. Does normally mate in autumn; gestation 150 days; young goats can be mated from 6 months.

5. *Concentrates:* Average 0.55 kg concentrate per litre, at £210 per tonne.

6. *Forage:* Average 0.9 kg DM forage per litre at £100 per tonne DM (part purchased, part home-grown). Goats can be grazed but are normally storage fed to avoid problems with worms, fencing, milk taints and pneumonia. Farmers able to produce maize silage will have a better forage conversion ratio.

7. *Miscellaneous:* Bedding £12, vet and med. £24 (includes treatment for out-of-season breeding, vaccination against Johnes and humane disposal of unsaleable kids), sundries £19.

8. *Stocking rate:* Based on home-grown forage.

9. *Labour:* 1 full-time person per 100 goats is a guide, but very dependent on technology employed.

10. *Markets:* Herd sizes in the UK range from 50 to 3,000 milking does. Average herd size is growing rapidly as established producers expand with the market at about 15% average annual growth. Successful businesses have been built on producer processing and retailing, as bulk purchasers of goats milk are few and far between. Prolificacy and technical improvements allow higher annual growth than the market and there is a cycle in milk and stock prices.

Contact: *The British Goat Society* (Bovey Tracey, Devon (tel. 01626 833168)) registers pedigree animals and publishes a monthly newsletter.

Acknowledgements: The above information originally supplied by *Dr. T. Mottram*, Silsoe Research Institute, Bedford MK45 4HS, amended since by the author.

ANGORA GOATS

Angora goats produce mohair; angora rabbits produce angora; cashgora is produced by angora cross dairy goats; cashmere is produced by improved feral goats (valuable 'down' has to be separated from guard hairs; thus, with cashmere production, 'yield of down' must not be confused with 'weight of clip' as percentage down is low and can vary widely). Goat meat is called 'chevon'.

UK mohair output is currently around 8 tonnes per year, which indicates a population of between 1500 and 2,000 animals. The figures below are for a commercial enterprise. Many UK angora flocks are kept on a semi-commercial or hobby basis, in which case different criteria may apply – does retained longer, mortality rates lower, doe/buck ratio different.

Performance:

Kids per Doe per Year (1)	1.4
Fibre: Doe/Buck, 2 clips, 3 & 4kg/clip respectively (2)	6.3 kg
Kids (1.4), first and second clips (3)	4.3 kg
Whethers/Replacement Does (0.9), third clip (3)	2.7 kg

	£
Fibre Sales:	
Doe/Buck: 6.3kg @ £2.28/kg (3)	14.4
Kids: 4.3kg @ £5.50/kg (3)	23.9
Whethers/Replacements: 2.7kg @ £4.00/kg (3)	10.8
Stock Sales:	
Does: 0.5 females sold for breeding @ £50.00 each (1)(4)	25.0
Whethers: 0.7 males sold for meat @ £20.00 each (1)(4)	14.0
Culls: 0.17 does @ £20 each (1)(4)	3.4
Less Replacements (Buck only) (4)	1.2
Output per Doe	**90.3**

Variable Costs:		
Concentrates	does (plus buck): 90kg @ £200/tonne (5)	18.0
	kids (to clip 2): 50kg/hd @ £260/tonne (5)	18.2
	replacements: 15kg/head @ £210/tonne (5)	2.8
Vet and Med (6)		8.0
Miscellaneous (6)		16.5
Total Variable Costs per Doe		**63.5**

Gross Margin per Doe before Forage Costs	**26.7**
Forage Variable Costs (10.0 Does per hectare @ £175/ha) (7)	17.5
Gross Margin per Doe	**9.2**
Gross Margin per Forage hectare (10.0 ha)	92.4
Gross Margin per Forage acre (24.7 acres)	37.4

Notes

1. 1.5 kids born alive per doe mated; 2% mortality to each clip. Of 0.7 surviving doe kids, the majority (0.5) are sold for breeding, the remainder (0.2) are retained for replacements. Culls (0.17) and casualties are equal to the number of replacements (unless the flock size is changing). Progeny are sold after 2 clips for breeding or after 3 clips for meat. Stock may be retained for further shearing. This has become more common, as the demand for breeding stock is small, fibre quality has improved and there is little market for meat.

2. The data for Breeding Does include output and inputs for breeding bucks. Assumes 25 does to one buck.

3. Angora goats are usually clipped twice a year. Yield increases over first four clips, but quality decreases with age. Prices can be volatile, being dependent on fashion and on the world market dominated by South Africa and Texas. Demand and prices are highest for the high quality kid fibre <25 microns in diameter. The following yields and prices have been used:-

    Clip 1: 1.1 kg, £6.00 per kg; clip 2: 2.0 kg, £6.00 per kg; clip 3: 3.0 kg, £4.50 per kg; adult doe: 3.0 kg, adult buck 4.0 kg, £2.78 per kg.

    British Mohair Marketing arranges a collection once a year, currently in September. The fibre is professionally graded and then offered for sale by tender. There is a handling charge of 50p per kg of fibre. Membership of BMM costs £30. (Some producers improve their return by processing and using the fibre themselves or selling to local spinners. Commercial processing costs are significant: combing about £2.20 per kg and spinning about £8 per kg).

4. Stock sales. Breeding stock in commercial flocks are culled after six years on average. Subsequent shearing stock culled after a further 4 clips. Value of all cull stock: £20 each. Depending on quality, the skin can be worth £10 before curing or up to £120 after curing. Replacement costs: does, £80; bucks, £200. Shearing stock, £20 (as transfer from breeding enterprise). Show quality stock command a premium.

5. Concentrates. Quantities: Kids - 50 kg to clip 2, 15 kg to clip 3; Adults - breeding adults 90 kg per year, shearlings 40 kg per year.

6. Veterinary costs can be high. Miscellaneous costs include £2.50 to £2.50 per shearing per head (it may be more) and bedding materials.

7. Angora goats require more management than sheep. Fencing requirements are similar but housing costs rather higher. Margins are particularly sensitive to the value and number of breeding stock sold, yield and value of fibre, kidding percentage and meat values. There is a market for meat from older animals but no reliable market has yet been developed specifically for younger animals. Angoras are probably most successfully run as a subsidiary enterprise on a farm rather than a stand alone operation.

Contact: *British Angora Goat Society*: www.britishangoragoats.org.uk

Acknowledgements: Stephen Whitley, Corrymoor Angoras, Stockland, Honiton, Devon EX14 9DY socks@corrymoor.com www.corrymoor.com

GRAZING LIVESTOCK UNITS

Dairy cows	1.00	Lowland ewes	0.11
Beef cows (excl. calf)	0.75	Upland ewes	0.08
Heifers in calf (rearing)	0.80	Hill ewes	0.06
Bulls	0.65	Breeding ewe hoggets:	
		½ to 1 year	0.06
Other cattle (excl. intensive beef):		Other sheep, over 1 year	0.08
0-1 year old	0.34	Store lambs, under 1 year	0.04
1-2 years old	0.65	Rams	0.08
2 years old and over	0.80		

Source: as advised by DEFRA for the Farm Business Survey.

Other Livestock Units

Breeding sows	0.44	Broilers	0.0017
Gilts in pig	0.20	Other table chicken	0.004
Maiden gilts	0.18	Turkeys	0.005
Boars	0.35	Ducks, geese, other poultry..	0.003
Other pigs	0.17	Horses	0.80
Cocks, hens, pullets in lay	0.017	Milch goats	0.16
Pullets, 1 week to point of lay	0.003	Other goats	0.11

Source: as advised by DEFRA for the Farm Business Survey.

Notes

1. Total livestock units on a farm should be calculated by multiplying the above ratios by the *monthly livestock numbers averaged over the whole year*.

2. The ratios are based on feed requirements. Strictly speaking, when calculating stocking density, allowances should also be made for differences in output (e.g. milk yield per cow or liveweight gain per head), breed (e.g. Friesians v. Jerseys) and quantities of non-forage feed consumed.

FORAGE VARIABLE COSTS

£ per hectare (acre) / year	Grass Dairying (1)	Grass Other (1)	Grass Clover Ley	Forage Maize (2)	Kale
Yield tonnes/ha (tons/acre)	50	45	40 (16)	40 (16)	45 (18)
Seed per year	20 (8)	14 (6)	21 (9)	148 (60)	70 (28)
Fertiliser	313 (127)	227 (92)	78 (32)	260 (105)	261 (106)
Sprays	10 (4)	7 (3)	12 (5)	37 (15)	42 (17)
Total	343 (139)	249 (101)	111 (45)	445 (180)	373 (151)
Cost per tonne fresh weight	6.85	5.53	2.78	11.14	8.30

	Fodder Beet	Forage Rape	Turnips	Stubble Turnips	Swedes
Yield tonnes/ha (tons/acre)	70 (28)	35 (14)	65 (26)	35 (14)	70 (28)
Seed	130 (53)	23 (9)	22 (9)	35 (14)	155 (63)
Fertiliser	325 (132)	174 (70)	263 (107)	190 (77)	263 (107)
Sprays	135 (55)	20 (8)	43 (17)	22 (9)	45 (18)
Total	590 (239)	217 (88)	328 (133)	247 (100)	463 (188)
Cost per tonne fresh weight	8.43	6.20	5.05	7.04	6.62

1. These are average figures. Intensively silaged and grazed grass may have much higher fertiliser costs in particular - even as much as £400/ha (200/acre) for some dairying systems. The seed costs will vary according to the proportion of permanent pasture and the length of leys. Fertiliser inputs are often less on permanent pasture too, but this depends on the attitude of the farmer/manager, which will also be reflected in the stocking rates and productive levels per animal achieved.

2. Contract work on maize: drilling £42 (16); harvesting £93 (37), or £153 (62) to include carting and clamping. The area grown in the United Kingdom was 146,000ha in 2007 and 137,000 ha in 2006.

   Standing maize crops are typically sold for between £600 and £700/ha (£243-283/acre) but can be as high as £850/ha (£350/acre), depending on the potential yield of the crop and local supply and demand.

   Whole Crop Cereals (winter wheat; fermented). Variable costs are as for combined crop (see Section 2) plus contract harvesting at £180 per ha (£72 per acre). Fresh yield averages 27.5 tonnes per ha (11 tons per acre) harvested in late June with a 35% dry matter. Urea treatment (for higher dry matter): add £200 per ha (£80 per acre) for urea prills.

   Labour: forage and conservation labour, pages 148.

   Conservation machinery, page 163.

Grass Silage and Hay Costs and Value

Estimated average costs (for 2009) of producing and harvesting, on a full costs basis (i.e. including rental value of the land, all labour, share of general overheads, etc.) are: Hay: £95 per tonne; Silage: £32 per tonne.

Approximately half the silage cost is for growing the grass and half for harvesting and storage. The per cent breakdown of total costs is typically as follows:

Variable Costs:		Fertiliser	Seeds and Sprays	Contract	Sundries
Silage................................		36	1	9	4
Hay....................................		29	1	2	2

Fixed Costs:	Rent	Labour	Tractors	Deprec. & Reps.	FYM/Lime
Silage...........	18	8	14	8	4
Hay..............	22	13	17	11	4

Sale Value of hay and (far less common because of its bulk) silage vary widely according to the region and type of season (supply/demand situation), quality and time of year.

Hay (pick-up baled) has an average ex-farm sale value of £70 to £85 per tonne. Seed hay (main range November to May £100 to £120) and £65.00-£85.00 for meadow hay (main range November to May £70 to £80); prices are higher in the west than the east and more after a dry summer (giving low yields of grass) than a wet one. Prices tend to be higher for horses. Big bale hay is £20 to £30/tonne cheaper.

Grass silage is typically valued at about £35 a tonne delivered (up to £50 when forage is very short in an area and less if it is plentiful), maize silage approx. £30 a tonne.

Relative Costs of Grazing, Conserved Grass, etc.

	Yield DM tonnes/ha (acre)	Cost per tonne DM (£)	MJ per kg DM	Pence per MJ of ME in DM
Grazed Grass............................	10 (4.1)	47	12.8	0.46
Kale (direct drilled).................	6.9 (2.8)	75	11.0	0.80
Forage Turnips (direct drilled)	6.9 (2.8)	77	10.2	0.94
Grass Silage	10 (4.1)	47	10.9	0.49
Big Bale Silage	10 (4.1)	46	10.8	0.53
Purchased Hay (1)...................		78	8.8	0.88
Brewers' Grains (2)		145	11.7	1.25
Concentrates (3)......................		232	12.8	1.82

(1) at £65 per tonne   (2) at £35 per tonne   (3) 14% CP 14% Moisture, delivered in bulk, £200 per tonne

Notes

In interpreting the above figures for use in planning feed use on farm, it is important to remember that own land, labour and capital for equipment are required for home-produced fodder but not for purchased feed, and much more storage is required

The consumption of fodder is limited by its bulk although this very much depends upon its quality/digestibility.

Clearly, the cost of forage will vary enormously depending on growing conditions, soil fertility and type, intensity of farming practice and management ability.

FODDER CROPS, GRASSES AND CLOVERS
SEED PRICES (2009) AND SEED RATES

Crop	Price	Seed Rate	Cost
	£/Kg	Kg/Ha	£/Ha
Fodder Kale	£9.40-£11.50	5-7.5	50-71
Swedes	£42.00	Precision drill 0.75	35
		seed drill 3.75	155
Stubble Turnips	£4.80- £12.00	3.75 kg drilled,	18 - 45
		5.0 kg broadcast	24 - 60
Rape	£2.35	10	23
Mustard	£3.00	20 to 25	60 - 75
Rape and Turnip mix	£4.20/kg mix	1.25 kg rape	21
		3.75 kg turnips	
Kale, Swede & Turnips	£16/kg mix	1.5 kg kale,	60
		0.5 kg swede,	
		1.75 kg turnips	
1 year leys	£2.00 - £2.25	35- 55	73 -120
2 year leys	£2.00	35kg	70 - 90
4-6 year leys	£2.80	35 - 40	100 - 117
Long-term Ley	£3.00	30 - 45	100 - 130
White Clover Ley	£3.50	30	105
Red Clover Ley	£3.10 - 3.60	30	95 – 110
Game Cover mixture	£3.00	25	75
Game Maize	£2.60	27.5	71
Forage Maize: Silage			128 - 168
Vetch/Tares	£1.65	100 to 125 kg	165-205
Westerwold Ryegrass	£2.00	35 kg	70
Italian Ryegrass	£2.40	33 to 50 kg	80 - 120
Perennial Ryegrass	£2.70	35 to 40 kg	94 - 108
Hybrid Ryegrass	£2.80	30 to 40 kg	84 - 112
Cocksfoot	£4.00	20 to 25 kg	80 - 100
Red Clover	£6.00	15	90
Alsike Clover	£3.90	18 to 22 kg	70 - 85
White Clover	£7.50	5 kg	37
Timothy/M. Fescue ley	£4.00	31kg	124
Timothy	£3.35		
Meadow Fescue	£3.10		
Lucerne	£6.50 (inoculated)	20 kg	130
Sainfoin	£2.80	60 to 90 kg	170 - 250
Forage Rye	£0.90	180 kg	162
Millet	£2.11	25	53
Quinoa & Kale cover Mix	£9.10	7.5	68
Field Corner Mixture	£13.50	25	335
Horse grazing	£2.00 - 5.00	35kg	70 - 200
Gallop mixture	£3.20	100-250	320 - 800

These figures are all inflated from the 2008 price list by 7%. This is thought likely to be the minimum rise for the 2009 year, and could be considerably more in some cases.

3. PIGS, POULTRY, TROUT, RABBIT

PIGS

1. Breeding and Rearing (to 32 kg liveweight):

per sow per year and per 32 kg pig reared

Performance Level	*Average*		*High*	
	per sow	per pig	per sow	per pig
	£	£	£	£
Weaners: (ave) 21.6 (1) @ £38.00 (3)	821	38.00		
(high) 24.7 (2) @ £38.00 (3)			939	38.00
Less Livestock Depreciation (4)	37	1.70	41	1.68
Output	784	36.30	898	36.32
Variable Costs:				
Food (5)	531	24.59	549	22.22
Miscellaneous (6)	70	3.24	70	2.83
Total Variable Costs	601	27.83	619	25.05
Gross Margin (per year)	183	8.47	279	11.27

Notes

1. Weaners per sow - average: 9.80 reared per litter, 2.2 litters per year = 21.6 weaners per sow per year. (The average has now recovered following falls in the early 2000's due to the wasting diseases PMWS and PDNS).

2. Weaners per sow - high: 10.50 reared per litter, 2.35 litters per year = 24.7 weaners per sow per year. For Outdoor Breeding performance figures see page 89.

3. Price – assumed pig cycle average. (See note 4 on page 89). Prices for 32kg weaners have varied from £15 to £45 during the past decade. They have been between £30 and £35 in the last three years, but have recently firmed.

4. Average livestock depreciation assumes an in-pig gilt purchase price of £155, a cull value per sow of £95 and a 43% replacement rate (i.e. approximately 6 litters per sow life). Sow mortality 4%. Boars (1 per 24 sows) purchased at £650 (40% a year replacement), sold at £90. 'High' compared with 'Average': higher gilt purchase prices and slightly fewer sows per boar assumed.

5. Food – 2.50 tonnes per sow: sow 1.34, boar (per sow) 0.05, weaner feed (per sow) 1.11. Price of feed consumed: £213 per tonne; (average of 56% sow (and boar) feed (at £175) and 43% piglet and rearing feed (at £260), and of home-mixed and purchased compounds). High performance: lower sow feed but extra piglet rearing feed for additional weaners. Piglets weaned at average 3.75 weeks, 7.25kg weight.

6. Average: vet. and med. £40, transport £11, straw and bedding £10, miscellaneous £9. (Electricity and gas [£18] and water [£9] included in fixed costs below).

7. Direct Labour Cost per sow: average £210, good £165; per weaner: average £9.67, good £6.70. This figure does not include labour used for 'overhead' activities – repairs etc. For futher fixed costs information see page 186.

8. Building Costs: see page 195.

Acknowledgement: The main data source for the margins within the Pigs section is the Pig Yearbook (Meat and Livestock Commission), but the pig and feed price assumptions are entirely the author's responsibility. Small differences in the relationship between these can of course cause large differences in margins. Big variations can occur between farms. The weaner price is crucial as regards the relative margins between breeding and rearing, and finishing.

2. Feeding (from 32 kg liveweight): per pig

A. Average Performance

	Pork £	Cutter £	Bacon £
Sale Value	74.50	84.50	94.70
Less Weaner Cost (1)	38.00	38.00	38.00
Mortality Charge	1.70	1.80	1.90
Output	34.80	44.70	54.80
Variable Costs:			
Food	26.80	34.60	41.50
Miscellaneous	4.50	5.00	5.50
Total Variable Costs	31.30	39.60	47.00
Gross Margin	**3.50**	**5.10**	**7.80**
Liveweight (kg)	76	87	97
Deadweight (kg)	56	65	74
Killing Out %	74%	75%	76%
Price per Deadweight (p)	133	130	128
Price per Liveweight (p)	98.0	97.1	97.6
Food Conversion Rate	2.65	2.70	2.75
Food per Pig (kg)	122	154	184
Average Cost of Food per tonne (£) (2)	£220	£225	£225
Food Cost per Kg l/w Gain (p)	58.30	60.75	61.88
Liveweight Gain per Day (kg)	0.62	0.65	0.67
Feeding Period (weeks)	10.6	12.5	14.3
Mortality (%)	4.5	4.7	5.0
Direct Labour Costs per Pig (£)	4.90	5.80	6.70

B. High Performance (same pig price)

Food Conversion Rate	2.55	2.62	2.7
Food per Pig (kg)	117	149	181
Food Cost per Pig (£5/t less than ave.)	25.22	32.85	39.80
Food Cost per Kg l/w Gain (p)	54.83	57.64	59.40
Gross Margin per Pig	**5.80**	**7.50**	**9.70**
Direct Labour Costs per Pig	3.70	4.30	4.80

(1) Weaner cost assumes on farm transfer. If purchased (i.e., feeding only) transport and purchasing costs have to be added: these are very variable but average about £1.75 per weaner.

(2) Average of home-mixed and purchased compounds. There can be big variations in feed costs per tonne between farms, according to whether the food is purchased as compounds or home-mixed, bought in bulk or in bags, size of unit, etc.

Labour: see page 159. Building Costs: see page 195.

Sensitivity Analysis. The effect of changes in important variables (other things being equal) are as follows;

Change in Gross Margin (£)	Porker	Cutter	Baconer
Price: 5p per kg dw difference	2.80	3.25	3.70
Food Cost per tonne: £10 difference	1.22	1.54	1.84
Food Conversion Rate: 0.1 difference ...	1.01	1.28	1.51

The effect of differences in the cost per weaner is obvious.

3. Combined Breeding, Rearing, and Feeding: per pig

Performance Level*	Pork £ Ave.	High	Cutter £ Ave.	High	Bacon £ Ave.	High
Sale Value	74.50	74.50	84.50	84.50	94.70	94.70
Sow and Boar Deprcn	1.70	1.68	1.70	1.68	1.70	1.68
Mortality Charge	1.70	1.50	1.80	1.60	1.90	1.70
Output	**71.10**	**71.32**	**81.00**	**81.22**	**91.10**	**91.32**
Food	51.39	47.42	59.19	55.12	66.09	62.02
Miscellaneous	7.74	6.83	8.24	7.33	8.74	8.33
Total Variable Costs	**59.13**	**54.25**	**67.43**	**62.45**	**74.83**	**70.35**
Gross Margin per Pig	**11.97**	**17.07**	**13.57**	**18.77**	**16.27**	**20.97**
Gross Margin per Sow	**259**	**422**	**293**	**464**	**351**	**518**
Labour Costs per Pig	13.76	9.85	14.66	10.45	15.56	10.95
Labour Costs per Sow	297	243	317	258	336	270

* Performance levels refer to breeding and rearing differences as on pages 86-87 and, for feeding, differences in food conversion rate, food costs and labour cost only.

4. Prices - General

Pig prices are notoriously difficult to predict. Over the last three years the GB average pig price (DAPP Eurospec) has ranged from below 100p per kg deadweight to 135ppkg as the time of writing (July 2008). The majority of UK pigs are now taken to baconer weight. The level shown in the finisher margins for baconers above, of 128p, is an estimated average for late 2008 through 2009.

5. Further Performance Data

Source: The Meat and Livestock Commission's 'Pig Yearbook 2008' (data for the year ended Sept. 2007).

	Performance Level		
A. Breeding	Average	Top Third*	Top 10%*
Sow replacements (%)	46.6	47.0	49.8
Sow sales and deaths (%)	41.6	47.1	56.6
Sow mortality (%)	3.4	3.3	4.3
Litters per sow per year	2.22	2.33	2.37
Pigs reared per litter	9.7	10.4	10.9
Pigs reared per sow per year	21.6	24.3	25.9
Weight of pigs produced (kg)	7.6	7.5	7.4
Average weaning age (days)	26.7	26.0	26.5
Sow feed per sow per year (tonnes) .	1.34	1.34	1.44
Feed per pig reared (kg)	70	61	56
Sow feed cost per tonne (£)	131	129	131
Sow feed cost per sow per year (£) .	180	179	193
Feed cost per pig reared (£)	7.71	7.09	6.93

* selected on basis of pigs reared per sow per year.

B. Rearing	Average	Top Third*
Weight of pigs at start (kg)	7.4	7.0
Weight of pigs produced (kg)	35.3	34.7
Mortality (%)	2.7	2.0
Feed conversion ratio	1.8	1.7
Daily Gain (g)	453	465
Feed cost per tonne (£)	214	196
Feed cost per kg gain (p)	38.8	34.0
Feed cost per pig reared (£)	10.84	9.41

C. Feeding	Average	Top Third*	Top 10%*
Weight of pigs at start (kg)	26.6	33.3	30.1
Weight of pigs produced (kg)	98.8	102.0	100.4
Mortality (%)	4.8	3.5	2.8
Feed conversion ratio	2.73	2.77	2.65
Daily Gain (g)	673	753	746
Feed cost per tonne (£)	133	108	104
Feed cost per kg gain (£)	36.2	30.1	27.6
Feed cost per pig reared (£)	26.14	20.67	19.38

*   selected on basis of feed cost per kg liveweight gain.

Feed conversion ratio for rearing and feeding combined, from 7.5kg to 99kg liveweight is approximately 2.47.

6. Outdoor v Indoor Performance

Breeding	Outdoor	Indoor
Sow replacements (%)	45.8	47.7
Sow sales and deaths (%)	36.9	46.7
Sow mortality (%)	3.1	3.9
Litters per sow per year	2.19	2.25
Pigs reared per litter	9.5	10.0
Pigs reared per sow per year	20.9	22.4
Weight of pigs produced (kg)	7.6	7.4
Average weaning age (days)	26.5	27.1
Sow feed per sow per year (tonnes) .	1.30	1.36
Feed per pig reared (kg)	70	66
Sow feed cost per tonne (£)	133	128
Sow feed cost per sow per year (£) .	177	179
Feed cost per pig reared (£)	7.25	7.83

Stocking Rate for outdoor pigs is mainly between 12 and 25 per hectare (5 and 10 per acre), 20 (8) being the most common. Good drainage is essential. A low rainfall and mild climate are also highly desirable. In 2003, MLC's Agrosoft puts the cost of establishing a sow herd on a greenfield site at £1,800 per sow place for an indoor unit and about £600 per sow place for an outdoor unit.

Data on the split of indoor and outdoor herds is hard to come by. However, it is thought that well over a third of the UK breeding sow herd is now kept outdoors. A somewhat smaller proportion (probably <10%) of pigs are finished outdoors.

Further costing information can be found in 'Pig Production in England 2006-07' produced by Askham Bryan College, York on behalf of Rural Business Research. See www.ruralbusinessresearch.co.uk

EGG PRODUCTION

(brown egg layers, 52 week laying period)

Level of Performance . .	Cages				Free Range	
	Average		High		Average	
	per bird	per doz eggs	per bird	per doz eggs	per bird	per doz eggs
	£	p	£	p	£	p
Egg Returns	14.82	57.0	15.39	57.0	22.75	91.0
Less Livestock Deprcn . .	3.04	11.7	3.04	11.3	3.24	13.0
Output	**11.78**	**45.3**	**12.35**	**45.7**	**19.51**	**78.0**
Variable Costs:						
Food	8.93	34.3	8.93	33.1	10.90	43.6
Miscellaneous	1.69	6.5	1.69	6.3	1.64	6.6
Total Variable Costs	**10.62**	**40.8**	**10.62**	**39.3**	**12.54**	**50.2**
Gross Margin	**1.17**	**4.5**	**1.74**	**6.4**	**6.97**	**27.9**

Notes:

Hen-housed data are used throughout, i.e. the total costs and returns are divided by the number of birds housed at the commencement of the laying period. IPPC permit charges have not been included (Integrated Pollution Prevention and Control).

Due to the volatility of feed prices, large variations in input costs and returns can occur.

A. Cage Production

1. The yields assumed are:

    Average .... 312 (26.00 dozen)

    High...................................... 324 (27.00 dozen)

2. The average price assumed (for 2009), 57p per dozen, includes all quantity and quality bonuses. Farmer to shop and consumer prices are well above packer to producer levels and normally 35p and 65p per dozen premiums respectively are required.

3. Livestock depreciation—the average point of lay pullet is priced at £3.10 (16/17 weeks old).

4. The food price assumed (for 2009) is £210 per tonne. The feed cost is dependent on breed, housing and environmental conditions, quantity purchased and type of ration. Quantity of feed used = 42.5 kg for caged birds.

5. Direct Labour Costs: average £1.31 per bird, premium £1.00. See page 160.

    Housing Costs: see page 195. Deadstock depreciation averages about £1 per caged bird.

B. Free Range Production

1. Egg yields: 300 (25 dozen).

2. Average price: 91p per dozen.

3. Quantity of feed used = 47.4 kg. Price £230 per tonne.

4. Direct Labour Costs: average £4.17 per bird, dependent on automation.

Acknowledgement: The figures in the whole of the poultry section are provided by John Newton, ADAS, Wergs Road, Wolverhampton.

REARING PULLETS

(Average per bird reared)

	£
Value of 16/17 weeks old bird.............................	3.10
Less Chicks 1.01 (1) @ 60p (including levy)..................	0.61
Output...	**2.49**
Variable Costs:	
Food: 6.25 kg @ £210 per tonne......................	1.31
Miscellaneous (2)...................................	0.80
Total Variable Costs	**2.11**
Gross Margin.....................................	**0.38**

1. Assumes 3 per cent mortality, but 2 per cent allowed in price.

2. Excluding transport (18p), but including full vaccination costs.

   Labour (37p); deadstock depreciation (46p).

TABLE POULTRY

A Broilers (per bird sold at 41 days)	p
Returns 2.37 kg per bird @ 72.0p per kg lw	170.6
Less Cost of Chick..................................	29.5
Output..	**141.1**
Variable Costs:	
Food: 4.12 kg @ £277 per tonne......................	114.1
Miscellaneous......................................	16.5
Total Variable Costs	**130.6**
Gross Margin.....................................	**10.5**

Capital cost of housing and equipment: £6.65 per broiler space (depreciation cost approximately 5.7p per bird sold). Housing Costs: see page 195.

Labour: 4.9p, excluding catching and cleaning out (4.8p) but includes management; see page 160.

B All Year Round Turkey (per bird sold at 20 weeks, sexed stags)	£
Returns 14.3 kg per bird @ £2.58 per kg O.R.	36.9
Less Cost of Poult..................................	2.0
Output..	**34.9**
Variable Costs:	
Food: 50 kg @ £267 per tonne........................	13.4
Miscellaneous......................................	4.5
Total Variable Costs	**17.9**
Gross Margin.....................................	**17.0**

10% mortality allowed in cost of poult figures.

Note: Rearing turkeys all the year round now tends to be just in the hands of a few large companies. Cheap imports has led to many smaller operators giving up.

C Christmas Turkey (Traditional Farm Fresh - indoor reared)

	Light £	Medium £	Heavy £
Returns per bird sold	25.85	29.05	27.96
Less Cost of Poult	4.26	4.26	3.57
Output	**21.59**	**24.79**	**24.39**
Variable Costs:			
Food	6.37	8.30	8.89
Miscellaneous....................	11.78	12.17	12.58
Total Variable Costs	**18.15**	**20.47**	**21.47**
Gross Margin.....................	**3.44**	**4.32**	**2.92**
Killing Age (weeks)	18	22	22
Live Weight (kg)	7.2	8.3	12.0
Oven Ready Weight (kg)	6.1	6.9	9.8
Food Conversion	3.2	3.7	2.8
Food per Bird (kg)	22.7	30.4	33.3
Food Cost per tonne	£280	£273	£267

1. 7, 8 and 10% mortality allowed for in cost of poult figures for light, medium and heavy weights respectively.

2. Light and medium = slow growing sexed hens.
   Heavy = stags (as hatched).

3. Price per kilogram:
   Christmas (fresh, eviscerated): hens 385 - 460p range; stags 250 - 320p range.

4. Miscellaneous costs include processing / marketing

Note: With both turkey enterprises considerable variations will occur between individual strains and because of different production systems and feeding regimes. Free range systems for example will show higher costs and returns. The figures should therefore be used only as rough guidelines.

D Large roaster chickens (per bird sold at 12 weeks; Christmas - males only)

	£
Returns 4.8 kg per bird @ £3.00 per kg O.R.	14.40
Less Cost of Chick....................................	0.77
Output...	**13.63**
Variable Costs:	
Food: 14.3 kg @ £267 per tonne......................	3.82
Miscellaneous.....................................	1.44
Total Variable Costs	**5.26**
Gross Margin......................................	**8.37**

10% mortality allowed for in cost of chick figures.

E Ducks (Pekin type) (per bird sold at 7 weeks)

	£
Returns 2.3 kg per bird @ £3.20 per kg O.R.	7.36
Less Cost of Duckling	0.80
Output	**6.56**
Variable Costs:	
Food: 8.2 kg @ £210 per tonne	1.72
Miscellaneous	1.95
Total Variable Costs	**3.67**
Gross Margin	**2.89**

Day-old costs allow for 10% mortality.

F Geese (Traditional Farm Fresh - free range and dry plucked)

	£
Returns 6.5 kg per bird @ £9.50 per kg O.R.	61.75
Less Cost of Gosling	5.20
Output	**56.55**
Variable Costs:	
Food: 64 kg @ £320 per tonne	20.48
Miscellaneous	11.30
Total Variable Costs	**31.78**
Gross Margin	**24.77**

Notes: Day-old costs allow for 6% mortality.

Farm gate output values used

Miscellaneous costs include processing and marketing

RAINBOW TROUT

	£ per tonne of fish
Returns: 1 tonne of fish @ £1.75 per kg	1,750
Less 4000 fingerlings @ 5.5p each	220
Output	**1,530**
Variable Costs:	
Food: 1 tonne @ £825 per tonne	825
Vet and med; Miscellaneous	125
Miscellaneous	20
Total Variable Costs	**970**
Gross Margin	**560**

Notes

1. Fish growing to 350g from fingerlings at 4.5g.

2. Prices are estimated ex-farm to processor or wholesaler. Higher prices of up to £4.20 per kg can be achieved by selling direct to retailers, caterers and consumers at, say farmers markets, but significant additional costs are associated with such sales.

3. Fingerlings price: varies according to quantity ordered and time of year.

4. Average feeding period, 10 months. Mortality, from fingerling to market size, 15%. Food conversion ratio 1.05:1. The price for fish food is for a pigmented high oil expanded pellet.

5. Current capital costs for construction of earth pond unit approximately £60 per cubic metre, to include buildings, holding systems and installation of water supply and services, but excluding land.

6. Labour requirement: the basic norm has in the past been 1 man per 50 tonnes of fish produced per annum on a table fish farm, but to remain competitive farmers now need to produce at least 150 tonnes per annum of table fish per man.

The figures given above must only be considered illustrative and cannot reflect the complexities of trout farming. Trout farming varies across the UK – from Cage Farming in Scottish lochs (freshwater and marine) through to 'traditional' river farming. It also encompasses both the table and restocking sectors. As such feed costs, conversion rates etc do vary which obviously has an effect on the costings for the enterprise. Differences in water temperature will also impact significantly on food conversion ratios, mortality figures etc.

Acknowledgement: British Trout Association, The Rural Centre, West Mains, Ingliston, Edinburgh, EH28 8NZ. Tel: 0131 472 4080 .www.britishtrout.co.uk.

MEAT RABBITS

Although the consumption of rabbit meat in the UK is low, at less than 2oz per person per year, most of it is imported. Commercial rabbit production is an intensive livestock enterprise and will probably require planning permission and building regulation approval from the Local Authority.

A meat rabbit unit needs a weather- and vermin-proof building, which is insulated, well-drained and has good ventilation, lighting and a water supply. Housing can be fully environment controlled to give good feed conversion rates and better winter conditions for both stock and personnel, or be natural environment, which has lower capital and running costs and possibly keeps animals healthier. Rabbits are kept in wire cages, usually in one tier, ideally suspended; a single tier system needs 10-12 square feet per cage. Feed hoppers, drinkers and nest boxes are required. Some experimental work to provide less intensive conditions for the animals, possibly with outside access, is in progress, but is at an early stage.

New Zealand White or Californian stock is used. Young does are bought in at 12 weeks and mated at 16-20 weeks. Bucks are bought at 16 weeks and first mated at 20 weeks. A ratio of one buck to 10-20 does is recommended. Gestation is 31 days. Average litter size is 8-9, of which 6-7 should be successfully fattened. Re-mating can be immediately post-partum or up to 6 weeks afterwards; the average is about 21 days. A doe can have a useful life of 10-12 litters over 18 months; less productive animals may be culled sooner. An overall mortality rate of up to 12.5% can be expected.

Young rabbits are weaned at 35-42 days at about 2.5-3 lb and then fed ad-lib until they are ready for marketing at 5.5-6.5lb liveweight at 11-13 weeks. Food conversion rate, including the doe's feed and a share of the buck's is around 4:1. A balanced ration can be obtained for £165 per tonne in bulk but may cost up to £185 per tonne. A doe should produce around 50 meat rabbits each year but experienced producers would aim for 60-70. Health, hygiene and good stockmanship are crucial to the enterprise. One full-time person can look after 250-300 does and their progeny.

There are only a few buyers and processors of meat rabbits in the UK and they do not cover all parts of the country. Hence transport costs may have to be allowed for. The demand for rabbit meat is seasonal - more is eaten in the winter than the summer, which can pose marketing problems. Producers are advised to adjust their production by 15 to 20% in summer to allow for this. An individual producer may develop local markets but this will require initiative. There may be a market for the manure but again this would have to be developed.

Meat Rabbit Costs and Gross Margin

Capital Costs	£	No. per 50 does	£ per 50 does
Doe at 12 weeks	10	50	500
Buck at 16 weeks	12	3	36
Cage	10	87	870
Drinker	5	87	435
Nest Box	4	50	200
Building (new):			
(10 sq.ft/cage at £3/sq.ft x 1.75) 52.50/doe			2,625

Gross Margin	£/doe/year	£/50 does/year
48 young @ 2.60 kg @ £1.30/kg (1)	162.2	8,112
Less Depreciation (2)	4.6	228
Output	**157.7**	**7,884**
Variable Costs:		
Feed	97.3	4,867
Vet and med	1.7	85
Bedding	1.8	90
Miscellaneous (including electricity)	4.0	200
Total Variable Costs	**104.8**	**5,242**
Gross Margin	**52.8**	**2,642**

1. £1.20 to £1.40 depending on delivery and collection

2. Cull value: Does £1.5 over 2 years. Bucks £1.5 over 3 years. Both 10% mortality.

3. Food conversion 4:1 at £195 per tonne including allowance for doe and share of buck.

Acknowledgement: David Blythe, *Woldsway Foods Ltd.* Tel: 01754 890 641. www.woldsway.co.uk

4. RENEWABLE ENERGY

GENERAL

The rapidly emerging renewable energy industrial sector offers many opportunities to farmers and land based entrepreneurs. Some forms of renewable energy generation such as wind turbines can be located on agricultural land, others, such as bioethanol have a fundamental dependence on agriculture for its raw materials.

Renewable energy is a relatively novel concept in industrial terms even though virtually all technologies are not new and are well understood. Wind power and wood heating clearly have long histories, as has anaerobic digestion having been harnessed by man for centuries. Even biofuels were available for the Second World War and second generation biofuels, whilst well understood are simply prohibitively expensive. What is new is the increasing focus on these technologies as a means to combating climate change.

The Renewable Energy industry is developing in response to incentives to cut the emissions of climate changing green house gases (GHGs) as a response to human activities. The main GHGs are:

- Carbon Dioxide, which accounts for up to a quarter of the green house gas effect

- Methane accounts for between 4% and 9% of the effect but is about 25 times more potent by volume than carbon dioxide

- Nitrous Oxide, which, whilst very low in concentration in the atmosphere, is about 300 times more potent than carbon dioxide

- Water Vapour. Whilst this is the most voluminous and causes between a third and two thirds of the green house effect, human activity has a negligible effect on it.

Since 1997, 169 countries have signed a commitment to reduce their emissions of GHGs; the Kyoto Protocol. The UK has a legally binding target under the Protocol to reduce its GHG emissions to 12.5% below 1990 levels between 2008 and 2012. It also has another domestic goal to reduce carbon dioxide emissions (one of the main greenhouse gases) by 20% below 1990 levels by 2010. The March 2007 Draft Climate Change Bill outlines how Government intends to enshrine the commitments in the 2003 Energy White Paper ('Our Energy Future, Creating a Low Carbon Economy') to reduce CO_2 emissions by 60% on 1990 levels by 2050; and to achieve "real progress" by 2020 (equating to reductions of 26-32%). This is further reinforced in the May 2007 Energy White Paper, 'Meeting the Energy Challenge'.

SUPPORT AND GRANTS

Under the Single Payment Scheme, an **Energy Aid Payment** is available to growers of €45 per hectare (less modulation deductions in 2009 of 19% see Section III ~ Support). This is subject to a Maximum Guaranteed Area throughout the EU of 2.0 million hectares. This was exceeded in 2007 meaning payments were reduced pro-rata. The grant is normally split between the grower and processor as the latter has administration to cover and guarantees to finance. We are not expecting an overshoot for the 2008 harvest. The CAP Health Check (see Section III) proposes its abolition from 2010 which would mean 2009 harvest would be its last year.

In the UK, the area claimed against the Energy Aid payment rose from its launch in 2004 to 2007 then fell dramatically in 2008 as follows:

Energy Aid UK Area

Year	2004	2005	2006	2007	2008
Hectares	32,972	99,351	182,394	242,413	53,520

The **Energy Crops Scheme** is part of the Rural Development Programme for England and is managed by Natural England. It finances the establishment of Miscanthus and Short Rotation Coppice (SRC of Willow, Poplar, Ash, Alder, Hazel, Silver Birch, Sycamore, Sweet Chestnut and Lime). Applicants submit estimates of the likely costs. If they are within a range of 'typical costs' then the grant is paid at 40% of the actual expenditure. In Scotland, support for planting SRC willow or poplar provides 40% planting grant (50% in LFAs) up to a maximum of £1,540/ha meaning the grant is worth up to £616 (£770 LFAs) per hectare.

The **Bio-energy Capital Grants Scheme** (England only), whilst not part of the Rural Development fund supports the installation of biomass fuelled CHP (Combined Heat and power) projects in England. It opens in 'rounds'. The scheme provides funding of up to 40% to a maximum of £100,000 of the difference in capital cost of installing a biomass CHP and a fossil fuel alternative. Eligibility extends to biogas for CHP. About £4 million is available for this financial year (2008/9). Future rounds of application are scheduled through to 2010.

The **Bio-energy Infrastructure Scheme** (England) is designed to help develop the supply chain to harvest, store, process and supply biomass for heat, power and electricity end users. Growers set up producer groups to supply biomass to energy end-users.

Whilst currently closed, DEFRA anticipates opening a new round in 2008. Eligible costs are likely to include legal and administrative work in setting up the group, rental of office accommodation, purchase/rental of office and IT equipment etc. The scheme doesn't fund planting or growing biomass, or standard items of farm equipment.

The **Wood Energy Business Scheme** (Wales) is currently closed, although a successor scheme is being developed to provide support to the emerging wood fuel sector. This will probably provide capital support for wood heating and combined heat and power generators to stimulate further demand. It will also support the production and supply chain.

BIOMASS FOR POWER

Energy crops are a form of renewable energy. They are grown to be used for heat and electricity generation or to produce transport fuels. They are considered 'carbon neutral' which means the carbon released on burning is only what they (recently) took up into the plant when growing, thereby not releasing additional carbon from fossil reserves beyond the requirements for fertiliser and chemicals, mechanical cultivation, harvest and transport to end-use location.

This section covers crops that are grown to be burnt directly to produce heat and/or electricity. The plant material is chopped, chipped, or baled and is generally either used in boilers in dedicated biomass power stations, or mixed with coal for co-firing in conventional power stations. Biomass includes short rotation coppice, miscanthus, straw, canary reed grass and switch grass as well as forest residues.

The Renewables Obligation

The European Union's **Renewables Directive** that came into force in 2001 encourages Member States to adopt national targets of deriving energy from renewable sources. The UK Government has introduced legislation requiring 10% of UK electricity to be generated from renewable resources by 2010 and 20% by 2020. In 2005 it was 4.2%. There are policy incentives for generation of renewable electricity and road fuel but not yet heat or gas. These incentives operate in a very similar manner to each other. The mechanism for achieving electricity from renewable sources in the UK is the **Renewables Obligation** (RO). Renewables Obligation Certificates (ROCs) are issued to electricity suppliers for providing electricity from renewable sources.

The RO sets a target for licensed electricity suppliers to generate a minimum percentage of their electricity from renewable sources each year (this rises annually). Each supplier is awarded a certificate (ROC) for each mega Watt hour (mWh) electricity that comes from renewable sources. If they do not have sufficient ROCs to meet their target, they are charged £30/mWh up to the target (index linked to 2003 making £35.76 in 2008/09). This money is recirculated equally to all certificates after each year end meaning ROCS are worth more than the penalty. Thus ROCs have a market value; their average price in April 2008 was £49.50/MWh. Electricity suppliers can fulfil their RO by purchasing ROCs from other generators. Farmers generating renewable electricity can sell the ROCs, having no obligation to keep them.

Renewables Obligation Target for Renewable Electricity Generation and Penalty

Year*	Renewables Obligation Target	Non-compliance Penalty per mWh
2002/03	3.0 %	£30.00
2003/04	4.3 %	£30.51
2004/05	4.9 %	£31.59
2005/06	5.5 %	£32.33
2006/07	6.7 %	£33.24
2007/08	7.9 %	£34.30
2008/09	9.1 %	£35.76
2009/10	9.7 %	Index linked
2010/11	10.4 %	increments
Annually thereafter to	+1 %	
2015/16	15.4 %	

* The ROC year is 1ˢᵗ April to 31ˢᵗ March

Generators can also claim 1 LEC (Climate Change Levy Exemption Certificate) for each 1MWh electricity produced. Utilities need to source these LECs so they can exempt business consumers from Climate change levy - which is £4.41 on 1 MWh of electricity

Short Rotation Coppice

Short Rotation Coppice (SRC) is a fast growing species of willow or (less often) poplar that when harvested, chipped and dried can be used as a fuel for heat or power generation. In the UK the majority of SRC is willow because in part to problems with mechanical planting of poplar.

SRC willow needs access to moisture but grows on any cultivated land. It requires a seedbed similar to that of a conventional arable crop, with particular attention to weed control. Planting is carried out in the spring using unrooted cuttings at a rate of 15,000/ha. Rabbit (or deer) fencing may be necessary. Pest and weed control is essential until canopy closure is achieved in the second year. In the autumn after planting, some growers cut back the willow to encourage multi-stemmed stools. This allows herbicide application and encourages a more competitive canopy. Some growers omit this cut-back when weed control is good, thereby achieving a commercial harvest sooner. Crops are usually harvested on a 3 year cycle. In poor conditions it may be left for 4 years, but in good conditions possibly only 2 years. In best conditions, stems would grow too thick to harvest if left any longer. Crops should last for more than 20 years. Most growers apply some fertiliser post harvest. Sewage sludge is commonly used as are animal manures and some apply inorganic fertilisers. In general, approximately 60 kg/ha N is sufficient to maintain growth through the harvest cycle.

The harvested crop can be stored on-farm either as billets or chips. It is then processed according to the needs of the user or processor. Many grind and pellet their crop, increasing density and improving transport efficiency but adding to costs. Pellets flow better in automated fuel feed systems and are sometimes preferred for co-firing (with coal) as the willow has been milled prior to pelleting easing the load on the generator's mills. Pellets obviously command a premium price over chip. SRC wood chip historically sold for £45/odt (oven dried tonne) delivered, however there are reports within the industry of substantially greater prices in 2008 in response to rising commodity prices, many of which compete with SRC wood chip in the energy markets. The first harvest should yield 25-30odt/ha (oven dried tonnes), subsequent ones 32-35odt/ha.

The following gives a broad indication of likely costs and net annual returns. Account has been taken of the Energy Crops Scheme at 40% of costs.

SRC Establishment Costs:	£/ha
Fencing (optional)	200
Pre-planting spraying	30
Post-planting spraying	50
Fertiliser	55
Cultivations	50
Planting	350
Cuttings	750
Cut-back	45
Energy Crops Scheme Grant	- 612
Total Establishment	*918*

Annual Net Returns: Output 27 odt at £45 every third year; £405/year plus Energy Aid Payment net of deductions of approximately £15/ha. Variable costs per year including fertiliser and sprays are £55/ha, harvesting £100/ha, transport and handling £100/ha and processing £100/ha making a total of £355. Note, this equates to harvesting etc, each costing £350 every 3 years. Remember to amortise the cost of planting (including fencing etc) over the forecast period of the crop. Use the Amortisation Table in section VIII.

Gross Margin for SRC Chips (Amortised over 20 years)

	Per Harvest	Per Year
	£	£
Yield: 33odt/ha at £45/odt	1,485	495
Energy Crops Scheme *	85	28
Output:	**1,570 (636)**	**523 (212)**
Variable Costs:		
Amortised Planting Cost**	259 (105)	86 (35)
Fertiliser/spray	180 (73)	60 (24)
Harvest	450 (182)	150 (61)
Transport & Handling	330 (134)	110 (45)
Total Variable Costs	**1,219 (494)**	**406 (164)**
Gross Margin per ha (acre)	351 (142)	117 (47)

* €45 at 78p/€ less 19% modulation
** £918 amortised over 20 years at 7%

Miscanthus (Elephant Grass)

Miscanthus is a perennial energy and fibre crop, indigenous to Africa and Asia, now grown commercially in the UK. It differs from short-rotation coppice as it is harvested annually using existing farm machinery. The crop is expected to have a useful life of 15-20 years.

There is a range of other uses for miscanthus beyond energy generation. After suitable treatment it makes valuable animal bedding, for which there is a ready market. It can go into paper making and biopolymer manufacture or be used to produce a number of bio-degradable products, such as flowerpots.

Potential cropping zones in the UK are widespread but the crop is vulnerable to late spring frosts. Trials have performed well in Central Scotland and the area in Yorkshire is growing to supply a local power generator (Drax). It is suitable for a wide range of soil types and pH values but is not recommended for drought prone soils where again yield can be reduced.

The crop is propagated from rhizomes. New technology has improved planting techniques with a work-rate of 10-20ha per day. Weed control is necessary at establishment and in the following spring. A mature crop should suppress any weed growth. So far in the UK no significant pathogens and pests have been encountered. Agro-chemical use is therefore minimal

Fertiliser requirement is low. Leaf mulch recycles nutrient, but cannot replenish that removed from harvest. In the first year, there is little growth so fertiliser is not thought necessary. Current ongoing research suggests the mature crop removes 7kg P and 100kg K/ha/year. The plant being deep rooted may access minerals from deeper than most other crops. The mature crop removes about 75kg N/ha/year, some of this is replaced by soil mineralisation and aerial deposition but trials indicate a response from 35-45kg/ha/year. Sewage sludge is an ideal fertiliser. Commercial crops often use none but eventually the minerals would run low. The figures in the Miscanthus gross margin schedule below include fertiliser at 00/05/30 kg of $N/P_2O_5/K_2O$ per hectare.

Each spring the crop produces new shoots, usually in April, which grow into strong erect stems up to 4 metres in height by late August. They resemble bamboo canes and contain solid pith. The plants senesce in the autumn, nutrients pass down into the rhizomes and a deep leaf litter forms. All foliage dies after the first frost and the stems desiccate to 50% moisture content during winter. The leafless canes are harvested between March and April, before the crop shoots again. The robust rhizome network provides a platform for harvesting machinery.

The harvest method depends on end use. For energy the crop is cut with a mower conditioner and then baled into 500-600kg Heston bales. These are stored outside before being taken to the power station. For other end uses a modified maize harvester can be used. New machinery is being developed to make operations more efficient and cheaper.

In the UK the likely yield of a mature crop should be 12-15 oven dried tonnes (odt)/ha/year. In the year after establishment only as much as 50 to 60% of the full yield is obtained. The price for miscanthus ranges enormously between £25 to £55/odt (ex-farm). Its energy value is potentially higher than this. Horse bedding can retail for as much as £100/tonne in bulk to £240/tonne, de-dusted in 20kg bags.

There are probably about 6,000ha of miscanthus in the UK although this is difficult to measure. Initially much of the crop was used for propagation material but now it is being planted for both energy and fibre end uses. A number of other biomass projects, supported by BERR, are in train. Small on-farm boilers, to produce heat and energy, have been developed which also offer potential for miscanthus.

New techniques are making the planting process cheaper and tend to cost in the region of £1,600 to £2,000 per hectare. Planting miscanthus for long term power contracts can involve an agreement whereby planting costs fall to £1,250, meaning net costs after the grant can be as low as £750. Some agro-chemicals will probably be required in the first year.

Amortised Gross Margin for Miscanthus over 3 time periods

Crop Longevity (years)..................	**5 years**	**15 Years**	**20 years**
Yield: 12.5odt/ha (5odt/acre) @ £45/odt	**£**		
Miscanthus*................................	391	506	520
Energy Crop Supplement............	28	28	28
Output:...	419 (170)	534 (217)	548 (222)
Variable Costs:			
Amortised Planting Cost**.........	245 (99)	110 (45)	95 (38)
Fertiliser/spray............................	30 (12)	30 (12)	30 (12)
Harvest, bale and haul/store........	157 (64)	202 (82)	208 (84)
Total Variable Costs.....................	432 (175)	342 (139)	333 (135)
Gross Margin per ha (acre)	-13 (-5)	192 (78)	215 (87)

* calculated as average yield over period including 1ˢᵗ year (no harvest) and 2ⁿᵈ season (½ yield)

** Based on £1,675 less £670 planting grant (40%) amortised at 7% for longevity of crop

Acknowledgement: Andrew Riche; Rothamstead.

LIQUID BIOFUELS

Liquid biofuels are road transport fuels produced from plants, including several mainstream farm crops. Biodiesel is produced from oilseed crops such as oilseed rape, soybeans and palm and is a replacement for mineral diesel. Bioethanol is a petrol replacement, produced from starch/sugar-based crops including wheat, maize and sugar beet or cane. A 'second generation' of biofuels is being developed which will use cellulosic feedstock. This will enable a higher energy return per hectare of cropped land and the opportunity to process household, manufacturing and agricultural organic wastes. Its production is currently not financially viable so may be some years from large-scale commercial production.

Policy

In the UK, a **fuel excise duty discount** of 20ppl is available for biofuels (only for the biofuel component of fuel). This discount is in place until April 2010 when it ends. Planned future changes to Fuel Excise Duty rates had been scheduled for October 2008 (to 52.35ppl) and April 2009 (to 54.19ppl) but these changes have been shelved until the next budget (April 2009). Announcements may be made in the pre-budget report in November 2008 or the Budget Statement in March 2009 Duty rates are as follows:

Budget 2008 Fuel Excise Duty:	*1-Apr 2008*
Mineral Fuel *ppl*	50.35
Bioethanol *ppl*	30.35
Biodiesel *ppl*...............................	30.35
Biodiesel for non-road use *ppl* ...	9.69
Natural Gas (inc Biogas) *p/kg**..	13.70

* The duty differential applicable to biogas is equivalent to 40.88p on a litre of petrol. It will remain at this level until at least Budget 2012.

On 15ᵗʰ April 2008, the **Renewable Transport Fuel Obligation** (RTFO) began. It encourages road fuel suppliers to incorporate a minimum amount of biofuel in their sales. The RTFO started in 2008/9 with a target biofuel inclusion rate of 2.5% of aggregate road transport fuel by volume, increasing to 3.75% in 2009/10, reaching 5% in 2010/11. For every litre of biofuel that excise duty is paid on, a Renewable Transport Fuel Certificate

(RTFC) will be issued. Companies supplying at least 450,000 litres of mineral fuel to the UK market annually must participate by either incorporating sufficient biofuel into their sales, buying RTFCs from another biofuel provider or pay a 15ppl 'buy-out' penalty (fine).

This 'buy-out' penalty, coupled with the 20ppl excise duty discount, gives (mineral) fuel companies a financial incentive to incorporate biofuel into their road-fuel sales of 35ppl over mineral based fuel (less the additional costs of biofuel production). After April 2010, the emphasis will move from duty exemption to buy-out price as the principal support mechanism. As a compelling incentive, the 'buy-out fund' generated, is redistributed equally to every RTFC issued by the year-end. This makes RTFC's worth more than 15p. It also means that the further away the UK is from hitting the annual target, the greater the incentive. As the incorporation percentage nears the target, biofuel incentives fall towards 35ppl. These subsidies are essential to make the industry viable, without them, there would be no biofuels.

RTFO and Excise Duty Incentives for Biofuels

Biofuel Year [1]	2007-2008	2008-2009	2009-2010	2010-2011
RTFO Obligation [2]	0.0%	2.5%	3.75%	5.0%
Buy-Out Penalty *ppl*	15.0	15.0	15.0	30.0
Duty Discount *ppl* [3]	20.0	20.0	20.0	0.0

[1] The biofuel accounting year is from 15th April to 14th April
[2] The RTFO inclusion obligation is by volume and percentage of fuel sales/use
[3] Fuel Excise Duty reduction from fossil fuel Excise Duty per litre

Supply

By 2010, UK road fuel use will be about 40 million tonnes (diesel exceeding petrol use by about 55:45) meaning 2m tonnes of biofuel will be required. The RTFO does not differentiate between biofuels so one may dominate the market. Splitting the market proportionately would require roughly 1.1 m tonnes of biodiesel and 0.9m of bioethanol. This would need 2.6 m tonnes OSR (or equivalent feedstock) covering 800 thousand hectares (at 3.25t/ha) and 3m tonnes of wheat (or equivalent feedstock) covering 380 thousand hectares (at 8.00t/ha). The UK could use its exportable surplus, for wheat, but cannot produce that much additional oilseed rape at today's yields.

Over 30 other countries have biofuel policies. Whilst nationally we can redirect an exportable surplus, this is not possible globally as there is no surplus grain production. More land must be converted into arable cropping or higher yields achieved from existing land to supply this new market.

Farmers options on whether to grow a crop to supply biofuel facility can, at this stage in most cases be made relatively simply by allowing the market to decide. As the crops used in biofuel production are, in the most part, mainstream crops that could also be sold to other consumers, the processor that bids the farmer the highest value deal ought to win the contract. Clearly headline price is important, but also other contractual details including the risk of rejection or cost of claims, and the value versus the limitations of claiming the Energy Aid Payment should be considered

ANAEROBIC DIGESTION

Anaerobic Digestion (AD) is the digestion of non-woody organic material in the absence of oxygen by micro-organisms to produce biogas (a mixture of 60% carbon dioxide CO_2 and 40% methane CH_4) and digestate (a useful soil conditioner). The biogas is collected and normally used in a combined heat and power (CHP) generator to produce heat and electricity for use or sale. The biogas can also be purified by removing the CO_2 and contaminant gasses (less than 1%) making bio-methane for use as road fuel or in place of natural gas. It is a natural process and is well understood by mankind having been harnessed for many years.

A very wide range of feedstock can be used. Livestock manure provides a cheap supply with high levels of micro-organisms but has a low biogas yield. Energy crops such as maize silage offer high yields and are commonly used in several AD business models. Non-farm waste streams from food processing companies offer a high return, with potential to earn revenue from gate fees and also high biogas yields too. Regulatory controls are greater when importing others' waste streams, especially if animal by products are likely to be included.

There are several types of AD plant, all better suited to different situations and feedstocks. The rate of turnover of digestate is controlled by the rate at which feedstock enters the digester less the small (usually 3-10%) fall in volume from the production into biogas. Depending on feedstock and system used, digestion can take as little as a week up to 2 months in some circumstances.

Example On-Farm Feedstocks for Anaerobic Digestion

Feedstock	Biogas Yield m³/t feedstock	Value of Biogas £/t feedstock*
Cattle/pig slurry	15 – 25	2.90 – 4.80
Poultry manure	30 – 100	5.80 – 19.26
Maize silage	200 – 220	38.50 – 42.40
Grass silage	160 – 200	30.80 – 38.50
Whole crop wheat	185	35.60
Maize grain	560	108
Rolled wheat grain	610	117.50
Crude glycerine	580 – 1,000	112 – 190
Rape meal	620	120
Fats	Up to 1,200	up to 230

* 5.2p/kWh electricity, 1p/kWh heat, £49.50/ROC, 1ROC/mWh electricity

Policy

When biogas is used to generate electricity, ROCs can be claimed as part of the Renewables Obligation (see previous section). Bio-methane for road transport is eligible for RTFCs (see Biofuels section above). The UK Government has accepted a proposal that electricity generated from AD should be eligible for 2 ROCs per mWh as opposed to 1 (see The Renewables Obligation 3 pages above). This has not yet been ratified by The European Commission (June 2008). AD can also benefit from the Climate Change Levy, and the Landfill Tax.

Economics

The two major costs associated with AD are usually the capital set up and feedstock (if home grown or purchased feed is used). Operating and maintenance costs such as insurance, labour and utilities are usually relatively low. An average size plant (2,500m³ digester and 350kW CHP generator) would cost in the region of £1-2 million. Depending on feedstock, temperature and other settings, this size plant could digest in the region of 20,000 tonnes of feedstock per year with a 45 day retention time (spent in the digester) or 30,000t with a 30 day retention period.

Revenue from this system using the assumptions from the table above, an average gas yield per tonne feedstock of 120m³/tonne and an efficiency of 85% would return income before costs of about £390,000 and potentially £560,000 if the double ROC policy is implemented.

WIND TURBINES

There are currently slightly over 2,000 wind turbines spread across 175 grid-connected wind farms throughout the UK. Small scale turbines can have capacities of as little as 100 watts (W) up to models of 800 kilowatts (kW). Wind farms are becoming larger; the average size a decade ago was 7mW and is expected to be as large as 50mW by 2010, albeit with considerable offshore wind farm growth.

Wind turbines in good locations can produce energy equivalent to their rated capacity for around 30% of the year, according to the Energy Saving Trust. For example: for a turbine rated at 4kW this calculates as 4kW x 30% x 8760 (hours in a year) = 10,512 kWh per year. If this electricity is sold at 10 pence per kWh (including ROC), then a return of £1,051 per year is possible.

Typical costs for a range of turbine capacities are in the region of the following table. Good quality constructions should have an operational life of 20 years.

Guideline Figures for Capital and Revenue of Wind Turbines

Capacity kW	Capital Cost	Monthly Output (kWh)	Revenue/yr at 10p/kWh e*
2.50	10,000	550	£660
5.0	20,000	1,300	£1,560
15	47,000	3,200	£3,850
75	95,000	16,000	£19,200
800	700,000	173,000	£208,000

* at 5p/kWh and 5p/kWh ROC, kWh e = kilo Watt hour of electricity

Planning permission is required and consultation with neighbours and stakeholders for all scale turbines. For farms planning to exceed 50mW, automatic referral to the Department for Trade and Industry will take place.

The land surrounding a wind turbine is usually un-affected, apart from access required up to the base of the tower. A minimum wind speed of 4 to 5 meters per second (m/s) is required; they operate at their rated capacity at 11-15m/s. Many turbines have automatic shut-down mechanisms when wind speeds exceed about 25m/s to avoid damage.

Many schemes are operated by developers with land rented to them by the land owner for 20 years. In this situation, a rent will be payable to the landowner, usually at about 2-4% of income. Access to the turbines must be possible, but land between the turbines can be farmed normally. Other benefits like road improvements may also be included. An option to develop a site could be worth £1,000 to £5,000 per year.

A large (800mW) wind turbine has a standard hub height of 76m, a height at the maximum blade position of 102m, and a blade diameter of 53m. The area of wind captured by this size blade is 0.88ha.

5. OTHER ENTERPRISES

MUSHROOMS

The mushroom industry has changed considerably during the past 5 years or so. A significant number of businesses of all sizes and in different parts of the country have ceased production and few if any new growers have entered the business. Less than 75 firms remain in production. Those that remain are either highly efficient enterprises with strong links to supermarkets or small low cost family-run businesses selling largely to wholesalers. The reasons for this are static consumption levels and competition from cheap imports. There are a few organic mushroom producers who sell at a premium.

Among the firms that remain there have also been changes in the method of production. Traditionally, the majority of UK growers employed Phase 1 compost, which they pasteurised and spawn-ran on the premises, to fill moveable trays or shelves in their growing rooms. Currently, the most prevalent system (perhaps 70% of all growers) uses purchased Phase 2 compost (pasteurised, with spawn added). This is supplied in shrink-wrapped blocks but it is also available in plastic bags as well as in bulk. Phase 3 compost (fully spawn-run) in blocks or bags is used by some growers. Organic Phase 2 and Phase 3 compost is also available.

Type of Compost Used	Phase 2	Phase 3
	per tonne compost	
Mushroom Yield/tonne compost	250 kg	300 kg
	£	£
Mushroom Price/kg	1.80	1.80
Spent Compost/tonne	2.00	2.00
Output	**452.0**	**542.0**
Variable Costs:		
Compost (incl. delivery)	95.0	135.0
Casing	15.0	15.0
Operations & growing labour at 6p/kg	15.0	18.0
Supervision & picking labour at 48p/kg	120.0	144.0
Packing materials at 21p/kg	52.5	63.0
Packing labour at 10p/kg	25.0	30.0
Energy costs at 10p/kg	25.0	30.0
Other costs at 15p/kg	37.5	45.0
Total Variable Costs	**385.0**	**480.0**
Margin / tonne compost	**67.0**	**62.0**
Variable Costs / kg mushrooms	1.54	1.60
Margin / kg mushrooms	0.27	0.21

N.B. All labour is included but labour for growing, if not picking and packing, could well be regular.

Output: Growers using Phase 2 compost will fill on an 8-week cycle and produce 6.5 crops per year. Phase 3 compost can be filled on a 6-week cycle and allows 8.5 crops per year. Yields are expressed as kg per square metre of bed or kg per tonne of compost. Commercial yields are 25-35kg/sq m of bed area per crop (250-350kg per tonne of compost) using Phase 2 or 3 compost, but only 18-20kg/sq metre (180-200kg/tonne of compost) using Phase 1. Phase 1 compost costs £25/tonne, Phase 2 £85/tonne and Phase 3 £125/tonne plus delivery which can add £6-15/tonne, depending on distance and size of load.

Labour costs: If Phase 2 or 3 compost is used, labour for growing amounts to around 10% of all labour costs while picking is 75% and packing 15%. Using Phase 1 compost labour cost for growing is significantly greater, perhaps 40p/kg or 40% of total labour, but the initial compost is cheaper.

Prices: Mushroom prices are in the range of £2.00/kg supplied to a supermarket to £1.00 or less sold on the wholesale market. Small growers marketing through a producer organisation would get around £1.60/kg delivered. At present 60% of the crop is sold by growers direct to supermarkets. Prices can be volatile and oversupply can lead to mushrooms being sold at a loss. Imports now account for 65% of all mushrooms sold in the UK, and 60% of the value of sales. Almost all imports are from the Netherlands and the Republic of Ireland.

Returns: The data suggest that ex-farm it costs £1.54 to produce 1kg of mushrooms using Phase 2 compost and £1.60 using Phase 3 compost. This does not take into account management or finance costs. The yield of the crop and the number of cycles each year are, of course, crucial.

Establishment Costs: A mushroom farm using Phase 2 compost on an 8-week cycle would require 8 rooms each with a 200sq m capacity. A farm using Phase 3 compost on a 6-week cycle would need 6 rooms of 200sq m capacity. In both cases one growing room would be filled each week using 20 tonnes of compost. To set up such a production system would require a capital investment of £200,000-£300,000 for the rooms, trays or shelves, heating and cooling systems, packing area, hard standings and equipment. If Phase 1 compost is used then buildings and equipment for composting, peak heating and spawning are also required.

Acknowledgement: Mushroom Growers Association, c/o Snowcap Mushrooms, Broadway, Yaxley, Peterborough, Cambs. PE7 3EF: www.mushroomgrowers.org.

TURF

The market for turf remains good at present, but the strength of the sector is closely linked with the health of the economy, and particularly the building industry. A slowdown in construction will have an adverse effect, and competition within the sector is strong, particularly among the producers of general contract grade turf. The market is now predominantly supplied with seed sown turf or cultivated lawn turf. Pasture turf is still available in certain areas, but overall its importance is small and declining. Suitable pasture for turf lifting is hard to find and it can now be cheaper to grow cultivated turf than treat and prepare existing pasture. Special seed mixtures and cultivation techniques produce a range of types of turfgrass that can be matched to particular sites and uses. In some cases special soil mixes are provided for the site as well as the turf. The Turfgrass Growers Association (TGA) has introduced quality standards and buyers are increasingly specifying the precise type of turf they require. It is estimated that there are around 16,000 ha (40,000 acres) of turfgrass grown in the UK. Although several turfgrass companies were originally set up by farmers, the business has moved away from mainstream farming. However, farms may be involved in the following ways:

1. Selling existing pasture turf to a turf company

This is the traditional option but it now represents very little of the turf market and its share will continue to decline. The opportunity will be open to very few farmers indeed. The approach may be by the farmer to the company or vice-versa. Minimum 5-6 year ley/pasture generally needed for spring or autumn lifting, 8-10 year grass is better for summer cutting.

Important features: good root structure, number and type of weeds, level, well-drained, stone-free land; good access; timing (farmer wants lifting completed in time to drill next crop).

Payment varies between £750-£1,500 per hectare (£300-£600 per acre), but mainly £900-£1,200 per ha (£360-£480 per acre). There is usually an initial payment plus further payments as turf is lifted. There may be a penalty clause if lifting delays prevent subsequent timely drilling. Lifting can take from two months to even a year. It can be done at any time of year except when there is snow on the ground. The turf company usually sprays against broadleaved weeds, fertilises and mows before lifting; the farmer may do these tasks, for payment. He may graze the land, for a rent, if lifting is delayed.

Apparently the effect on the land is not detrimental; some say there are benefits (removal of accumulated pests, etc. in the top half inch of grass, roots and topsoil).

Some local authorities require planning consent for turf stripping. In some instances it has been refused on the grounds that pasture turf is not an agricultural crop. Cultivated turf, however, is deemed to be an agricultural crop. On tenanted land landlord's permission is necessary to cut pasture turf.

2. *Farmer cutting, lifting and selling pasture turf himself*

Extremely uncommon. The turf must be treated, as in option 1. A small turf cutting machine can be hired for about £60 a day. This slices off the turf which must then be cut into lengths and picked up by hand. Two or three workers are required. It is slow going even in good conditions. The wastage figure is commonly 10-20% of the area, perhaps more. To hire a machine which cuts and picks up the turf may be possible but the charge will be considerably more.

Turf has a short life once cut and stacked - a maximum 1 to 2 days in summer, 3 to 4 days in winter, depending on temperature.

3. *Renting land to a turf company for production of cultivated turf*

Turf companies rent land for turfgrass production in addition to using their own land. As before, well-drained, stone-free land with good access is required. Typically the land is rented on a per crop basis and one or two crops grown. A turf crop usually takes 12 to 18 months from preparation to harvest but autumn sown crops may be harvested within 12 months. Rent levels depend on the quality of the land, the provision of irrigation and the profitability of competing agricultural enterprises. Currently rents are in the order of £650-£1,200 per hectare per crop (£265-£485 per acre) or £500-£750 per ha per year (£200-£300 per acre).

4. *Cultivated turf production*

On their own land turf producers can grow turf continuously, taking a crop every 18 months to two years on average. On rented land (as in option 3), they take one or two crops and move on. Usually they produce a quick growing type of turf which sells quickly on rented land and cultivate more specialist and slower growing turf on their own land. A high level of agronomic expertise and considerable investment in machinery are needed and labour requirements are heavy. As the business is very competitive a high degree of marketing expertise is essential. While the bulk of the trade goes into general landscaping or garden centres there is an increase in the number of contracts where the quality and type of turf is specified. It is estimated that a turf farm would need to be 150-200 hectares (400-500 acres) or more in size to be viable – in order to justify the machinery and equipment necessary and to produce a succession of turf for the market. There are significant economies of scale. The cost of specialist machinery for turf production can be £350,000. The new one-man harvesting machine costs in the order of £120,000-£200,000 but significantly reduces labour costs.

Costs and Returns

Variable Costs plus Rent:	£/ha	(£/ac)
Seed	750-1,100	(300-445)
Fertiliser	400-800	(160-325)
Herbicide	90-150	(35-60)
Fungicide	75-185	(30-75)
Rent (for 15 months)	650-1,200	(365-525)
Total Costs	1,965-3,435	(795-1,390)

It may be necessary to irrigate and on occasions use netting to grow the grass through for certain sites.

Labour

Special seed bed preparation (including subsoiling and stone burying), regular mowing (twice a week May/June), picking up clippings, harvesting (2 men on harvester plus one loading lorry) between 0.2-0.4 hectares per day (0.5-1.0 acre). The new one-man harvester can do 2 ha (5 acres) a day.

Total costs of the order of £4,942-£7,413 per ha (£12,000-£3,000 per acre), approximately 56-83p per sq.m. (47-69p per sq.yd.)

Value of Turf (on the field)

	per sq. m	per sq. yd.	per ha*	per acre*
Pasture turf	38-43p	32-36p	£3,420-£3,850	£1,380-£1,570
Hardwearing, domestic general contract	75-95p	65-80p	£6,840-£8,550	£2,755-£3,470
Football, hockey, prestige landscape	115-145p	95-120p	£10,260-£12,825	£4,150-£5,200
High quality/specialist**	190-475p	160-405p	£17,100-£42,750	£6,910-£17,290

* assuming 90% recovery, but some producers work on 85%.

** for some contracts the price may be higher.

Delivery charges 45-55p per sq.m.

Acknowledgements: Turfgrass Growers Association, 133 Eastgate, Louth, Lincolnshire, LN11 9QG. Telephone: 01507 607722. www.turfgrass.co.uk. *Robert Laycock,* Dial Cottage, North End, Seaton Ross, York, YO42 4LX. www.robertlaycock.co.uk.

GOLF

The boom in golf course construction that was seen in the early 1990s, when almost 70 a year were being built, is long over. Golf is still very popular in the UK but the supply of courses comfortably exceeds demand in most areas. According to Sport England, almost a million and a half people play golf each month, making it the seventh most popular sport and recreational activity in the country behind recreational walking, swimming, going to the gym, recreational cycling, football and running/jogging. This equates to 3.6% of the adult population of England playing golf at least once a month.

Despite having just under 900,000 club members, the dominance in the golf market of private members clubs has waned and a very large proportion of the market is occupied by proprietary golf clubs (built for profit by individuals or companies). Over the past 3-4 years the market has weakened, with over two thirds of the 940 companies monitored by one organisation seeing a fall in sales. This indicates that any market growth is being shared by a small number of proprietary companies, with private members club seeing a further downwards trend in number of members and rounds played.

Currently there are only a few courses under construction, but numerous courses are trying to upgrade old facilities to cope with the new competition. This includes many of private members courses who are having to protect their businesses by investing in courses and facilities to reduce membership attrition. It is virtually impossible to build a new facility for less than the cost of existing trading courses.

Range development has increased with nearly 400 ranges in the UK, but again many are having to diversify to attract business

The opportunity for farmers to be involved in golf course development is so low as to be negligible. There may be isolated opportunities however - there are a few hotels wishing to add golf to their facilities and needing to acquire farmland. But, restrictive planning policies on development in the countryside make gaining planning permission for all but urban fringe locations extremely difficult. In addition, recent rises in agricultural land values means that the viability of any golf project is threatened by land costs alone, even for hotel companies.

It is important that any new golf facility is near a substantial centre of population that can support the course. A rule of thumb measure is that a population of 25,000 within a 20-minute drive will support an 18-hole course. In some areas this has dropped to one course per 17,000 - resulting in a lack of long term future for many courses.

One ray of hope for farmers is the emerging trend for courses within urban areas to be developed for housing. This generates the need for extremely cash-rich golf clubs to relocate – usually to the urban fringe close to their old location. This is likely to continue as land in urban areas comes under greater pressure caused by Government policies to restrict built development to 'brownfield' sites.

Accidents on course continue and the number increase as the level of golfing skill in new players fails to improve. The space needed for facilities also increases as longer and longer courses are required.

Type of facility
- 18-hole 7000 yard plus course: 70-80 ha (170-195 acres) with Clubhouse and Pro Shop (600 sq. metres), parking, proper access and maintenance buildings. It takes between 1 and 2 years to construct.
- 9-hole course: 35-40 ha (84-95 acres).
- 9-hole Par 3 course: 7 ha (17 acres).
- 6-hole Par 3 or 4 course: 14 ha (34 acres).
- Driving range: 4 ha (10 acres).
- Pitch and putt course: 1.5 ha (4 acres).

Type of business organisation
- To sell land with planning permission. The cost of development of an average new course will be significantly more than the value of the facility when it is complete. Thus little or no premium over agricultural value can be expected unless the situation or planning consent offers something exceptional.
- To let land to a developer/operator. Assuming the latter pays for constructing the course, a long lease will be required. Rental levels will depend on the expected profitability of the facility.
- To form a joint company with a developer/operator. This obviously means the farmer shares in the success or failure. The land would be all or part of the farmer's equity. A well constructed agreement is essential.
- To develop and operate the course himself. The farmer would need good knowledge of golf and exceptional management ability besides access to substantial capital. In the present circumstances it is not to be recommended.

Construction methods and cost
- Specialist golf course constructor:
  18-hole course (60-75 ha): £2.5m-£3.5m according to drainage, earthmoving and irrigation, but excluding green keepers building and machinery.
  9-hole course (35-40 ha): £800,000-£1.2m.
  9-hole par 3 course (7 ha): £600,000-£900,000.
  6-hole par 3 or 4 course (14 ha): £500,000-£800,000.
  Driving range (4 ha): £250,000-£800,000, to include offices, storage, equipment, fencing and floodlighting.
  Full inventory of new machinery for 18-hole course: £460,000.
  Clubhouse (600 sq. metres): from £700,000 or £1.8m fitted out.

- Direct labour may reduce costs by around a third.

- Using own farm labour it is possible to reduce costs but it is very risky in terms of resultant course quality.

It is crucial to obtain professional advice at the outset for investment appraisal, feasibility study and a business plan. Changes to the national planning system places some obligation on Local Authorities to make allowance for the needs of all sports in their areas but in many emerging plans such information is often missing.

Large scale developments require Environmental Impact Assessments to be submitted with a planning application. These can cost anything from £80,000 to £150,000 on top of the golf designers and architects fees. The design and environmental fees are all at risk if planning approval is not gained.

Returns

Many existing businesses are seeing none or only marginal growth, whereas a successful well-run golf business has in the past achieved more than a 15% return on capital. These returns on new courses are now extremely rare. It would have to be a special circumstance to recommend the construction of a new stand-alone golf development in the UK today. Some situations exist, but it is very wise to proceed cautiously and be certain of the expected financial returns. Associated residential development could make developments profitable, but even this is now debateable in the current climate.

Acknowledgement: PGA Design Consulting Ltd., The Old Church, Neath Road, Bristol BS5 9AP. Telephone: 0117 952 7585. www.pgadc.com

BED AND BREAKFAST

It is estimated that around 2,000 farms across the UK offer B&B. Some are seasonal and informally run but many are open for much of the year, inspected under the auspices of the National Tourist Boards and/or the AA, and are members of a Regional Tourist Board and/or an organisation such as Farm Stay UK.

A bed and breakfast enterprise can be rewarding in both financial and social terms. However, the person running the business should enjoy meeting people, have good social skills and be prepared to work long hours. Other members of the family must be willing to share their home with visitors and to lose a certain amount of privacy. In a crowded market, and with rising customer expectations, the standard of the product is increasingly important. The aim must be to provide a standard of accommodation equal to that found in hotels. This is likely to involve some refurbishment of the farmhouse; either before starting the enterprise, to upgrade an existing B&B to modern standards, or just ongoing repair of wear and tear. Very little grant assistance is available to cover capital costs in setting-up a B&B. Any support is likely to be on a regional basis. The relevant Regional Development Agency (RDA) should be contacted as a first step. As with all new ventures, it is good practice, and essential if seeking additional finance, to create a well-thought-out business plan containing realistic projections.

Although they are not necessarily onerous for smaller operations, it is vital to know the planning, legislative and financial requirements involved in B&B provision. '*The Pink Booklet - a practical guide to legislation for accommodation providers*' produced by VisitBritain covers all the points which have to be addressed. In addition a great deal of help and advice is provided by National Tourist Boards (which in England is VisitBritain), the Regional Tourist Boards, and the Regional Development Agencies. A series of information pamphlets is available and one-day tourism training courses are run. In particular, The Daily Telegraph publish a paperback 'Starting and Running a Bed & Breakfast – a Practical Guide to Setting up and Managing a B&B Business' (.www.howtobooks.co.uk) whilst VisitBritain has produced two excellent booklets entitled 'How to Run Quality Self-catering Accommodation' and 'How to Run a Quality B&B'.

Marketing is very important. It can be done through a national organisation, in local Tourist Information Centres, in newspapers and magazines, and by word of mouth. Some establishments produce an attractive brochure or card giving details of the B&B, its location, facilities, and quality standards rating. Copies are left at tourist information centres etc and sent to prospective visitors. The internet is an important tool for the promotion of farmhouse B&Bs. Indeed, nowadays it's almost imperative to have a website and e-mail address, whilst many operators are also subscribing to online booking and availability systems.

As there is considerable competition it is useful if the enterprise can offer something special or different such as accommodation for visitors' horses, a welcome for pets or use of a tennis court or pool. Establishments that can accommodate bigger parties are gaining in popularity. The number of B&Bs offering an evening meal has tended to decline in recent years, but providing locally grown produce can also be a draw. If evening meals are not offered it helps to have good local restaurants and pubs that customers can be directed to.

To join a marketing organisation it is important for the B&B to have a Quality Assurance Standard rating. These are awarded either by the official National Tourist Board inspectorate (which in England is Quality in Tourism), or the AA. The rating is at one of five levels, expressed as stars. It is based on guest care and the quality of what is provided following an unannounced overnight inspection visit. The inspection fee depends on the number of bedrooms and the level of charges. The rated establishment gets a listing in the VisitBritain guides and on their internet site. In some areas membership of a Regional Tourist Board is an option; this confers additional benefits including a reduction in inspection fees, access to legal advice, and discounted rates for promotional activities and training courses.

Prices charged will reflect the quality of accommodation and location but cannot be far out of line with other local B&Bs and small hotels. Prices can also vary depending on length of stay and time of year. The price range for one person per night ranges from £20 to over £40. The average is around £30 on the basis of two adults sharing a room. A higher rate usually applies for single occupancy of a double room. There are regional differences with higher prices generally being charged in the south and east, and lower ones in the west and north.

The receipts from the enterprise can be calculated as follows: If the B&B is open for 40 weeks of the year at £30 per person per night, given a 60% occupancy rate the gross return per bed will be just over £5,000. Most farmhouse B&Bs have 4-6 bed spaces, which would generate a gross return of between £20,000 to £30,000 p.a.

As every farmhouse B&B is different and some costs are difficult to apportion between guests and family, it is hard to provide realistic average costings. The following provides some pointers. Variable costs are food, electricity and heating, laundry, cleaning materials and additional help. There will also be regular redecoration costs, repairs, and replacement and renewal of glassware, china, cutlery, towels and bed linen. Variable costs if no non-family labour is used might average about 20% of the nightly charge. If casual labour has to be included variable costs could amount to 30-35% of the nightly charge. Fixed costs will include insurance, business rates (if they apply), membership of a marketing organisation, regular advertising, repayments on any loans taken out for building and equipment to start the business and regular labour; they are likely to average 30-35% of charges.

Contact: Farm Stay UK, NAC, Stoneleigh Park, Warwickshire, CV8 2LG. Tel: 02476 696 909. www.farmstayuk.co.uk *VisitBritain* (formerly English Tourism Council), Thames Tower, Black's Road, Hammersmith, London W6 9EL. Tel: 020 8563 3000. www.visitbritain.com. *Quality in Tourism*, Farncombe House, Braodway, Worcs. WR12 7LJ. Tel: 0845 300 6996. www.qualityintourism.com.

CHRISTMAS TREES

About 8 million trees are sold a year in the UK: 7.9 million of them home-grown. Five years ago 80% were Norway Spruce, but this is now down to less than 25%, with Nordman Fir, which retains its needles longer, at 55% (95% in urban areas) and Fraser Fir, a US favourite, 12%. The most popular size has been increasing and is now 5 to 7 feet. Only 5% are sold rooted, although public interest in 'living trees' is now increasing.

Imported trees in the past have accounted for 20% of total sales, but imports for Christmas 2005 fell to a few hundred thousand, and this trend has continued, putting pressure on supplies and resulting in higher wholesale prices. Christmas trees are not eligible for the Single Payment, and as a result, many growers throughout the EU have grubbed-up trees, or are not replanting. The supply of trees in mainland Europe has therefore been substantially reduced. UK Christmas tree growers, unlike those in other countries, have never received subsidies and have not cut back production significantly. In addition changes in the Pound-Euro exchange rate has made imports relatively more expensive.

There are some 400 British growers across all parts of the country, with plantations ranging from less than one hectare to 1,000 ha. It is estimated that there are 60 million trees being grown, on some 25,000 ha. The average grower sells 6 to 7,000 a year from about 20 ha. The majority of sales are through the big garden centres, which require a uniform tree, netted and palletised, but there are successful 'choose and cut' operations and the enterprise works well on a farm with a farm shop. Producers need to sell 10 to 15,000 a year to justify buying machinery to assist in cultivation

The enterprise is slow to make a return. Norway Spruce is harvested in years 5 to 7, Nordman and Fraser Firs in years 7 to 9, making the enterprise vulnerable to changing market conditions. About 30% of the crop is harvested in the first harvesting year, 40% in the second, 30% in the third. All species need a well-drained site free from late frosts, with good access. As with any crop, the better the land, the better the crop.

Rabbit fencing (£2 per m) and possibly deer fencing (£5.50 per m) are pre-requisites. Spacing is possible from 60cm x 60cm to 1.8m x 1.8m, but 1.2m x 1.2m is recommended. This gives 5,500 plants per ha allowing for 80% land loss for headlands, access, etc. Losses of 5 to 10% in the first year means 300-500 replacements are needed in second year. Norway Spruce transplants 20p-50p each, Nordman Fir 30-60p. Planting, by hand or machine, 10-15p/per plant.

Variable Inputs: Fertiliser in a split top dressing of 350 kg/ha 12:11:18 + Mg and TE in late March and mid-September. Herbicides for weed control: residual herbicide, as cereals, in first year; subsequently an over-spray in October/November plus spot weeding until the canopy closes over. Weed control costs have been affected by rising herbicide costs and are likely to be 35p/per plant over the life of the tree. Pesticides: aphicide three times a year for Norway Spruce, once for Nordman Fir at £30 per ha per application. Acaricide from year 3 to harvest: £180 per ha per year for Norway Spruce, £100 for Nordman Fir.

Pruning and Shaping: This is essential to produce the shape of tree the market demands. Norway Spruce: shaping 15p per tree per year from year 3 or 4. Nordman Fir: basal pruning in year 3 or 4 at 15p-20p per tree plus shaping in the same year at 15p per tree and bud-rubbing every year except harvest at 5-10p per tree per year.

Harvesting: Done over 3 to 6 weeks, for dispatch Nov 20th to Dec. 12th. A full-time person is needed per 3,000 trees sold, or one person per week per 400-500 trees. Cost: Norway Spruce 60-80p per tree, Nordman Fir 70-90p; Norway Spruce may be dipped or sprayed to reduce needle drop. Marketing costs around 10% of output.

Machinery: Inter-row plantation tractors £15,000-£65,000; stump clearing machines £7,000-£25,000; palletiser £13,000-£14,000; mist blowers £8,000-£10,000; hydraulic netting funnel £8,000-£10,000; manual netting funnel £175.

Labour: Planting and pruning can be done in January/February and tagging for height and quality in October/November. Thus it fits in well with combinable cropping.

Whilst the gross margins given are high, these will only be achieved by a high level of expertise and commitment and the long period before any return is obtained must also be stressed, together with the risk this entails.

	Nordman Fir		Norway Spruce	
	£/ha	(£/ac)	£/ha	(£/ac)
4000 5 to 7 foot trees per ha @ price of ..	£3.50 - 4.00 / ft		£1.70 / ft	
Output (average)	90,000	(36,423)	40,800	(16,512)
Variable Costs:*				
Plants	2,655	(1,074)	2,065	(836)
Planting	740	(299)	740	(299)
Fertiliser	1,310	(530)	980	(397)
Weed control	1,650	(668)	1,650	(668)
Pesticides	740	(299)	1,080	(437)
Pruning and shaping	4,540	(1,837)	2,480	(1,004)
Harvesting	4,400	(1,781)	3,850	(1,558)
Marketing	9,000	(3,642)	4,080	(1,651)
Total Variable Costs	25,035	(10,132)	16,925	(6,849)
Gross Margin (whole period)	64,965	(26,291)	23,875	(9,662)
Gross Margin per year over 8 & 6 years	8,121	(3,286)	3,979	(1,610)

*   Labour assumed to be casuals.

Acknowledgements: British Christmas Tree Growers Association, 13 Wolrige Road, Edinburgh, EH16 6HX. Tel: 0131 664 1100 www.bctga.co.uk.

FORESTRY

(Estimated for 2009)

A. ESTABLISHMENT COSTS (BEFORE GRANT)

1. *Unit Cost of Operations*

Year/s	Operation		Estimated Cost (£)
1.	Trees for planting		
	(i) Bare rooted:		
		Conifers	150-250 per 1,000
		Broadleaves	250-350 per 1,000
	(ii) Rooted in small peat blocks:		
		Conifers	150-250 per 1,000
		Broadleaves	300-360 per 1,000
1.	Tree Protection		
	(i) Fencing (materials and erection)		
		Rabbit	3·50-5.00 per metre
		Stock	3·00-3·75 per metre
		Deer	5·00-7·00 per metre
		Deer and Rabbit	7·00-9·00 per metre
		Split post and rail	6·00-7·00 per metre
	(ii) Tree guards/shelters		
		Spiral and canes (450mm)	35-50 per 100
		Plastic tubes (1,200mm)	70-85 per 100
		Stakes	45-70 per 100
1.	Spot spraying		100-120 per 1,000 trees
1.	Hand planting at approximately 2m spacing		
		Conifers	160-190 per ha
		Broadleaves*	450-650 per ha
	Machine planting (loams and sand)		140-160 per ha
2-3.	Replacing dead trees**		
		Operation	60-120 per ha
		Plant supply	40-50 per ha
1-4.	Weeding per operation		
		Herbicide***	80-120 per ha weeded
2.	Inter-row mowing		100-250 per ha

Costs specific to location			Upland	Lowland
1.	Ground Preparation:	ploughing	100-150 per ha	50- 80 per ha
		mounding	250-350 per ha	250-350 per ha
1.	Drainage		80- 100 per ha	—
1.	Fertilising		100-250 per ha	—

*   Includes cost of erecting guards/shelters.

** Replacing dead trees (beating up) may be necessary, once in the second year and again in the third year. Costs depend on number of trees.

*** Up to 2 weeding operations may be necessary in each of the first 4 years in extreme situations. Costs are inclusive of materials.

Access roads may need to be constructed and can typically cost between £6,000 and £22,000 per kilometre (£9,600 to £35,000 per mile) depending on availability of road stone and the number of culverts and bridges required.

2. *Total Establishment Costs up to Year 3.*

(i) Conifer—Lowland Sites

On a fairly typical lowland site, requiring little or no clearing or draining, the approximate cost before grant of establishing a conifer plantation would be in the range £1,200-£1,800 per hectare. Up to 8 separate weeding operations may be required.

(ii) Conifer—Upland Sites

Establishing a similar conifer plantation on an upland site could cost £1,100 to £1,600 per hectare. Normally some form of site preparation and drainage is required but only one weeding operation may be necessary. Overall costs tend to be £100-£200 per ha less than on lowland sites.

(iii) Hardwoods

Costs of establishing hardwood plantations are highly dependent on the fencing and/or tree protection required. If tubes are needed the overall costs will be influenced by the number of plants per hectare. Costs could be in the range £1,600-£2,500 per ha. Site conditions normally mean that hardwoods being grown for timber production are restricted to lowland sites.

(iv) Farm Woodlands

Establishment costs for farm woodlands may be lower than those indicated for hardwoods in (iii) above if lower planting densities are used. Initial establishment costs in the first year of the order of £1,800 per ha for woods under 3 ha and £1,600 per ha for woods of 3 to 10 ha would be typical.

(v) Size Factor

Savings in fencing and other economies of scale may reduce average costs per ha by 10 to 20% where large plantations are being established; conversely costs for small woods may easily be 25% higher per ha established.

(vi) Method of Establishment

A range of organisations and individuals undertake forestry contracting work and competitive tendering can help to control costs.

3. *Re-Stocking Costs*

Once trees on a site have been felled the Forestry Commission usually requires the site to be restocked as one of the conditions of awarding a felling licence. Re-stocking can either be done by planting or through natural regeneration by leaving a proportion of the existing trees standing and using seed from these trees to re-stock the site. Only minimum site preparation is usually required if using natural regeneration. There is no longer any grant for simply restocking woodland, although grant is available for 'regeneration' where the species mix is being altered. (see Grant section).

The costs of establishment given above, and those for maintenance given below in section B, are estimates for England. Costs in Scotland tend to be somewhat lower.

B. MAINTENANCE COSTS

Once trees have been established they will normally require some maintenance and management work each year. For trees being grown primarily for timber production on a large scale, operations required may include ride maintenance, fence maintenance, pest control, fire protection, management fee and insurance premiums. Costs will normally fall within the range £10-£50 per ha per annum depending upon the size of the plantation and the complexity of management. In upland areas one or more fertilising operations are occasionally applied in the first 20 years in the life of a tree depending on the quality of the site. Estimated cost £100-£250 per ha, depending on elements applied. For trees being grown for sporting and amenity purposes, annual maintenance costs are likely to be less and may range up to about £10 per ha.

A brashing operation which involves removing branches up to two metres may be required for access reasons as the crop matures. Opening up inspection racks over 5-10% of the crop may cost £35-£65 per ha. Brashing 40-50% of the crop could cost £150-£350 per ha.

C. PRODUCTION

Production is usually measured in terms of cubic metres (m³) of marketable timber per hectare and will vary according to the quality of the site, species planted and thinning policy. Sites in lowland Britain planted to conifers typically produce an average of 12 to 18 m³ of timber per ha per year over the rotation as a whole and would accordingly be assessed as falling in yield classes 12 to 18. Under traditional management systems, thinning begins 18 to 25 years after planting and is repeated at intervals of approximately 5 years until the wood is clear-felled at between 40 and 60 years. Approximately 40-45% of total production will be from thinnings. Broadleaves typically produce an average of between 4 and 8 m³ of timber per hectare per year and fall in yield classes 4 to 8. A felling licence must be obtained from the Forestry Commission before any felling takes place, unless a Forest Plan has already been approved by them. Grants are available for preparing a Forest Plan which covers a 10 year period (see Grants section).

Prior to a thinning sale the trees normally have to be marked and measured at an estimated cost of 35 - 40p per m³, which is equivalent to £100-£150 per hectare depending on species, crop density and age. For a clear-felling sale the cost can range from £250 to £350 per ha, or about £1 per m³ where a full tariff applies, i.e. where each tree is counted and sample measurements of individual trees are taken.

D. PRICES

Prices for standing timber are extremely variable, depending on species, tree size and quality, ease of extraction from site, geographical location (nearness to end user), quantity being sold, world market prices and effectiveness of marketing method used. The use of wood for energy generation is beginning to open up a new market for poorer quality hardwood and conifer logs and forest residues.

Conifers

Average prices paid for standing coniferous timber sold from Forest Enterprise areas in the year to 31ˢᵗ March 2007, were:

Harvesting stage	Average tree size (m³)	Price (£ per m³)		
		England	Wales	Scotland
1st Thinning	Up to 0.074	2.32	1.52	3.87
	0.075-0.124	9.00	3.36	3.33
Subsequent	0.125-0.174	9.40	5.57	3.41
Thinnings	0.175-0.224	10.56	5.23	4.09
	0.225-0.274	9.83	2.92	7.75
	0.275-0.424	10.09	5.60	6.70
	0.425-0.499	12.85	5.67	10.56
Clearfelling	0.500-0.599	9.99	6.59	5.03
	0.600-0.699	11.08	5.20	5.68
	0.700-0.799	15.58	7.35	6.59
	0.800-0.899	17.63	4.08	13.74
	0.900-0.999	13.30	2.42	7.62
	1.000 and over	20.33	15.75	10.89

Source: Forest Enterprise, July 2007

Hardwoods

The hardwood trade is very complex. Merchants normally assess and value all but the smallest trees on a stem by stem basis. Actual prices fetched can show considerable variation depending on species, size, form, quality and marketing expertise of the seller. Felling usually takes place in the winter months.

Some indicative prices for hardwoods are given below, but it is important to note that actual prices fetched can vary quite widely. Wood quality is particularly important in determining prices.

Harvesting stage	Tree size range (m^3)	Price range £ per m^3	Possible use
First thinnings	<0.13	0-12	Firewood, board products and pulp wood. Poles for refineries and turnery.
Subsequent Thinnings	0.13-0.3	5-20	Smaller sizes and lower quality
	0.3-0.6	8-22	material may go for fencing or
	0.6 -1.0	10-40	for use in the mining industry.
Clearfellings	1.0-2.0	15-80	Trees over 30 cm in diameter and of better quality may go for planking, furniture or joinery. High quality material may go for veneers and can fetch between £150 and £300 per m^3 depending on species and specifications.
	2+	25-150	

Prices for Oak, Ash, Sycamore, Cherry and Elm tend to be significantly higher than for Beech, which seldom exceeds about £45 per m^3 standing even for stands containing significant volumes of first quality planking.

E. TIMBER MARKETING

In-house marketing by the owner or agent can be cost effective but only if they have detailed, up-to-date knowledge of timber buyers in the market place. The alternative is marketing through a forestry manager or management company, but this can be expensive and is not guaranteed to test the open market fully.

Nationwide electronic sales of timber by auction and tender are now available for all types and quantities of timber. This cost effective, no-sale-no-fee (1·5 to 2·3% sales commission) method offers full exposure to the trade and should realise the correct market value. (Beacon Forestry: www.beaconforestry.co.uk). For small, unusual or low value timber parcels free advertising is available on the Ecolots website and in a free magazine (www.ecolots.co.uk or tel: 01721 724 788).

F. MARKET VALUE OF ESTABLISHED PLANTATIONS AND WOODS

The value of woods depends on many factors, such as location, access, species, age and soil type. The table on the following page gives an indication of the range of current (2008) market values of commercial woodlands of different ages, based on recent market sales.

From years 20 to 25 onwards prices of commercial woods will also be increasingly influenced by the quantity of merchantable timber they contain. Depending on the time of clear-felling, the timber may be worth between £900 to £6,000 per hectare (£360 to £2,500 per acre).

Woods that are relatively small with high amenity or Ancient Woodland status can often command a premium over prices fetched for commercial woodlands as can those that are freehold and include minerals and sporting rights. This is particularly the case in southern England. Conversely conservation designation can restrict value by preventing economic forest management.

The value of woods containing mature hardwoods will depend on the quality and value of the timber they contain and the quality of access.

Market Value of Commercial Sitka Spruce Woodlands

Age of Commercial Woods and Plantations	Price Range for crop and land	
	£/ha	£/acre
0-5 years	400- 625	(160-600)
6-10 years	1,000-2,500	(400-1,000)
11-15 years	1,500-2,750	(600-1,100)
16-20 years	2,000-3,000	(800-1,200)
21-25 years	2,500-3,500	(1,000 - 1,400)

G. GRANTS

With devolution, each part of the United Kingdom has introduced new schemes that replace the previous Woodland Grant Scheme (WGS) and the Farm Woodland Premium Scheme (FWPS). In England, the English Woodland Grant Scheme (EWGS) opened in July 2005 (with some elements becoming available later that year). The Scottish Forestry Grant Scheme (SFGS) was introduced in June 2002. In Wales, the Better Woodlands for Wales (BWW) programme began in April 2006, with planting grants subsequently being brought under the BWW umbrella.

English Woodland Grant Scheme

Initially this scheme will operate in a similar manner across the whole of England. However, it is envisaged that in time variations in levels of support will be introduced on a regional basis to meet the needs of each region.

Applicants to the EWGS need an approved agent to apply for a grant for them, have an IACS number for their wood, and have their application submitted electronically. The EWGS comprises six components and applications can be made for combinations of these components where appropriate.

1. *Woodland Management Planning Grant:* available as a contribution towards the cost of producing plans for existing woodlands, and which meet the UK Woodland Assurance Standard. Rates of grant contribution are £10 per hectare for the first 100 hectares and £5 thereafter. There is a minimum payment of £300 for plans covering more than 3 hectares but less than 30 hectares.

2. *Woodland Assessment Grant:* available as a contribution towards the costs of obtaining additional information about the woodland in relation to ecology, landscape, historic and heritage assessments, and to determine stakeholder interests. A fixed hourly rate of £35 is payable plus a contribution at 80% of a set range of standard assessment costs.

3. *Woodland Management Grant:* aid for providing public benefits and to undertake sustainable woodland management. Potentially eligible activities include public access, maintaining boundaries, protecting archaeological features, management of old wood habitat and open space, soil and ground water protection, controlling non-native species, pest control, woodland health and monitoring sustainability. The rate of grant is in line with ELS payments at £30 per hectare per year.

4. *Woodland Regeneration Grant:* a contribution towards the cost of regenerating woodland after felling. The aim is to promote the replacement of felled woodland whilst changing woodland types for increased public benefit. Grant rates depend on the type of wood being felled and the type of wood which replaces it:

Type of woodland felled	Type of woodland being regenerated	Grant (£/ha)
Conifer plantation	Native species	1,100
	Broadleaved species	950
	Conifer species	360
Broadleaved plantation	Native species	1,100
	Broadleaved species	950
Conifer plantation on Ancient Woodland Site	Native species	1,760
	Broadleaved species	950
	Conifer species	0
Broadleaved plantation on Ancient Woodland Site	Native species	1,760
	Broadleaved species	950
Ancient and other semi-natural woodland	Native species	1,100

5. *Woodland Improvement Grant:* a contribution towards the cost of work to improve the quality of woodland for social, environmental, and economic benefits. Initially the rate of grant is set at 50% of agreed costs in a five-year plan. The focus is on improving access, biodiversity, and protecting SSSIs. In the course of time regions may choose to vary the rate of contributions or priority areas to reflect regional differences. There will be a maximum grant contribution of £100,000.

6. *Woodland Creation Grants:* aids the establishment of new woodlands. This element of the EWGS is competitive and will be assessed on a points-scoring system with the applications that giving the greatest benefits being selected. Woodland creation may be by natural regeneration or by direct seeding. The rates of grant will depend on the type of woodland; Standard (3 ha or more), Small Standard (less than 3 ha), Native Species Only, Community (designed for public access), or Special Broadleaved (species appropriate for growth at wide spacing). Planting density requirements, percentage open space and percentage of shrub element are set for for each woodland type. Rates of grant are as follows:

Woodland category	Broadleaves £/ha	Conifers £/ha
Standard, Native and Community	1,800	1,200
Special Broadleaved	700	n/a

In addition to the above grant an extra £500 per ha is paid for woodland established within five miles of 100,000 people or within the National Forest Area, or where there is an agreement to provide for public access and there is an identified need. Woodland meeting both of these requirements will be eligible to claim £1000 per ha.

Payment is made 80% on the completion of the work, with the final 20% payable after 5 years as long as the plantation is maintained. Applications usually have to be made in the summer prior to the winter/spring when the planting will take place.

Planting on Agricultural Land: Annual payments are available under the EWGS for converting agricultural land to woodland (similar to the old FWPS). Payments will continue for 15 years when new woodlands comprise more than 50% broadleaved species, and 10 years when the percentage broadleaves is less than 50% (or fast growing broadleaved species such as poplar). Payment rates will depend on the agricultural land use category being converted to woodland. Current rates are set out below, although they may be subject to revision in future years;

Agricultural Land Category	Annual payment (£/ha)		
	Non-Less Favoured Area (LFA)	LFA: Disadvantaged Areas	LFA: Severely Disadvantaged
Arable Land*	300	230	160
Improved Grassland.................	260	200	140
Other Cropped Land	260	200	140
Unimproved Land....................	ineligible	60	60

* defined as land that used to be eligible for AAPS under the old IACS system

More details of the EWGS are available on the Forestry Commission website (www.forestry.gov.uk). There are deadlines for the submission of application forms for the different components of the scheme as funding is limited. Early discussion with one of Forestry Commission England Conservancy offices is advised. Help and advice can also be obtained from the EWGS helpline Tel: 01223 346004.

H. WOODLAND AND THE SINGLE PAYMENT

In general, land being used to grow trees is not eligible to activate Single Payment entitlements. However, farm woodland planted on arable land under the English Woodland Grant Scheme (EWGS) and the previous Woodland Grant Scheme / Farm Woodland Premium Scheme (FWPS) can be counted towards a farmer's set-aside obligation under the Single Payment Scheme. Farmers receive the annual payments under the FWPS / Woodland Creation Grant payments, not set-aside payments. Short-rotation coppice is not eligible for entry into woodland grant schemes but where it is planted on set-aside land, such land will remain eligible for the Single Payment.

I. TAXATION

Income from commercial woodlands is no longer subject to income tax, and tax relief cannot be claimed for the cost of establishing new woodlands.

In general EWGS grants are tax free but annual payments under the Farm Woodland Premium Scheme (and now Woodland Creation Grants) are regarded as compensation for agricultural income forgone and are liable to income tax.

The sale of timber does not attract Capital Gains Tax, although the disposal of the underlying land may give rise to an assessment.

Woodlands which are managed commercially or which are ancillary to a farming business may be eligible for either Business Property Relief or Agricultural Relief for Inheritance Tax purposes.

Acknowledgement: The above estimates are based in part on information supplied by John Clegg Consulting Ltd.

A magazine, 'Forestry and British Timber', is published monthly (Miller Freeman, Telephone 01732-377651).

A NOTE ON DIVERSIFICATION

Well calculated diversification should be encouraged. Non-agricultural enterprises managed in conjunction with the farming operation can offer several benefits to the business. These include:

- Spreading risks of returns; if the economics of agricultural production declines, revenue from non-commodity based enterprises may boost business income.

- Resource efficiency; most farm systems have quieter and busier periods for staff and management which may be switched into other roles for examples.

- Increasing profit.

Any new enterprise will have its own risks associated with it. These must be clearly and objectively calculated (this will be a requirement of borrowed money is necessary). Each resource employed will have its own opportunity cost (what could it be earning if it was not being used for this new venture?). Cash (return on capital) is the obvious one, what could it earn in a high interest account? Labour is less straight forward. For example, a B&B might require minimal new capital under some circumstances, but tie somebody to the house at key times of the day, restricting other employment opportunities.

Before any major investment or change in business structure to incorporate new diversifications, business plans and market research to assess the likely income potential are critical. Most new enterprises require new skills (such as different production systems, new marketing techniques and sales techniques). These take time and dedication to acquire. Developing new ideas and expanding a novel business venture can be exciting and time consuming; maintaining sufficient management time on the existing farm business is a common problem.

Nevertheless, many ventures exist where entrepreneurial skills have achieved notable success. Conversion of surplus farm buildings, for offices, workshops, retail and storage, has been the primary farm diversification activity up to date. A 2006 DEFRA survey found that 46% of farms had diversification activity generating an average income of £10,900 pa. But if letting farm buildings is stripped out, the percentage of diversified farms falls to 19%. It also shows that arable farms tend to be more diversified than livestock and farms in the South East are more diversified than elsewhere in the UK.

Some 'diversification' enterprises have been included above. There are many others, which include;

Novel Crops	Sporting	Tourism
• Alpacas	• Fisheries	• Caravans / Camping
• Herbs	• Game Shooting	• Holiday Cottages
• Carp and Crayfish	• Stalking	• B & B
• Llamas	• Clay Pigeon Shooting	Barn Conversions
• Quails	Horses	• Business Lets
• Snails	• Riding School	• Dwelling Let
	• Trekking	Vertical integration
	Adventure Games	• Yoghurt, ice cream, etc.
	• Motor Sports	• Farm Shop

6. ORGANIC FARMING

The Organic Sector:

As at January 2008, 3.9% of UK agricultural land (excluding common grazing) was in organic production on 5,506 holdings. The percentage in England is 3.9%. In January 2008 the area (in hectares) devoted to organic production was as follows:

	Fully Organic	In conversion	Total	% of Agric. Area	of UK Organic Area	% of UK Organic Producers
England	258,744	89,037	347,781	3.7	51.0	68
Wales	65,127	30,908	96,035	6.4	14.1	16
Scotland	193,133	34,759	227,892	4.1	33.4	12
N. Ireland	7,229	3,188	10,488	1.0	1.5	4
2008	*524,303*	*157,893*	*682,196*	*3.9*	*100*	*100*
2007	*498,646*	*121,137*	*619,783*	*3.6*		
2006	*533,902*	*85,951*	*619,853*	*3.6*		

The amount has risen significantly in recent years for a number of reasons: poor prices for conventionally produced crops and livestock, good premium price levels, and increasing demand - owing largely to health concerns. There is also grant aid to help producers during the required conversion period (see next page). The market potential is shown by the fact that around 34% of primary organic produce sold through UK multiple retailers is currently imported (down from 54% in 2003). Demand has risen considerably in recent years. UK retail sales are £1.4 billion. This is approximately 2.3% of total food sales. The Government's aim is to increase the UK share of the total domestic market to at least 70%. However, some organic farmers have reverted to conventional production primarily because of declining premiums (see next page). Imports of organic fruit and vegetables, often of lower standards, are especially high.

Many hill and upland livestock farms have converted to organic production – with inputs already low, management changes need only be small. Similar factors have meant that a sizeable number of lowland beef and sheep producers have also embraced organic production. There is also a strong organic dairy sector although the ongoing 'credit crunch' and associated likely recession is swaying consumers away from organic consumption and 'transitional' farmers are therefore returning to conventional production methods. The cropping sector appears to have lagged behind other parts of the industry – causing difficulty in sourcing organic feed in many cases. Approximately 18.5% of organic land in England is in crops, just over 12% in the UK as a whole.

Below is the land use estimates of producers of organic and in conversion crop areas and livestock numbers recorded in January for the applicable years:

Organic Land Use according to Crop Type '000 ha	2005	2006	2007	2008	year on year % change
Cereals	39.3	47.7	47.5	51.5	*8.6*
Other crops	12.9	10.8	10.2	11.3	*10.8*
Fruit & Nut	1.7	1.7	1.8	2.0	*11.1*
Vegetables (inc. Potatoes)	14.1	13.7	15.5	16.9	*9.0*
Herbs & Ornamentals	0.3	0.8	0.7	0.6	*-14.3*
Temporary pasture	90.7	97.9	102.7	125.1	*21.8*
Permanent pasture	495.0	428.3	422.6	452.0	*7.0*
Woodland	5.8	6.7	8.2	11.5	*40.2*
Other	14.7	12.1	10.6	11.2	*5.7*
Total area ha	***674.5***	***619.7***	***619.8***	***682.1***	***10.1***

Organic Livestock Numbers '000 head	2005	2006	2007	2008	year on year % change
Cattle	174.8	214.3	244.8	250.4	2.3
Sheep	571.6	691.0	747.3	863.1	15.5
Pigs	43.7	30.0	32.9	50.4	53.2
Poultry	2,431.6	3,439.5	4,421.3	4,440.7	0.4
Goats	0.5	0.5	0.6	0.5	-16.7
Other Livestock	1.2	1.5	4.3	3.4	-20.9
Total head	**3,223.4**	**4,376.8**	**5,451.2**	**5,608.5**	

The economics to the farmer depend primarily upon the:

- relative yield compared with conventional farming;
- price premium compared with conventional farming.

In the case of cereals both research and experience suggests that yields of organic crops are typically between 60% and two-thirds of those of conventionally produced crops, but the much higher prices obtained have easily compensated for this to date, with feed wheat prices around £250 ex-farm and feed beans £280 per tonne ex-far , in addition to the obvious saving in fertiliser and spray costs. Hence the gross margin is normally much higher. However, there are also the wider whole farm effects to be considered, e.g., unless the farm already has a substantial percentage of its area down to leys this will probably have to be increased in order to maintain yields and this extra grass has to be utilised profitably – which is far from easy, and the extra capital requirements could be heavy.

Furthermore, there is a two year 'conversion period' to undergo before full price premiums can be claimed; (though note the aid scheme, below). Also, in the case of vegetable crops, quality (in the sense of appearance) can be badly affected by pests and diseases.

As regards relative cultivation costs, in one ADAS monitored study, these were reported to be 15% higher on the organically grown wheat (approximately £20 more per ha (£8 per acre) at present costs). However no spraying is required. Survey data have indicated overall labour requirements to be 10-30% higher than on conventional farms, with machinery costs generally similar.

In the case of livestock, premiums have been highly attractive. In some sectors, such as milk, this led to many producers converting to organic, creating an excess of supply over demand. This then collapsed the organic premium. A steady increase in demand has since re-balanced the milk market and average prices have returned to around 31p/litre. Organic milk price has risen more slowly than conventional milk price in most areas. It is a demonstration of the need to consider markets fully in a 'niche' sector like organic. Organic production of grazing livestock is generally speaking of greater value to the larger farm, especially on land that favours grass rather than cash crops, where the reduction in stocking rate caused by the lack of nitrogen fertilizer is less important. Concentrate feed costs per tonne are much higher.

Aid for Organic Farmers:

In England, support for organic farmers is through the Organic Entry Level Stewardship (OELS) (see Section III). In summary, this provides relatively high levels of support per hectare for the two-year conversion period. Rates then drop to a 'stewardship' level thereafter. Similar schemes, but with different categories and payment rates, are available in Wales and in Scotland.

Further Information:

No gross margin data for organic enterprises are included in this section because a specialist publication is available on the subject: the '2009 Organic Farm Management

Handbook', (8th Ed - Sept 2008) by Nic Lampkin, Mark Measures and Susanne Padel, University of Wales, Aberystwyth. Tel: 01970 622 248.

Additional information may be available from the following organisations:

DEFRA (Organic Food and Industrial Crops Division)
Nobel House, 17 Smith Square, London, SW1P 3JR. 0207 238 5605

Organic Farmers and Growers Limited
The Elim Centre, Lancaster Road, Shrewsbury, Shropshire, SY1 3LE. 01743 440 512

Soil Association
Bristol House, 40-56 Victoria Street, Bristol, BS1 6BY. 0117 929 0661

Elm Farm Research Centre
Hamstead Marshall, Newbury, Berkshire, RG20 0HR. 01488 658 298

Biodynamic Agricultural Association
The Secretary, Painswick Inn, Stroud, Glos. GL5 1QG. 01453 759 501

Organic Food Federation
1 Turbine Way, EcoTech Business Park, Swaffham, Norfolk, PE37 7XD. 01760 720 444

Organic Centre Wales
University of Wales, Aberystwyth, Ceredigion, SY23 3AL. 01970 622 248

Tesco Centre for Organic Agriculture
Nafferton Farm, Stocksfield, Northumberland, NE47 7XD. 01661 830 222

Scottish Agricultural College
Organic Farming Unit, Craibstone Estate, Bucksburn, Aberdeen,
AB21 9YA 01224 711 293

7. SUMMARY OF GROSS MARGINS

This page summarises the key figures of the gross margins over the previous pages. There are well in excess of 100 gross margins in the Pocketbook and additional data for other enterprises too. They cannot be directly compared on a like for like basis, as different resources are required in order to produce each one. Some, for example require higher quality land than others and some will require more overheads in terms of machinery, labour or buildings than others. Management requirement varies from one enterprise to another.

Summary of Arable Crop Gross Margins

Crop (£/Ha)	Price	Yield	Output	Variable Costs	Gross Margin
Winter Feed Wheat	£135	8.25	£1,114	£511	£602
Winter Milling Wheat	£147	7.55	£1,110	£551	£559
Spring Milling Wheat	£145	5.75	£835	£408	£427
Winter Feed Barley	£130	6.60	£858	£437	£421
Winter Malting Barley	£145	5.75	£834	£370	£463
Spring Malting Barley	£150	5.25	£788	£314	£474
Winter Oats	£125	6.50	£813	£341	£472
Spring Oats	£125	5.50	£688	£299	£388
Winter Rape	£300	3.25	£975	£465	£510
Spring Rape	£300	2.00	£600	£265	£335
Linseed	£400	1.75	£700	£285	£415
Winter Beans	£165	4.00	£695	£255	£440
Spring Beans	£175	3.70	£683	£236	£447
Blue Peas	£191	3.75	£751	£299	£453
Marofats	£215	3.40	£766	£318	£448
Lupins	£175	3.00	£560	£317	£243
Rye	£155	6.00	£930	£475	£455
Triticale	£130	5.00	£650	£373	£277
Naked Oats	£180	5.50	£990	£375	£615
Durum Wheat	£180	6.20	£1,116	£474	£642
Borage	£2,500	0.40	£1,000	£312	£688
Crambe	£160	2.50	£400	£337	£63
Hemp	£135	7.00	£945	£509	£436
Grain Maize	£150	7.00	£1,050	£435	£615
Millet	£250	3.50	£875	£330	£545
Sunflower	£350	2.00	£700	£305	£395
Vining Peas	£274	4.75	£1,300	£383	£917
Maincrop Potatoes	£121	45.00	£5,445	£3,010	£2,435
Early Potatoes	£175	22.00	£3,850	£2,321	£1,529
Sugarbeet	£29.50	62.00	£1,829	£867	£962

Summary of Livestock Gross Margins

Livestock		Output	Variable Costs	Gross Margin /Head	Gross margin £/Ha
Dairy					
Friesian Holsteins	per Cow	£1,590	£767	£823	£1,645
Channel Island	per Cow	£1,394	£700	£694	£1,665
Ayreshire	per Cow	£1,446	£658	£788	£1,890
Friesian Followers	per Head	£1,150	£474	£676	£933
Channel Followers	per Head	£695	£416	£279	£485
Ayreshire Followers	per Head	£595	£402	£193	£336
Beef Cattle					
Bucket Reared Calf 3 month	per Calf	£124	£90	£34	
Bucket Reared Calf 6 month	per Calf	£214	£172	£41	
Lowland Sucklers					
Spring Calving	per Cow	£297	£253	£44	£79
Autumn Calving	per Cow	£358	£317	£41	£67
Upland Sucklers					
Spring Calving	per Cow	£278	£238	£40	£65
Autumn Calving	per Cow	£360	£302	£58	£73
Summer Store Finishers	per Head	£148	£96	£52	£208
Winter Store Finishers	per Head	£176	£157	£19	£187
Continental Cereal beef	per Head	£599	£540	£58	
Holstein Cereal Beef	per Head	£632	£540	£92	
18 month Beef	per Head	£588	£435	£153	£520
Silage Beef	per Head	£574	£462	£112	£900
Lowland Spring Lamb	per Ewe	£56	£30	£25	£279
Early Lambing	per Ewe	£69	£58	£11	£150
Upland Flocks	per Ewe	£47	£36	£10	£99
Hill Flocks	per Ewe	£31	£23	£8	
Store Lambs	per Ewe	£14	£8	£6	£249
Pigs					
Weaners	per Sow	£784	£601	£183	
Pork	per Pig	£35	£31	£3.50	
Cutter	per Pig	£45	£40	£5.10	
Bacon	per Pig	£55	£47	£7.80	
Combined Pork	per Pig	£71	£59	£11.97	
Combined Cutter	per Pig	£81	£67	£13.57	
Combined Bacon	per Pig	£91	£75	£16.27	

Summary of Livestock Gross Margins (Continued)

Livestock		Output	Variable Costs	Gross Margin /Head	Gross margin £/Ha
Poultry					
Caged Eggs	per Bird	£11.78	£10.62	£1.17	
Free Range Eggs	per Bird	£19.51	£12.54	£6.97	
Pullets	/bird reared	£2.49	£2.11	£0.38	
Broilers	p/bird	141.14p	130.62p	10.52p	
All year turkey	£/Bird	£34.89	£17.85	£17.04	
Christmas Turkey	£/Bird	£24.79	£20.47	£4.32	
Large Roaster Chickens	£/Bird	£13.63	£5.26	£8.37	
Ducks	£/Bird	£6.56	£3.67	£2.89	
Geese	£/Bird	£56.55	£31.78	£24.77	
Other Livestock					
Breeding & Finishing Deer	per 100 hinds	£12,236	£5,857	£6,379	£351
Deer Calves	per 100 hinds	£5,735	£4,132	£1,603	£104
Finishing Stag Calves	per 200 hinds	£19,320	£6,866	£12,454	£685
Ostriches	per Bird	£356	£324	£32	
Wild Boar	per Sow	£1,134	£740	£394	
Dairy Sheep	per Ewe	£309	£194	£115	£1,265
Dairy Goats	per Doe	£296	£219	£77	£612
Angora Goats	per Doe	£90	£81	£9	£92
Trout	per tonne fish	£1,530	£970	£560	
Rabbit	per 50 does	£7,884	£5,242	£2,642	

III GOVERNMENT SUPPORT

1. INTRODUCTION

Agricultural support to farmers and the rural economy is largely provided through the European Union's Common Agricultural Policy (CAP), and delivered in the UK by the devolved Governments of England, Wales, Scotland and Northern Ireland. The World Trade Organisation (WTO) provides a higher tier in the hierarchy of agricultural support policy and has driven the past changes in the CAP. With the apparent collapse in July 2008 of the WTO Doha Development Round no immediate further WTO driven changes are anticipated. The Doha Round was working towards an agreement that would have meant the EU reducing barriers to imports (mainly tariffs and tariff quotas) and this could have had the effect of reducing prices to UK farmers. Now the existing tariff regime largely continues and it is likely to be several years before WTO talks resume.

The CAP has two main budgets (or pillars). Pillar 1 includes the Single Payment Scheme (SPS) which provides direct aid to farm businesses and also Market Support for agricultural produce – once the mainstay of CAP support, but now much reduced in importance. Then Pillar 2 is support through the Rural Development legislation which is increasing in importance in the EU and provides direct support to farmers and also to rural communities. As an indication of the relative importance of Pillar 1 and Pillar 2 support to English farmers it is estimated that in the period 2007-13 Pillar 1 will amount to approximately 73% and Pillar 2 27%. Market support (which is not paid direct to farmers) is not included but is now a very small proportion of total CAP support.

Further details of the main CAP mechanisms are given in the following paragraphs: in individual situations businesses should always check with the latest legislation and their devolved administrations' publications.

2. SINGLE PAYMENT SCHEME

Major reforms of Pillar 1 of the CAP were agreed in 2003. They came into effect, for the most part, on the 1st January 2005. Then in November 2005 a major reform of the Sugar Regime was agreed including price cuts and compensation to farmers starting with the 2006 sugar beet crop. In 2007 a reform of the Fruit and Vegetable regime was agreed. These subsequent reforms have now been incorporated into the Single Payment legislation and there have been some significant simplifications. Currently there is an ongoing 'Health Check' of the SPS by EU agriculture ministers and decisions are expected late in 2008. Little change is expected for the 2009 year, but from 2010 onwards some relatively minor changes should be expected. There is a section at the end outlining the Health Check proposals.

THE BASICS

The major, essential change is ***decoupling***. This means that farm support is no longer linked to what is being produced on the farm during the year, i.e. to the crops being grown or the livestock kept. The 'Single Payment' (still often referred to as the 'Single Farm Payment') is being made according to what was being produced, by each individual farmer who made the claims, during the three years 2000-2002 (the reference period), expressed on a £ per hectare basis. While it was originally conceived (by most people at least) that these would be paid directly to the individuals who originally made the claims ('historic entitlements') an alternative method of distributing the total entitlements gained increasing support during the later months of 2003: paying it as a flat-rate regional average payment per hectare. Various 'hybrids' – combinations of the two methods – were also advocated.

The governments in the various EU member states finally made widely different decisions regarding the distribution of the payment: often varying in different regions within their countries. Differences even occurred within the UK. Essentially (with some relatively small variations), Scotland and Wales decided to adopt an individual historic entitlements basis, Northern Ireland a static hybrid.

For England the government opted for what may be regarded as a complex 'sophisticated' method: generally referred to as a 'dynamic hybrid' or 'delayed flat-rate'. It consists of some of each, historic and regional average, with the proportions changing over an eight-year period: starting mainly historic and changing in annual steps to become entirely regional average, as follows:

Transitional Percentages from Historic to Regional Component in English SPS

Year	2005	2006	2007	2008	2009	2010	2011	2012
% historic	90	85	70	55	40	25	10	0
% regional	10	15	30	45	60	75	90	100

The regional payments in England will differ according to topography, with three types: lowland (or non SDA), non moorland severely disadvantaged areas (SDAs) and moorland SDA. Payments for the second of these will be approximately 80% of those in the lowland and those for moorland about 14% (i.e. about a sixth of those in non-moorland SDAs).

In order to receive payment recipients will have to be farming 'eligible' land (see below). They must also satisfy 'cross-compliance' rules, which are in two parts: 'Statutory Management Requirements' (directives, largely already in force, on public and plant health, animal welfare and the environment) and keeping the land in 'Good Agricultural and Environmental Condition'. They apply to the entire holding. The rules in England include no cultivating, fertilising or spraying within two metres of the centre line of any hedge or ditch (after July 2005), no hedge cutting between 1st March and 31st July and providing a soil management plan. The area of permanent pasture in each region must be maintained (this is a government responsibility to monitor not an individual farmer responsibility – though farmers ploughing permanent pasture must carry out an environmental impact assessment).

A claimant's total reference amount (or historic entitlement) was calculated by multiplying the area and headage claims in the reference period by the 2005 aid rates in euros per hectare, per head or per litre. These were as follows:

2005 Aid Rates used for Calculating Reference Amount

Arable Area: €/ha		**Livestock:** €/head	
England	371.07	Suckler Cow Premium	237.5
Scotland non-LFA	357.21	Beef Special Premium (steers) .	150
Scotland LFA	328.23	Beef Special Premium (bulls) . .	210
Wales non-LFA	325.71	Slaughter Premium	80
Wales LFA	318.15	Extensification (lower rate) . . .	40
N.Ireland non-LFA	328.86	Extensification (higher rate) . . .	80
N.Ireland LFA	316.89	Sheep Annual Premium (SAP) .	21.79
Other Crops:		SAP LFA Supplement	7
Hops.	480.00	**Dairy:** (€/litre)	
Dried Fodder Aid (€/tonne) . . .	68.83	2005	0.02435
		2006	0.03654

Sugar: Compensation for sugar reform price cuts has increased farmers' reference amounts on the basis of their contract tonnage for the 2005 crop. For 2006 the whole amount of £6.58 per tonne was paid separately after receipt of the Single Payment, subject to modulation deductions. For 2007 onwards compensation has been incorporated into the recipient's reference amount and will be subject to the increasing deductions (only 40% remaining in 2009) under the English regional average scheme.

OTHER POINTS

The other important points are as follows:

- As the payments are calculated in euros the £: euro exchange rate remains important, as pre-2005. The rate used is that prevailing on 30th September each year. For the first three years the rate was € = 68-69p. For 2008 onwards the rate assumed in the Pocketbook is 78p, an increase of 12% over 2007.

- Initial entitlements were awarded to the IACS claimant of agricultural land in 2005. They are transferable/tradable: and can be sold with or without land, or if leased only with an equivalent area of land.

- Most farmland is 'eligible', comprising arable land and permanent pasture but excluding woodland and land in non-agricultural use. Initially 'permanent crops' (essentially orchards and vineyards) were excluded, but new legislation allows this land to be eligible. The land has to be 'at the farmer's disposal', initially for at least ten months (the 10 month rule), but from 2008 the land has to be at the farmer's disposal for just 15th May (the application deadline).

- From 2008 land growing soft fruit, vegetables and potatoes (fvp crops) can activate any entitlements (this applies to all UK land). This change removed the need for 'FVP Authorised Entitlements' in England.

- Set-aside Entitlements were issued to farmers in 2005, in Scotland and Wales at 10% of the Arable Area Payment claims in the years 2000-02. In England they were based on 8% in English lowland (1.3% in non-moorland SDA) of arable land in 2005. Now that compulsory set-aside has been abandoned by the EU (confirmed for 2009 following 0% in 2008) it is expected that set-aside entitlements will remain and that farmers will be able to validate them with any eligible land.

- In 2005 only, farmers could opt for the historic payments to which they were entitled to be paid in full on a smaller area of land than that previously farmed. This provision applied in England, and to a much lesser extent elsewhere.

- A Dairy Premium was introduced in 2004 as compensation for intervention price cuts. Details of the payments in 2005 and 2006 are given on page 130. These were decoupled in 2005 and added to reference amounts based on quota held at 31st March 2005. In England, as with all other payments, the annual historic element will be calculated by multiplying by the relevant annual percentage, and therefore worth less than in Wales and Scotland.

- There are supplements (euros/ha) for protein crops (55.57) and energy crops (45). These continue in 2009, but may go in 2010 – see Health Check.

DEDUCTIONS TO THE SINGLE PAYMENT

Initial deductions: A 'National Ceiling', based on past national subsidy receipts led to a 0.17% reduction in England only. Across the UK 4.2% was deducted for the *'National Reserve'*, to provide payments for special cases, e.g. new entrants since the end of 2002 and purchasers of extra land. These two deductions were made before issuing the initial entitlements in 2005. Up to 10% of direct aids from each sector can be deducted to set up a 'National Envelope' to support specific types of farming or improve product quality/marketing; in the UK this is only being used in Scotland (for beef).

Modulation: There is compulsory *'Modulation'* (for all EU member states) to fund EU-wide Rural Development projects; this was 3% in 2005 , 4% in 2006 and 5% in 2007 and thereafter; member states will keep 1% themselves and each will get back at least 80% of its own total; the first 5,000 euros of aid on every farm is exempt. Member states may add 'voluntary' modulation to the above. For the UK the currently agreed voluntary modulation rates are shown below for each devolved administration, EU compulsory rates are also shown and should be added to national rates to arrive at total annual modulation deductions:

Currently Agreed UK and EU Modulation Rates

%	2005	2006	2007	2008	2009	2010	2011	2012
Scotland	3.5	4.5	5	8	8.5	9	9	9
Wales	1.5	0.5	0	2.5	4.2	5.8	6.5	6.5
N.Ireland		4.5	4.5	6	7	8	9	9
England	2	6	12	13	14	14	14	14
EU	3	4	5	5	5	5	5	5

Financial Discipline: EU Farm Ministers decide annually what percentage reductions are needed to keep spending within stipulated budget thresholds; as with EU modulation the first 5,000 euros of aid per farm will be exempt. No Financial Discipline has been deducted so far and none is expected for 2008 or for 2009, but for budgeting it may be prudent to allow 1% in 2010, 2% in 2011 and 3% in 2012.

WINNERS AND LOSERS

The gradual change to a flat-rate area payment in England will clearly create winners and losers. By 2012 a farm in 100% combinable crops will lose around €13/ha (from approximately €343/ha to €330/ha), probably increasing to around €86/ha after deductions. The loss in euro terms is being offset at current conversion rates by the weak pound and if it were not for the high deductions in England the payment would now increase over time. Growers of unsupported crops in the past, such as potatoes and soft fruit, will gain the whole of the payment, though at the cost of having to obey cross-compliance rules. Sugar beet growers saw their single payments increase in 2006, but there will be a steep decline after 2009 to the regional average rate in 2012. In the case of dairy farmers the higher their historic milk yield and stocking rate the more they will lose, especially if they have a flying herd, i.e. no followers; a low-yielding, extensively stocked dairy farm with many followers may lose little or even gain. Intensive beef producers could lose considerably; a low stocking rate suckler herd could be no worse off. Lowland sheep would have to be stocked at a very high rate historically to lose from the new system; most should gain, some significantly.

TOTAL PAYMENTS PER FARM

It is obvious from the above that every farm will have a different total payment per hectare each year as far as the historic payments are concerned. In Wales and Scotland these differences will persist until they have to change from the wholly historic system, as is likely after 2012. In England the differences will gradually iron out as a higher and higher proportion becomes a flat-rate per hectare across all 'lowland' (or all non-moorland SDA or all moorland SDA in the case of the other two areas).

The following are estimates of the flat-rate area payments in 2012 in the three areas (or sub-regions) of England, with 1€ = 78p from 2008 onwards. 'Lowland' covers all non-SDA (Severely Disadvantaged Area) land, which is more than 84% of farmed land. The estimates are made by Andersons and include allowance for the inclusion of Dairy Premium and Sugar Beet compensation in the flat-rate area payments.

Estimated 2012 Flat Rate Area Payments in England

	Lowland £/ha (acre)	Non-Moorland SDA £/ha (acre)	Moorland SDA £/ha (acre)
Payments before deductions....	258 (104)	205 (83)	35 (14)
Payments after deductions	201 (81)	160 (65)	27 (11)

The deductions (22% from modulation and financial discipline by 2012, i.e. 4 years ahead) can obviously only be assumed; they may well be higher, for several reasons: the future entry into the EU of more, poorer member states, increasing demands for a faster transference of funds to rural/environmental expenditure, changes to modulation rates following the Health Check.

Arable Example: As a first example, let us take a 100% combinable cropping farm in England. Assuming the same currency conversion and deductions as above the table below gives actual figures up to 2007 and estimates for 2008 onwards: the implication is that net payments are likely to increase in 2008 because of currency and then decline only marginally by 2012.

Single Payment Calculation for Example Arable Farm

	A. Before Deductions			B. After Deductions
	Historic Part	Flat-rate Part	Total	Total
Year	£	£	£	£
2005	215	19	234	222
2006	200	31	231	208
2007	169	66	235	195
2008	148	112	260	213
2009	108	150	258	209
2010	68	191	259	207
2011	27	231	258	204
2012	0	258	258	201

Beef Example: As a second example, let us assume a lowland farm with a considerable amount of intensive or semi-intensive beef, giving a gross historic payment of approximately £400/ha (at 2005 exchange rate). The example could also apply to a very intensive dairy farm (i.e. high yield and high stocking rate), except that the figures would be higher in year 2006 than 2005 (because the dairy premium rises, before levelling off). Clearly the rate of the loss compared with pre 2005 increases over time – more quickly than the first example.

Single Payment Calculation for Example Lowland Beef Farm

	A. Before Deductions			B. After Deductions
	Historic Part	Flat-rate Part	Total	Total
Year	£	£	£	£
2005	348	19	367	349
2006	324	31	355	319
2007	274	66	340	282
2008	241	112	353	289
2009	175	150	325	263
2010	110	191	301	241
2011	44	231	275	218

| | A. Before Deductions | | | B. After Deductions |
Year	Historic Part £	Flat-rate Part £	Total £	Total £
2012	0	258	258	201

Lowland Sheep: Finally, as a third example, let us assume a lowland sheep farm extensively stocked, giving an historic payment of only £100/ha (at 2005 currency rate).

Single Payment Calculation for Example Lowland Sheep Farm

| | A. Before Deductions | | | B. After Deductions |
Year	Historic Part £	Flat-rate Part £	Total £	Total £
2005	89	19	108	103
2006	83	31	114	103
2007	70	66	136	113
2008	62	111	173	142
2009	45	150	193	158
2010	29	191	220	176
2011	11	231	242	191
2012	0	258	258	201

In this example the farmer gains from the new system increasingly over time, and this is accelerated by the assumed currency gain from 2008.

IMPLICATIONS OF DECOUPLING ON PRODUCTION

Reasons for Little Change: Despite the enormity of the change made in the gross margins – and even more so in net margins, or profits – of the major enterprises affected, the impact on production (areas planted and number of livestock reared) would appear to have been relatively small so far. They may be greater in subsequent years, although with the current high prices for many arable crops the immediate outlook for these enterprises is for an increase in area grown, quite possibly at the expense of grazing livestock production.

There are a number of reasons for the small impact so far:

- The changes, though considerable, will take time to 'register' for many producers. The instinct to 'wait and see' will be strong. Simple inertia will also play a part. Also in England the continued delay in completing the 2005 and 2006 application process has contributed to the inertia.

- Many will continue to sow and to rear as in the past because 'it is what they do': it is what their farm life (which is often the major part of their life) is about. The Single Farm Payment, in many (perhaps most) cases at least will enable this to be done – even if it could be regarded as subsidising unprofitable production.

- If ones own labour, whether manual or managerial, capital and land is charged at 'the going rate', or opportunity cost, most enterprises that might previously have shown a profit, with an area and headage payment, will no longer do so. However, if one stays farming (or even if one does not) many of these costs will still have to be borne, i.e. they are unavoidable, or inescapable by reducing, or even stopping, production. On many farms, especially small and medium sized ones, little would be saved in the way of 'fixed' costs: they really *are* largely, 'fixed'. Hence even a low gross margin may still be leaving an addition to the net income that one would otherwise not have.

- The same point as above needs also to be remembered when considering leaving poorer fields fallow while still cropping the rest. The only actual costs saved on those fields may be the variable costs (primarily seed, fertiliser and sprays) and some fuel and repairs, a total for cereals of around £520/ha (£210/acre), which would be covered by a wheat yield of only 4 tonnes/ha (1.6/acre) at £130/tonne. However, there would be benefits of greater timeliness on the rest in difficult seasons and casual labour and 'catch up' contract work may be saved on some farms.

- Many arable farmers made heavy investments in expensive new machinery following the high prices for the 2003 and now the 2007 harvest crops, many of them with a view to farming more land, particularly in contract farming arrangements; they are unlikely to want to see such investments wasted. Similarly, well established farmers will not want to lose their skilled workers.

Reasons for Change: The recent rapid increase in costs of production, particularly in feed, fertiliser and fuel, may be the trigger for a bigger withdrawal from production in some circumstances. Much will depend on whether the recent increase in most output prices can be maintained or improved on and on other factors such as bovine TB and Bluetongue. A number of other situations have led to change and these may increasingly be important:

- An increasing number of farmers, particularly those who are older, with no obvious successors, or others simply tired of the work involved, the uncertainties and the paperwork, can opt for a simpler system of farming, with very low inputs, taking care to abide by cross-compliance rules.

- Those who have most of their farm operations done by contractors, will be in different position than those described above with truly 'fixed' costs. Clearly the contractor's cost is saved if one ceases production, which could be crucial, especially where yields are only average or below.

- The higher the crop yields, or present levels of enterprise profitability, the more clearly it will pay to continue to farm similarly as in the past. Those in the opposite situation who are still farming either have very low (escapable) fixed costs or another source of income. These will be among those likely to turn to more extensive farming, as described above.

- More farmers are expected to introduce, or expand existing, diversification enterprises, partly, even entirely in some cases, replacing farm enterprises. For many, however, this is easier said than done.

- With regard to the so called 'variable' costs, primarily seed, fertilizer and sprays, the initial thought might be to reduce them. However, if the right (economic) level of these was being applied before (where, as an economist would put it, marginal cost roughly equates to marginal revenue) then it remains the right amount. Reducing these costs will reduce the net margin (or remaining gross margin) from the crop, with or without an aid payment. The exception might be some economies, cutting out waste, but these should already have been attended to, regardless of policy changes. However, farmers planning 2009 cropping may well be right to reduce nitrogen levels at current levels.

- Another exception to the general 'little change' tenor above is sugar beet production. Most of the growers delivering to the Allscott and York factories in 2006 have now abandoned beet growing, but most of their contract tonnage has been taken up by growers in East Anglia and the East Midlands, largely through existing growers increasing the scale of their beet growing operations. This trend is likely to continue as the high cereal and oilseed prices attract some to give up beet growing, but their tonnage so far has been taken up by increasingly specialist large scale growers on land capable of growing very high yields. The rapid increase in costs of growing sugar beet may result in contract tonnage not being grown if prices do not improve.

THE HEALTH CHECK

Formal proposals were published on 20th May 2008, and are due to be finally agreed before the end of 2008. There are likely to be changes, but in summary the proposals are to:

- permanently end set-aside (this has been confirmed by the Commission from 2009)

- further limit the scope of the cereals intervention system

- manage the end of milk quotas on 31st March 2015 through quota increases of 1% for 5 years starting in April 2009

- change support systems in the dairy regime

- open the option for countries to change from a historic to a regional (or hybrid) payment system (applies to Wales and Scotland in the UK) starting in 2010

- phase out most 're-coupled' aids (applies in the UK only to the energy and protein crop supplements in 2010, and to dried fodder in 2011). In theory individual reference amounts for those who have been claiming these coupled aids should be increased, but for English growers this may not be worth much with the move to flat rate payments by 2012.

- increase the minimum SPS claim size to 1 Ha (or €250)

- use the modulation system to create new monies for Rural Development, and particularly to target larger recipients with higher percentages of modulation (see below)

- add new priorities to where Rural Development funds can be spent (see below)

- rewrite the rules on 'National Envelopes' to make them more flexible

One of the most controversial proposals, and therefore less likely to be agreed, is the increased EU modulation and, particularly for the UK, the targeting of larger businesses with higher rates. The proposed figures for compulsory EU modulation are set out in the table below. All new receipts from the extra EU modulation would stay in the UK.

Proposed 'Compulsory' EU Modulation

SPS Income Band:	2008 (current)	2009	2010	2011	2012
Small – below €5,000	0%	0%	0%	0%	0%
Basic - €5,000 to €100,000	**5%**	**7%**	**9%**	**11%**	**13%**
€100,000 to €200,000	5%	10%	12%	14%	16%
€200,000 to €300,000	5%	13%	15%	17%	19%
Over €300,000	5%	16%	18%	20%	22%

It is likely that UK national modulation would reduce if these higher European rates are agreed, and it appears that combined EU and national modulation could not go above the rates shown above. This would be some comfort to very large English growers as the top rate in 2012 would only increase from 19% to 22%. However for large Welsh and Scottish farmers the top rate of 22% would be considerably more than present expectations – see table in p132 above. The money raised through extra modulation will go into new Rural Development spending areas – climate change, water management, renewable energy and biodiversity.

3. MARKET SUPPORT

Market support measures are the other part of Pillar 1 funding, including intervention buying, export subsidies, quotas/set-aside and tariff barriers. Most of these mechanisms are being phased out and are of little significance directly to farmers. The main exception is tariffs which are unlikely to change much in the short term following the collapse of WTO talks – see the introduction to this section. Milk quotas still remain, although it is planned to remove them after 31st March 2015. Individual UK producers have seen their quota increase by a total of 3.5% over the last three years, and more is proposed.

Sugar prices are still supported within the EU. Following the 2006 reforms 'institutional' sugar prices have been cut over four years to reach a minimum EU beet price of €26.4 per tonne in 2009 (€26.7 in 2008). These are being translated into beet prices though the Inter-Professional Agreement. For 2008 at €1=78p this would give a price of about £22.60 per tonne before transport and late delivery bonus (LDB) estimated at £3.50. For 2009 British Sugar is offering the option of a guaranteed minimum price of £24 per tonne with in addition the full potential upside due to movements in currency and wheat price, or a fixed guaranteed price of £26 per tonne. Under both options transport and LDB would add about £4.75 per tonne.

British Sugar reduced contract offers to growers by 10% for 2008 in anticipation of further EU restructuring and it now looks like this will be the final 'institutional' led cut of contract tonnage. Some compensation will be paid for the recent cut based on contract tonnage held for each of the growing seasons 2005, 2006 and 2007. Payments will be made in June 2009 and February 2010, but their value was not known when going to print.

4. RURAL DEVELOPMENT

Rural Development or Pillar 2 of the CAP supports environmental protection and improvement of the countryside, and encourages sustainable enterprises and thriving rural communities. A range of support measures are allowed under four 'axes', with a minimum percentage of each Member State's budget in each:

- Axis 1 Competitiveness (min 10%): includes training young farmers, advice, food quality, production groups etc.

- Axis 2 Land Management (min 25%): includes agri-environmental schemes, hill farming (LFA support), forestry and animal welfare.

- Axis 3 Diversification (min 10%): includes grant aid for non-farming business, tourism, rural services etc.

- Axis 4 LEADER schemes (min 5%): funds local partnership programmes to address specific problems in certain areas.

Each country has a 7-year Rural Development programme running from 2007-13. In the UK these have now all been launched. A brief description is given below. For further details contact the relevant agency in England, Wales and Scotland.

ENGLAND

The stated strategy for the Rural Development Programme England (RDPE) is:

- To build profitable, innovative and competitive farming, food and forestry sectors, that meet the need of consumers and make a net positive contribution to the environment.

- To improve the environment and countryside.

- To enhance opportunity in rural areas in a way that harnesses and builds on environmental quality.

The overall budget for the RDPE for the period 2007-2013 is €5,185 million made up of €3,217 million (62%) from EU funds and the remainder (38%) from national funds. The total funding split into axes is given below:-

	€	%
Axis 1 – Competitiveness	448m	9
Axis 2 – Land Management	4,183m	81
Axis 3 – Diversification	334m	6
Axis 4 – Leader	220m	4
	5,185m	100

Axis 2 Schemes

The vast majority of spending in England is in Axis 2 or the Land Management Schemes. These are being administered by Natural England. The available schemes are:

- Environmental Stewardship Scheme (ESS)

- Hill Farm Allowance Scheme (England) (HFAS)

- England Woodland Grant Scheme (EWGS)

- Energy Crops Scheme (ECS)

Environmental Stewardship Scheme (ESS)

The Environmental Stewardship Scheme was launched in 2005 to replace the Environmental Sensitive Areas, Countryside Stewardship and Organic Farming schemes. The scheme comprises three elements:-

- Entry Level Stewardship (ELS)

- Organic Entry Level Stewardship (OELS)

- Higher Level Stewardship (HLS)

ELS is intended to encourage a large number of farmers across a wide area to adopt simple environmental management practices such as hedgerow management, stone wall maintenance, low input grassland, buffer strips and arable options. The scheme is non-competitive and open to all as long as scheme requirements are met. Points are awarded for each management option adopted. There is a large range of management options including hedgerow management, one side 11 points/100m, both sides 22points/100m; 2m, 4m, 6m buffer strips attracting 10, 20 and 30 points /100m respectively; overwintered stubbles gain 120 points/ha and beetle banks 580 points/ha. Applicants have to achieve a minimum number of 30 points per hectare to be accepted into ELS. An annual payment of £30 per hectare will be made. ELS agreements last for five years. Above the moorland line in the LFAs the payment is £8 per hectare for parcels of land over 15ha.

OELS is open to all organic farmers with land which is registered as organic or in conversion and not currently receiving aid under the Organic Farming Scheme (closed to new applicants). OELS has similar options to those under ELS and participants will receive annual payments of £30 per hectare for carrying out the organic options on the organic land plus an additional £30 per hectare for farming the land organically. There will also be an option to apply for organic conversion with a payment of £600 per hectare per year for top fruit orchards and £175 for improved land. To participate in this latter option land must not already have been converted to full organic production and applicants must have registered the land with an organic inspection body. OELS agreements last for five years. Where a business has a mix of organic and conventional land a single OELS must be made and payments will be at £30 per hectare on the ELS eligible land and £60 per hectare on the organic land.

HLS is targeted towards achieving significant environmental benefits in high priority areas with the objectives being wildlife conservation, protecting historic environments, maintaining and enhancing landscape quality, encouraging public access and resource protection. Applicants have to produce a Farm Environment Plan (FEP) and will usually have to participate in ELS. Only applications that give the best value in meeting the scheme aims will be accepted. Payment will depend on the management options adopted, and can include a mix of capital items and per hectare payments. HLS agreements will normally be for ten years with a break clause for either party after five years. RDAs are now operating a pre-application screening process so that potential applicants do not get involved in unneccessary work and expenditure.

Hill Farm Allowance (HFA) Scheme

This scheme provides support for beef and sheep farming in the Less Favoured Areas. It will continue in 2009 after which it will be replaced by the Uplands Entry Level Stewardship (UELS) scheme. Under the existing scheme area payments will be made to farmers who extensively graze eligible land with sheep breeding flocks and suckler cows in Less Favoured Areas (LFAs). The scheme does not support LFA land used for dairy farming or other new enterprises such as deer farming. To be eligible for payments the following criteria must be met by the applicant:

- have at least ten hectares of eligible LFA land in England on the previous year's Single Payment Scheme application form. (The 2009 scheme uses the 2008 SP5 application form)

- undertake to farm in the LFA for five years from the first payment

- have a stocking density of at least 0.15LU/ha. It may be possible to qualify at lower rates where agri-environment or other recognised environmental measures require this. If stocking rates are above 1.4LU/ha there will have to be an inspection in the first year this happens, and at least once every three years thereafter, to ensure that land is not being overgrazed

- meet the requirements of 'Good Farming Practice' and not use prohibited substances.

Payments are made up of a Basic Payment *and* an optional Environmental Enhancement:

Basic HFA Payments:

£/ha	2007	2008	2009*
Moorland	13.32	14.12	*14.12*
Common Land	13.32	14.12	*14.12*
Other DA Land	19.03	-	-
Other SDA Land	35.20	37.31	*37.31*

*Payment in 2009 is expected to be similar to that in 2008.

Full rate is paid on the first 350ha, half rate on the next 350ha. No payment is paid on land in excess of 700ha. As from 2008 no payment will be made on Disadvantaged Land.

Environmental Enhancements: producers can increase their basic payments by 10% or 20% by undertaking mixed farming practices and animal husbandry that satisfies certain criteria.

England Woodland Grant Scheme(EWGS)

The previous Woodland Grant Scheme (WGS) and the Farm Woodland Premium Scheme (FWPS) have been replaced by the England Woodland Grant Scheme (EWGS), administered jointly by Natural England and the Forestry Commission. Details of the scheme are set out in the Forestry section at 115.

Energy Crops Scheme (ECS)

The Energy Crops Scheme provides aid for the planting of Short Rotation Coppice (SRC) and Miscanthus (elephant grass). Poplar, willow, ash, alder, hazel, silver birch, sycamore, sweet chestnut and lime have been added to the list of trees that are eligible for the SRC grant.

Unlike the previous Energy Crops Scheme, there is not a fixed 'per Ha' grant rate for each crop. Instead, grant aid will be paid at 40% of the actual expenditure. Applicants have to submit invoices showing their actual costs. Applicants will be required to provide estimates of likely costs as part of the application process if these estimates are consistent with an Independent Verification of typical costs then the application can be accepted on a single quote. Where estimated costs are higher than the Independent Verification applicants will be required to provide written evidence to explain the variation – this may also involve getting further quotes.

Any land is eligible for the ECS, either agricultural or non-agricultural, but not land already under forestry, energy crops, or common land. There is a minimum application size of 3 hectares. Grant is paid in full on submission of costs. No English Woodland Grant Scheme payments are available on these crops. Land planted to these crops remains eligible for the Single Payment in addition to payments under this scheme. The rules on distance to the end-user are likely to be amended for 2009 plantings – rather than being based on a simple distance measure, applications will instead be judged on a carbon balance calculation.

Axes 1,3,4 Schemes

This part of the RDPE is administered by eight Regional Development Agencies (RDAs). Each RDA has come up with its own priorities and schemes. Support is in the form of capital grants to fund a percentage of eligible expenditure. There may also be funding for training and advice, including individual farm business advice, but this will vary considerably between RDAs. Funding is limited and will be competitive. Compared to previous programmes, RDAs are mostly looking for a small number of larger projects, and hence a tendency to encourage collaboration and cooperation. Schemes tend to cover the following broad areas:

- Adding value to farming and forestry products

- Diversification of farming businesses

- Collaboration/cooperation between land-based businesses

- Renewable energy and water conservation and management

For scheme details the relevant RDA should be contacted:

South East: SEEDA – www.seeda.co.uk

South West: SWERDA – www.southwestrda.org.uk

West Midlands: Advantage West Midlands – www.advantagewm.co.uk

East Midlands: EMDA – www.emda.org.uk

East of England: EEDA – www.eeda.org.uk

Yorkshire/Humberside: Yorkshire Forward – www.yorkshire-forward.com

North East: One North East - www.onenortheast.co.uk

North West: NWRDA – www.nwda.co.uk

WALES

The stated strategy for the Wales Rural Development Programme (WRDP) is:

- to stimulate a dynamic and innovative agricultural sector.

- Encourage sustainable production methods with a view to improving the environment.

- Improve the quality of life in rural areas and encourage diversification of the rural economy.

- Build capacity and innovation in rural areas.

The overall budget is a total of €985 million made up of €377 million (38%) from EU funds and the remainder (62%) from national funds. The total funding split into axes is given below:-

	€	%
Axis 1 – Competitivness	122m	12
Axis 2 – Land Management	722m	73
Axis 3 – Diversification	94m	10
Axis 4 – Leader	47m	5
	985m	100

Axis 2 Schemes

These land management schemes account for 73% of Rural Development funding in Wales. Most of the previous land management schemes carry on in the short term, but the future of Tir Mynydd (Hill Farming Scheme) is uncertain and a replacement scheme is planned for 2009. There is also a comprehensive review in 2008 of all agri-environmental support in Wales and this may lead to changes in the other schemes. The schemes in the WRDP are:

- Tir Gofal

- Tir Cynnal

- Organic Farming Scheme (OFS)

- Better Woodlands for Wales (BWW)

- Tir Mynydd (probably replaced in 2009)

Tir Gofal, which means 'land in care' is an integrated agri-environmental scheme, with 10 year agreements with a 5 year break clause. The whole farm must be entered and there is a combination of mandatory and optional land management payments, and capital grants.

Tir Cynnal is a whole farm entry level type scheme first introduced in 2005. Application is via the Single Application Form (SAF). Applicants enter their whole farm with a 10 year agreement with a 5 year break clause. Payments are made per hectare in bands with the first 20 hectares at £45 per hectare reducing to any area over 200 hectares at £2 per hectare.

The **OFS** is a five year agreement covering land in conversion and/or fully organic.

BWW helps fund the improved management of existing woodland and funds the creation of new woods in Wales. The scheme is run in conjunction with the Forestry Commission.

The existing **Tir Mynydd** scheme is based on payments for land in the LFA areas as entered on the previous year's SAF. Payments have been at £19 per hectare for disadvantaged areas and £30 per hectare for severely disadvantaged areas with these rates paid up to the first £140 hectares. Reduced rates are paid above 140 hectares but there is no upper limit. Above 640 hectares the percentage paid is 30% of the full payment. For 2009 it is likely that Tir Mynydd will close in its existing form and be replaced by an agri-environmental type scheme.

Axes 1, 3 And 4 Schemes

The WRDP covering these three axes has an emphasis on collaboration and co-operation in the whole food chain. At the centre of the strategy is the processing and marketing grant scheme (PMGS) which covers food and forestry. Grant is available for adding value to agricultural products and for marketing. The rate of Grant is 40% of eligible costs (50% in some designated areas). Eligible expenditure includes erection of buildings as well as product development, market research etc. There will also be assistance for diversification and tourism and farm business advice through Farming Connect.

SCOTLAND

The overall strategy for the Scotland Rural Development Programme (SRDP) is to:

- support business viability

- add value to the rural economy and facilitate increased market orientation.

- Support a coherent and integrated approach to meet environmental objectives.

- Encourage private enterprise and entrepreneurship, improve services and infrastructure at local level and support Scotland's cultural opportunities.

- Support capacity building and innovation.

The overall budget from the SRDP is €2,131million of which €676 million (32%) is from European funds and the remainder (68%) from national funds. The total funding split into axes is given below:-

	€	%
Axis 1 – Competitivness	306m	14
Axis 2 – Land Management	1,469m	69
Axis 3 – Diversification	248m	12
Axis 4 – Leader	108m	5
	2,131m	100

Rural Development Contracts

The SRDP is delivered through a single mechanism known as Rural Development Contracts (RDCs), and is divided into three tiers:-

Tier I: The Single Payment Scheme – through the cross-compliance requirements a basic level of environmental protection, food safety and animal welfare is provided.

Tier II: Land Manager's Options - Farmers choose from a menu of options with application at the same time as the Single Application Form (SAF).

Tier III: Rural Priorities – This element is discretionary and competitive and it covers the areas that were previously aided under schemes such as the Rural Stewardship Scheme (RSS), Organic Aid Scheme (OAS), Farm Business Development Scheme (FBDS) and Forestry Support. Now a New Entrants scheme has been added, there is also aid for processing and marketing which is available at the farm level through the SRDP, but larger scale projects are funded directly by Scottish Government.

Hill Farming Support (LFASS) is outside the RDCs and will continue in 2009 on a similar basis to 2007 and 2008. There will be a replacement put in place for 2010 which is likely to pay land managers for environmental benefits similar to what is planned for England and Wales. The other main support for farmers in Scotland outside the RDCs is the Whole Farm Review, which grant aids a business review, action plan and implementation up to a maximum of £1,850.

CLOSED SCHEMES

There are many schemes across the UK that are now closed to new applicants but are still providing annual payments to some farmers. Some were available across all the devolved regions such as the Environmentally Sensitive Areas (ESA) schemes and the Hill Farm Allowance schemes. The other major agri-environmental schemes include the Countryside Stewardship (CSS) in England, Tir Gofal in Wales, and Rural Stewardship (RSS) in Scotland. The table below summarises the latest payments made under these agri-environmental schemes across the UK, also including Tir Cynnal and the LMCS in Scotland:

Environment Schemes Payments, 2006 (provisional)

		£ million
England:	Organic Farming Scheme	2.6
	Environmentally Sensitive Areas	63.8
	Countryside Stewardship	106.5
	Hill Farm Allowance	27.2
Wales:	Organic Farming Scheme	3.1
	Environmentally Sensitive Areas	4.2
	Tir Mynydd	34.8
	Tir Gofal	24.2
	Tir Cynnal	5.9
Scotland:	Organic Aid Scheme	3.5
	Environmentally Sensitive Areas	6.3
	Rural Stewardship	20.8
	Less Favoured Area Support Scheme	100.3
	Land Management Contract Scheme	21.8
N. Ireland	Organic Farming Scheme	0.4
	New Environmentally Sensitive Areas	4.8
	Countryside Management Scheme	10.2
	Less Favoured Area Compensatory Allowances	21.0

Source: DEFRA, SGRPID, DARD, WAGDEPC. Agriculture in the UK 2007.

IV. LABOUR

1. LABOUR COST

1. Statutory Minimum Wage Rates

The following rates are taken from the proposed Agricultural Wages Board Order for the year from 1st October 2008. They are subject to ratification. The minimum weekly rates relate to a 39-hour standard week of normal hours worked on any five days between Monday and Saturday.

A. Normal Hours (Standard Rates)

Grade			39 Hr Weekly Rate	Hourly Rate	Overtime per Hour
			£	£	£
1.	Initial Grade	Over 16 years...................	223.86	5.74	8.61
		Under 16 years.................	-	2.87	4.31
2.	***Standard Worker*****......................................**		***244.14***	***6.26***	***9.39***
3.	Lead Worker		228.32	6.89	10.34
4.	Craft Grade		287.82	7.39	11.09
5.	Supervisory Grade		304.98	7.82	11.73
6.	Farm Management Grade		329.55	8.45	12.68
	Apprentice:	Year 1................................	137.67	3.53	5.30
		Year 2 ~ 16-18 years	137.67	3.53	5.30
		Year 2 ~ 19-21 years	186.03	4.77	7.16
		Year 2 ~ 22 years and over	223.47	5.73	8.60

Night work rates are £1.23 per hour; standby rates £24.81 per day; dog rates £6.86 per week.

B. Flexible Working

Grade		Number of days basic hours worked	Weekly Rate	Hourly Rate	Overtime per Hour
			£	£	£
1.	Initial Grade (16+ only).......	4 to 5	235.17	6.03	8.61
		6	239.46	6.14	8.61
2.	Standard Worker..................	4 to 5	256.43	6.57	9.39
		6	261.30	6.70	9.39
3.	Lead Worker	4 to 5	281.97	7.23	10.34
		6	287.43	7.37	10.34
4.	Craft Grade	4 to 5	302.64	7.76	11.09
		6	308.49	7.91	11.09
5.	Supervisory Grade	4 to 5	320.19	8.21	11.73
		6	326.43	8.37	11.73
6.	Farm Management Grade	4 to 5	345.93	8.87	12.68
		6	352.56	9.04	12.68

Notes

1. The new grading structure, comprising six grades instead of the previous five, was introduced in 2005. Flexible working rates were set for each of the six new grades. In 2006 the Basic Trainee Grade was renamed the Initial Grade. All age differentials were abolished apart from the under 16 category in the Initial Grade.

2. Part standby duty days are paid at half the rates given above.

3. A deduction up to £31.22 a week or £4.46 a day for non-house accommodation can be made. There are specified provisions for sick pay, paid bereavement leave and paid paternity leave (3 days).

Full details are available from the Agricultural Wages Board for England and Wales (Telephone: 0207 238 6523).

Holiday Pay

Holidays with pay. The number of days holiday that workers are entitled to in a year depends on the number of days worked each week. Those working full-time, 5 days a week, have 23 days per year. There are rules as to timing.

For part-time workers the number of days worked per week is based on the total hours worked over the 12 months ending on the last 5th April.

2. Average Earnings 2008

Average Earnings and Hours Worked by Type of Full Time Permanent Worker

Type of Worker	Number of Workers	Basic Hours	Overtime Hours	Basic Pay	Over-Time	Total Pay
Grade 1	1,244	36.6	1.8	11,476	510	11,986
Grade 2	21,992	38.7	6.3	13,765	1,790	15,555
Grade 3	4,123	39.5	5.1	14,809	2,380	17,189
Grade 4	13,180	38.5	8.9	14,895	3,864	18,759
Grade 5	6,169	39.8	6.2	17,033	2,842	19,875
Grade 6	1,965	37.8	7.3	16,629	3,152	19,781

Type of Worker	Total Pay	Total Hours	average £/Hr
Foreman/Woman	331.34	37.35	8.87
Dairy Herdsperson	256.97	34.65	7.42
Other Stockperson	307.37	41.09	7.48
Tractor Driver	347.90	45.39	7.66
Horticultural Worker	223.31	33.61	6.64
General Farm Worker	275.48	39.38	7.00
Other Manual Farm Worker	201.13	30.43	6.61
Farm Manager	360.05	40.24	8.95

Notes

1. The data in these 2 tables is for the year to March 2008 from DEFRA's quarterly earnings and Hours Surveys

2. They are weighted weekly equivalent figures and include overtime and holiday pay

3. Only for workers aged 20 or over

4. Covers all grades of worker

5. Excludes office workers

6. Excludes salaried staff (with no set hours)

3. Typical Annual Labour Cost

Estimated for the 2009 calendar year, based on a Standard Worker.

	Average Annual Cost(1)	Average Weekly Cost	Average Hourly Cost(2)
	£	£	£
Minimum Wage (basic standard worker rate)	12,688	244.00	7.23
National Insurance Contribution and Employers Liability Insurance	1,751	33.67	
Minimum Cost	14,439	277.67	8.22
Overtime, average 10 hrs per working week (45) @ £9.39 (+ NIC, ELI)	4809	92.48	
	19,248	370.15	8.73
'Premium' over basic rate average £46.00 per week (+ NIC, ELI)	2,722	52.34	
Total Cost (3,4)	21,970	422.50	9.96

NIC = National Insurance Employer Contribution = 12.8%;

ELI = Employer's Liability Insurance = 1%

Notes:

1. Estimated average annual cost higher than 2007 AWB rate as figures based on calendar year rather than Oct-Oct AWB year.

2. Hours, excluding overtime, based on 45 weeks (of 39 hours) per year, i.e. statutory holidays (23 days), public holidays (8 days) and illness (4 days), have been deducted.

3. Annual cost (or net value) of cottages, value of perquisites, contribution towards payment of the council tax, etc., would have to be added where appropriate.

4. Total average worker's gross earnings on the above assumptions = £19,306 a year, £371 a week, £8.75 an hour including overtime.

2. LABOUR HOURS AVAILABLE FOR FIELD WORK

(per man per month)

	Total Ordinary Hours (1)	Adjusted Ordinary Hours (2)	% Workable	Available Ordinary Hours (3)	Available Overtime Hours (4)	**Total Available Hours**	Total Available '8-hour Days' (5)
January	177	148	50	74	28 (61)	102 (135)	13 (17)
February	160	134	50	67	33 (55)	100 (122)	12½ (15)
March	172	149	60	89	69 (82)	158 (171)	20 (21½)
April	161	139	65	90	86	176	22
May	171	151	70	106	110	216	27
June	170	150	75	112	112	224	28
July	177	157	75	118	113	231	29
August	169	150	75	112	104	216	27
September	172	152	70	106	82 (69)	188 (195)	23½ (24½)
October	177	153	65	99	63 (83)	162 (182)	20 (23)
November	172	144	50	72	26 (59)	98 (131)	12 (16½)
December	161	135	50	67	25 (65)	92 (132)	11½ (16½)

(1) 40 hour week, less public holidays. No deductions have been made for other holidays because they may be taken at various times of the year.

(2) After deducting (a) for illness (10 per cent Nov. to Feb., 7½% March, April and Oct., 5% May to Sept.), and (b) for contingencies and non-delayable maintenance (½ hour per day).

(3) Adjusted Ordinary Hours x percentage Workable.

(4) Maximum 4 overtime hours per day summer, 3 hours winter, and 12 to 14 hours' work at weekends, according to season. Same adjustments for illness and percentage workable as for ordinary hours. Figures in brackets indicate hours available if headlights used up to limit of overtime stated. The percentage overtime (without headlights) available from weekend work as opposed to evenings = (January to December respectively): 100, 78, 58, 50, 40, 40, 41, 42, 53, 67, 100, 100.

(5) Total available hours ÷ 8.

Notes

(1) These figures relate to medium land. The percentage workability will be higher with light soils and less with particularly heavy soils. On heavy soils, of course, the land may be virtually 100 per cent unworkable between late November and early March (or still later, according to the season), particularly if undrained. A rough estimate of variations in workability according to soil type (compared with the figures in the above table) are as follows. Heavy land — March, October, November: one-third less; April: one-fifth less; September: 10% less; May to August: no difference. Light land — October to April: one-sixth more; May and September: 10% more; June to August: no difference.

(2) When these figures are used for planning, it must be remembered that indoor work, e.g. livestock tending or potato riddling, can be continued over the full working-week, i.e. the hours available are the Adjusted Ordinary Hours, plus overtime. Also, some handwork in the field has to continue even in rain, e.g. sprout picking.

(3) To be precise, percentage workability varies according to the particular operation, e.g. compare ploughing and drilling.

(4) Furthermore, some operations are limited by factors other than soil workability, e.g. combine-harvesting by grain moisture content.

(5) Factors touched upon briefly above are discussed fully in Duckham's 'The Farming Year'.

3. SEASONAL LABOUR REQUIREMENTS FOR

CROPS AND GRASS

On the following pages, data on labour requirements for various crops and types of livestock are given. Two levels are shown: average and premium. The average figures relate to the whole range of conditions and farm size, i.e. small and medium-sized farms as well as large; the figures give all farms equal weight. The premium rates do not denote the maximum rates possible, for instance by the use of especially high-powered tractors under ideal conditions, but relate to rates of work estimated to be obtainable over the whole season, averaging good and bad conditions, with the use of wide implements, relatively large tractors (75 to 90 kW) (100-120 hp) and high capacity equipment in 8 hectare fields and over, where no time is wasted. Most farmers with more than 200 hectares (500 acres) of arable land are likely to achieve at least the premium levels shown. Those with over 400 hectares (1,000 acres) will have still bigger machines and therefore faster work rates, and thus require 15 to 25% less labour than even the premium levels given.

The rates of work include preparation, travelling to fields, allow for minor breakdowns and other stoppages. They relate broadly to medium and medium-heavy land; some jobs, such as ploughing, may be done more quickly on light soils. Operations such as combine harvesting can obviously vary according to many factors to do with the topography and other natural features of the farm.

The usual times of year when each operation takes place are shown; these relate to lowland conditions in the south-eastern half of Britain. They will obviously vary between seasons, soil types, latitude and altitude. In particular, on light land, land can be ploughed over a longer winter period and a high proportion of cultivations for spring crops may be completed in February in many seasons. All such factors must be allowed for in individual farm planning. Conditions in different seasons will also affect, for instance, the number and type of cultivations required in seedbed preparation. Typical monthly breakdowns of requirements are given for various crops.

To illustrate the type of questions that need to be asked for full details of seasonal labour requirements on the individual farm, 'Critical Questions affecting Timing' are listed for cereals. Similar questions would, of course, need to be asked for other crops.

WINTER CEREALS

Operations	Labour-hours per hectare		Time of Year
	Average	Premium	
Plough (1)	1.4	1.0	July to October (according to previous crop)
Cultivate (often power harrow)	1.0	0.7	September to October (according to previous crop) (½ Aug if ploughed in July)
Drill (often with power harrows) followed by roll	1.1	0.7	Mid-September to 3rd week October (according to previous crop and soil)
Apply Fertiliser	0.3	0.2	
Spray	0.3	0.2	October-November
Top Dress (three times [2])	0.9	0.6	March and April
Spray (three or four [2])		1.0	0.5 Spring/early summer
Combine, Cart Grain, Barn Work	2.5	1.9	Mid-Aug to approx. 10th Sept
Later Barn Work (3)	0.7	0.4	September to June
Total	**9.2**	**6.2**	
Straw: Bale	1.3	0.8	Mid-August to end
Cart	3.5	2.6	September

Typical Monthly Breakdown

Month	Average	Premium	Notes
October	2.4	1.7	Approx. 60% of Ploughing,
November	—	—	Cults., Drill, Harrow
December	—	—	
January	—	—	
February	—	—	
March	0.4	0.2	Part Top Dress
April	0.8	0.5	Part Top Dress, Spraying
May	0.3	0.2	Spraying
June	0.3	0.2	Spraying
July	—	—	
August	1.7 (+2.4 Straw)	1.3 (+1.7 Straw)	⅔ of harvesting (4)
September (harvest)	0.9 (+2.4 Straw)	0.6 (+1.7 Straw)	⅓ of harvesting (4)
September (prepn. drill)	1.7	1.1	40% of Ploughing, Cults., Drill, Harrow

Notes

1. Some cereal crops are direct drilled or drilled after reduced, or minimal, cultivations, i.e. without traditional ploughing. Direct drilling reduces man-hours per hectare by about 2.5 (average) or 1.8 (premium), and minimal cultivations by about 1.2 (average) and 0.9 (premium).

2. Winter wheat; winter barley will often have one less top dressing and spraying and oats two less.

3. Later barn work excluded from monthly breakdown.

4. Winter wheat (see next page for harvest times for winter barley and oats).

SPRING CEREALS

Operations	Labour-Hours per hectare		Time of Year
	Average	Premium	
Plough (1)	1.4	1.0	July to October (according to previous crop and soil type)
Cultivate (often power harrow)	1.0	0.7	March (½ in second half February on light land)
Apply Fertiliser	0.3	0.2	
Drill (often with power harrow), plus roll	1.2	0.8	March (½ at end February on light land)
Top Dress (once, some possibly twice)	0.4	0.2	
Spray (two or three)	0.7	0.3	May
Combine, Cart Grain, Barn Work	2.4	1.8	Last ¾ of August (affected by variety and season)
Later Barn Work (2)	0.6	0.4	September to June
Total	**8.0**	**5.4**	
Straw: Bale (unmanned sledge)	1.3	0.8	Mid-August to end
Cart	3.5	2.6	September

Typical Monthly Breakdown

Month	Average	Premium	Notes
October	0.4	0.3	Ploughing. How much in
November	0.8	0.5	October depends on area
December	0.2	0.2	W. Wheat, Potatoes, etc.
January	—	—	
February	—	—	
March	2.4	1.6	All Cults. Drilling, Rolling, (nearly half in February on light land)
April	—	—	
May	1.1	0.6	Spray and Top dress
June	—	—	
July	—	—	
August(3)	2.4 (+2.6 Straw)	1.8 (+1.8 Straw)	Harvesting
September	— (+2.2 Straw)	(+1.6 Straw)	

Notes

1. Later barn work excluded.

2. Spring barley; spring wheat and oats partly September (see page 151).

In a *normal* (i.e. neither early or late) *season*:

WINTER WHEAT

Drilling mid-September to 3rd week October.
Harvesting mid-August to approx. 10th September.

WINTER BARLEY

As for winter wheat, except that:
Ploughing unlikely to start before cereal harvest, as usually follows a cereal crop.
Harvesting some weeks earlier: mid July to approx. 10th August.

WINTER OATS

As for winter wheat, except that:
Drilling usually first full half of October.
Harvesting earlier (late July or first half of August).

SPRING BARLEY

Drilling end of February to end of March or early April.
Harvesting last half to ¾ of August.

SPRING WHEAT

As for spring barley, except that:
Drilling is on average one or two weeks earlier (should be finished in March) — lose more if later than barley.
Harvesting, on average, is two weeks later: last week of August/first half of September (two-thirds in September).

SPRING OATS

As for spring barley, except that:

Drilling is usually a little earlier.

Harvesting is later than spring barley, earlier than spring wheat: end of August/beginning of September.

Critical Questions affecting Timing (Autumn-sown Cereals)

1. Previous crops (affects time available and need for ploughing and cultivations).
2. Will the crop be ploughed traditionally, chisel ploughed, minimally cultivated, or direct drilled?
3. Earliest and latest drilling date, by choice.
4. Effect on yield if drilling is delayed.
5. Autumn weed control?
6. In the spring: (a) whether crop is rolled, and when,
    (b) whether crop is harrowed, and when,
    (c) time of top dressings,
    (d) number of spray applications.
7. (a) Average period for harvesting.
   (b) Earliest dates for starting and finishing harvest, and latest dates for starting and finishing harvest, ignoring extreme seasons (one year in ten).

Critical Questions affecting Timing (Spring-sown Cereals)

1. Previous crops.
2. Will the crop be ploughed traditionally, chisel ploughed, minimally cultivated, or direct drilled?
3. Months when winter ploughing is possible, on average. (Where relevant).
4. Is spring ploughing satisfactory? (Where relevant).
5. Average period of cultivations and drilling.
6. Earliest dates for starting and finishing spring cultivations/drilling and latest dates for starting and finishing cultivations/drilling, ignoring extreme seasons (1 year in 10).
7. Effect on yield if drilling is delayed.
8. Is the crop rolled (a) within a few days of drilling or (b) later?
9. (a) Average period of harvesting.
   (b) Earliest dates for starting and finishing harvest, and latest dates for starting and finishing harvest, ignoring extreme seasons (one year in ten).

MAINCROP POTATOES

| Operations | Labour-Hours per hectare | | Time of Year |
	Average	Premium	
Plough	1.4	1.0	September to December
Cultivating, Ridging, Destoning/			
Clod sep. (as required)	6.5	5.0	March, early April
Plant and Apply Fertiliser (1)	4.5	3.5	Last quarter of March, first
Apply Herbicide..........................	0.3	0.2	three-quarters of April
Spray for Blight (av. 6 times)	1.2	0.9	July, first half August
Burn off Haulm..........................	0.3	0.2	End September, early
			October
Harvest, Cart, Clamp (2).............	15.0	10.0	End September, October
Work on Indoor Clamp...............	4.8	3.2	November
Riddle, Bag, Load	40.0	30.0	October to May
Total..	**74.0**	**54.0**	

(1) Automatic planter. Hand-fed planters: approx. 12 hrs plus 8 (could be casual labour).

(2) Mechanical harvester, excluding up to 25 hours for picking off on harvester—usually casual labour. None may be needed on clod and stone-free soils. Hand harvesting: additional approx. 80 hours of casual labour.

Typical Monthly Breakdown

Month	Average	Premium	Notes
October..	12.2	8.2	80% of harvest, ½ burn off
November.....................................	5.9	4.0	Clamp work and ¾ plough
December	0.3	0.2	¼ plough
January	—	—	
February	—	—	
March	7.8	6.0	All fert', ½ cults', ¼ plant
April	3.5	2.7	½ cult's, ¾ plant
May	—	—	
June	—	—	
July	0.9	0.7	3 blight sprays
August...	0.3	0.2	1 blight spray
September	3.1	2.0	20% harvest, ½ burn off

Note: These figures exclude casual labour and riddling.

EARLY POTATOES

| Operations | Labour-Hours per hectare | | Time of Year |
	Average	Premium	
Plough	1.4 (1)	1.0 (1)	September to December
Cultivating, etc............................	6.5 (1)	5.0 (1)	Late February, early March
Plant and Apply Fertiliser	4.5 (1)	3.5 (1)	Late February, early March
Apply Herbicide..........................	0.3 (1)	0.2 (1)	1st half March (some in
			February on light land or
			in early season)
Further Spraying	0.3 (1)	0.2 (1)	
After-Cultivation/Spray	0.3 (1)	0.2 (1)	April, early May
Harvest, bag, load	30.0 (1)	25.0 (2)	2nd week June onwards.
			All June or till mid-July

(1) Excluding 80 hours picking—usually casuals.

(2) Excluding 60 hours picking—usually casuals.

SECOND EARLY POTATOES

Operations	Average	Premium	Time of Year
	Labour-Hours per hectare		
Plough	1.4 (1)	1.0 (1)	September to December
Cultivating, etc	6.5 (1)	5.0 (1)	March
Plant and Apply Fertiliser	4.5 (1)	3.5 (1)	March
Apply Herbicide	0.3 (1)	0.2 (1)	Half 2nd half March, half 1st half April
Further Spraying	0.9 (1)	0.7 (1)	End April, May, early June
Harvest	15.0 (1)	10.0 (2)	Mid-July to end August

(1) Spinner or elevator-digger, excluding picking and riddling—usually casual labour.

(2) Mechanical harvester, excluding picking off on harvester and riddling—usually casual labour.

SUGAR BEET

Operations	Average	Premium	Time of Year
	Labour-Hours per hectare		
Plough	1.4	1.0	September to December
Seedbed Cults	3.2	2.2	Mainly March (some early April. Some late February
Load, Cart, Apply Fertiliser	0.7	0.4	in good seasons)
Drill (and Flat Roll)	1.8	1.1	Between mid-March and mid-April
Spray (herbicide: pre- and post-emergence)	0.6	0.3	Late March/April
Spray (x 2)	0.6	0.3	May/June
Spray (aphis)	0.3	0.2	July
Harvest (machine)	14.0	9.0	End September, October, November
Load	3.4	2.5	End September to early January
Total	**26.0**	**17.0**	

Typical Monthly Breakdown

Month	Average	Premium	Notes
October	7.2	4.6	45% harvest; + loading
November	8.2	5.3	45% harvest; ¾ ploughing; + loading
December	1.0	0.8	¼ ploughing; + loading
January	0.5	0.4	Loading
February	—	—	
March	3.8	2.3	Fert., most cults., some drilling
April	2.5	1.7	Some cults., most of drilling
May	0.3	0.2	Spray
June	0.3	0.15	Spray
July	0.2	0.15	Spray
August	—	—	
September	2.0	1.4	10% harvesting; + loading

VINING PEAS

Operations	Labour-Hours per hectare		Time of Year
	Average	Premium	
Plough...............................	1.4	1.0	September to December
Cults, Fert. and Drill..................	2.3	1.6	Mid-Feb. to April
Post Drilling and Spraying..........	1.5	0.8	
Harvesting..................................	19.0	14.0	July and early August
Total............................	**24.2**	**17.4**	

Note

Drilling is staggered in small areas through the season, ranging from early varieties to late varieties.

DRIED PEAS

Month	Labour-Hours per hectare		Notes
	Average	Premium	
October..	1.2	0.8	
November....................................	0.8	0.5	Stubble cult., Plough
December.....................................	—	—	
January..	—	—	
February......................................	0.2	0.1	Cult. x 2, harrow; drill & fert.
March..	2.8	1.9	(80% March); light harrow
April..	0.6	0.4	roll; and spray
May...	2.5	1.2	
June...	0.2	0.2	Scare pigeons; spray
July..	1.8	1.1	Possible spray desiccant;
August...	2.2	1.3	combine and cart, dry
September....................................	0.5	0.3	Stubble cult.

Assumes direct combining.

FIELD BEANS

A. Winter Beans

Operations	Labour-Hours per hectare		Time of Year
	Average	Premium	
Broadcast Seed............................	0.6	0.4	
Apply Fertiliser...........................	0.3	0.2	
Plough...	1.4	1.0	September/October
Power Harrow..............................	1.0	0.8	
Spray (pre-emergence)................	0.3	0.15	
Spraying (two or three times).....	0.8	0.35	Spring
Combine and cart and			
Barn-work....................................	3.0	2.4	August

B. Spring Beans

Operations	Labour-Hours per hectare		Time of Year
	Average	Premium	
Plough	1.4	1.0	September to December
Cultivate (often power harrow)	1.0	0.7	
Apply Fertiliser	0.3	0.2	
Drill, Roll	1.2	0.8	End Feb, early March
Spray (two or three times)	0.8	0.4	
Combine and cart and Barn-work	3.0	2.4	September

OILSEED RAPE

(Autumn Sown - Desiccated)

Month	Labour-Hours per hectare		Notes
	Average	Premium	
October			
November	0.6	0.3	Spray herbicide and
December			insecticide if necessary
January	—	—	
February	—	—	
March			
April	0.8	0.4	Top dress twice
May	—	—	
June	—	—	Desiccate (1st half July);
July	2.4	1.7	combine (½ 2nd half July
August	2.0	1.4	½ 1st half Aug.); dry
August	1.6	0.9	Cults. (x 2), spray, drill, fert.;
September	1.6	0.9	harrow, roll, barn work (0.5)

HERBAGE SEED *(first production year)*

A. Undersown

Operations	Labour-Hours per hectare		Time of Year
	Average	Premium	
Undersow	0.6	0.4	March, April
Roll {	(0.6)	(0.4)	Straight after drilling
	0.4	0.3	September
	0.4	0.3	Late February, March
Harvest (by Combine): Mow	1.4	0.9	3 to 4 days before combining
Combine and Cart	4.5	3.5	Ital. Ryegrasses and Early *Perennials: late July.* *Intermed. Perennials: late July/early August.* *Late Perennials/White Clover: mid-August*
	6.0	4.5	Meadow Fescue: early July
	7.0	5.0	Cocksfoot: early July
	10.0	7.0	Timothy: mid-August Red Clover: late September

B. Direct Drilled in Autumn

Operations	Labour-Hours per hectare		Time of Year
	Average	Premium	
Plough	1.4	1.0	
Seedbed Cults	2.2	1.6	Depends on previous crop—
Load, Cart, Apply Fertiliser	0.3	0.2	Usually July or August
Drill (with harrows behind)	0.8	0.6	As early as previous crop allows. This may be up to mid-Sept for ryegrass without detriment to the yield.
Roll (soon after drilling)	0.6	0.4	Meadow fescue and cocksfoot are best sown no later than July and it is risky to sow Timothy much later than this.

GRASS

A. Production

Operations	Labour-Hours per hectare		Time of Year
	Average	Premium	
Plough	1.4	1.0	Autumn drilling: may not
Seedbed Cults	2.2	1.6	
Load, Cart, Apply Fertiliser	0.3	0.2	
Drill*	0.7	0.5	Mid-March to mid-April (1) or end July to mid-Sept.
Roll	0.6	0.4	Soon after drilling
Load, Cart, Apply Fertiliser*:			
(three lots)	0.9	0.6	March to mid-August (2)
Top*	1.3	0.8	Mid-June to mid-July; if grazed only.

Notes

1. Spring drilling may continue to mid-May to enable extra cleaning cultivations or the application of farmyard manure.

2. P. and K. may be applied in September—especially on undersown ley in year sown.

* Only these operations apply where the seeds are undersown in a spring cereal crop soon after drilling. One extra harrowing and rolling is needed if undersown in an autumn-sown cereal crop.

B. Conservation

Operations	Labour-Hours per hectare Average	Premium	Time of Year
Plough	1.4	1.0	Autumn drilling: may not
Hay (5.5 tonnes per hectare)			
Mow	1.2	0.9	
Turn, etc	2.6	1.9	Two-thirds June, one-third
Bale	1.3	0.9	July
Cart	6.0	4.5	
Total per hectare	11.1	8.2	
Total per tonne	2.0	1.5	
Silage (17 tonnes per hectare)			
Mow	1.2	0.9	
Turn, etc	0.7	0.5	Two-thirds May, one-third
Load	2.3	1.7	June
Cart	3.0	2.3	
Clamp	2.3	1.7	
Total per hectare	9.5	7.1	
Total per tonne	0.56	0.42	

Specialised Equipment Prices for Grass Conservation: see page 163.

Typical Monthly Breakdown

A. Production (figures averaged over the life of the ley)

	1-year ley undersown in spring		3-year ley undersown in autumn (1)		1-year ley drilled		3-year ley drilled	
	Ave.	Prem.	Ave.	Prem.	Ave.	Prem.	Ave.	Prem.
March	0.9	0.5	0.7	0.5	0.6	0.3	0.6	0.3
April	0.9	0.5	0.7	0.5	0.6	0.3	0.6	0.3
May	0.6	0.3	0.6	0.3	0.6	0.3	0.6	0.3
June	0.6	0.3	0.6	0.3	0.6	0.3	0.6	0.3
July	0.6	0.3	0.6	0.3	0.6	0.3	0.6	0.3
August	0.3	0.2	0.3	0.2	5.0	3.4	1.9	1.4
September	0.6	0.3	0.3	0.2	3.2	2.2	1.4	1.0

Note

1. On land ploughed after a cereal crop, drilled early August to mid-September.

	1-year ley drilled in autumn (1)		3-year ley drilled in spring		Permanent Pasture	
	Ave.	Prem.	Ave.	Prem.	Ave.	Prem.
March	3.0	2.1	1.4	1.0	0.6	0.3
April	1.8	1.2	0.9	0.7	0.6	0.3
May	0.3	0.3	0.6	0.3	0.6	0.3
June	0.6	0.3	0.6	0.3	0.6	0.3
July	0.6	0.3	0.6	0.3	0.6	0.3
August	0.3	0.2	0.2	0.2	0.3	0.2
September	—	—	—	0.2	0.2	0.2
October	0.9	0.5	0.6	0.3	—	—
November	1.4	1.0	1.0	0.3	—	—
December	0.7	0.5	0.6	0.2	—	—

B. Conservation

| | Hay | | | | Silage | | | |
| | per hectare | | per tonne | | per hectare | | per tonne | |
	Av.	Prem.	Av.	Prem.	Av.	Prem.	Av.	Prem.
May	—	—	—	—	6.3	4.7	0.37	0.28
June	7.4	5.6	1.3	1.0	3.2	2.4	0.19	0.14
July................	3.7	2.6	0.7	0.5	—	—	—	—

KALE

(Growing only)

A. Production

| | Labour-Hours per hectare | | |
Operations	Average	Premium	Time of Year
Plough...	1.4	1.0	September onwards
Seedbed Cults	2.2	1.6	March, April, early May
Fertiliser.....................................	0.3	0.2	April, early May
Drill..	1.3	1.0	May
Roll..	0.6	0.4	Straight after drilling
Spray (weedkiller).......................	0.3	0.2	6 weeks after drilling

B. Catch Crop

Kale may be drilled up to the first week of July; the crop will be smaller but either an early bite or silage crop may have been taken from a ley earlier in the year, or the ground may have been fallowed and thoroughly cleaned during the spring and early summer. The smaller crop is also easier to graze using an electric fence.

The above operations will still apply although the times of the year will obviously be different, but there may be an additional three or so rotavations and two or three heavy cultivations if fallowed for the first half of the year or ploughed after an early bite. This means approximately an extra 10 (average) or 8 (premium) man-hours per hectare in April, May, June.

FIELD SCALE VEGETABLES

(Labour hours per hectare unless otherwise stated)

Cabbage Transplanting	Hand 150-160. Spring cabbage, Sept.-Oct.; summer, April; autumn, May-June Machine (3.5 gang). Spring cabbage 75, summer 85, autumn 100. Pulling and dipping plants. 20 per hectare transplanted.
Cabbage Harvesting	Early spring cabbage, 210, Feb.-April; hearted spring, 250, April-June; summer, 220, June-July; autumn, 220, Oct.-Dec.
Brussels Sprouts Transplanting	45 (machine) to 55 (hand), May-June.
Brussels Sprouts Picking	320-400: picked over 3-5 times, maximum approx. 3 hectares per picker per season. Early sprouts, Aug.-Dec.; late, Nov.-Mar.
Peas Hand Pulling	475-525 (150 per tonne). Early, June; maincrop, July-Aug.
Runner Beans (Picked)	Harvesting. 625 (175 per tonne), July-Sept.
Runner Beans (Stick)	Harvesting. 675, July-Sept.
Runner Beans (Stick)	Erecting Canes and String. 100-150, May-June.

Carrot Harvesting.	Elevator-digger: 260 (1 man + 12 casuals, 20 hours per hectare). Earlies, July-Aug.; maincrop, Sept.-Feb.
	Harvester: 30 (3 men, 10 hours per hectare). Riddle and Grade: (1° per tonne), Dec.-Feb.
Beetroot Harvest and Clamp.	25, Oct.-Dec. 12-15 man-hours per tonne to wash and pack.

Source: The Farm as a Business, Aids to Management, Section 6: Labour and Machinery (M.A.F.F.). (N.B. This data is now very dated, but it is still the latest known to the author.)

4. LABOUR FOR LIVESTOCK

DAIRY COWS

Time Required per Cow Depending on Yield.

Yield of Cow	5,500	7,000	8,000	9,000
	hours per cow per month			
January	2.0	2.5	3.1	3.8
February	1.9	2.5	3.1	3.8
March	1.8	2.5	3.1	3.8
April	1.6	2.4	3.0	3.8
May	1.6	2.1	2.7	3.5
June	1.6	2.1	2.6	3.2
July	1.6	2.1	2.6	3.2
August	1.6	2.1	2.6	3.2
September	1.6	2.2	2.8	3.5
October	1.8	2.4	3.1	3.8
November	1.9	2.5	3.1	3.8
December	2.0	2.5	3.1	3.8
Total per Cow per Year	21	27.9	34.9	43.2
Average Seconds per Litre	*13.7*	*14.3*	*15.7*	*17.3*

No time is allocated here for dairy young stock. This schedule is based on a 100-cow herd. Low yielding cows tend to spend more time at grass and less housed. High milk yielders take more management time.
13.7 seconds per litre = 1 man per 725,000L
17.3 seconds per litre = 1 man per 575,000L
The most labour efficient milk producing operations in the UK achieve over 800,000 litres per employed man.

Hours staff Requirement per Cow per Year.

	Cow Annual Milk Yield (L)			
	5,500	7,000	8,000	9,000
Cows per Herd				
60	21.9	29.1	36.4	45.0
100	21.0	27.9	34.9	43.2
150	20.0	26.6	33.2	41.1
300	17.5	23.3	29.1	36.0
500	15.0	19.9	24.9	30.9

Labour Cost Per Litre

	Cow Annual Milk Yield (L)			
ppl	5,500	7,000	8,000	9,000
Cows per Herd				
60..	3.75	3.92	4.29	4.72
100..	3.6	3.76	4.11	4.53
150..	3.43	3.58	3.92	4.31
300..	3.00	3.13	3.43	3.77
500..	2.57	2.68	2.92	3.23

Note

Earnings. The average earnings of 'dairy herdsmen' in 2009 are estimated to be approximately £26,100 a year and working 2770 hours (10 hours for 277 days). This labour cost includes relief milking etc but no cover for young stock or fieldwork, such as hay and silage making

DAIRY FOLLOWERS AND BEEF

Note

No recent survey work has been published on labour requirements for beef animals and dairy followers. The following data can therefore only be taken as 'best estimates'. They are for average performance under average conditions, excluding fieldwork.
Substantial variations can occur from farm to farm, e.g. through differing management styles or economies of scale with differing herd sizes.

A. Calves (per head, early weaning)

	Labour hours per month	
Age Group	Average	Premium
0-3 months..	2.3	1.6
3-6 months..	0.9	0.6
(av. 0-6 months..	1.6	1.1)
6-12 months, yarded....................................	1.1	0.8
6-12 months, summer grazed..........................	0.3	0.2
(av. 0-12 months, during winter (1)................	1.3	0.9)
(av. 0-12 months, during summer (1)................	0.9	0.6)

Note

1. Assuming 6 to 12-month olds housed in winter and grazed in summer, and calvings or calf purchases fairly evenly spaced throughout the year.

B. Stores (per head)

Yearling, housed....................................	1.0	0.7
2 year olds and over, housed......................	1.4	0.8
Out-wintered store..................................	0.7	0.5
12 months and over, summer grazed.............	0.2	0.1

C. Dairy Followers

(Per 'replacement unit', i.e. calf + yearling + in-calf heifer.) (1)		
During winter.......................................	2.9	2.0
During summer......................................	1.2	0.8

1. Assuming calvings fairly evenly spaced throughout the year and heifers calving at 2 to 2.5 years old.

D. *Beef Finishing* (per head)

Housed...	1.8	1.2
Summer Grazed..................................	0.2	0.1
Intensive Beef (0-12 months)...................	1.3	1.0

E. *Suckler Herds (per cow)*

Lowland Single suckling (av. whole year)......	0.9	0.6
Lowland Multiple suckling (av. whole year)...	2.9	2.1
Upland/Hill Single suckling (av. whole year)...	1.1	0.7

SHEEP
(per ewe)

	Labour hours per month	
	Average	Premium (4)
January...	0.3	0.2
February..	0.3	0.2
March..	1.0 (1)	0.7
April...	0.4	0.25
May...	0.3	0.2
June..	0.4 (2)	0.3
July...	0.2	0.15
August...	0.2	0.15
September...	0.25	0.15
October..	0.25	0.15
November...	0.2	0.15
December...	0.2	0.15
Total..	4.0 (3)	2.75

1. Assuming mainly March lambing.

2. 0.3 if shearing is by contract.

3. A full-time shepherd, i.e. one who did no other work on the farm, would have to have a flock of at least 600 ewes for the average 4 hours per ewe per year to be achieved, assuming full-time assistance during lambing time.

4. In a national survey conducted in 1999 the average annual requirement for flocks exceeding 500 ewes was 2.9 hours.

PIGS

Age Group	Labour hours per month	
	Average	Premium
Breeding and Rearing, per sow...............................	1.5	1.20
(Average 130 sows per worker, Premium 160)		
Feeding only, per 10 pigs......................................	1.6	1.25
No. at a time, per worker:		
Average 1,200 per man, Premium 1,600		
No. per year, per worker:		
Average: 6,000 porkers, 4,800 cutters, 4,450 baconers		
Premium: 8,000 porkers, 6,400 cutters, 5,750 baconers		
Breeding, Rearing and Feeding, per sow (with progeny)		
Porkers, average 90 sows per worker, premium 110.........	2.4	2.0
Cutters, average 80-85 sows per worker, premium 100-105	2.6	2.1
Baconers, average 75-80 sows per worker, premium 95-100	2.8	2.2

POULTRY
(large scale, automated)

	Labour hours per month
Laying hens: battery cages (18,000 per full-time worker)	1.1 per 100
free range	4 per 100
Broilers: 32,500 at a time per full-time worker*	
(225,000 a year)	1.0 per 100

* N.B. additional help needed for catching and cleaning out (included in labour hours per month)

V. MACHINERY

1. AGRICULTURAL MACHINERY PRICES

This schedule of prices is estimated for spring 2009 purchase of new machinery, net of discounts and ex. V.A.T. Machinery inflation has been subdued over the last decade compared with most other benchmark inflation indicators (mainstream and agricultural). Over the seven years between 1997 and 2004, machinery inflation totalled only 1.1 per cent. Since then, inflationary pressures have affected machinery prices by much more, with overall rises in 2005 of 8%, 2006, 4.2% and 2007 of 5.4%. Over the forthcoming year, it is expected that the cost of machinery is likely to increase by considerably more as several factors have simultaneously affected the cost of inputs to make the machines. These include the cost of steel, the doubling of the cost of fuel required to make the machinery and the weakening of sterling by 18% against the euro, the region where much machinery is imported from.

1. Tractors

		£
(a)	Two-Wheel Drive	
	43-49 kW (57-66 hp)	20,000-23,700
	50-56 kW (67-75 hp)	21,200-26,800
	57-66 kW (76-89 hp)	24,200-29,500
	67-75 kW (90-100 hp)	26,800-31,900
(b)		Four-Wheel Drive
	43-50 kW (57-67 hp)	19,400-28,300
	56-65 kW (75-87 hp)	26,800-33,000
	66-75 kW (88-100 hp)	33,000-38,400
	76-90 kW (101-120 hp)	36,600-46,000
	94-105 kW (125-140 hp)	44,300-55,100
	115-134 kW (154-180 hp)	55,100-66,900
	140-165 kW (187-220 hp)	64,400-70,800
	170-200 kW (228-268 hp)	82,200-94,400
(c)		High Road Speed (50 Km /hour)
	15-130 kW (155-175 hp)	60,000-73,700
	140-165 kW (188-221 hp)	73,700-85,900
(d)		Crawlers
	175-225 kW (230-300 hp) rubber track	132,000-145,000
	225-300 kW (340-400 hp) rubber track	152,000-177,000
	336-410 kW (450-550 hp) rubber track	184,000-203,000

2. Cultivating Equipment

£

(a) Ploughs	Fixed width	Variable width	
		Mechanical Adjustment	Hydraulic Adjustment
Reversible:			
3-furrow	7,400-8,200	8,200-10,400	—
4-furrow	8,700-9,800	9,500-12,900	12,900-18,800
5-furrow	9,800-11,000	11,100-14,600	15,100-19,500
6-furrow		14,300-18,300	17,300-21,400
6-furrow (semi-mounted)		16,800-19,400	19,200-18,900
7-furrow (semi-mounted)		18,100-20,700	20,000-25,400
8-furrow (semi-mounted)		23,100-25,900	23,900-29,000
9-furrow (semi-mounted)			27,800-33,600

(b) *Furrow Presses*

1.6-1.8 m double row	2,900-3,600
2.0-2.4 m double row	3,400-4,600
2.6-3.0 m double row	4,400-6,500
3.2-3.6 m double row	6,500-8,100
3.8-4.0 m double row	7,800-9,000
Front Press Arm – hydraulic	1,500-1,600

(c) *Front Presses (excluding linkage)*

1.5 m single row	2,300-2,600
3.0 m single row	3,500-4,900
4.0 m single row — hydraulic folding	5,200-6,400

(d) *Front Press Linkage*

1.5 to 2.0 tonne	2,000-2,300
3.5 to 5.5 tonne	2,700-3,400

(e) *Other Cultivating Equipment*

Sub Soiler 2-3 leg		2,600-3,300
Soil Looseners	(3 m)	6,000-7,300
	(4 m)	9,300-10,600
Vibrating Compaction Breaker	(2-2.5m)	6,800-8,100
	(3 m)	9,300-10,600
Straw Incorporating Disc Cultivator	(2.5-3 m)	7,600-8,800
Stubble Cultivator	(3 m):	5,200-6,000
(heavy duty)	(4 m): hydraulic folding	9,300-10,600
	(6 m): hydraulic folding	13,400-16,100
Spring-tine Cultivator	(3-4 m):	2,200-3,200
	(5-6 m): hydraulic folding	6,000-7,200
Combination Harrows	(2.5-4 m)	4,500-7,100
	(5-6 m): hydraulic folding	12,000-12,900
Levelling Harrows	(2.5-4.2 m)	1,600-2,600
	(3.7-6.1 m): hydraulic folding.	3,300-4,900
Disc Harrows	(2.7-3.6 m): trailed	12,100-13,300
	(4.25-6.25 m): trailed, , folding	21,300-31,100
Harrows (5-6 m): light-medium, hydraulic folding		2,100-2,500
Rotovator	(up to 100 kW tractor)	7,100-8,400
	(150 kW tractor)	11,500-12,900
Power Harrow (with packer roller)		
	(2.5-3 m)	6,400-7,300
	(3.5-4m)	9,200-10,700
	(5-6m): folding	20,100-22,600
Rolls: triple gang, hydraulic folding	(6 m)	7,100-8,400
five gang, " "	(12m)	17,000-18,700

3. *Fertiliser Distributors, Seed Drills, Sprayers* £

(a) *Fertiliser Distributors*

Mounted Spinners

(500-750 litre)	1,600-2,100
(700-1,200 litre): twin disc, hydraulic control1	2,300-2,900
(1,300-1,700 litre): twin disc, hydraulic control	3,800-4,200
(1,650-2,300 litre): twin disc, electronic control	6,400-7,000

| | | (3,200 litre): twin disc, electronic control.................. | 8,300-8,500 |
| | | Bag lifter (850-1,000kg) .... | 1,600-1,900 |

(b) *Seed Drills*

Grain: mounted	3 m, gravity fed, 25 row	6,400-7,900
	3-4 m, pneumatic, 24-32 row ..	13,100-16,000
	6 m, pneumatic, 48 row	26,000-30,600

(c) *Combined Cultivator and Pneumatic Drill*

| 3-4 m, 24-32 row .... | 18,500-22,200 |
| 6 m, 48 row.............................. | 37,200-42,000 |

(d) *Combined Power Harrow and Pneumatic Drill*

| 3-4 m, 24-32 row .... | 19,700-26,400 |
| 6 m, 48 row.............................. | 35,600-52,200 |

(e) *Direct Drill*

| 6m, 32 chisel openers.. | 64,800-72,000 |

(f) *Sprayers*

Mounted, 600-800 litre tank, 12 m boom............................	3,800-4,300
Mounted, 1,000-1,300 litre tank, 20-24 m hydraulic boom ..	15,700-19,800
Mounted, Air Assisted, 1,000 litre tank, 18 m boom............	22,200-26,600
Trailed, Air Assisted, 2,500-3,000 litre tank, 24 m boom.....	39,600-45,600
Trailed, 2,500-3,000 litre tank 18-24 m boom	29,400-33,000
Trailed, 3,000-3,500 litre tank 24-30 m boom	34,200-39,600
Self-propelled, 24-36 m boom, 4-wheel drive......................	76,000-92,000

4. Grass Conservation and Handling Equipment

£

(a) *Silage Equipment*

Forage Harvester: trailed, precision chop............................	25,200-33,300
Self-propelled (3 m pick-up 280-375 hp).............................	127,000-144,000
Maize attachment, 4-6 row	25,200-33,000
Silage Trailer, 12 tonne, tandem axle	6,900-8,300
Silage Trailer, 14 tonne, tandem axle	7,800-9,800
Silage Trailer, 16 tonne, tandem axle	9,700-11,000
Buckrake (push off)	2,000-2,300

(b) *Haymaking Equipment*

Mower (1.6-1.8 m, 2 drum)	2,400-3,200
Mower (2.0-2.4 m, 5-6 disc).....................................	4,300-4,900
Mower (disc) Conditioner, mounted (2.4-3.2 m)	8,900-10,200
Mower (disc) Conditioner, trailed (2.8-3.2 m)......................	14,000-15,200
Tedder (5-7 m, 4-6 rotors)	4,400-7,000
Windrower, (3.9-4.2 m)	4,200-4,800
Balers and Bale Handling: see 5(c) and (d) below

(c) *Silage Handling Equipment*

Silage shear bucket (1-1.2 m)..	2,300-3,400
Silage grab...	1,700-2,200
Big Bale Silage Feeder, mounted	6,400-8,300
Diet-feeder Wagon (8-14 m)	22,200-26,800
Clamp Silage Mixer (12-18m^3)	21,500-27,400

5. Grain and Straw Harvesting and Handling Equipment £

(a) Combines

Engine size kW (hp)	Cutterbar width metres (feet)	
150-165 (200-220)	4.5-5.0 (14-16)	105,000-110,000
165-185 (220-249)	4.5-5.5 (14-18)	112,000-153,000
186-223 (250-299)	5.4-6.1 (18-20)	122,000-166,000
223-298 (300-399)	6.0-7.7 (20-25)	147,000-234,000
Over 300 (400 up to 530)	9.0-9.15 (25-30)	222,000-342,000

(b) Yield monitoring/mapping *7,200-9,000*

(c) Pick-up Balers (twine tying)

Small rectangular bales	10,000-11,200
Small rectangular bales, heavy duty models	12,500-15,000
Big round bales, twine tying and net wrap	17,500-21,200
High density rectangular bales	68,000-75,500

(d) Bale Wrappers

Big Bale Wrapper: mounted/trailed	10,000-11,300
Big Square Bale Wrapper: mounted	15,000-16,300
Combined Baler and Wrapper	41,300-48,500
Bale Trailers, 5-8 tonne	3,100-4,100
Accumulator, flat 8, mechanical	2,100-2,700
Loader, flat 8	880-1,200
Big Bale Spike	200-320
Big Bale Handler	650-950
Big Bale Shredder, silage or straw	6,300-7,500

(e) Drying, Handling, Food Processing Equipment

Grain driers and Grain storage: see pages 163 and 181	
Cleaner/grader, 10-20 tonnes/hour	9,400-13,300
Grain augers 100 mm, 3.3-7.3 m	590-770
Grain augers 150 mm, 6-8.5 m, with trolley	1,900-2,400
Grain conveyors, (25-50t/hour)	1,400-1,900 + 140-180 per m
Specific gravity separator, (5-10t/hour)	15,000-17,800
Bucket elevator, (25-50t/hour)	2,000-2,700 + 180-240 per m
Hammer mill, 7.5-15 kW	3,400-3,800
Roller mill, 4-5.5 kW	3,000-3,500
Mixer, 750-1000 kg	3,800-4,500
Mill and mixer, 1,000-1,300kg, 3.7-5.5 kW	6,200-7,600
Grain weigher, 25 tonne/hour	1,900-2,200

6. Potato, Sugar Beet and Vegetable Machinery £

(a) Potato Machinery

Stone separator, 1.6 m (1 bed)		42,000-48,000
Bedformer, 2 row		3,800-4,200
Bed cultivator, 1.7-1.8 m (1 bed)		7,900-8,500
Planter:	2 row mounted	10,200-12,700
	4 row mounted	31,800-36,000
Haulm pulveriser:	2 row	6,400-7,200
	2 row cross conveyor	9,800-10,000
Elevator-Digger,	2 row	6,400-7,200
Harvesters (trailed):	2 row, elevator manned/unmanned	70,000-83,000

	2 row, 6 tonne bunker	90,000-106,000
	4 row, self-propelled	125,000-180,000
Store loader (heavy duty)		23,800-28,000
Flat belt conveyor, 3-8 m		2,200-3,600
Soil elevator (rubber belt)		6,600-7,200
Self-unloading hopper, 3-5 tonnes		9,600-10,800
Clod separator		9,600-10,800
Sizer, 5-30 tonnes/hour		9,600-14,400
Sponge drier, 0.9-1.2m		13,200-14,400
Barrel washer, 8-10 tonnes/hour		19,200-21,600
Roller inspection table, 1.2 x 2.4 m		3,600-4,200
Weigher, automatic, 8-10 tonnes/hour		6,000-7,200
Box tipper with cross conveyor		16,800-19,200
Box filer, automatic		14,400-15,600
Bag stitcher (hand held)		950-1,200
Complete out of store grading line:	20 tonnes/hour	36,000-44,000
	30 tonnes/hour	84,000-90,000
Box filler (30 tonnes/hour)		13,200-16,200

(b) **Sugar Beet Machinery**

Precision Drill:	6 row (pneumatic)	10,200-12,000
	12 row-18 row (pneumatic)	20,400-31,800
Hoe:	6 row-12 row (heavy duty)	6,700-12,700
Harvesters:	Trailed, 2 row, tanker	63,600-70,000
	Trailed, 3 row, tanker	76,800-84,000
	Trailed, 4 row, tanker	89,000-96,000
Self-propelled, 6 row, 18 tonne tank		304,000-343,000
Cleaner-loader, with engine, 1-3 tonnes per minute		25,200-28,800
Fodder beet harvester		7,000-7,700

(c) **Vegetable Machinery**

Onion windrower		9,400-10,800
Root crop digger:	1 webb	6,600-7,200
	2 webbs	7,700-9,000
Top lifting vegetable harvester:	single row, bunker	50,000-57,600
	twin row, bunker/elevator	89,000-108,000
	four row, elevator	114,000-134,000
	four row, self-propelled	305,000-330,000
Leek harvester (mounted)		19,000-31,800

7. General   £

Trailer, 4 tonne tipping	2,400-2,800
Trailer, 5-6 tonne tipping; grain/silage	3,200-3,900/3,900-4,400
Trailer, 10 tonne tipping, tandem axle; grain/silage	5,800-6,300/7,000-7,600
F.Y.M. Spreaders, (6 - 8 tonne)	5,000-6,400
F.Y.M. Spreaders, (10 - 12 tonne)	7,000-9,900
F.Y.M. Spreaders, (12 - 14 tonne)	9,000-13,000
Loaders, front mounted	4,400-5,000
Pallet loader, self levelling (1,000-1,600 kg)	5,000-6,300
Materials Handler, telescopic boom (2.5-3.0 tonne)	40,800-48,000
Skid steer loader (500-600 kg)	16,800-19,200
Slurry Stores (metal), including base for 120 day storage period for:	
100 cows	£250 per cow

200 cows	£230 per cow
400 cows	£200 per cow
Vacuum Tankers (5,000-6,000 litre)	5,000-5,600
Low Ground Pressure Tankers (9,000-11,000 litre)	10,800-12,800
Slurry pump	3,800-4,400
Cattle crush	1000-1,400
Cattle crush with weigher	2,000-2,300
Cattle trailer (twin-axle)	2,300-3,000
Yard scrapers	660-850
Rotary brush (2-2.5 m)	1,800-2,300
Grassland roll, ballastable (2.5-3 m)	1,100-1,300
Pasture topper (2.0-3.0 m)	2,300-3,200
Hedger: hydraulic angling; flail head	11,600-14,400
Ditcher: fully slewing	9,000-10,200
Carrier box	600-700
Post hole digger/driver	1,200-1,550/1,900-3,000
Saw bench	1,900-2,200
Log splitter	750-950

2. TYPICAL CONTRACTORS' CHARGES, AVERAGE FARMERS' COSTS, AND RATES OF WORK FOR VARIOUS FARM OPERATIONS

Contractors' charges vary widely according to many factors: those given below are estimates for 2009. Farmer-contractors often charge less, since their overheads and machinery fixed costs are largely considered covered by their own farming operations, but the service may not always be so complete, including specialist advice.

Farmers' own costs (which include the value of the farmers' own manual labour) vary even more widely; those given below (estimated for 2009) are averages in every respect — covering different types of soil, size of farm, and so on; they are based on accounting cost procedures in that labour, tractor and machinery fuel, repairs and depreciation are included — but no allowance has been added for general farm overheads, interest on capital, supervision/management or under-occupied labour during slack times. They assume four-wheel drive 75-90 kW (100-120 hp) tractors for ploughing, heavy cultivation and other work with a high power requirement. Four-wheel drive 55-65 kW (75-87 hp) tractors are assumed to be used for most other operations. The figures should not be used for partial budgeting.

For a typical set of farm operations, excluding harvesting, the breakdown of the farmers' costs averages very approximately one third each for labour, tractors and implements/machines. The larger the farm, the lower the labour element and the higher the machine element are likely to be and vice versa. However the input from contractors may affect these costs.

The contract charges and average farmers' costs are put side-by-side for tabular convenience, not to facilitate comparisons. Apart from the fact that contractors' charges must cover expenses omitted from the farmers' cost, the advisability or otherwise of hiring a contractor for a particular job depends on many factors, varying widely according to farm circumstances; furthermore, there are advantages and disadvantages not reflected in a cost comparison alone.

Assumptions: The contractors' costs are particularly sensitive to many factors. These include input costs, capital machinery prices, and demand versus local competition. Of these, fuel has doubled in the preceding 12 months and at the time the data was struck, was at 65ppl for tractor diesel and the average price inflation of machinery is forecast to be as much as 20% for some sectors for the year to September 2009. These two factors alone may have considerable effect on the movement of these prices throughout the year. Fuel is included in the contractors' costings.

Machinery rings. Prices charged by farmers offering services through machinery rings are extremely variable but are generally between average farmers' costs and contractors' charges. There are exceptions, which mainly relate to relatively expensive items of machinery (e.g. precision drills, destoners and combine harvesters), where the charges for services offered through machinery rings are close to and often less than average farmers' costs.

Four-wheel drive 120-150 kW (150-200 hp) tractors are assumed where appropriate to achieve the 'Premium' rates of work (which will be achieved on most farms with more than 200 hectares (500 acres) of arable land); obviously, still larger wheeled tractors and crawlers could achieve still faster rates of work, particularly on light land. The rates of work include preparation, travelling to and from the fields and allow for minor breakdowns and other stoppages. See further page 148, first paragraph.

All charges and costs below are per hectare unless otherwise stated.

Average Contractors and Farmers Costs of Performing Certain Mechanical Operations.

Operation	Contract Charge	Farmer's Average Cost	Rate of Work (Ha per 8 Hr day)	
	£/ha	£/ha	Average	Premium
Cultivations				
Ploughing (light/heavy soils)	48.40-52.10	54-71	5-6½	7½-9
with furrow press	Extra £7.70	62-83	4½-6%	7-8½
Deep Ploughing (over 300 mm)	58.30	87-108	3-3¾	5-6½
Rotovating ploughed land	57.00	93	4½	6
grass		139	3	4
Subsoiling	48.20	49	6	10
Stubble Cultivating	33.10	27	12	16
Heavy Disc Cultivating	39.90	39	10	15
Disc Harrowing	32.90	20	12	16
Chain Harrowing	14.80			
Power Harrowing	40.30	37	10	15
Spring tine Harrowing	23.70	20	12	18
Seedbed Harrowing	21.20	17	12	20
Rolling (flat 3-4 tonne)	20.10	28	6	10
(ring, set of 3, 6 m)	14.20	15	15	25
Fertiliser Distributing				
(including loading and carting):				
Broadcast (125-375 kg/ha)	10.10 (fert. in field)	7.80	30	60
Broadcast (500-750 kg/ha)		12.60	22.5	45
Broadcast (1,000-1,250 kg/ha).		19.00	15	30
Pneumatic (125-375 kg/ha)		17.60	25	40
Liquid Fertilising	21.10			
Drilling:				
Cereals : conventional	30.40	25.80	14	18
Cereals : combi-drilling	52.90	46.30	10	14
Direct Drilling	43.20			
One-pass tillage train	46.70			
Grass Broadcasting	16.70	19.00	11	15
Roots/Maize (inc. fertiliser)	42.90	77.60	3½ (4 row)	5 (6 row)
Sugar Beet - precision drill	43.50	45.60	6 (6 row)	10 (12 row)
Destoning potato land	216.00	230	3.25	4
Potato Planting automatic		149	2½ (2 row)	3½
Potato Ridging	50.00	36.00	5½	7
Spraying (excl. materials):				
(extra £1-£2 for < 20ha)	16.00			
Low volume (to 175 l/ha)	11.20	9.80	35	75
Medium vol.(200-300 l/ha)		11.40	30	60
High vol. (over 800 l/ha)		20.30	25	50
Tractor Hoeing Sugar Beet		45.30	5	8

Operation	Contract Charge £/ha	Farmer's Average Cost £/ha	Rate of Work (Ha per 8 Hr day) Average	Premium
Combine Harvesting:				
Combine Harvesting Cereals:			(hectares per hour)	
100 ha/year		146	¾-1	1-1¾
200 ha/year	79.50	96	1	1½
300 ha/year		84	1½	2
600 ha/year		73	2¾	3¼
Carting to barn add	29.20	21.20/hr		
Straw Chopper incorporated	6.00			
Seed Autocast on combine	11.10			
Straw chopping (sep. operation).	40.40			
Combining				
Oilseed rape (windrowed)	80.70	as cereals + 10%	⅔-1	¾-1¼
Oilseed rape (direct)	80.90			
Beans	80.00	as cereals + 10%	⅔-1	¾-1¼
Peas	82.80	As cereals	¾-1	1-1½
Windrowing Oilseed Rape	42.00		1.2	1.4
Potato Harvesting				
2-row unmanned	556		0.75	2
2-row manned inc. carting	950			
Sugar Beet Harvesting				
Excluding Carting	272	233	3.5	4.5
Extra for Carting	30.90			

Baling (Inc. string)				
small	44p/bale	26.0p/bale	0.8	1.25
80x70cm	2.55/bale			
120x70cm	3.90.bale			
120x130cm	5.75/bale			
round	2.25/bale	2.18		
Bale wrapping: silage	4.50/bale			
haylage	5.50/bale			

Crop Drying (inc. intake and pre-cleaning)		
Cereals:	*per tonne*	
by 6 per cent	16.50	13.70
by 10 per cent	19.70	16.30
Oilseed Rape:		
by 5 per cent	20.60	13.00
by 10 per cent	26.60	16.30
Cleaning without drying (£/t)	9.00	
Mobile Seed Cleaning		
(cereals inc. SPD)	58-64/t plus Royalty	
Grain Storage (/tonne per week)	35p	(see page 173)
Handling into store (per tonne)	1.75	£1.50
Handling out of store (/tonne)	1.75	£1.50

Operation	Contract Charge £/ha	Farmer's Average Cost £/ha	Rate of Work (Ha per 8 Hr day) Average	Premium
Grass Mowing/Topping				
Grass Mowing	26.20	28.00	8	12
Topping	27.40			
Swath Turning/Tedding	15.50	18.90	11	15
Forage Harvesting:				
First cut	62.00			
Other cuts	55.40			
Forage harvesting, carting and ensiling grass				
First cut	124.00			
Other cuts	115.00			
carting and ensiling maize				
25-30 tonnes/ha	152.00			
Manure Handling etc.				
F.Y.M.: Tractor and Spreader	35.00/hr			
F.Y.M.: Tractor and Loader	28.75/hr			
Slurry Spreading ~ Tanker	32.30/hr			
Umbilical	52.00/hr			
Lime Spreading	3.65/t			
General Rural Maintenance				
Hedge Cutting	27.15/hr			
Fence Erection per metre				
Post & Wire inc wire	3.10/m			
Post & netting inc. netting	4.00/m			
Post & rail inc. wood	11.00/m			
Tractor inc. driver and fuel	27.90/hr	20.00-32.00/hr (60 -120hp)		
Trailer (with driver and tractor)	30.00/hr	add £5.50 to above		
Livestock Husbandry				
Sheep Shearing	1.30/head			
Sheep Crutching	55p/head			
Foot Trimming ~ Sheep	62p/head			
~ Cattle	12.00/head			
General Sheep Husbandry	10.00/hour			
General Cattle Husbandry	10.00/hour			

Acknowledgement. The above estimates for contractors' charges are based in part on information kindly supplied by the National Association of Agricultural Contractors.

Contract Charge for All Operations (Cereals and Combinable Break Crops, 'stubble to stubble' i.e. up to and including Combine Harvesting and Carting the Grain to Store): £240 to £320/ha (£100-130/acre). Variations depend upon such factors as distance away, area contracted, size of fields, type of terrain, quality of soil and level of inputs (as affecting weight of crop to be harvested and carted) and local competition.

Management Agreements. The contract charge can be as low as £200/ha (£80/acre) where a significant proportion of the returns is also taken by the contractor or a neighbouring farmer after payment of a prior charge to the landowner. This was usually between £220 and £270/ha (£90-£100/acre) in 1995-8, but is now likely to average £200 to £210/ha (£80-£85/acre) owing to the fall in farm profitability. The percentage share of total gross margin less these two deductions and the running costs has been typically 70%-80% to the contractor and 20%-30% to the landowner. Arrangements where lower basic payments are made, a second band of payment rate may be introduced.

One sometimes sees farmers' total power and machinery costs compared with stubble to stubble contractors' charges. It has of course to be remembered that the former include many cost items not included in the latter, e.g. the cost of farm vehicles, fixed plant such as grain stores and general farm maintenance.

GRAIN HAULAGE COSTS

The average costs per tonne of grain (and oilseed) haulage in Great Britain over the past four seasons are summarised by the HGCA's haulage survey carried out each December. The summarised results for the years 2004 to 2007 are tabulated below:

Summary table of the HGCA Haulage Survey Results

	2004	2005	2006	2007
10 miles	£4.05	£4.29	£4.09	£4.18
20 miles	£4.52	£4.77	£4.57	£4.69
40 miles	£5.47	£5.74	£5.53	£5.72
60 miles	£6.42	£6.71	£6.50	£6.74
100 miles	£8.31	£8.65	£8.43	£8.78
150 miles	£10.68	£11.08	£10.84	£11.34

3. TRACTOR HOURS

(per annum)

A. *Crops*	per hectare	
	Average	Premium
Cereals	9	7
Straw Harvesting	3.5	2.5
Potatoes	25	15
Sugar Beet	20	12
Vining Peas	20	12
Dried Peas	10	8
Field Beans	9	7
Oilseed Rape	9	7
Herbage Seeds:		
1 year undersown or 3 year direct drilled	7	5
1 year direct drilled	11	8
Hops (machine picked)	125	—
Kale (grazed)	8	6
Turnips/Swedes: folded/lifted	12/35	10/25
Fallow	12	7
Ley Establishment:		
Undersown	2	1
Direct Seed	7	4
Making Hay	12	8
Making Silage:		
1st Cut	12	8
2nd Cut	9	6
Grazing:		
Temporary Grass	3	2.5
Permanent Grass	2	1.5

B. *Livestock*	per head
	Average
Dairy Cows	6
Other Cattle over 2 years	5
Other Cattle 1-2 years	4
Other Cattle ½-1 year	2.25
Calves 0-½ year	2.25
Housed bullocks................................	3
Sheep, per ewe	1.25
Store sheep....................................	0.8
Sows	1.75
Other pigs over 2 months........................	1
Laying Birds	0.04

1. For livestock, annual requirements are the per head requirements above multiplied by average numbers during the year (i.e. average numbers at end of each month).

2. As with labour, the number of tractors required by a farm depends more on the seasonal requirements and number required at any one time than on total annual tractor hours. These can be calculated from the seasonal labour data provided earlier in this book. The soil type and size/power of tractors purchased are obviously other relevant factors.

Tractor Power Requirements		hp/acre		hp/ha		kW/ha	
		av.	prem.	av.	prem.	av.	prem.
Combinable crops:	heavy land	.75	.65	1.85	1.5	1.4	1.1
	light land	.5	.45	1.25	1	0.95	0.75
Mixed cropping:	heavy land	1	.75	2.5	1.85	1.85	1.4
	light land	.7	.5	1.75	1.25	1.3	1.95

UK Agricultural Tractor Sales per Year (over 50 HP)

Year	Average Tractor Size kW (HP)	Number of Units Sold	Per Cent change y/y
2002	88.48 (118.6)	13,878	+20.4%
2003	94.0 (126.0)	14,445	+4.1%
2004	96.1 (128.8)	14,750	+ 2.1%
2005	95.2 (127.6)	13,068	-11.4%
2006	95.7 (128.3)	13,566	+ 3.8%
2007	100.0 (134.0)	15,540	+14.6%
2008 (to May)			+ >10%

(Data from the Agricultural Engineers Association).

4. TRACTOR COSTS

(Estimates for 2009)

	Two-Wheel Drive 43-49 kW (56-66 h.p.) £22,200		Four-Wheel Drive 56-65kW (75-85 h.p.) £31,000	
Initial Cost				
	per year £	per hour £	per year £	per hour £
Depreciation	1,332	2.66	1,938	3.88
Insurance	264	0.53	337	0.67
Repairs and Maintenance	888	1.78	1,240	2.48
Fuel and Oil	2,626	5.25	4,191	8.38
Total	5,110	10.22	7,705	15.41

	Four-Wheel Drive			
	76-90 kW (101-120 h.p.) £45,600		115-134 kW (154-180 h.p.) £51,000	
Initial Cost				
	per year £	per hour £	per year £	per hour £
Depreciation	2,964	5.93	4,270	8.54
Insurance	456	0.91	568	1.14
Repairs and Maintenance	1,824	3.65	2,440	4.88
Fuel and Oil	5,802	11.60	8,059	16.12
Total	11,047	22.09	15,337	30.67

	Crawlers			
	60 kW (80 h.p.) £27,600		200 kW (266 h.p.) £140,000	
Initial Cost				
	per year £	per hour £	per year £	per hour £
Depreciation	1,932	3.86	9,800	19.60
Insurance	294	0.59	1,215	2.43
Repairs and Maintenance	1,104	2.21	5,600	11.20
Fuel and Oil	4,126	8.25	13,754	27.51
Total	7,456	14.91	30,369	60.74

Depreciation is based on the assumption that small two-wheel drive tractors are sold for 40% of their original value after ten years and that small, medium and large four-wheel drive tractors (including crawlers) are sold for 37.5, 35 and 30% respectively of their original value after ten years. Annual repair costs have been calculated at 4 per cent of initial cost for all tractors. No interest on capital has been included. Fuel has been charged at 65 pence per litre.

The hourly figures are based on a use of 500 hours per year. A greater annual use than this will mean higher annual costs but possibly lower hourly costs. On large arable farms and contracting businesses, many tractors do over 750 hours per year, or even 1,000 in some cases. Earlier replacement at a given annual use will increase depreciation costs per hour but should reduce repair costs. The hourly figures are averages for all types of work: heavy operations such as ploughing obviously have a higher cost than light work.

5. ESTIMATING ANNUAL MACHINERY COSTS

Annual machinery costs consist of depreciation, repairs, fuel and oil, contract charges, and vehicle tax and insurance. These can be budgeted in three ways, assuming there is no available information on past machinery costs on the farm:

(a) Per hectare, by looking up an average figure for the district, according to the size and type of farm. Approximate levels are shown in the tables of whole farm fixed costs (186). This is obviously a very rough and ready measure.

(b) Per standard tractor hour. The crop area and livestock numbers can be multiplied by the appropriate standard (average) tractor hours per hectare and per head as given on page 174. The total can then be multiplied by the machinery cost per standard tractor hour as calculated from farm surveys. The following average figures (estimated for 2008/09) are based on 2001-2004 levels in South-East England.

Machinery Cost per Standard Tractor Hour per Farm Type (in South-East England)

Farm Type	Cost per Standard Tractor Hour
Mainly Sheep/Cattle, over 100 ha............................	£13.00
Sheep/Cattle and Arable, over 100 ha	£18.00
Mainly Sheep/Cattle, under 100 ha	£19.00
Mainly Dairying, under 60 ha..............................	£23.00
Mainly Dairying, over 120 ha..............................	£23.00
Mainly Arable, over 200 ha	£23.00
Dairying and Arable...	£23.00
Sheep/Cattle and Arable, under 100 ha.....................	£23.00
Mainly Dairying, 60-120 ha	£23.00
Mainly Arable, 100-200 ha.................................	£27.00
Mainly Arable, under 100 ha...............................	£42.00

Premium levels are about 15 per cent lower.

The capital element of leasing (but not the interest) is included in depreciation.

The percentage composition of the total cost (based on Cambridge, Reading and Wye Farm Business Survey data) varies with size and type of farm but averages approximately:

Depreciation	Repairs	Fuel/Elec.	Contract	VTI*
32	20	24	19	5

*Vehicle tax and insurance.

This method may be used as a check on the per hectare calculation.

(N.B. The standard tractor hour is used only as a convenient measure of machinery input. The costs incorporate not only tractor costs but all other power and machinery expenses, including field machinery and implements, fixed equipment, vans, use of farm car, etc.)

(c) Fully detailed calculation, costing and depreciating each machine in turn, including tractors, estimating repairs and fuel costs for each, and adding the charges for any contract work. The following tables give, for different types of machine, estimated life, annual depreciation, and estimated repairs according to annual use.

1. Estimated Useful Life (years) of Power Operated Machinery in relation to normal use

Equipment	25	50	100	200	300
	Annual Use (hours)				
Group 1:					
Ploughs, Cultivators, Toothed harrows, Hoes, Rolls, Ridgers, Potato planting attachments, Grain cleaners……………..	12+	12+	12+	12	10
Group 2:					
Disc harrows, Corn drills, Grain drying machines, Food grinders and mixers……	12+	12+	12	10	8
Group 3:					
Combine harvesters, Pick-up balers, Rotary cultivators, Hydraulic loaders…...	12+	12+	12	9	7
Group 4:					
Mowers, Forage harvesters, Swath turners, Side-delivery rakes, Tedders, Hedge cutting machines, Semi-automatic potato planters and transplanters, Unit root drills, Mechanical root thinners……	12+	12	11	8	6
Group 5:					
Fertiliser distributors, Combine drills, Farmyard manure spreaders, Elevator Potato diggers, Spraying machines, Pea cutter windrowers………………	10	10	9	8	7
Miscellaneous:					
Beet harvesters……………………….	11	10	9	6	5
Potato harvesters……………………	—	8	7	5	—
Milking machinery…………………	—	—	—	25	20

	500	750	1,000	1,500	2,000	2,500
	Annual Use (hours)					
Tractors…………	12+	12	10	7	6	5
Electric motors...	12+	12+	12+	12+	12	12

178

2. Depreciation: Average annual fall in value

(per cent of new price)

Age of Machine	Complex. High Depreciation Rate e.g. potato harvesters, mobile pea viners, etc.	Established machines with many moving parts, e.g. tractors, combines, balers, forage harvesters	Simple equipment with few moving parts, e.g. ploughs, trailers
	%	%	%
1	40	30	20
2	27½	20	15
3	20*	16*	12½
4	17½†	14½	11½
5	15‡	13†	10½*
6	13½	12	9½
7	12	11	9
8	11	10‡	8½†
9	(10)	9½	8
10	(9½)	8½	7½‡

* Typical frequency of renewal with heavy use.

† Typical frequency of renewal with average use.

‡Typical frequency of renewal with light use.

Tractors. For the results of a study giving variations in tractor depreciation according to size and annual use as well as age when sold see P. Wilson and S. Davis, 'Estimating Depreciation in Tractors in the UK (etc)', 'Farm Management', Vol. 10, No. 4, Winter 1998/99, pp. 183-193.

3. Depreciation: Percentage rates

A. Straight-Line

Trade-in, Second-hand or Scrap Value as % of New Price

Years Retained	5%	10%	20%	25%	33%	40%	50%	60%
3	—	—	—	—	—	20	16	13
4	—	—	—	—	17	15	12	—
5	—	—	—	15	13	12	—	—
6	—	—	13	12	11	10	—	—
8	—	11	10	9	—	—	—	—
10	9	9	8	—	—	—	—	—
12	8	7	—	—	—	—	—	—
15	6	—	—	—	—	—	—	—

Example: If a machine costing £10,000 is retained for 8 years, at the end of which the trade-in value is 20% of the new price (i.e. £2,000), the average depreciation per annum has been £8,000 over 8 years = £1,000 (i.e. 10% of the new price).

Formula to calculate percentage = ((NP – TiV) / AoM) / NP x 100

NP   New Price

TiV   Trade in Value

AoM   Age of Machine

B. Diminishing Balances

Trade-in, Second-hand or Scrap Value as % of New Price

Years Retained	5%	10%	20%	25%	33%	40%	50%	60%
3	—	—	—	—	—	26	21	16
4	—	—	—	—	24	20	16	—
5	—	—	—	24	20	17	—	—
6	—	—	23	20	17	14	—	—
8	—	25	18	16	—	—	—	—
10	25	20	15	—	—	—	—	—
12	22	17	—	—	—	—	—	—
15	18	—	—	—	—	—	—	—

Example: If a machine costing £10,000 is retained for 4 years, at the end of which the trade-in value is 40% of the new replacement price, the annual depreciation on the diminishing balances method is: Year 1, £2,000 (i.e. 20% of £10,000); Year 2, £1,600 (i.e. 20% of £8,000 [the written-down value]); Year 3, £1,280 (i.e. 20% of £6,400); Year 4, £1,024 (20% of £5,120). The total written-down value at the end of Year 4 is therefore £4,096 (i.e. £10,000 less the total depreciation of £5,904). This is approximately 41% of the new price. (Taking the percentages in the above table to decimal places would give the trade-in prices stated more precisely).

4. Estimated Annual Cost of spares and repairs as a percentage of purchase price* at various levels of use

	Approximate Annual Use (hours)				Additional use per 100 hours
	500	750	1,000	1,500	ADD
	%	%	%	%	%
Tractors...	5.0	6.7	8.0	10.5	0.5

	Approximate Annual Use (hours)				Additional use per 100 hours
	50	100	150	200	ADD
Harvesting Machinery:	%	%	%	%	%
Combine Harvesters, self-propelled and engine-driven........................	1.5	2.5	3.5	4.5	2.0
Combine Harvesters, p.t.o. driven, metered-chop forage harvesters, pick-up balers, potato harvesters, sugar beet harvesters.....................	3.0	5.0	6.0	7.0	2.0
Other Implements and Machines:					
Group 1					
Ploughs, Cultivators, Toothed harrows, Hoes, Elevator potato diggers......................................	4.5	8.0	11.0	14.0	6.0
Group 2:					
Rotary cultivators, Mowers, Pea cutter-windrowers..................	4.0	7.0	9.5	12.0	5.0
Group 3:					
Disc harrows, Fertiliser distributors, Farmyard manure spreaders, Combine drills, Potato planters with fertiliser attachment, Sprayers, Hedge-cutting machines..	3.0	5.5	7.5	9.5	4.0
Group 4:					
Swath turners, Tedders, Side-delivery rakes, Unit drills, Flail forage harvesters, Semi-automatic potato planters and transplanters, Down-the-row thinners.............................	2.5	4.5	6.5	8.5	4.0
Group 5:					
Corn drills, Milking machines, Hydraulic loaders, Potato planting Attachments..............................	2.0	4.0	5.5	7.0	3.0
Group 6:					
Grain driers, Grain cleaners, Rolls, Hammer mills, Feed mixers Threshers..................................	1.5	2.0	2.5	3.0	0.5

* When it is known that a high purchase price is due to high quality and durability or a low price corresponds to a high rate of wear and tear, adjustments to the figures should be made.

6. IRRIGATION COSTS

(Estimated for 2009)

A. Capital Costs

1. Pumps (delivering from 20 to 200 cubic metres per hour from a surface water source, all with portable suction and delivery fittings)

Tractor pto shaft driven c/w monitoring equipment	£2,900-5,600
Diesel engine driven c/w monitoring equipment	£5,200-22,000
Electric motor driven (c/w switch gear)	£2,700-39,000
Optional remote/wireless monitoring controls	£2,200-5,600

2. Pipelines (averages per m)

Portable: (excl. valve take offs) 50mm, £2.70; 75 mm, £3.25; 100 mm, £4.90; 125 mm, £5.90; 150 mm, £8.50; (incl. valve take offs) 75 mm, £5.10; 100 mm, £6.50; 125 mm, £7.50; 150mm, £10.80.

Permanent Underground P.V.C. pipe 12.5 bar rating (supply and laying) per metre: 75 mm, £4.90; 100 mm, £6.00; 150/160 mm, £8.40; 200 mm, £11.90; 250mm, £16.00.

Hydrants: 100 mm x 100 mm, £216; 150 mm x 125 mm, £260.

3. Application Systems

   (a) Traditional portable hand move sprinkler systems

       75mm (3 inch) diameter. Sprinkler line assemblies:

1 move/day/six day cycle	£850/ha
2 moves/day/six day cycle	£450/ha
3 moves/day/six day cycle	£310/ha

   (b) Solid set sprinkler lines – semi-permanent systems

       63mm dia. pipework assemblies at

18m x 18m triangulated spacings	£1,475/ha
As above but infra-red automated hand-held controls	£1,700/ha

   (c) Drip irrigation systems

       16.5mm non-recoverable tape (excluding header mains, control valves and filtration equipment)   £400/ha

   (d) Hose reel systems using rain guns (average cost per machine)

		Manual controls	Electric Controls
Small	6-15m³/hr	£4,300	–
Medium	20-40m³/hr	£10,800	£12,400
Large	40-80m³/hr	£15,100	£16,700

   (e) Hose reel systems using irrigation booms (average cost per unit)

Small including	20m boom	£ 7,800
Medium including	40/50m boom	£14,500
Large including	70/80m boom	£29,000

   (f) Pivot and linear systems

Small pivot	200m radius (12.5ha)	£1,400/ha full circle
Large pivot	600m radius (113ha)	£835/ha full circle
Linear machine (dependent on length)		£1,600-2,250/ha

4. *Total*

If no source works are needed, as with water from a river, or pond, total capital costs are likely to vary between £1,100 and £2,150 per hectare requiring irrigation at regular intervals, depending on the levels of sophistication and automation of the system installed.

B. *Water Sources*

An abstraction licence is required if more than 20m^3 of water per day are taken from surface or underground sources. If abstracting more than 10mi^3 per day in Scotland, you must obtain authorisation from SEPA. If abstracting less than 10mi^3 per day in Scotland, and comply with certain General Binding Rules (GBR) you do not require authorisation. Abstraction charges vary widely, depending on the region, season and whether or not the source is supported by Environment Agency operations. Winter abstraction charges (authorised between 1st November to 31st March) typically range from £2 to £3 per 1000m^3 and summer rates (authorised between 1st April to 31st October) from £15 to £30 per 1000m^3 for sources that are not supported by the Environment Agency operations. Abstraction charges during the summer can be up to £100 per 1000m^3 in areas where supplies are supported by Environment Agency operations. A charge of £3 per 1000m^3 equals 75p per 25mm hectare whilst a charge of £25 per 1000m^3 would cost £6.25 per hectare per 25mm application. Mains water at 107p per m^3 would cost £265 per application of 25mm per hectare.

New time limited abstraction licences are difficult to obtain, especially for summer abstraction. Hence there is an increasing trend towards constructing reservoirs that can be used to store water abstracted during the winter months. The cost of clay-lined reservoirs varies widely but would typically be of the order of £1 per m^3 of water stored. The cost of storing 4546m^3 (1 million gallons) could easily be £4,000. This price could double if the reservoir is lined and fenced.

A subsistence charge is payable, calculated by a formula combining the following factors together:

- Volume – annual licensed
- Whether the source is Environment Agency unsupported, supported or tidal
- Season – summer, winter or all year round
- Level of losses
- A minimum charge of £25

An application charge of £135 and advertising administration charge of £100 is due, alongside a standard unit charge (SUC), a charge for the region in which the abstraction is authorised to be made. For 2008/09 they are:

Region	2008/09 Standard Unit Charges (£/1000m^3)
Anglian	25.18
Midlands	14.31
Northumbria	25.36
Yorkshire	11.17
North West	13.22
Southern	18.42
South West including Wessex	19.71
Thames	13.53
EA Wales	13.49

C. Overall Operating Costs

Because of variations in individual farm circumstances in terms of source works and the irrigation system used the overall cost of applying 25mm per hectare can range widely, from £60 to £120. Very sophisticated systems distributing mains water over intensive specialist crops could be much more expensive.

Note:

The (approximate) imperial equivalents for metric values commonly used in irrigation are as follows:

1 cubic metre = 1,000 litres = 220 gallons.

A pump capacity of 100 cubic metres per hour is equivalent to 22,000 gallons per hour (366 gallons per minute).

In terms of water storage 1,000 cubic metres (1 million litres) is equivalent to 220,000 gallons (1 million gallons = 4,546 cubic metres).

1,000 cubic metres is sufficient to apply 25 millimetres of water over 4 hectares, which is approximately equivalent to applying 1 inch over 10 acres. An acre inch is therefore 101 cubic meters (22,000 gallons), or a hectare centimetre is 100 cubic meters.

7. FIELD DRAINAGE

(Estimated for 2009)

1. Installation (costs per metre of excavating a trench, supplying and laying the pipe and backfilling with soil).

Plastic pipes:	60mm diameter	1.70—2.00
	80mm diameter	2.00—2.55
	100mm diameter	2.90—3.10
	125mm diameter	3.90—4.20
	150mm diameter	4.40—5.00
	300mm diameter	12.00—13.50

The above rates apply to schemes of 5 hectares or more; smaller areas and patching up work can cost up to 50% more.

Supplying and laying permeable backfill to within 375mm of ground level will add between £2.60 and £3.30 per metre to costs.

Digging new open ditches (1.8m top width, 0.9m depth) costs £1.90-£2.45 per metre compared with improving existing ditches at £1.35 to £1.90 per metre.

Subsoiling or mole draining will cost in the region of £54-£70 per hectare.

2. *Total*

Costs per hectare for complete schemes will vary depending on the distance between laterals, soil type, size of area to be drained, region of the country and the time of year when the work is to be undertaken. The cost of a scheme with 20m spacing between laterals and using permeable backfill will typically be in the range £2,450 to £2,950 per hectare (£970-£1,200 per acre). Backfilling with soil, rather than with permeable material such as washed gravel, may reduce the cost by almost half but is only possible on certain types of soil. Equally, certain soil types which are particularly suitable for mole drainage may permit spacing between laterals to be increased to 40m or even 80m in some instances. Where this is possible costs will be reduced proportionately.

8. GRAIN DRYING AND STORAGE COSTS

(Estimated for 2009)

A. Drying

Capital Costs: vary widely according to type and capacity of drier. A standard 20 tonne per hour heated air drier, suitable for a 350 hectare arable unit would cost in the region of £110,000 including the wet bin and associated handling requirements (to feed drier and empty it). Over 10 years, this capital cost represents £5 for every tonne of grain regardless of drying requirements. Over 16 years it will fall to £3.10. Amortised (including finance) at 8% and assuming only 75% of the grain requires drying, over the 16 year period, this figure rises to £13.29/tonne dried. A 20 tonne per hour operating for 12 hours a day 7 days a week for 6 weeks could theoretically cope with 10,000 tonnes of grain. Under this 'full' capacity, the amortised capital cost per tonne over 15 years falls to £1.24/tonne.

Annual fixed costs: being fitted and immobile, grain dryers have a low resale value. *Depreciation* is therefore calculated as the capital value divided by the longevity and tonnes per year. This ranges from £5.50 to £2.30 per tonne. *Maintenance* tends to be low at around 2% of purchase value, rising as the dryer ages. *Insurance*; £12 per £1,000 of current value.

Running costs: *Fuel*: A useful 'rule of thumb' is 1 litre of fuel per 1% moisture per tonne. Thus drying each tonne by an average of 5% points at 65ppl makes £3.25 per tonne. *Electricity* use is 17.5Kw/hr for the burner and dischargers, as much again for the handling apparatus, totalling 35Kw/hr. Over a season, (approximately 150 hours use) at 12p/kWh is £630. This represents 20p per tonne grain.

Little labour is required for modern automatic driers unless grain has to be passed over the drier several times.

Central grain stores have grain drying services of about £5.50 to £11.75 per tonne for 5% moisture drying for members and non-members respectively.

B. Storage

Capital Costs: from approximately £80 per tonne (on-floor storage in a purpose-built building) to over £230 per tonne for an elaborate plant, including pit, elevator, conveyors, ventilated storage bins etc. in a new building.

Typical costs are given on page 195.

Depreciation and Interest: £175 per tonne depreciated over 20 years, with 6 per cent interest, equals £15.25 per annum; over 15 years, at 8 per cent interest, £20.45. (In highly mechanized bulk plants, part of this may be charged against harvesting and drying rather than entirely against storage).

Fuel and Repairs: £2.60 per tonne.

Extra Drying: Additional drying costs will be borne if storage necessitates further moisture reduction. Average £5.00 per tonne where own drier, £6.50 if dried on contract, for an additional 4% moisture extraction.

*Loss of Weigh*t: the value of the weight of grain lost should be considered as an additional cost of storage if storage requires extra drying. 2% = £2.40 to £3.20 per tonne.

Interest on Grain Stored: 70p/month (£8.67/year compound) at £120/t grain at 7% interest to £1.20/month (£15/year compounded) at £160/t grain, at 9% interest.

Contract Storage: typically £1.75 per tonne per month with a handling charge of around £2.00 per tonne for loading into store and out of store.

VI. OTHER FIXED COSTS DATA

1. WHOLE FARM FIXED COSTS

The following are a *broad indication* of the levels of fixed costs (£) per hectare (acre) for various types and sizes of farm, estimated for 2009, *including the value of unpaid family manual labour*, including that of the farmer and his wife.

The figures are based on the actual results from the Farm Business Survey (FBS) for the 2006-07 year, adjusted for subsequent changes in costs. The FBS is conducted by a consortium of Universities and Colleges across England on behalf of DEFRA. Although the survey is limited to England, the figures within this section are likely to be broadly applicable to most parts of the UK. The FBS has undergone an overhaul in the last couple of years. Specific regional reports are no longer published - although they can be accessed via the FBS website (see www.farmbusinesssurvey.co.uk). In addition, the farm types have been standardised across the country. They are now based on DEFRA's standard farm classifications. This has meant that some categories of farm have disappeared (mainly the 'mixed' ones such as dairy & arable, and arable & lowland livestock).

All of these costs can of course vary widely according to many factors, especially the intensity of farming, e.g. the number of cows per 100 hectares on dairy farms, or the hectares of intensive crops on general cropping farms.

Furthermore, *the figures provided are only averages. 'Premium' farms of the same level of intensity can have labour, machinery and general overhead costs at least 20% lower.* However, the most profitable farms are often more intensive. They therefore have higher fixed costs associated with the great intensity - but with substantially higher total farm gross margins. Thus it is the net amount (TGM-TFC) that matters.

Regarding the 'small' categories; these relate only to full-time holdings and do not include very intensive holdings occupying very small areas.

The term 'fixed costs' is used here as it is in gross margin analysis and planning; a full explanation of the differences between fixed and variable costs in this context is given on pages 1 and 2. *Note that all casual labour and contract work has been included under fixed costs.* In calculating enterprise gross margins on the individual farm these costs are normally allocated as variable costs if they are specific to a particular enterprise and vary approximately in proportion to its size, i.e. are approximately constant per hectare of a particular crop or per head of livestock. Otherwise they are included as fixed costs. In both cases, however, they could be regarded as substitutes for regular labour and/or the farmer's own machinery - which are both items of fixed cost. It is therefore simpler if both are included, fully, as fixed costs. If one is comparing results from accounts set out on a gross margin basis, and some or all of the casual labour and contract work have been included as variable costs (especially on cropping farms, e.g. for potato harvesting using casual labour or a contractor's machine), the necessary adjustments need to be made in making the comparisons.

Notes

Unpaid Labour. Refers to the value of unpaid family manual labour, including that of the farmer and his wife.

Machinery Depreciation. This is based on current (i.e. replacement) cost. This gives a truer reflection of the real loss of value of machinery (as is apparent when replacement becomes necessary). It also allows easier comparison between different businesses. However, many farm accounts calculate depreciation on the 'historic' (i.e. original) cost of the machinery. This will tend to produce a lower figure. Depending on the age of the machine, and bearing in mind recent strong increases in machinery prices, the historic method may underestimate depreciation by 10-20%. Note that both the Depreciation item and Repairs include vehicles.

Leasing Charges: The capital element, but not the interest, is included in depreciation; the proportion paid as interest varies according to the rate of interest paid and the length of the leasing period, but is typically 7 to 10 per cent.

Machinery Running Costs. This includes fuel, oil, repairs, servicing and vehicle tax and insurance. Separate figures for these elements are no longer available. As a general rule, fuel might make up a little over half of all such costs.

Rental Value. Unlike previously, this now only relates to the ***actual*** rent paid by the average farm in that particular category. It is ***no longer*** an imputed rent for all land farmed by the business. Thus, a fully owned-occupied farm will have no rental costs.

General Overheads include general farm maintenance and repairs, office expenses, water, insurance, fees, subscriptions, etc.

In making comparisons with fixed costs taken from farm accounts it is important to note that in the figures below unpaid manual labour and a rental value for leased land are included. Very low 'target' figures given in press articles often omit these items and can therefore be misleading; usually, too, they relate only to large, very well appointed farms. If an 'opportunity cost' for owner-occupied land (often fully paid for many years ago) is included, then the cost level rises further. Note too that the figures given below do not include management, whether paid or unpaid, nor interest on capital - again whether paid or unpaid. The margin after deducting the fixed costs below from the total gross margin plus any other farm receipts represents the total return to the management supplied and the capital utilised.

Labour, machinery and buildings are the main items of 'fixed' costs subject to change with major alterations in farm policy. Each has a separate section in this book.

Mainly Dairying

	Under 75 ha		75 - 125 ha		Over 125 ha	
	(Under 185 acres)		(185 - 310 acres)		(Over 310 acres)	
Regular Labour (paid)	80	(32)	115	(47)	200	(81)
Regular Labour (unpaid)	575	(233)	375	(152)	185	(75)
Casual Labour	20	(8)	20	(8)	20	(8)
Total Labour	**675**	**(273)**	**510**	**(206)**	**405**	**(164)**
Machinery Depreciation	95	(38)	100	(40)	100	(40)
Machinery Running Costs	140	(57)	145	(59)	140	(57)
Contract	90	(36)	95	(38)	95	(38)
Total Power & Machinery...	**325**	**(132)**	**340**	**(138)**	**335**	**(136)**
Farm Maintenance	35	(14)	35	(14)	30	(12)
Water & Electricity	140	(57)	135	(55)	120	(49)
General Overhead Expenses ..	100	(40)	65	(26)	55	(22)
Total Overheads	**275**	**(111)**	**235**	**(95)**	**205**	**(83)**
Rent & Interest	145	(59)	135	(55)	120	(49)
Total Fixed Costs	**1420**	**(575)**	**1220**	**(494)**	**1065**	**(431)**

Mainly Cereals

	Under 175 ha (Under 430 acres)		175 - 300 ha (430 - 740 acres)		Over 300 ha (Over 740 acres)	
Regular Labour (paid)	65	(26)	90	(36)	105	(42)
Regular Labour (unpaid)	225	(91)	100	(40)	50	(20)
Casual Labour	30	(12)	20	(8)	15	(6)
Total Labour	**320**	**(130)**	**210**	**(85)**	**170**	**(69)**
Machinery Depreciation	90	(36)	80	(32)	85	(34)
Machinery Running Costs	130	(53)	120	(49)	100	(40)
Contract	75	(30)	65	(26)	45	(18)
Total Power & Machinery...	**295**	**(119)**	**265**	**(107)**	**230**	**(93)**
Farm Maintenance	35	(14)	30	(12)	25	(10)
Water & Electricity	70	(28)	60	(24)	55	(22)
General Overhead Expenses ..	60	(24)	55	(22)	40	(16)
Total Overheads	**165**	**(67)**	**145**	**(59)**	**120**	**(49)**
Rent & Interest	110	(45)	95	(38)	90	(36)
Total Fixed Costs	**890**	**(360)**	**715**	**(289)**	**610**	**(247)**

Large-Scale Cereal Farms (over 500 ha (1,250 acres))

Data from the Farm Business Survey indicates there are further economies of scale for cereals farms at even larger farm sizes. There are likely to be wide variations depending on the precise scale of these businesses (some of which are very large). The following figures may be used as a guide; Labour - £135 per ha (of which paid labour £105); Power & Machinery - £190 per ha; Other Overheads - £100 per ha; Rent & Interest - £90 per ha. This totals £515 per ha (£208 per acre).

Data for larger-scale General Cropping farms (see below) is not so conclusive. Costs on a 'per ha' basis do not necessarily seem to fall as farm size increases. This may be due to the larger proportion of (higher cost) root crops and vegetables seen on larger farm sizes.

General Cropping

	Under 150 ha (Under 370 acres)		150 - 225 ha (370 - 560 acres)		Over 225 ha (Over 560 acres)	
Regular Labour (paid)	95	(38)	140	(57)	160	(65)
Regular Labour (unpaid)	235	(95)	125	(51)	55	(22)
Casual Labour	35	(14)	30	(12)	25	(10)
Total Labour	**365**	**(148)**	**295**	**(119)**	**240**	**(97)**
Machinery Depreciation	110	(45)	125	(51)	110	(45)
Machinery Running Costs	150	(61)	165	(67)	155	(63)
Contract	70	(28)	80	(32)	90	(36)
Total Power & Machinery...	**330**	**(134)**	**370**	**(150)**	**355**	**(144)**
Farm Maintenance	35	(14)	30	(12)	25	(10)
Water & Electricity	85	(34)	85	(34)	75	(30)
General Overhead Expenses ..	70	(28)	60	(24)	50	(20)
Total Overheads	**190**	**(77)**	**175**	**(71)**	**150**	**(61)**
Rent & Interest	140	(57)	125	(51)	120	(49)
Total Fixed Costs	**1025**	**(415)**	**965**	**(391)**	**865**	**(350)**

* With potatoes and/or sugar beet and/or field vegetables; grade 1 or 2 land.

Mainly Sheep/Cattle (lowland)

	Under 90 ha (Under 220 acres)		90 - 125 ha (220 - 310 acres)		Over 125 ha (Over 310 acres)	
Regular Labour (paid)	60	(24)	45	(18)	40	(16)
Regular Labour (unpaid)	330	(134)	210	(85)	160	(65)
Casual Labour	20	(8)	15	(6)	15	(6)
Total Labour	**410**	**(166)**	**270**	**(109)**	**215**	**(87)**
Machinery Depreciation	75	(30)	70	(28)	65	(26)
Machinery Running Costs	130	(53)	120	(49)	110	(45)
Contract	55	(22)	45	(18)	40	(16)
Total Power & Machinery...	**260**	**(105)**	**235**	**(95)**	**215**	**(87)**
Farm Maintenance	35	(14)	30	(12)	25	(10)
Water & Electricity	85	(34)	65	(26)	55	(22)
General Overhead Expenses ..	60	(24)	45	(18)	45	(18)
Total Overheads	**180**	**(73)**	**140**	**(57)**	**125**	**(51)**
Rent & Interest	100	(40)	90	(36)	95	(38)
Total Fixed Costs	**950**	**(384)**	**735**	**(297)**	**650**	**(263)**

Mainly Sheep/Cattle (upland)

	Under 130 ha (Under 320 acres)		130 - 230 ha (320 - 570 acres)		Over 230 ha (Over 570 acres)	
Regular Labour (paid)	35	(14)	25	(10)	30	(12)
Regular Labour (unpaid)	300	(121)	200	(81)	180	(73)
Casual Labour	10	(4)	10	(4)	10	(4)
Total Labour	**345**	**(140)**	**235**	**(95)**	**220**	**(89)**
Machinery Depreciation	50	(20)	40	(16)	40	(16)
Machinery Running Costs	80	(32)	70	(28)	65	(26)
Contract	25	(10)	20	(8)	20	(8)
Total Power & Machinery...	**155**	**(63)**	**130**	**(53)**	**125**	**(51)**
Farm Maintenance	25	(10)	20	(8)	15	(6)
Water & Electricity	50	(20)	40	(16)	35	(14)
General Overhead Expenses ..	35	(14)	30	(12)	20	(8)
Total Overheads	**110**	**(45)**	**90**	**(36)**	**70**	**(28)**
Rent & Interest	65	(26)	60	(24)	65	(26)
Total Fixed Costs	**675**	**(273)**	**515**	**(208)**	**480**	**(194)**

Other Farm Types

For whole-farm cost data for **Horticultural** holdings see page 36.

The other main DEFRA farm types are '**Mixed**', **Pigs**, and **Poultry**. As the name suggests, the Mixed category includes all farms where one enterprise is not sufficiently dominant for it to be allocated to one of the categories above. As it includes many different mixes of enterprises, the figures are unlikely to be useful for budgeting purposes.

Due to the intensity of the Pig and Poultry farm types, the presentation of 'per ha' figures is largely meaningless. For Pig farms, the following 'per Sow' figures may be used as a guide; Labour - £275 per sow (of which paid labour £250); Power & Machinery - £160 per sow; Other Overheads - £110 per sow; Rent & Interest - £100 per sow. This totals £645 per sow.

2. RENTS

There are three main types of agricultural tenancy in England and Wales: Full or Agricultural Holdings Act (AHA) 1986, Farm Business Tenancies (FBTs, under the 1995 Act) and Seasonal Lets of less than 1 year. No new AHA tenancies can be created. The influence of the Single Payment Scheme provisions which started in 2005 needs to be taken into account when comparing rent levels. The situation will vary from farm to farm and differ between the different regions of the countries of the UK. The tenant is the only person who can claim the Single Payment (SP), except in some seasonal agreements where the landlord may be able to claim. In an AHA tenancy agreement the rental is struck independently of the Single Payment in that the tenant will have been awarded the Single Payment entitlements in 2005 and at the end of the tenancy the ownership remains with the tenant or his/her successors. With FBTs the assumption is that the tenant is claiming a 'full' SP, and if land becomes available without SP entitlements then rental levels will be lower than those shown below.

Unless otherwise stated the figures in this section relate to farms let with a combination of crops, grass and rough grazing in England; they include housing and buildings, as available.

Agricultural Holdings Act Tenancies: It should be borne in mind that rough grazing may be included in the figures given in the table below and that DEFRA has not updated the Tenanted Land Survey since 2006. Some farms are likely to be let at below competitive rates, for various reasons. Rents for land had been tending to fall up to 2007 but this was offset by higher rents for housing and buildings so that overall per hectare rents were stable. The surge in many commodity prices in 2007 and 2008 has now affected rental levels. Where rentals were reviewed in 2007 increases of up to 20% were sometimes obtained. By mid 2008 with rapid input cost increases (especially fuel, fertiliser and feed) much lower settlements have been made, usually in the range of 5-10%.

The average rent for lowland, excluding woodland and rough grazing for farms under full Agricultural Tenancies is likely to be approximately £173 per ha, £70 per acre, in 2009. The levels on large mixed arable farms (i.e. including potatoes, sugar beet and/or vegetables) on very good soil, or well-equipped dairy farms, will tend to average £185 to £245 per hectare, £75 to £100 per acre. Rents on moderate, below average, quality farms, particularly with full repairing and insuring leases are likely to average £125 to £140 per hectare, £50 to £55 per acre.

Farm Business Tenancies: Rents will remain higher than those above for AHA tenancies, although still lower on average than those initially offered when such first tenancies became available, in 1996, at a relatively prosperous time. Farmers who already own land, with little or no mortgage, can afford to offer a higher figure than bidders with no other farms. For cereals land of reasonable quality recent offers have tended to follow the price of a tonne of wheat, and offers of over £400 per hectare (£160 per acre) have been reported for 3-5 year agreements. However typically FBT rentals for arable land are much lower and a 2008 opinion based survey from RICS reported below, gives the average for England and Wales for arable FBT rents at £259 per hectare, £105 per acre.

Tenanted Land Survey - England 2006: The figures are rounded to the nearest 50p/ha or 25p/acre.

Average Rent by Type of Agreement:	£/ha (acre)
Full Agricultural Tenancies	114 (46.25)
Farm Business Tenancies for 1 year and over	133 (53.75)
Seasonal Lets of less than one year	102 (41.25)

Average Rent by Farm Type: (£ per ha [acre])	Full Agricultural Tenancies		Farm Business Tenancies*
	Land Only	**Other**	**All Agreements**
Cereal	129.00 (52.25)	127.50 (51.50)	148.50 (60.00)
General Cropping	114.00 (46.25)	142.50 (57.75)	167.00 (67.50)
Dairy	106.50 (43.00)	137.50 (55.75)	168.50 (68.25)
Cattle and Sheep (Lowland)	93.50 (37.75)	111.50 (45.25)	89.00 (36.00)
Cattle and Sheep (LFA)	29.00 (11.75)	40.00 (16.25)	42.00 (17.00)
All	101.00 (40.75)	116.00 (47.00)	133.00 (53.75)

for a year and over

Source of Data

DEFRA (Farming Statistics): Tenanted Land Survey - England, 2006. The survey's results were based on approximately 7,300 agreements, covering 9% of all tenanted land in England by area. This survey is now under review and will probably be replaced by a new survey in 2009 from FBS data.

RICS Rural Land Market Survey 2008: published in July 2008 the following were average rents for England and Wales and should be treated with caution as they are opinion based, and reflect recently stuck rental levels.

Average Rent	Full Agricultural Tenancy £ per Ha (acre)	Farm Business Tenancy £ per Ha (acre)
Arable	163 (66)	259 (105)
Pasture	119 (48)	177 (72)

3. LAND PRICES

SALE VALUE OF FARMLAND, ENGLAND AND WALES

(1) Auction Sales (with Vacant Possession only) :
Oxford Institute/Savills(1) series, 1937-2000

Year	Current Prices		Real Values(2)		Index (3)	Year	Current Prices		Real Values(2)		Index (3)
1937-9	0	(24)	2030	(822)	33	1982	4557	(1844)	8373	(3389)	136
1945	111	(45)	2246	(909)	37	1983	5145	(2082)	9041	(3659)	147
1955	198	(80)	3274	(1325)	53	1984	4888	(1978)	8180	(3310)	133
1960	198	(80)	2643	(1070)	43	1985	4781	(1935)	7542	(3052)	123
1965	304	(123)	3608	(1460)	59	1986	4193	(1697)	6398	(2589)	104
1970	581	(235)	5857	(2370)	95	1987	4944	(2001)	7242	(2931)	118
1971	605	(245)	4872	(1972)	79	1988	6716	(2718)	9376	(3794)	153
1971	647	(262)	4761	(1927)	77	1989	6558	(2654)	8493	(3437)	138
1972	1473	(596)	9603	(3886)	156	1990	6346	(2568)	7505	(3037)	122
1973	1871	(757)	11793	(4773)	192	1991	6007	(2431)	6708	(2715)	109
1974	1572	(636)	8529	(3452)	139	1992	5441	(2202)	5859	(2371)	95
1975	1332	(539)	5817	(2354)	95	1993	5456	(2208)	5783	(2340)	94
1976	1814	(734)	6798	(2751)	111	1994	5028	(2035)	5204	(2106)	85
1977	2449	(991)	7922	(3206)	129	1995	6140	(2484)	6140	(2485)	100
1988	3279	(1327)	9794	(3964)	160	1996	8797	(3560)	8591	(3477)	140
1979	4371	(1769)	11513	(4659)	188	1997	8065	(3263)	7636	(3090)	124
1980	4265	(1726)	9521	(3853)	155	1998	7250	(2934)	6637	(2686)	108
1981	4272	(1729)	8525	(3450)	139	1999	13920	(5634)	12565	(5085)	205
						2000	7895	(3196)	7125	(2885)	116

(1) Savills after 1988. (2) At 1995 general price levels. (3) Real Values, 1995 = 100.

From 1970, figures were based on sales reports in the Estates Gazette and the Farmers Weekly, plus some unpublished sales, with a minimum size of 10 hectares.

The series was discontinued after 2000.

(2) Current Agricultural Land Prices

A CALP/RICS Farmland Price Index (England and Wales) began in 1995. It covers sales of vacant possession land in England and Wales, excluding residential value where more than 50% of total sale price; value of milk quota excluded. It is calculated by dividing total value of sales by total area sold. Figures for the most recent quarters are subject to revision as further information becomes available. In 2006 twice as much land was sold as in 2005 and that year saw an increase of 30% compared to 2004. The higher area sold in 2006 did not see lower prices reflecting a strong market. With lower areas sold in 2007 and so far in 2008 the strong land market has been confirmed with a provisional increase in the first half of 2008 of over 20%.

CALP/RICS Farmland Price Index 1995-2008

		Number of Sales	Area sold '000		Weighted Average Price		Index 1995
			Ha	(acres)	Ha	(acres)	=100
1995	Q1	73	3.9	(9.6)	5,187	(2,099)	100
1997	Q1	118	6.5	(16.1)	6,906	(2,795)	133
	Q2	208	9.1	(22.5)	7,263	(2,939)	140
	Q3	210	8.8	(21.7)	7,870	(3,185)	152
	Q4	183	8.5	(21.0)	7,166	(2,900)	138

		Number of Sales	Area sold '000		Weighted Average Price		Index 1995 =100
			Ha	(acres)	Ha	(acres)	
1998	Q1	113	5.2	(12.8)	7,364	(3,033)	145
	Q2	133	5.5	(13.6)	7,545	(3,053)	146
	Q3	164	7.1	(17.5)	6,411	(2,594)	124
	Q4	149	7.9	(19.5)	6,812	(2,757)	131
1999	Q1	84	3.6	(8.9)	6,376	(2,580)	123
	Q2	138	4.5	(11.1)	7,337	(2,969)	141
	Q3	152	9.0	(22.2)	7,186	(2,908)	139
	Q4	15	6.9	(17.0)	7,204	(2,915)	139
2000	Q1	90	3.9	(9.6)	7,660	(3,100)	148
	Q2	120	4.9	(12.1)	7,211	(2,918)	139
	Q3	134	7.2	(17.8)	7,082	(2,866)	137
	Q4	128	5.9	(14.6)	6,461	(2,615)	125
2001	Q1	73	4.5	(11.1)	7,273	(2,943)	140
	Q2	70	4.3	(10.6)	7,967	(3,224)	154
	Q3	137	7.5	(18.5)	7,169	(2,901)	138
	Q4	130	5.8	(14.3)	7,327	(2,965)	141
2002	Q1	71	3.0	(7.4)	7,906	(3,200)	152
	Q2	87	3.4	(8.4)	7,579	(3,067)	146
	Q3	135	6.6	(16.3)	7,694	(3,114)	148
	Q4	154	6.0	(14.8)	6,390	(2,586)	123
2003	Q1	69	2.5	(6.2)	7,817	(3,163)	151
	Q2	80	3.4	(8.4)	7,910	(3,201)	152
	Q3	67	3.3	(8.2)	7,629	(3,087)	147
	Q4	85	4.1	(10.1)	8,367	(3,386)	161
2004	Q1	46	1.8	(4.4)	9,526	(3,855)	184
	Q2	75	2.8	(6.9)	9,255	(3,745)	178
	Q3	53	2.1	(5.2)	10,670	(4,318)	206
	Q4	89	2.6	(6.4)	9,828	(3,977)	189
2005	Q1	65	3.7	(9.1)	9,713	(3,712)	174
	Q2	76	2.3	(5.7)	9,608	(3,888)	172
	Q3	82	4.6	(11.4)	9,386	(3,798)	163
	Q4	82	4.1	(10.1)	9,307	(3,766)	167
2006	Q1	91	6.0	(14.8)	9,228	(3,735)	165
	Q2	82	3.4	(8.4)	9,527	(3,856)	171
	H2	234	15.0	(37.1)	9,892	(4,003)	177
2007	H1	141	7.0	(17.3)	10,765	(4,357)	193
	H2	230	10.8	(26.7)	12,646	(5,118)	229
2008	H1	211	7.1	(17.5)	15,298	(6,191)	273

(3)   Other Land Price Series

In past editions of the Pocketbook, Inland Revenue and Valuation Office (VO) land price returns have been published, covering 30 years up to 1996/97 and 1993-2004 respectively. These series contained detailed splits between vacant possession and tenanted land, farms (including houses and buildings) and bare land, and also by size, land class and region. This information is still available from past editions of the Pocketbook (available at the same contact details). Data in the VO series does not continue beyond 2004, although limited information is available on the website, www.voa.gov.uk

Much of the data included in this section is available in **Farmland Market**, a Farmers Weekly publication in association with RICS, and includes other land and rental statistics, articles and opinion.

SALE VALUE OF FORESTS AND WOODLANDS

(1) *Forests*

The figures in this section relate to planted land sold (over 25 hectares) so that values include the value of the property (land) and the timber. Timber prices have risen significantly in the last year along with most world commodities. The number of transactions reduced in the year to September 2007, but area sold increased by 8% compared to last year. The average transaction value was £726,000, an annual increase of 160%, but there were two large portfolio sales of particularly valuable forests included in the year.

In the forest sector average prices were up 80% in the year to September 2007 compared to 2006. On average 2007 saw higher yield class sales and forests located nearer to markets. Adjusting for these factors, average values in like for like sales have increased by 35-40% over the past year, compared to an adjusted increase last year of 20%.

For forests the figures are for the UK and are predominantly upland with at least 50% coniferous content. Values vary with many factors and only size of block and age are recorded here, but yield class is also important. Some of the very large changes in value shown below indicate better quality and well located land compared to 2006.

Value of Forestland according to:

A. By Size Range (approx.)	2006	2007
	£/ha (£/acre)	£/ha (£/acre)
Below 51 hectares..................................	3,300 (1,337)	3,600 (1,457)
51 to 100 hectares	2,600 (1,053)	3,600 (1,457)
101 to 200 hectares	2,500 (1,012)	2,900 (1,174)
Above 200 hectares................................	2,200 (874)	4,400 (1,780)

B. By Age Band	2006	2007
	£/ha (£/acre)	£/ha (£/acre)
Young (1 to 10 years)	1,900 (769)	1,950 (789)
Mid-rotation (11 to 20 years).................	1,850 (749)	2,800 (1,133)
Semi-mature (21 to 30 years)	1,950 (789)	4,150 (1,679)
Mature (over 30 years)..........................	2,350 (951)	4,700 (1,902)
Mature (over 40 years)..........................	3,450 (1,397)	3,750 (1,517)

(2) *Woodlands*

Small woodland values continued to increase, attributable to the general rise in land values and keen demand for amenity, sporting and development hope value. Values are at their highest adjacent to centres of population and for properties of high amenity value. Sales in the South of England are often recorded in the £8-12,000/ha range, whereas £2-5,000/ha is more typical for more remote properties, or where amenity values are lower. Woodlands are sometimes being split and marketed in very small blocks and have often been sold in the £8-12,000 per ha range throughout the UK.

Source: UPM Tilhill and Savills, Forest Market Report.

4. BUILDINGS

BUILDING COSTS

Building costs are notoriously variable. Many factors influence a contractor's price, including distance from his yard, size of contract, site access, site conditions, complexity of work, familiarity with the type of work and his current work load. There will also be differences in efficiency and standard of work between contractors and, as is often the case with farm buildings, the absence of detailed specification by the client may mean that different contractors will not have quoted for identical buildings. The number of extras that are found to be required after a contract has been agreed will also vary.

The costs given below can only be taken as an approximate guide. They refer to new buildings, erected by contractor on a clear level site and exclude VAT and any grants that may be available. The costs were provided by SAC Buildings Design Services, Aberdeen, in 2008. More detailed information is available in the following publications. The books and journals giving general building cost information generally assume knowledge of how to take off quantities for building work.

Specialised Information on Farm Building Costs

Farm Building Cost Guide published by SAC Building Design Services, Aberdeen.

Standard Costs Part 1: Specifications; Part 2: Costs. Published by DEFRA and the Agricultural Departments in Scotland, Wales and Northern Ireland. Used when claiming government grants on a standard-cost basis.

General Building Cost Information

Books are produced by a number of publishers with annual or more frequent new editions and updates. Examples are Laxton's Building Price Book, Spon's Architects' and Builders' Price Book, and Wessex Comprehensive Building Price Book. Regularly updated cost information is also given in several professional and trade journals.

1. Constituent Parts

Frame, Roof and Foundations   *per m² floor area*

1. Open-sided timber framed pole barn with round pole uprights on concrete bases, sawn timber rafters and purlins, high-tensile galvanised steel cladding to roof and gable ends above eaves, hardcore floor, eaves height 4.8 m, 9 m span, no side cladding, rainwater drainage to soakaways.   £57.50

2. Open-sided steel portal-framed building with fibre-cement or plastic coated steel cladding to roof and gables above eaves, hardcore floor, eaves height 4.8 m, no side cladding, rainwater drainage to soakaways.

9 m span	£/110
13.2 m span	£95
18 m span	£90

3. Cost breakdown of 2 above;

Materials:		
	portal frame and purlins	26%
	foundations	3%
	roofing	16%
	rainwater and drainage	3%
	hardcore and blinding	2%
	Total Materials	50%

Erection:	portal frame and purlins	19%
	foundations	2%
	roofing	19%
	rainwater and drainage	5%
	hardcore and blinding	5%
	Total Erection	50%

Roof cladding   *per m²*

1. Natural grey fibre-cement, 146 mm corrugations fixed with drive screws

Materials	£12.50	
Fixing	£/12.00	
Total		/24.50

2. Extra for coloured sheet   £1.90

3. Deduct for translucent sheets   £0.12

4. Deduct for PVC-coated steel   £4.50

5. Deduct for high-tensile corrugated galvanised steel sheeting   £7.80

6. PVC 150 mm half-round gutter on fascia brackets, including stop-ends and outlets   £23.00

7. PVC 100 mm rainwater pipe with fixings, swan-neck and shoe   £41.00

                                                                  per m run

8. Fibre-cement close-fitting ridge   £35.20

9. Fibre-cement ventilating ridge   £38.00

Walls and Cladding   *per m²*

1. Concrete blockwork, fair faced and pointed both sides

150 mm thick	£41.50
215 mm thick	£59.00
215 mm thick hollow blocks	£61.50
215 mm thick hollow blocks, filled and reinforced	£75.10

2. Extra for rendering or roughcast to blockwork on one side   £19.75

3. Vertical spaced boarding 21x 145 mm with 19 mm gaps including horizontal rails, all pressure treated   £24.50

4. Fibre-cement vertical cladding, including rails   £38.20

5. Corrugated high-tensile steel side cladding, including rails   £30.65

6. Wall element: 215 mm thick blockwork, including strip foundation (base 750 mm below ground level), 2.5 m height above ground level   £155 per m run

Floors   *per m²*

1. Concrete floor 100 mm thick, Gen 3 mix, on 150 mm hardcore, including excavation: £31.50

Breakdown:
(a)	excavate, level and compact	£2.85
(b)	hardcore	£4.40
(c)	blinding	£2.10
(d)	damp-proofmembrane	£1.80
(e)	premixed concrete spread and compacted	£16.70

(f)	float finish	£3.65

2. Extra to above for
   (a) 150 mm instead of 100 mm — £5.25
   (b) laying concrete to falls — £1.48
   (c) broom or textured finish — £1.80
   (d) Carborundum dust non-slip finish — £3.05
   (e) insulating concrete — £8.85

3. Reinforced concrete slatted floors for cattle
   (a) cattle loading — £67.50
   (b) tractor loading — £75.10

4. Reinforced concrete slats for pigs — £49.35

5. Insulating floor, including excavation and base
   (a) 27 mm expanded polystyrene, 38 mm screed — £43.60
   (b) insulating concrete with lightweight aggregate — £34.70
   (c) as (b) with 20 mm screed — £44.10

6. Form channel in concrete — £4.10 per m run

7. Excavate for cast 1 m3 in-situ concrete bases for stanchions each — £112.00

Services and Fittings   *per m²*

1. Drainage: 100 mm PVC pipe laid in trench, including 750 mm deep excavation and backfil — £22.30 per m run
   Breakdown:
   (a) excavate and backfill — £14.20
   (b) 100 mm PVC pipe laid — £8.10
   Extras:
   (c) add to (a) for 1 m deep — £3.35
   (d) add to (b) for 150 mm pipe — £5.90

2. Excavate soakaway and fill with stones — £97.00 each

3. Trap and grid top, 100 mm PVC — £18.80 each

4. Yard gully with heavy duty road grating 400 x 300 mm — £176 each

5. Inspection chamber 900 mm deep, 450 x 600 mm opening and medium duty cast iron cover — £352 each

6. Above-ground vitreous enamel slurry tank on concrete base, 1000 m³ — £45000 each

7. Reception pit, 20 m³ — £4050 each

8. Slurry channel beneath (not including) slats, 1.8 m deep, 3m wide — £410 per m run

9. Lighting: 1.5 m 60W single fluorescent unit, including wiring and switch — £120 each
   Extras:
   (a) PVC conduit — £5.75
   (b) screwed steel conduit — £10.00

10. Power: 13A switched outlet — £18.20 each

11. Diagonal feed fence, fixed, including posts (painted) — £80 per m run

12. Tombstone feed fence, fixed, including posts (painted) — £94 per m run

13. Feed bunker — £54 per m run

14. Hay rack, wall fixing — £61 per m run

15.	Cubicle division, galvanised, fixed in place	£81 each
16.	Fencing: three-rail timber with posts, all pressure treated	£23.65 per m run
17.	Gate, 3 m wide, galvanised steel, including posts set in concrete	
	(a) medium duty	£195 each
	(b) heavy duty	£270 each
	Deduct for painted instead of galvanised finish	£33.50

2. Complete Buildings

Fully Covered and Enclosed Barn

Portal frame, 18 m span, 6 m bays, 6 m to eaves, 3 m high blockwork walls with sheet cladding above, 6 m sliding doors at either end, 150mm thick concrete floor   £168 per m² floor area

Cows and Cattle Housing

1.	Covered strawed yard, enclosed with ventilated cladding, concrete floor, pens only, with 4.0 m² per head floor area	£650 per head
2.	Extra to 1 for 4.0 m wide double-sided feeding passage, barrier and troughs	£270 per head
3.	Kennel building	£410 per head
4.	Portal framed building with cubicles	£1300 per head
5.	Extra to 4 for feed stance, feeding passage, barriers and troughs	£565 per head
6.	Extra to 4 for slatting of cubicle passages	£570 per head
7.	Covered collecting yard, 1.1 m² per cow	£195 per head
8.	Milking parlour building, example: 5.5 x 11.5 m for 8/16 parlour	£15,500
9.	Parlour equipment, herringbone parlours:	
	(a) low level, 1 stall per point	£3,440 per point
	(b) pipeline	£3,175 per point
	(c) extra for meter and auto cluster removal	£1,950 per point
	(d) auto feed dispenser	£810 per point
10.	Dairy building	£280 per m² floor area
11.	Bulk tank and washer	£6.40 per litre
12.	Loose box, 16 m² floor area laid to falls, rendered walls	£290 per m² floor area
13.	Bull pen and open run	£10,500
14.	Cattle crush and 20 m race	£4,500
15.	Slatted floor cattle building for 120 growing cattle (1.7 m² pen space per head) with drive-through feed passage/troughs	£1,200 per head

Silage

		per tonne stored
1.	Timber panel clamp on concrete base with effluent tank	£60
2.	Precast concrete panel clamp with effluent tank	£85
3.	Glass-lined forage tower and unloader	£210

Waste Storage

		per m³ stored
1.	Lined lagoon with safety fence	£35.50
2.	Glass-lined steel slurry silo	
	small (400 m³)	£50
	medium (1,200 m³)	£45
	large (3,600 m³)	£40
3.	GRP below-ground effluent tank, encased in concrete	
	small (12 m³)	£440
	large (36 m³)	£385

Sheep Housing

1.	Penning, troughs, feed barriers and drinkers installed in suitable existing building	£30.50 per ewe
2.	Purpose-built sheep shed with 1.35 m² pen space per ewe concentrate troughs, feed passage and barrier for forage feeding	£190 per ewe
	Extras:	
	(a) softwood slatted floor panels, materials only	£7.35 per m²
	(b) slatted panels as (a), made up, plus supports	£24.75 per m²

Pig Housing

		per sow and litter
1.	Farrowing and rearing	
	(a) Prefabricated farrowing pens with crates, side creep areas, part-slatted floors, including foundations, electrical and plumbing work	£3,025
	(b) Steel-framed farrowing house with insulated blockwork walls, part-slatted pens with side creeps in rooms of eight with off main passage	£3,475
	(c) Flat-deck rearing house 3-6 weeks with fully perforated floors to pens, 0.25 m² per pig pen area	£124 per weaner
	(d) Prefabricated verandah house including foundations, electrical and plumbing work, 0.3m² per pig internal lying area	£100 per weaner

		per baconer
2.	Finishing	
	(a) Prefabricated fattening house with part-slatted floors, trough feeding	£225
	(b) Prefabricated fattening house with part-slatted floors, floor fed	£210
	(c) Steel framed building with insulated blockwork walls, part-slatted floors, trough fed	£85
	(d) Automatic feeding systems for items (a), (b) and (c) above:	
	dry-feed system with ad-lib hoppers	£605
	dry on-floor feeding	£12
	wet feeding	£17.90

		per sow
3.	Dry sows and boars	
	(a) Yards with floor feeding	£325
	(b) Sow cubicle system	£540

(c)	Yards with electronic feeders	£890
(d)	Yards with individual feeders	£990
(e)	Two-yard system with flat-rate feeding	£1,100
(f)	Boar pens as part of sow house	£2,365 each

4. Complete pig unit

Building costs calculated on basis of three-week weaning, 23 pigs per sow per year to bacon, excl. external slurry or dung storage, feed storage and handling/weighing facilities:

(a)	Breeding and rearing only	£1,760 per sow
(b)	Breeding with progeny to bacon	£3,200 per sow

Poultry Housing and Equipment — *per bird*

1.	Intensive enriched cages with automatic feeding and egg collection; (new traditional cages were banned from 1st January 2003; only enriched cages complete with nest box, perches and scratching area are now allowed)	£19.80-£22.50
2.	Perchery/barn	£18.50-£22.50
3.	Free Range: new sites stocked at 9 birds per m²,	£22.50-£30.00
	existing sites stocked at 11.7 birds per m²	£18.25-£24.00
	smaller mobile units will cost	£26.00 plus
4.	Broiler Breeders, deep litter, 0.167 m² per bird	£24.80
5.	Pullets (cage and floor reared)	£12.50
6.	Broilers, deep litter, 0.05 m² per bird	£7.20-£8.00
7.	Turkeys, 20,000 pole barn fattening unit (cost varies with size of unit and degree of automation)	£17.80-£24.20

Grain Storage and Drying — *per tonne stored*

1.	Intake pit, conveyor, elevator, overhead conveyor and catwalk, storage bins within existing building	£180
	extra for low volume ventilation of bins	£70
2.	As 1 in new building	£260
3.	Portable grain walling for on-floor storage in existing building	£41.50
4.	On floor grain storage in purpose-built building	£100
	Extras:	
	(a) low volume ventilation	£7.35-£8.10
	(b) on-floor drying with above-ground main duct and laterals	£110.00
	(c) add to (b) for below-ground laterals	£13.50
5.	Sealed towers for moist grain, including loading and unloading equipment	£142-£160

Potato Storage — *per tonne stored*

1.	Pallet-box store with recirculation fans	£190
	Pallet boxes, 1 tonne	£64
2.	Bulk store, building only	£175
	Ventilation system: fans, main duct, below-floor lateral ducts	£40

Roads and Fences

	per m length
3.2 m wide hardcore road with drainage ditches using locally excavated material	£25.50
using imported hardcore (£6.15/m³)	£38.70
extra for bitumen macadam surfacing, two coats	£46.20
Traditional 7-wire stock fence	£5.60
High tensile 7-wire stock fence	£4.00

Construction Equipment Hire

	hourly rate, with driver
Excavator	£20-£27.50
Tipping lorry	£32.00
10-tonne crane	£36

	weekly rate
Concrete mixer, 100 litre (5/3)	£4
Compressor and heavy breaker	£115

STANDARD COSTS

Standard costs are published by the Scottish Executive on the basis of the cost of farm or casual labour and new materials. They do not include an allowance for overheads and profit: in most cases building contractors would add 15-30% to cover them. Standard costs are therefore usually lower, sometimes by a larger percentage than this, particularly where the labour content of the item is high. The following examples are based on standard costs issued in 2002. Farm buildings costs generally will have risen by about 35% between that year and mid-2008. Crown copyright material is reproduced from standard costs with permission of the Controller of HMSO and the Queen's Printer for Scotland.

	per m² floor area
Open-sided framed building with cladding to roof and gable peaks only, hardcore floor, rainwater drainage to soakaways:	
9 x 18 m	£35
13.2 x 24m	£32.50

	per m² wall or roof
Corrugated cladding to roof or walls, including supports (purlins or rails):	
fibre cement sheeting	£16.80
extra for coloured sheeting	£0.80
extra for PVC coated steel instead of fibre cement	£0.60
deduct for metallic coated (e.g. galvanised) steel	£4.90
Spaced boarding	£18.80

Wall element, concrete blockwork 190-324 mm thick with strip foundation (base 750 mm below ground level) and 2.5 mm height above ground level	£92 per m run
Extra for rendering blockwork on one side	£6.50 per m²
Concrete floor, 100 mm thick, including excavation, hardcore and waterproof membrane	£11.50 per m²
Concrete floor, 150 mm thick as above	£15.50 per m²
Reinforced concrete slats for cattle (supports not included)	£47.50 per m²

Yard gully with heavy grating	£251 each
Drainage pipes, 100 mm, jointed in UPVC, clayware or spun concrete including 900 mm trench and backfill	£10.70 per m run
Drainage pipes 150 mm as above	£19.00 per m run
Tank for water, effluent etc., 20 m³	£2,966 each
Gate, 3 m wide, steel, including posts concreted in: light duty	£106.40 each
cattle yard type	£141.90 each

Fully covered enclosed building with concrete floor, and rainwater drainage to soakaways	*per m² floor area*
10 x 18 m	£72.50
15 x 24 m	£54.60

Storage Requirements

Bulk (cubic metres (feet) per tonne):

Beans		1.2	(43)
Wheat, peas		1.3	(46)
Barley, rye, oilseed rape, linseed, fodder beet		1.4	(50)
Oats		1.9	(68)
Potatoes		1.6	(57)
Dry bulb onions		2.0	(71)
Concentrates:	meal	2.0	(71)
	cubes	1.6	(57)
Grass silage:	18% DM	1.3	(46)
	30% DM	1.6	(57)
Maize silage		1.3	(46)
Silage: large round bales		2.5	(88)
Wheat straw ⎤		13.0	(464)
Barley straw ⎬ small bales		11.5	(411)
Hay ⎦		6.0	(214)
Wheat straw ⎤		20.0	(714)
Barley straw ⎬ large round bales		18.0	(643)
Hay ⎦		8.0	(286)
Brewers' grains		0.9	(32)

(With straw and hay the storage requirement clearly depends on the packing density; the above are simply typical averages).

Boxes (floor area in square metres (feet) per tonne):

Potatoes:	0.5 tonne boxes, 5 boxes high	0.52	(5.6)
	1.0 tonne boxes, 4 boxes high	0.52	(5.6)
	1.0 tonne boxes, 5 boxes high	0.45	(4.8)

Bags (floor area in square metres (feet) per tonne):

Feedingstuffs:	2 bags high	1.6	(17)
Fertiliser:	6 bags high	1.1	(12)
	10 bags high	0.7	(8)

VII TAXATION

Note: no responsibility can be taken for any errors or omissions in the information presented in this section or for any action taken on the basis of the information provided. Professional advice should always be sought before taking any decision that may affect your tax position.

1. INCOME TAX

1. RATES OF INCOME TAX (2008-09)

	Income Band	Dividends	Interest	Other Income
Starting rate	Up to £2,230*	10	10	20
Basic rate	£2,231 to £34,800**	10	20	20
Higher rate	Over £34,800	32.5	40	40

* For 2008-09 the lower rate of 10% still applies to other savings income (primarily bank and building society interest) up to a limit of £2,320. This 10% rate is not available if taxable non-savings income exceeds £2,320.

** As a result of the Chancellor of the Exchequer's announcement on 13 May 2008, the threshold is reduced from the previously announced £36,000.

2. ALLOWANCES AND RELIEFS (2008-09)

A. Personal Allowance

This is £6,035 (£9,030 if aged 65 to 74 and £9,180 if aged over 75 on 5th April 2009, subject to total income not exceeding the statutory income limit (£21,800 for 2008-09)). The Personal Allowance is increased by £600 over the previously announced £5,435 following the Chancellor of the Exchequer's statement on 13 May 2008.

B. Married Couples Allowance

This was abolished from the tax year ended 6th April 2001 except for couples where at least one spouse was born before 6th April 1935. From 2005-06 the allowance is available to couples in a civil partnership where at least one partner was born before 6th April 1935. The relief is given as a reduction in income tax restricted to the lower of 10% of the allowance (£2,540 for 2008-09) or the total tax liability.

C. Personal Pension Schemes

Tax relief is obtainable for contributions to a pension. The rules on maximum contributions have been simplified; there is an annual allowance of £235,000 for 2008-09 (£225,000 for 2007-08) and a lifetime allowance of £1,650,000 in 2008-09 (£1,600,000 in 2007-08). Maximum contributions under the simplified Stakeholder Pension rules are £3,600 per year.

2. PRIVATE COMPANY TAXATION

1. RATES OF CORPORATION TAX (2008-09)

The rates set out in the table below apply to profits made in the financial year (FY) ending 1st April 2008 to 31st March 2009. Profits are chargeable at the following rates;

	Profits band	per cent tax	
		FY08	*FY09*
Small companies' rate	Up to £300,000	21	*22*
Upper marginal rate	£300,000 to £1.5m	29.75	*29.5*
Main companies' rate	Over £1.5m	28	*28*

Note: The marginal rates shown above are divided by the number of associated companies.

2. COMPANY TAXATION – OTHER ISSUES

A. Capital Gains

Capital gains of companies are charged at the appropriate rate of Corporation Tax. The indexation allowance is still available to reduce capital gains made by Companies.

B. Quotas

Milk quota purchased by a company after 1st April 2002 will attract Corporation Tax relief at the rate of depreciation selected in the accounting policies of the company or 4% per year if not depreciated in the accounts of the company.

C. Distributions

Dividends are not deductible in arriving at the amount of Corporation Tax profit. However, the recipient of distributions will be credited with a tax payment of 10% of distributions received, which will be deemed to discharge the liability of lower (10%) and basic rate (22%) taxpayers; however, higher rate taxpayers will have to pay additional tax of 25% of the net dividend; dividends are treated as the top slice of income.

D. Losses

Carry back restricted to one year. Losses can be carried forward and offset against profits of the same trade.

Editorial Note: *The continuing increase in the rate of small companies Corporation Tax from 20% in FY07 to 22% in FY09 will make the benefits of incorporation less attractive. In addition, the reduction in the value of milk quotas make the benefits of incorporating to write-off the cost of the quota acquired by the company less attractive.*

3. AGRICULTURAL BUSINESSES: OTHER ITEMS

1. ASSESSING SELF-EMPLOYED PROFITS

Since 1997-98 self-employed people have been assessed for tax in any tax year on the basis of the profits recorded in the annual accounts which end in that tax year, i.e. on a 'current year basis'.

2. LIVESTOCK

Dairy cows or breeding livestock may be treated on the herd basis or on a trading stock basis;

A. Herd Basis

Under the herd basis valuation changes are not included in the trading account, nor are additions to the herd, but sales from the herd and replacements are. On the sale of all or a substantial proportion (normally taken as 20% or more) of the herd, no tax is paid on any profit over the original cost price, nor is there any relief for loss.

Editorial Note: *The high values of cattle at present make it less likely that a new farming business will want to elect for the herd basis although each case must be judged on its merits.*

B. Trading Stock Basis

Purchases, sales and valuation changes are all included in the trading account. Under this method stock should be valued at the lower of cost (or cost of production) and net realisable value. Where animals are home-produced and it is not possible to ascertain actual costs from farm records the 'deemed' cost may be used. This is 60% of market value for cattle and 75% for sheep and pigs.

3. STOCK VALUATION: CROPS

Crops should generally be valued at the cost of production (or net realisable value, if lower). Costs which are directly attributable to buying, producing and growing the crops should be included. The deemed cost method allows 75% of market value to be used although this method should only be used where it is not possible to ascertain actual costs.

4. ALLOWANCES FOR CAPITAL EXPENDITURE

A. Machinery and Plant

(i) The same rules apply whether the machinery and plant is new or second hand. An annual writing down allowance of 20% p.a. (25% p.a. up to April 2008) is available on a reducing balance basis on capital expenditure incurred on the provision of plant and machinery. Qualifying expenditure is added to the asset 'pool' and the writing down allowances are given on the residue of expenditure in that pool. A hybrid rate of writing down allowance applies for periods spanning April 2008. The 50% First Year Allowances for small and medium-sized businesses have been discontinued from April 2008.

(ii) A new Annual Investment Allowance ('AIA') has been introduced from 6th April 2008 (1st April 2008 for companies). This gives 100% relief for the first £50,000 of qualifying expenditure incurred in an accounting period. The limit is proportionally increased or decreased where the chargeable period is longer or shorter than a year. A group of companies can only receive a single allowance. Expenditure on cars does not qualify, although expenditure on long life assets, or on 'integral features' can be claimed.

(iii) A new 10% rate applies to expenditure incurred on certain listed 'integral features' in a building and on long life assets on or after April 2008. Long life asset expenditure brought forward will obtain the 10% rate (6% up to April 2008).

(iv) 100% First year allowances can be claimed for expenditure incurred by any business on designated energy-saving plant and machinery and environmentally beneficial technologies and products. The lists of items which qualify can be found on the Government's Energy Technology Product lists which can be found on www.eca.gov.uk.

(v) For chargeable periods beginning on or after 6th April 2008 (1st April 2008 for Companies), a Writing Down Allowance of up to £1,000 can be claimed in respect of the main pool and/or the special rate pool where the unrelieved expenditure in that pool is £1,000 or less.

B. Cars

Motor cars costing more than £12,000 are included in a separate 'pool' in the year of purchase, on which a 20% writing down allowance is available. The allowance is restricted to a maximum of £3,000 for motor cars with a written-down value of more than £12,000. Special rules apply where a motor car is only partly used for business purposes. There is a 100% first year allowance for new cars with emissions of less than 110g/km CO_2 (120g/km for expenditure incurred before 1st April 2008). This applies to cars registered after 16th April 2002.

C. Machinery Leasing

Tax allowances for rental payments on financial leases are spread to reflect the commercial depreciation of the asset. This may mean that full tax relief for rental payments may not be gained in the years in which the payments are made.

D. Buildings

Farm buildings, fencing, drainage and other improvements (including up to one-third of farmhouses) qualify for a writing-down allowance of 4% annually, given equally over 25 years. These annual allowances are to be phased out by the 2010-11 tax year. For 2008-09, the rate has been reduced by 25% to 3%. Where an accounting period spans the financial year (31st March for companies, 5th April for individuals and partnerships), time apportionment applies to determine the amount of the allowance.

Editorial Note: The 2007 Budget saw the announcement of the phased withdrawal of Agricultural Buildings Allowances. The change includes the withdrawal of allowances on expenditure previously incurred. The changes make it even more important that any items of plant and equipment are identified in a building and the appropriate allowances claimed.

The new Annual Investment Allowance (AIA) makes the planning of capital expenditure more important where expenditure can be brought forward or deferred. Businesses who consistently spend in excess of the £50,000 pa AIA will need to review their spending policies to ascertain whether leasing or contract hire may be more efficient.

5. LOSSES

Losses can normally be set off against other income in the year in which they are incurred and in the prior year. If other income is insufficient in the year when the loss occurs and in the prior year, any unrelieved losses can be carried forward and set off against future profits from the same trade. Special rules apply to prevent abuse of loss relief provisions by 'hobby' farmers who are not running their farms on a commercial basis with a view to producing a profit: normally losses are disallowed against other income after 5 consecutive years of loss. Trading losses may be set against capital gains arising in the same year as the loss.

6. PROFIT AVERAGING

This relief is to enable farmers, other than companies, to average their taxable profits over two consecutive years. Where the difference between the profits of two consecutive years is 30% or more of the higher profits, the total profits for the two years are equally divided between the two years. Marginal relief is available where the difference is less than 30% but more than 25% of the higher profits. Profit for the purposes of tax averaging calculations is after the deduction of capital allowances. There is a two year limit in which to make the claim.

4. CAPITAL GAINS TAX

1. APPLICATION AND RATES

Applies to capital gains made by an individual. Capital gains accruing to companies are chargeable to Corporation Tax. A capital gain is the difference between the acquisition value and the sale price. The first £9,600 of capital gains realised by an individual in a tax year are covered by their annual exemption. Capital gains in excess of £9,600 are charged to tax at 18% on any disposals arising after 5 April 2008.

Exempt assets include a principal private residence (e.g. farm house, if non-exclusive business occupation applies) if occupied as such, normal life assurance policies, animals and tangible movable properly (i.e. chattels) disposed of for £6,000 or less.

Capital Gains Tax is chargeable only on the disposal (including gifts) of assets. Capital Gains Tax is not payable on death.

Payment of Capital Gains Tax is due on 31st January following the tax year of disposal on the self-assessment return.

2. RELIEFS

A. Losses

Should a transaction produce a loss, this may be set against any long term chargeable gains arising in the same year or, if these are insufficient, those accruing in subsequent years. Losses brought forward will be used only to the extent necessary to reduce untaxed gains for the year to £9,600.

Where a trading loss can be set against other income in the same or prior year for income tax purposes, any unused loss can be set against capital gains for those years.

B. Improvements

Spending that has increased the value of the asset can be offset against any gain. In the case of agricultural property, allowance would be made for any capital expenditure undertaken to improve the property, even though the expenditure may have obtained a buildings allowance referred to at 3(d) above.

C. Indexation and Taper Relief

Indexation and Taper relief for individuals has now been abolished for any disposals taking place on or after 6th April 2008. Indexation allowance is still available for capital gains arising in companies. We have not reproduced the Taper relief rules, but would refer you to the 2008 (38th Edition) Pocketbook for guidance on calculating the gains on any disposals prior to 5th April 2008.

D. Entrepreneurs Relief

Entrepreneur's relief applies to disposals by an individual on or after 6th April 2008. The relief, which must be claimed, gives a reduced effective rate of Capital Gains Tax of 10% for eligible gains of up to £1m. The limit of £1m is a lifetime limit per individual. The assets which qualify for entrepreneurs' relief are in line with those which qualified for business asset taper relief. This covers:

- a trading business carried on by an individual alone or in partnership;
- assets of such a trade following cessation;
- shares or securities in a trading company where the individual owns 5% or more and is an officer or employee

The conditions for the relief must have been satisfied throughout a qualifying period of a year before the disposal. The relief operates by reducing the amount of qualifying gains by four-ninths to arrive at the effective rate of 10%.

Editorial Note: *The new rules for Entrepreneur relief are complex, particularly in cases of disposals of part of the business. The rules are similar to the previous retirement relief and are particularly tricky in cases of disposals of farmland and related assets and trade. It is recommended that professional advice is sought where it is anticipated claiming this relief.*

E. Rollover

Payment of tax may be deferred on gains accruing from the sale of business assets (including land and buildings occupied and used for trade purposes, fixed plant and machinery, milk quotas, and from the sale of shares in a family business) if part or all of the proceeds are spent on acquiring new qualifying assets. The tax is deferred by deducting the gain from the acquisition price of the new asset. It can only be claimed if the new asset is acquired within 12 months before and 3 years after the disposal of the old assets. Disposal and acquisition dates for Capital Gains purposes are generally contract, not completion, dates.

F. Holdover

Payments of tax may be deferred where disposal is by gift. This relief only applies to gifts of business assets, land which qualifies for agricultural property relief at either the 100% or 50% rate under Inheritance Tax (see next section) and gifts which lead to an immediate charge to Inheritance Tax (e.g. gifts into a discretionary trust). The amount of the chargeable gain which would normally have accrued to the donor will be held over; the value at which the donee is deemed to acquire the asset will be its market value reduced by the amount of the donor's chargeable gain held over. The held over gain is reduced by any time apportionment, indexation allowance, or any retirement relief available to the donor, but not taper relief. Where deferral is not available, payment of tax by interest bearing annual instalments over 10 years will be allowed for gifts of land, controlling share holdings and minority share holdings in unquoted companies.

5. INHERITANCE TAX

1. APPLICATION AND RATES

This tax is charged on lifetime gifts and transfers on death. Rates for 2008-09 are as follows;

Slice of Chargeable Transfer	Rate per cent
£1- 312,000	0%
Over £312,000	40%

The nil rate band is potentially increased for surviving spouses or civil partners who died on or after 9 October 2007. From this date the nil rate band may be increased by the unused proportion of the deceased spouse or civil partners nil rate band.

Outright gifts to individuals are exempt from tax at the time of the gift. If the donor lives for a further seven years then the transfer is fully exempt. Gifts into accumulation and maintenance trusts and interest in possession trusts no longer receive special treatment - all other gifts will be taxed at half the above rates at the time of the transfer.

Tax is charged on the value of an individual's estate at death plus the value of all gifts made within seven years of death. Allowance is made for any tax paid on lifetime gifts included in the value of the estate on death. Relief is given for outright gifts made more than three years before death according to the following scale:

Years between gift and death	Percentage of the full charge to tax
0-3	100
3-4	80
4-5	60
5-6	40
6-7	20

Exemptions include: transfers between husband and wife; the first £3,000 of gift made by a donor in the income tax year and separately up to £250 per year to any number of persons; gifts made out of income which form part of normal expenditure; marriage gifts within limits of £5,000 for a parent, £2,500 for a lineal ancestor and £1,000 for other donors.

2. RELIEFS

A. Agricultural Property Relief

Relief may be available for agricultural land. Subject to a general rule that the agricultural land must have been occupied by the transferor (or by his controlled company) for two years, or owned by the transferor for 7 years and occupied for agricultural purposes by someone else before any relief is granted. The relief is at two different rates. If the basis of valuation is vacant possession (or there is the right to obtain it within 12 months), the taxable value of the land is reduced by 100%. If the basis of valuation is tenanted value, the taxable value of the land is reduced by 50% of that tenanted value. Ownership and occupation periods normally include prior periods of ownership or occupation by husbands and wives. From 1st September 1995, 100% relief applies to new lettings of agricultural land as Farm Business Tenancies.

Editorial Note: *There has been so much publicised activity and tax cases concerning APR claims, particularly attempts by the Inland Revenue to reduce or deny the relief on claims for farmhouses. Care must be taken to protect the relief particularly where the attached land is either let out on a Farm Business Tenancy or under a contract farming arrangement.*

B. Business Property Relief

Relief is also available in respect to 'business property' transferred during lifetime or on death. The relief extends to the business assets of a proprietor and the interest of a partner or controlling shareholder in the business capital of a company. The value of such property, providing certain tests are satisfied (e.g. it has been owned by the transferor for two years preceding transfer), is reduced by 100%. Where a partner or controlling shareholder owns assets (e.g. land) that the business uses, the value will be reduced by 50%. Shareholdings in unquoted companies receive a 100% reduction in market value.

Lifetime gifts of property eligible for Agricultural and Business Property Relief have to be retained (or replaced by similar property) until the death of the donor (or earlier death of the donee) if those reliefs are to be available when the tax (or additional tax) becomes payable subsequent to the donor's death

In the case of the transfer of property eligible for APR and BPR, the tax can be paid by annual instalments over ten years free of interest.

6. STAMP TAXES

1. STAMP DUTY

Stamp Duty is charged at 0.5 per cent of consideration paid on the transfer of shares and securities.

2. STAMP DUTY LAND TAX

Stamp duty land tax is charged on the transfer of an interest in land; both sales and leases. With sales of property the tax is levied on a percentage of the sale value of the property (special rules apply to land in disadvantaged areas);

Residential property	Rate	Non-residential and mixed use	Rate
Value up to £125,000..................	nil	Value up to £150,000..............	nil
£125,000 to £250,000	1%	£150,000 to £250,000..............	1%
£250,000 to £500,000	3%	£250,000 to £500,000..............	3%
Over £500,000	4%	Over £500,000.........................	4%

Stamp Duty Land Tax is payable on leases calculated according to the net present value of the rent payable over the term of the lease.

7. VALUE ADDED TAX

Agricultural businesses with a turnover of taxable goods and services in excess of £67,000 per annum (from 1st April 2008) are required to register for VAT. Businesses with a turnover below this limit may apply for voluntary registration. The standard rate of VAT is 17.5%. Most agricultural products are zero rated for VAT purposes. VAT has to be paid on certain inputs. Registered businesses are eligible to reclaim the tax paid where the goods or services purchased have been used in the production of zero-rated supplies.

A flat rate scheme is available to farmers as an alternative to registering for VAT. Farmers under the flat rate scheme do not have to submit tax returns or account for VAT and consequently cannot reclaim tax. They can, however, charge (and keep) a flat rate addition of 4% when they sell to VAT registered customers goods and services which qualify. This addition is not VAT but acts as compensation for losing input tax on purchases. The registered person paying the flat rate amount to the farmer can recover it as if it were VAT, subject to the normal rules for reclaiming. The local VAT office may refuse to issue a certificate to participate in the flat rate scheme if this would mean the farmer would recover substantially (£3,000) more than through the normal system.

On 25th April 2002 a new flat rate scheme was introduced for small businesses generally and is an alternative that farmers can use if they have taxable supplies of no more than £150,000 and a total business income of no more than £187,500. This scheme operates in a different way to the flat rate scheme for farmers in that a business charges the normal rate of VAT on sales. However, the VAT which the business has to remit to Customs and Excise is calculated by multiplying the value of gross sales by a rate specified for each particular trade sector. The rate for agriculture is 6% except for businesses supplying agricultural services, when the rate is 7.5%.

Editorial Note*: Farmers and landowners must always consider the VAT implications when considering any new or more farming activities on the land or within the buildings, particularly where supplies are made the public who cannot recover any VAT which may be charged on the service or goods provided from the farm.*

8. NATIONAL INSURANCE

The tables below set out the National Insurance contributions for the 2008-09 year;

A. **Class 1** (not contracted out)

Employee's weekly earnings	Employee	Employer
£105.00 or less	Nil	Nil
£105.01 to £770.00	11%	12.8%
Over £770.00	1%	12.8%

B. **Class 2**
Self-employed flat rate (exception
if earnings below £4,825 a year) .... £2.30 a week

C. **Class 3**
Non-employed (voluntary) flat rate.................... . £8.10 a week

D. **Class 4**
Self-employed. On profits or gains
between £5,435 and £40,040 .... 8%

over £40,040 .... 1%

Acknowledgement: The Author is grateful to *Howard Worth Chartered Accountants Agricultural Department* (Tel: 01606 369 000) for their assistance in updating this section of the Pocketbook.

VIII FARM BUSINESS MANAGEMENT

1. DEFINITIONS OF FARM MANAGEMENT TERMS

Mainly abstracted from 'Terms and Definitions used in Farm and Horticulture Management', M.A.F.F., 1970.

1. Valuations and Capital

Valuations. Valuation is essentially a process of estimation. Alternative bases are possible, according to the purpose intended. The basis should be consistent throughout the period of any series of figures.

(i) *Saleable crops in store.* At estimated market value less costs still to be incurred, e.g. for storage and marketing. Both may be estimated either at the expected date of sale or at the date of valuation.

(ii) *Growing crops.* Preferably at variable costs to the date of valuation, although estimated total cost can alternatively be used.

(iii) *Saleable crops ready for harvesting* but still in the ground. Preferably valued as bullet (i), less estimated harvesting costs, although they can alternatively be treated as bullet (ii).

(iv) *Fodder stocks (home-grown).* Preferably at variable costs when calculating gross margins. Alternatively at estimated market value (based on hay-equivalent value according to quality). Fodder crops still in the ground, e.g. kale, treated as bullet (ii).

(v) *Stocks of purchased materials (including fodder).* At cost (net of discounts).

(vi) *Machinery and equipment.* Original cost (net of investment grants), less accumulated depreciation to date of valuation – this gives a valuation on the 'historic' cost basis. Alternatively at estimated market value.

(vii) *Livestock.* At current market value, less cost of marketing. Fluctuations in market value expected to be temporary should be ignored.

Tenant's Capital. The estimated total value of capital on the farm, other than land and fixed equipment. There is no easy way of determining this sum precisely and estimates are made in several ways depending on the information available and the purpose for which the estimate is required. One method is to take the average of the opening and closing valuations (at either market value or cost) of livestock, crops, machinery and stores (feed, seed, fertilisers). See also pages 215 (following section).

Landlord's Capital. Value of the land and fixed equipment (including buildings).

2. Output Terms

Revenue (or Income). Receipts adjusted for debtors at the beginning and end of the accounting period. Items such as CAP support, grants, contract receipts and wayleaves are included.

Returns. Revenue adjusted for valuation changes (add closing, deduct opening, valuation).

Gross Output. Returns plus the value of produce consumed in the farmhouse or supplied to workers for which no payment is made, less purchases of livestock, livestock products and other produce bought for resale.

Enterprise Output. The total value of an enterprise, whether sold or retained on the farm. It therefore equals Gross Output of the enterprise plus the market value of any of the products kept on the farm (transfers out). Following 'decoupling' the Single Payment should not be apportioned to individual enterprises, but coupled support such as protein and energy crop per ha payments should be. Products transferred from another enterprise to be used in the production of the enterprise whose output is being calculated are deducted at market value (transfers in). Instead of the accounting year the "harvest year" can be used for crops; valuations are then not relevant.

(Enterprise) Output from Forage. Primarily the sum of the enterprise outputs of grazing livestock, but includes keep let and occasional sales, e.g. of surplus hay, together with an adjustment for changes in the valuation of stocks of home-grown fodder. However, fortuitous changes in stocks caused by yield variations due to the weather, the severity or length of the winter, or minor changes in livestock numbers or forage area can be either ignored (if small in relation to total annual usage) or included in miscellaneous output.

Adjusted Forage (Enterprise) Output is Output from Forage less rented keep and purchases of bulk fodder.

Standard Output. The average enterprise output per hectare of a crop or per head of livestock calculated from either national or local average price and average yield data.

3.   Input Terms

Expenditure. Payments adjusted for creditors at the beginning and end of the accounting period. Capital expenditure is not included.

Costs. Expenditure adjusted for valuation changes (add opening, deduct closing, valuation), with the following adjustments. Add: depreciation on capital expenditure including machinery, any loss made on machinery sales (add to depreciation) and the value of payments in kind to workers if not already included in their earnings. Deduct: purchases of livestock, livestock products and other produce bought for resale, any profit made on machinery (deduct from depreciation), allowance for private use of farm vehicles (deduct from machinery costs), the value of purchased stores used in the farmhouse (e.g. electricity) or sold off the farm (deduct from the relevant item).

Inputs. Costs with the following adjustments, made in order to put all farms on a similar basis for comparative purposes. Add: the value of unpaid family labour, including the manual labour of the farmer and his wife, and, in the case of owner-occupiers, an estimated rental value (based on average rents of similar farms in the area), less any cottage rents received. Deduct: any mortgage payments and other expenses of owner-occupation, interest payments and the cost of paid management. A proportion of the rental value of the farmhouse may also be deducted.

Fixed Costs. See pages (186 -189 whole Farm Fixed Costs).

Variable Costs. See page 1.

4.   Margin Terms

Management and Investment Income. Gross Output less Inputs. It represents the reward to management and the return on tenant's capital invested in the farm, whether borrowed or not. It is mainly used for comparative purposes, all farms having been put on a similar financial basis by the adjustments made to costs in calculating Inputs.

Net Farm Income. Management and Investment Income, less paid management, plus the value of the manual labour of the farmer and his wife. It represents the return to all tenant's type capital and the reward to the farmer for his manual labour and management.

Profit (or Loss). Gross Output less Costs. This represents the surplus or deficit before imputing any notional charges such as rental value or unpaid labour. In the accounts of owner-occupiers it includes any profit accruing from the ownership of land.

Gross Margin. See page 1.

Net Margin. A term sometimes used to denote Gross Margin less direct labour and machinery costs charged to an individual enterprise. This is not, however, nationally accepted terminology. Increasingly Net Margin in the enterprise context is being used to denote the profit of an enterprise by taking its gross output less its 'complete enterprise costs', but see page 3.

5. Area Terms

Total Hectares. All hectares comprising the farm.

Hectares. Total hectares less the area of woods, waste land, roads, buildings, etc.

Adjusted Hectares. Hectares reduced by the conversion of rough grazings into the equivalent hectares of average quality grassland. This is the figure often used for lowland farms when calculating "per hectare" results.

Forage Hectares. Total hectares of forage crops grown, less any hectares exclusively used by pigs or poultry and the area equivalent of any home-grown fodder fed to barley beef. Usually, too, the area of rough grazings is converted to its grassland equivalent (see Adjusted Hectares). Forage crops are all crops, grass and rough grazings grown specifically for grazing livestock, other than catch crops and crops harvested as grain and pulses.

Adjusted Forage Hectares. Forage hectares adjusted as follows. Add area equivalent of keep rented, deduct area equivalent of keep let; deduct the area equivalent of occasional sales of fodder, e.g. surplus hay, and seed cuts (note: hay and seed grown regularly for sale should be regarded as cash crops, not forage crops); add or deduct the area equivalent of planned changes in the valuation of stocks of home-grown fodder (fortuitous changes in stocks resulting from weather conditions may be ignored); convert rough grazings into their grassland equivalent if not already done. The following adjustments also may be made: add the area equivalent of catch crops and of grazing from cash crops of hay or seed: add the area equivalent of purchased fodder.

In calculations such as Gross Margins per Forage Hectare, Adjusted Forage Hectares are usually used. If the area equivalent of purchased fodder has been added the cost of purchased fodder must not be charged as a variable cost: this is probably the best calculation for comparative purposes. Alternatively, when considering all the grazing enterprises taken together, purchased fodder can be deducted as a variable cost and no addition made for its area equivalent.

2. CAPITAL REQUIREMENTS AND RETURN

(i)   *Tenant's Capital consists of:*

  (a) *Machinery.* Costs of new machinery are given on pages 163. Written-down values in 2009 are likely to be averaging £500-600 per hectare (£200-243 per acre) taking all farm types together. Average values for different farm types are given on page 216.

  (b) *Breeding Livestock.* The 2009 average of breeding livestock value per hectare will vary from zero to over £1,500 (£600) for an intensive dairy farm. Approximate average market values of various categories of breeding livestock (of mixed ages in the case of adult stock) are as follows (actual value will vary according to average age and weight, quality and breed):

Average market values of various breeding livestock

	Dairy Cows *(inc. Dry Cows)*
Holstein/Friesian:	£1,200
Channel Island:	£750
Other Dairy Cows:	£900
Beef Cows:	£600

	Dairy Followers		
	Holstein Friesians	Ayrshires and C.I. Breeds	Beef Cattle
In Calf Heifers	£1,500	£800	£850
1-2 years	£650	£450	£500
6-12 months	£450	£320	£350
Under 6 months	£300	£200	£250

	Other Livestock
Ewes	£60
Rams	£275
Sows and In-Pig Gilts	£110
Boars	£500

  (c) Working Capital. This is defined as the current assets of a business less its current liabilities. It is the liquid capital needed to finance the cash flow through the production cycle, the length of which varies considerably between different crop and livestock enterprises and different combinations of these enterprises. It can include the cost of purchased fattening stock, feed, seed, fertilisers, regular labour, machinery running costs, general overhead costs, rent and living expenses. This capital may be only £250 per hectare (£100 per acre) or so on an all-dairying farm but £900 or more per hectare (£365 per acre) on an all-cereals farm where the crop is stored until the spring. The only accurate way to estimate working capital requirement is to complete a full cash flow estimate for the production cycle of the business.

(ii) *Average Tenant's Capital* per hectare (per acre in brackets) for different farm types, as estimated for 2009, are as follows:

Farm Type Group	Average No. Hectares	Livestock	Crops, Cultivns., Stores	Machinery and Equipment*	Total Tenant's Capital	
		£	£	£	£	£
Mainly Dairying:						
under 75 ha..........	60	1000	290	650	1940	(785)
75 to 125 ha.........	90	1200	380	620	2200	(890)
Over 125 ha.........	190	1260	340	730	2330	(940)
Mainly Cereals:						
under 175 ha.........	160	25	350	480	855	(345)
175 to 300 ha.......	250	40	260	535	835	(340)
over 300 ha..........	570	45	280	520	845	(340)
General Cropping:						
under 150 ha.........	120	-	590	610	1200	(485)
150 to 225 ha........	180	-	700	720	1420	(575)
over 225 ha..........	400	-	660	680	1340	(540)
Mainly Sheep/Cattle (Lowground):						
Under 90 ha.........	80	340	135	490	965	(390)
90 to 125 ha............	110	420	120	420	960	(390)
Over 125 ha.........	260	310	110	300	720	(290)
Mainly Sheep/Cattle (Upland LFA):						
under 130 ha.........	115	310	60	310	680	(275)
130 to 230 ha.........	190	285	50	220	555	(225)
over 230 ha..........	365	300	40	210	550	(220)

* Based on current (i.e. replacement) costs.

Note: The above (deliberately rounded) data are based on Farm Business Survey results compiled annually by University/Colleges centres (as listed on page 4). None includes the value of milk quota on farms with dairying. Farm types have been changed from previous editions and the patterns of average tenant's capital on some types appears to be changing, albeit the data is now drawn from different groupings of farms. For example the Mainly Dairying type shows investment rising with size whereas in previous years the opposite was true. This needs to be investigated further, but it would appear that smaller farms are becoming less intensive whilst larger farms are investing significantly more than in the past.

(iii) Return on Capital

(a) *Tenant's capital*. Return on tenant's capital is calculated by taking the management and investment income (MII) of a business as a percentage of the tenant's capital (see definitions in VIII.1). Because MII is before deduction of any interest, this return is 'gross', i.e. before allowing for cost of finance. However, it should be borne in mind that MII includes no charge for management but that a rental value for owner-occupied land and the value of the unpaid labour of the farmer and wife have been deducted.

(b) *Landlord's Capital* (i.e. land, buildings, roads, etc.). The return on landlord's capital is calculated by taking the rental income, less any ownership expenses (mortgage, insurance, repairs etc.), expressed as a percentage of the land value. With farms in 2009 averaging, possibly £15,000 per hectare (£6,070 per acre) (see page 193) with vacant possession (assuming no special amenity or house value), an average lowland rent of, say, £173 per hectare (£70 per acre) (see p. 191), and assuming ownership expenses at £65 per hectare (£26 per acre), the (net) return (£108 per hectare (£44 per acre)) averages 0.72 per cent. If land is taken at its tenanted value, with a vacant possession premium of say one-third, the return increases to 1.08 per cent. If farm business tenancy rents were paid, at say 40% above the average level for established tenants (i.e. £240/ha [£97/acre]), the return would average 1.6 per cent with land at the vacant possession price assumed and 2.4 per cent with land at the tenanted value assumed. Full repairing and insurance leases clearly raise the returns above these levels. Above average quality farms acquire higher rents but also obviously command higher prices than the average levels quoted above.

(iv) *Return on Capital to Individual Enterprises* on a mixed farm is virtually impossible to ascertain, except perhaps for a full-time pig or poultry enterprise, nor would it be of very much use even if it could be determined. It would require the arbitrary allocation both of costs and capital inputs that are common to several, in some cases all, of the enterprises on the farm.

What is relevant and important is the extra (net) return from an enterprise either to be introduced or expanded, as calculated by a partial budget, related to the extra (net) capital needed. The 'net' in brackets relates, as regards return, to the addition to gross margins less any addition to (or plus any reduction in) 'fixed' costs, bearing in mind that another enterprise may have to be deleted or reduced in size; and, as regards capital, to the fact that deletion or reduction of another enterprise may release capital.

In most cases of 'marginal' substitution, it is differences in the value of breeding livestock and differences in variable costs that are particularly relevant, but the timing of both inputs and sales are also obviously very important.

(v) *'Marginal' Capital Requirements* for small changes in crop areas or livestock numbers can be estimated as follows:

Crops: variable costs till sale.

Dairy Cows and Egg Production: value of the cow* or hens, plus food until payment of product.

Other Breeding Livestock: average value of stock*, plus variable costs to sale (payment) of the progeny (e.g. lambs) – or their transfer to another enterprise (*e.g.* weaners to the pig fattening enterprise). Rearing Breeding Livestock (*e.g.* heifers, tegs, gilts, pullets): cost of the calf, lamb, weaner or chick, plus variable costs till they produce their first progeny/eggs.

Fattening Livestock and Production of Stores: cost of stock, plus variable costs till sale.

* Value of breeding stock, including dairy cows: either the average value over their entire breeding or milk producing life (see table on page 216) or their value when they first produce progeny can be taken. The latter will give the lower return on (marginal) capital and is thus the severer test.

Home-reared stock: where stock to be used for milk or egg production, breeding or fattening are home-reared, there are two possibilities:

(a) either they can be valued at variable costs of production when they are transferred from the rearing to the 'productive' enterprise; in this case the return on (marginal) capital will be estimated over the combined rearing and 'productive' enterprise.

(b) or they can be valued at market value at point of transfer. This is the procedure if one wishes to work out a return on (marginal) capital for the rearing and the 'productive' enterprises separately.

(vi) *Return on 'Marginal' Capital.* This is sometimes expressed as the gross margin less fuel and repair costs of the enterprise expanded as a percentage of the 'marginal', or extra, capital. However, two points have to be remembered:

    (a) If another enterprise has had to be reduced in size to enable the enterprise under consideration to be expanded, the capital released and the gross margin forfeited by reducing the size of the first enterprise must be brought into the calculation in estimating the net result of the change.

    (b) All the above statements on 'marginal' capital refer to small changes. If the change is large enough to cause changes in labour, machinery or building requirements the capital changes brought about may be considerably greater.

(vii) Return on Investments in Medium-Term and Long-Term Capital. Rate of Return and the Discounted Yield.

Example: If £5,000 investment results in an annual net return of £500 (after deducting depreciation, but ignoring interest payments):

$$\text{\textit{Rate of Return} on \textit{Initial} Capital} = \frac{500}{5,000} \times 100 = 10\%$$

$$\text{\textit{Rate of Return} on \textit{Average} Capital} = \frac{500}{2,500} \times 100 = 20\%$$

It is more accurate to calculate the '*Discounted Yield*', which is the discount rate that brings the present value of the net cash flows (which means ignoring depreciation) to the value of the investment.

The tables on pages 222 and 223 may be used.

'*Short-Cut' Estimates of the Discounted Yield on depreciating assets.* The Discounted Yield falls between the simple Rates of Return on Initial and Average Capital. In fact, for investments lasting 5 to 15 years, when the Rate of Return on Initial Capital is 10 per cent and on Average Capital 20 per cent, the Discounted Yield will be almost exactly halfway between, i.e. about 15 per cent. However, this is only so providing the anticipated annual net cash earnings are fairly constant — or fluctuate unpredictably around a fairly constant level.

There are three circumstances when the Discounted Yield will get closer to the Rate of Return on Initial Capital (i.e. the lower per cent return) and further from the Rate of Return on Average Capital:

    (a)   The longer the life of the investment.

    (b)   The higher the Rate of Return.

    (c)   The higher the net cash flow is in the later years of the investment compared with the earlier years.

When the opposite circumstances obtain, the Discounted Yield will be closer to the Rate of Return on Average Capital (i.e. the higher per cent return).

Granted that there are inevitably varying degrees of estimation and uncertainty in calculating future net annual earnings of investments, the following short-cuts might reasonably be used where the annual net cash earnings are expected to be fairly constant — or fluctuate unpredictably (e.g. through weather effects on yields) around a fairly constant level. (W.O. period = write-off period; R.R.I.C. = rate of return on initial capital).

1.   Where

    (i)   the W.O. period is 5 years or less,

    (ii)   the W.O. period is 6 - 10 years and the R.R.I.C. is 15 per cent or less,

(iii)   the W.O. period is 11 - 20 years and the R.R.I.C. is 10 per cent or less,

calculate the Return on Capital as being approximately midway between the Rates of Return on Initial and Average Capital, i.e. by calculating the Rate of Return on 2/3 of the original investment.

For example, following the earlier example above:

$$\frac{500}{3,333} \times 100 = 15\%.$$

2.   Where

(i)   the W.O. period is 6 to 10 years and the R.R.I.C. exceeds 15 per cent,

(ii)   the W.O. period is 11 to 20 years and the R.R.I.C. is between 10 per cent and 25 per cent,

(iii)   the W.O. period exceeds 20 years and the R.R.I.C. is 10 per cent or less,

calculate the Return on Capital on 80 per cent of the original investment.

For example, again following the earlier example:

$$\frac{500}{4,000} \times 100 = 12\tfrac{\circ}{}\%.$$

3.   Where

(i)   the W.O. period is 11 to 20 years and the R.R.I.C. exceeds 25 per cent,

(ii)   the W.O. period exceeds 20 years and the R.R.I.C. exceeds 10 per cent, take the Return on Capital to be the R.R.I.C.

In borderline cases, use method 1 rather than 2, or 2 rather than 3 if there is a tendency for the cash flow to be higher in the earlier years, e.g. because of tax allowances on machinery. Take 2 rather than 1, and 3 rather than 2, if the likelihood is that the cash flow will be lower in earlier years and increase in later years.

However, where the annual cash flow is expected to vary (apart from unpredictable fluctuations) it is safer to make the full D.C.F. calculation. This is particularly so where the variation is both up and down and where further periodic investments are to be made during the life of the project.

3. INTEREST RATES

(i)   *Rate of Interest on Bank Loans.* Typically 2.5% to 3.0% above Base Rate. Main range is 1.5% above to 4.0% above. Extremes are likely to be 0.8% above (minimum) and 7% above (maximum).

(ii) *Annual Percentage Rate (APR).* This is the effective rate of interest calculated on an annual basis and should be used when seeking to make a true comparison between interest charges on money borrowed from different sources. The APR allows for the fact that when interest is applied to accounts at half yearly, quarterly or monthly intervals an element of compounding will arise. For example, £100 borrowed for one year at a quoted annual nominal interest rate of 6% (e.g. 2% over base rate of 4%) with interest charged quarterly, will lead to an accumulated interest charge of £6.136 (i.e., giving an APR of just under 6.14%). The higher the annual nominal interest rate and the more frequently the interest charges are applied to the account, the more pronounced the compounding element becomes. For example, an annual nominal interest rate of 10% produces an APR of 10.25% with half yearly charging, 10.38% with quarterly charging and 10.47% with monthly charging and with a nominal rate as high as 20% the rates become 21%, 21.6% and 21.9% respectively.

In the case of some loans and hire purchase agreements, interest charges may be quoted as a flat rate on the original amount borrowed. The APR will be considerably greater than the flat rate if the loan is repaid by equal periodic instalments, comprising part capital and part interest, so that the borrowing is completely repaid by the end of the agreed term. For example, the APR for a loan at a flat rate of interest of 8% repaid by monthly instalments over 5 years will be 15%. The shorter the repayment period, and the more frequent the payments, the higher is the APR compared with the flat rate.

(iii) *The Real Rate of Interest.* When preparing simple profit and loss budgets to estimate the worthwhileness of an investment in a fixed asset (machinery, buildings, land), it is usual to price inputs and outputs at present-day values even when most costs and returns are expected to rise due to inflation over the life of the investment. Where this real terms approach is adopted a more realistic estimate of the effect on profitability can be gained by basing charges for capital on the real rate of interest rather than the APR. The real rate of interest is the APR adjusted for the annual rate at which prices relevant to the investment are expected to increase. A crude estimate of the real rate of interest can be obtained by simply subtracting the expected rate of price increase from the APR; for example, if the APR were 8% and the expected rate of inflation 3%, the real rate of interest would be 8 – 3 = 5%.

4. FINANCIAL RATIOS

1. *Common Ratios*

The following ratios are often quoted as rough guidelines:

		% of Gross Output
Variable Costs		30-40%
Labour	15-17½%	
Machinery	15-17½%	30-40%
Sundry Fixed Costs	5%	
Rent & Interest		15%
Margin*		15%

* to cover drawings, tax, capital repayments, reinvestments

It has to be borne in mind, however, that these are indeed only rough guidelines and need to be considered with great care. Values vary, for example, with type of farming and size of farm. Furthermore, it is often unclear how certain items are being measured, especially whether unpaid manual labour of the farmer and family has been included or whether a rental value has been allowed for owner-occupied land. In the table above variable costs at 30% or less would be found on cereals type farms, leaving 40% for labour, machinery and sundry fixed costs. On intensive livestock farms variable costs of 40% would be expected, leaving only 30% for fixed costs.

2. *Farm Survey Ratios*

The following are rounded averages based on farm surveys in recent years on a large sample of all types of farm, assuming a Management and Investment Income (see page 213) of 10% of Total Output is made. It is to be noted that Total Output includes the market value of any production retained for use/consumption on the farm (e.g. cereals for feed or seed), Unpaid Labour (value of manual labour supplied by the farmer and spouse) is included. Rent includes the rental value of owner-occupied land and Interest charges are not included in the costs. Casual labour and all Contract work are included in fixed costs. Obviously, costs are a lower proportion and the margin a higher proportion in profitable years, and vice-versa in low profit years. Obviously, too, within years the more profitable farms have lower percentage costs, leaving higher percentage margins and vice-versa.

Average Financial Ratios from Farm Business Survey

	% Total Output	% Total Gross Margin	% Total Fixed Costs
Variable Costs:			
(excl. casual labour and contract work)	32.5		
Fixed Costs:			
Labour: Paid (inc. casuals) }	20	30	33
Labour: Unpaid			
Power & Machinery (inc. contract work)	20	30	33
Labour & Machinery	40	60	66
Rent/Rental Value	12.5	19	21
General Overheads	7.5	11	13
Total Fixed Costs	60	90	100
Margin	**7.5**	**10**	-

Total Gross Margin = 67.5% of Total Output

3. *Lending Criteria*

Another set of standards widely used by lending and leasing institutions looks at total Finance Charges (rent, interest, leasing charges, etc.), as a percentage of Gross Output and Gross Margin;

Finance as a % of Gross Output	Finance as a % of Gross Margin	Lending Criteria
0-10%	0-15%	Normally very safe
11-15%	16-22.5%	Common range, should be safe
16-20%	23-29%	Care required
20% plus	30% plus	Potentially dangerous

As lenders will be well aware, however, these ratios too must be regarded with caution and in conjunction with the farm's level of net worth (% equity) and its trend in recent years, recent trends in its profitability and the potential borrower's record of expenditure both on and off the farm, together with his or her character and potential. Also, of course, some enterprises / types of farming are more risky than others.

Discounting Table A

Discount Factors for Calculating the Present Value of Future (irregular) Cash Flows

Year	Percentage																				
	3%	4%	5%	6%	7%	8%	9%	10%	11%	12%	13%	14%	15%	16%	18%	20%	25%
1	0.971	0.962	0.952	0.943	0.935	0.926	0.917	0.909	0.901	0.893	0.885	0.877	0.870	0.862	0.847	0.833	0.800
2	0.943	0.925	0.907	0.890	0.873	0.857	0.842	0.826	0.812	0.797	0.783	0.769	0.756	0.743	0.718	0.694	0.640
3	0.915	0.889	0.864	0.840	0.816	0.794	0.772	0.751	0.731	0.712	0.693	0.675	0.658	0.641	0.609	0.579	0.512
4	0.888	0.855	0.823	0.792	0.763	0.735	0.708	0.683	0.659	0.636	0.613	0.592	0.572	0.552	0.516	0.482	0.410
5	0.863	0.822	0.784	0.747	0.713	0.681	0.650	0.621	0.593	0.567	0.543	0.519	0.497	0.476	0.437	0.402	0.328
6	0.837	0.790	0.746	0.705	0.666	0.630	0.596	0.564	0.535	0.507	0.480	0.456	0.432	0.410	0.370	0.335	0.262
7	0.813	0.760	0.711	0.665	0.623	0.583	0.547	0.513	0.482	0.452	0.425	0.400	0.376	0.354	0.314	0.279	0.210
8	0.789	0.731	0.677	0.627	0.582	0.540	0.502	0.467	0.434	0.404	0.376	0.351	0.327	0.305	0.266	0.233	0.168
9	0.766	0.703	0.645	0.592	0.544	0.500	0.460	0.424	0.391	0.361	0.333	0.308	0.284	0.263	0.225	0.194	0.134
10	0.744	0.676	0.614	0.558	0.508	0.463	0.422	0.386	0.352	0.322	0.295	0.270	0.247	0.227	0.191	0.162	0.107
11	0.722	0.650	0.585	0.527	0.475	0.429	0.388	0.350	0.317	0.287	0.261	0.237	0.215	0.195	0.162	0.135	0.086
12	0.701	0.625	0.557	0.497	0.444	0.397	0.356	0.319	0.286	0.257	0.231	0.208	0.187	0.168	0.137	0.112	0.069
13	0.681	0.601	0.530	0.469	0.415	0.368	0.326	0.290	0.258	0.229	0.204	0.182	0.163	0.145	0.116	0.093	0.055
14	0.661	0.577	0.505	0.442	0.388	0.340	0.299	0.263	0.232	0.205	0.181	0.160	0.141	0.125	0.098	0.078	0.044
15	0.642	0.555	0.481	0.417	0.362	0.315	0.275	0.239	0.209	0.183	0.160	0.140	0.123	0.108	0.084	0.065	0.035
20	0.554	0.456	0.377	0.312	0.258	0.215	0.178	0.149	0.124	0.104	0.087	0.073	0.061	0.051	0.037	0.026	0.012
25	0.478	0.375	0.295	0.233	0.184	0.146	0.116	0.092	0.074	0.059	0.047	0.038	0.030	0.024	0.016	0.010	0.004
30	0.412	0.308	0.231	0.174	0.131	0.099	0.075	0.057	0.044	0.033	0.026	0.020	0.015	0.012	0.007	0.004	0.001

Example: The Present Value of £500 received 10 years from now, at 12 per cent discount rate of interest = 500 x 0.322 = £161.

Conversely, £161 invested now, at 12 per cent compound interest, will be worth £500 in 10 years' time.

222

Discounting Table B

Discount Factors for Calculating the Present Value of Future Annuity (i.e. Constant Annual Cash Fow) Receivable in Year 1 to n inclusive.

Year	3%	4%	5%	6%	7%	8%	9%	10%	11%	12%	13%	14%	15%	16%	18%	20%	25%
1	0.971	0.962	0.952	0.943	0.935	0.926	0.917	0.909	0.901	0.893	0.885	0.877	0.870	0.862	0.847	0.833	0.800
2	1.913	1.886	1.859	1.833	1.808	1.783	1.759	1.736	1.713	1.690	1.668	1.647	1.626	1.605	1.566	1.528	1.440
3	2.829	2.775	2.723	2.673	2.624	2.577	2.531	2.487	2.444	2.402	2.361	2.322	2.283	2.246	2.174	2.106	1.952
4	3.717	3.630	3.546	3.465	3.387	3.312	3.240	3.170	3.102	3.037	2.974	2.914	2.855	2.798	2.690	2.589	2.362
5	4.580	4.452	4.329	4.212	4.100	3.993	3.890	3.791	3.696	3.605	3.517	3.433	3.352	3.274	3.127	2.991	2.689
6	5.417	5.242	5.076	4.917	4.767	4.623	4.486	4.355	4.231	4.111	3.998	3.889	3.784	3.685	3.498	3.326	2.951
7	6.230	6.002	5.786	5.582	5.389	5.206	5.033	4.868	4.712	4.564	4.423	4.288	4.160	4.039	3.812	3.605	3.161
8	7.020	6.733	6.463	6.210	5.971	5.747	5.535	5.335	5.146	4.968	4.799	4.639	4.487	4.344	4.078	3.837	3.329
9	7.786	7.435	7.108	6.802	6.515	6.247	5.995	5.759	5.537	5.328	5.132	4.946	4.772	4.607	4.303	4.031	3.463
10	8.530	8.111	7.722	7.360	7.024	6.710	6.418	6.145	5.889	5.650	5.426	5.216	5.019	4.833	4.494	4.192	3.570
11	9.253	8.760	8.306	7.887	7.499	7.139	6.805	6.495	6.207	5.938	5.687	5.453	5.234	5.029	4.656	4.327	3.656
12	9.954	9.385	8.863	8.384	7.943	7.536	7.161	6.814	6.492	6.194	5.918	5.660	5.421	5.197	4.793	4.439	3.725
13	10.635	9.986	9.394	8.853	8.358	7.904	7.487	7.103	6.750	6.424	6.122	5.842	5.583	5.342	4.910	4.533	3.780
14	11.296	10.563	9.899	9.295	8.745	8.244	7.786	7.367	6.982	6.628	6.302	6.002	5.724	5.468	5.008	4.611	3.824
15	11.938	11.118	10.380	9.712	9.108	8.559	8.061	7.606	7.191	6.811	6.462	6.142	5.847	5.575	5.092	4.675	3.859
20	14.877	13.590	12.462	11.470	10.594	9.818	9.129	8.514	7.963	7.469	7.025	6.623	6.259	5.929	5.353	4.870	3.954
25	17.413	15.662	14.094	12.783	11.654	10.675	9.823	9.077	8.422	7.843	7.330	6.873	6.464	6.097	5.467	4.948	3.985
30	19.600	17.292	15.372	13.765	12.409	11.258	10.274	9.427	8.694	8.055	7.496	7.003	6.566	6.177	5.517	4.979	3.995

Example: The Present Value of £500 a year for the next 10 years, at 12 per cent discount rate of interest = 500 x 5.650 = £2,825. This is the same answer that would be obtained by multiplying 500 by each discount factor (at 12 per cent) in Table A for each year from 1 to 10, and adding together the ten resulting figures.

To obtain the Discounted Yield of a constant annual net cash flow, divide this into the original investment and look up the resulting figure in the table above, against the number of years. Example: an investment of £1,000 is estimated to produce £80 a year additional profit over 10 years (before charging interest). Add £100 depreciation a year = £180 annual net cash flow. 1000 / 180 = 5.56. This equals just over 12 per cent (the 10 years /12 per cent figure being 5.650).

223

Compounding Table A

The Future Money Value of £1 after n Years with no additional payments made

Rate of Interest

Year	3%	4%	5%	6%	7%	8%	9%	10%	11%	12%	13%	14%	15%	16%	18%	20%	25%
1	1.03	1.04	1.05	1.06	1.07	1.08	1.09	1.10	1.11	1.12	1.13	1.14	1.15	1.16	1.18	1.20	1.25
2	1.06	1.08	1.10	1.12	1.14	1.17	1.19	1.21	1.23	1.25	1.28	1.30	1.32	1.35	1.39	1.44	1.56
3	1.09	1.12	1.16	1.19	1.23	1.26	1.30	1.33	1.37	1.40	1.44	1.48	1.52	1.56	1.64	1.73	1.95
4	1.13	1.17	1.22	1.26	1.31	1.36	1.41	1.46	1.52	1.57	1.63	1.69	1.75	1.81	1.94	2.07	2.44
5	1.16	1.22	1.28	1.34	1.40	1.47	1.54	1.61	1.69	1.76	1.84	1.93	2.01	2.10	2.29	2.49	3.05
6	1.19	1.27	1.34	1.42	1.50	1.59	1.68	1.77	1.87	1.97	2.08	2.19	2.31	2.44	2.70	2.99	3.81
7	1.23	1.32	1.41	1.50	1.61	1.71	1.83	1.95	2.08	2.21	2.35	2.50	2.66	2.83	3.19	3.58	4.77
8	1.27	1.37	1.48	1.59	1.72	1.85	1.99	2.14	2.30	2.48	2.66	2.85	3.06	3.28	3.76	4.30	5.96
9	1.30	1.42	1.55	1.69	1.84	2.00	2.17	2.36	2.56	2.77	3.00	3.25	3.52	3.80	4.44	5.16	7.45
10	1.34	1.48	1.63	1.79	1.97	2.16	2.37	2.59	2.84	3.11	3.39	3.71	4.05	4.41	5.23	6.19	9.31
11	1.38	1.54	1.71	1.90	2.10	2.33	2.58	2.85	3.15	3.48	3.84	4.23	4.65	5.12	6.18	7.43	11.64
12	1.43	1.60	1.80	2.01	2.25	2.52	2.81	3.14	3.50	3.90	4.33	4.82	5.35	5.94	7.29	8.92	14.55
13	1.47	1.67	1.89	2.13	2.41	2.72	3.07	3.45	3.88	4.36	4.90	5.49	6.15	6.89	8.60	10.70	18.19
14	1.51	1.73	1.98	2.26	2.58	2.94	3.34	3.80	4.31	4.89	5.53	6.26	7.08	7.99	10.15	12.84	22.74
15	1.56	1.80	2.08	2.40	2.76	3.17	3.64	4.18	4.78	5.47	6.25	7.14	8.14	9.27	11.97	15.41	28.42
20	1.81	2.19	2.65	3.21	3.87	4.66	5.60	6.73	8.06	9.65	11.52	13.74	16.37	19.46	27.39	38.34	86.74
25	2.09	2.67	3.39	4.29	5.43	6.85	8.62	10.83	13.59	17.00	21.23	26.46	32.92	40.87	62.67	95.40	264.7
30	2.43	3.24	4.32	5.74	7.61	10.06	13.27	17.45	22.89	29.96	39.12	50.95	66.21	85.85	143.4	237.4	807.8

Compounding Table B

The Future Money Value of £1 after n Years*

Year								Rate of Interest									
	3%	4%	5%	6%	7%	8%	9%	10%	11%	12%	13%	14%	15%	16%	18%	20%	25%
1	1.03	1.04	1.05	1.06	1.07	1.08	1.09	1.10	1.11	1.12	1.13	1.14	1.15	1.16	1.18	1.20	1.25
2	2.09	2.12	2.15	2.18	2.21	2.25	2.28	2.31	2.34	2.37	2.41	2.44	2.47	2.51	2.57	2.64	2.81
3	3.18	3.25	3.31	3.37	3.44	3.51	3.57	3.64	3.71	3.78	3.85	3.92	3.99	4.07	4.22	4.37	4.77
4	4.31	4.42	4.53	4.64	4.75	4.87	4.98	5.11	5.23	5.35	5.48	5.61	5.74	5.88	6.15	6.44	7.21
5	5.47	5.63	5.80	5.98	6.15	6.34	6.52	6.72	6.91	7.12	7.32	7.54	7.75	7.98	8.44	8.93	10.26
6	6.66	6.90	7.14	7.39	7.65	7.92	8.20	8.49	8.78	9.09	9.40	9.73	10.07	10.41	11.14	11.92	14.07
7	7.89	8.21	8.55	8.90	9.26	9.64	10.03	10.44	10.86	11.30	11.76	12.23	12.73	13.24	14.33	15.50	18.84
8	9.16	9.58	10.03	10.49	10.98	11.49	12.02	12.58	13.16	13.78	14.42	15.09	15.79	16.52	18.09	19.80	24.80
9	10.46	11.01	11.58	12.18	12.82	13.49	14.19	14.94	15.72	16.55	17.42	18.34	19.30	20.32	22.52	24.96	32.25
10	11.81	12.49	13.21	13.97	14.78	15.65	16.56	17.53	18.56	19.65	20.81	22.04	23.35	24.73	27.76	31.15	41.57
11	13.19	14.03	14.92	15.87	16.89	17.98	19.14	20.38	21.71	23.13	24.65	26.27	28.00	29.85	33.93	38.58	53.21
12	14.62	15.63	16.71	17.88	19.14	20.50	21.95	23.52	25.21	27.03	28.98	31.09	33.35	35.79	41.22	47.50	67.76
13	16.09	17.29	18.60	20.02	21.55	23.21	25.02	26.97	29.09	31.39	33.88	36.58	39.50	42.67	49.82	58.20	85.95
14	17.60	19.02	20.58	22.28	24.13	26.15	28.36	30.77	33.41	36.28	39.42	42.84	46.58	50.66	59.97	71.04	108.7
15	19.16	20.82	22.66	24.67	26.89	29.32	32.00	34.95	38.19	41.75	45.67	49.98	54.72	59.93	71.94	86.44	137.1
20	27.68	30.97	34.72	38.99	43.87	49.42	55.76	63.00	71.27	80.70	91.47	103.8	117.8	133.8	173.0	224.0	428.7
25	37.55	43.31	50.11	58.16	67.68	78.95	92.32	108.2	127.0	149.3	175.8	207.3	244.7	289.1	404.3	566.4	1318
30	49.00	58.33	69.76	83.80	101.1	122.3	148.6	180.9	220.9	270.3	331.3	406.7	500.0	615.2	933.3	1418	4034

* Equal payments made at the beginning of each year.

Amortisation Table

Annual Charge to write off £1,000

Write-off Period (Years)	Rate of Interest															
	3	4	5	6	7	8	9	10	11	12	13	14	15	16	18	20
5	218	225	231	237	244	250	257	264	271	277	284	291	298	305	320	334
6	185	191	197	203	210	216	223	230	236	243	250	257	264	271	286	301
7	161	167	173	179	186	192	199	205	212	219	226	233	240	248	262	277
8	142	149	155	161	167	174	181	187	194	201	208	216	223	230	245	261
9	128	134	141	147	153	160	167	174	181	188	195	202	210	217	232	248
10	117	123	130	136	142	149	156	163	170	177	184	192	199	207	223	239
11	108	114	120	127	133	140	147	154	161	168	176	183	191	199	215	231
12	100	107	113	119	125	133	140	147	154	161	169	177	184	192	209	225
13	94	100	106	113	120	127	134	141	148	156	163	171	179	187	204	221
14	89	95	101	108	114	121	128	136	143	151	159	167	175	183	200	217
15	84	90	96	103	110	117	124	131	139	147	155	163	171	179	196	214
16	80	86	92	99	106	113	120	128	136	143	151	160	168	176	194	211
17	76	82	89	95	102	110	117	125	132	140	149	157	165	174	191	209
18	73	79	86	92	99	107	114	122	130	138	146	155	163	172	190	208
19	70	76	83	90	97	104	112	120	128	136	144	153	161	170	188	206
20	67	74	80	87	94	102	110	117	126	134	142	151	160	169	187	205
25	57	64	71	78	86	94	102	110	119	127	136	145	155	164	183	202
30	51	58	65	73	81	89	97	106	115	124	133	143	152	162	181	201
40	43	51	58	66	75	84	93	102	112	122	131	141	151	160	180	200

Example: £3,000 is borrowed to erect a building. The annual charge to service interest and capital repayment on the £3,000, repayable over 10 years at 12%, is 3 x £177 = £531. Where the write-off period of the building (10 years) is equal to the repayment period of the loan, then the average annual depreciation and interest will also equal £531.

The proportion of the total annual charge representing the average amount of capital repaid per annum can be readily determined by dividing the sum borrowed by the number of years of the loan: (in the above example this is £3,000 ÷ 10 = £300/year). The remainder is clearly the average amount of interest paid per annum: (in the above example, £531 – £300 = £231/year). The year to year variations between the two items (i.e. capital repaid and interest) are shown in the tables on pages 228 to 230, which demonstrate the way in which the capital repayment part increases and the interest part decreases over time.

Sinking Fund Table

The sum required to be set aside at the end of each year to make £1,000

								Rate of Interest								
No. of Years	3	4	5	6	7	8	9	10	11	12	13	14	15	16	18	20
5	188	185	181	177	174	170	167	164	161	157	154	151	148	145	140	134
6	155	151	147	143	140	136	133	130	126	123	120	117	114	111	106	101
7	131	127	123	119	116	112	109	105	102	99	96	93	90	88	82	77
8	112	109	105	101	97	94	91	87	84	81	78	76	73	70	65	61
9	98	94	91	87	83	80	77	74	71	68	65	62	60	57	52	48
10	87	83	80	76	72	69	66	63	60	57	54	52	49	47	43	39
11	78	74	70	67	63	60	57	54	51	48	46	43	41	39	35	31
12	70	67	63	59	56	53	50	47	44	41	39	37	34	32	29	25
13	64	60	56	53	50	47	44	41	38	36	33	31	29	27	24	21
14	59	55	51	48	44	41	38	36	33	31	29	27	25	23	20	17
15	54	50	46	43	40	37	34	31	29	27	25	23	21	19	16	14
16	50	46	42	39	36	33	30	28	26	23	21	20	18	16	14	11
17	46	42	39	35	32	30	27	25	22	20	19	17	15	14	11	9
18	43	39	36	32	29	27	24	22	20	18	16	15	13	12	10	8
19	40	36	33	30	27	24	22	20	18	16	14	13	11	10	8	6
20	37	34	30	27	24	22	20	17	16	14	12	11	10	9	7	5
25	27	24	21	18	16	14	12	10	9	7	6	5	5	4	3	2
30	21	18	15	13	11	9	7	6	5	4	3	3	2	2	1	1
40	13	11	8	6	5	4	3	2	2	1	1	1	1	—	—	—

Mortgage Repayment Data

Items per £1000 invested; where I = Interest, P = Principal repaid, L = Loan outstanding

Loan through 5 years	4%			5%			6%			8%			10%			12%		
	I	P	L	I	P	L	I	P	L	I	P	L	I	P	L	I	P	L
1	40	185	815	50	181	819	60	177	823	80	170	830	100	164	836	120	157	834
2	33	192	623	41	190	629	49	188	635	66	184	645	84	180	656	101	175	670
3	25	200	424	31	200	424	38	199	435	52	199	447	66	198	458	80	197	469
4	17	208	216	21	210	220	26	211	224	36	215	232	46	218	240	56	221	248
5	9	216	0	11	220	0	13	224	0	19	232	0	24	240	0	30	248	0
10 years																		
1	40	83	917	50	80	920	60	76	924	80	69	931	100	63	939	120	57	934
2	37	87	830	46	83	837	55	80	844	75	75	856	94	69	868	113	64	879
3	33	90	740	42	88	749	51	85	758	69	81	776	87	76	792	106	71	808
4	30	94	646	37	92	657	46	90	668	62	87	689	79	84	709	97	80	728
5	26	97	549	33	97	561	40	96	572	55	94	595	71	92	617	87	90	638
6	22	101	448	28	101	459	34	102	471	48	101	494	62	101	516	77	100	538
7	18	105	342	23	107	353	28	108	363	39	110	384	52	111	405	65	112	425
8	14	110	233	18	112	241	22	114	249	31	118	266	40	122	282	51	126	299
9	9	114	119	12	117	123	15	121	128	21	128	138	28	134	148	36	141	158
10	5	119	0	6	123	0	8	128	0	11	138	0	15	148	0	19	158	0

228

Mortgage Repayment Data (continued)

Loan through 20 years	4%			5%			6%			8%			10%			12%		
	I	P	L	I	P	L	I	P	L	I	P	L	I	P	L	I	P	L
1	40	34	966	50	30	970	60	27	973	80	22	978	100	17	983	120	14	986
5	34	39	818	43	37	833	53	34	847	72	30	872	92	26	893	112	22	912
10	26	48	597	33	47	620	41	46	642	58	44	683	76	41	722	95	38	756
15	15	58	328	20	60	347	26	61	367	38	64	407	51	66	445	66	68	483
20	3	71	0	4	76	0	5	82	0	8	94	0	11	107	0	14	120	0
25 years																		
1	40	24	976	50	21	979	60	18	982	80	14	986	100	10	990	120	7	993
5	36	28	870	45	25	884	55	23	897	75	19	920	95	15	938	116	12	952
10	30	34	712	38	33	736	47	31	760	66	27	802	86	24	838	107	21	868
15	22	42	519	29	41	548	37	41	576	54	40	629	72	39	677	91	37	720
20	13	51	285	18	53	307	23	55	330	35	59	374	48	62	418	63	65	460
25	2	62	0	3	68	0	4	74	0	7	87	0	10	100	0	14	114	0

Mortgage Repayment Data (continued)

Loan through	6%			8%			10%			12%			14%			16%		
30 years	I	P	L	I	P	L	I	P	L	I	P	L	I	P	L	I	P	L
1	60	13	987	80	9	991	100	6	994	120	4	996	140	3	997	160	2	998
5	57	16	929	77	12	948	97	9	963	118	7	974	138	5	986	158	3	987
10	51	21	833	71	18	872	92	14	903	113	11	927	134	9	951	155	7	960
15	44	29	706	63	26	760	83	23	807	104	20	846	126	17	890	147	15	903
20	34	38	535	51	38	596	69	37	652	88	36	701	108	35	751	130	32	782
25	21	51	306	33	56	355	46	60	402	61	63	488	83	60	494	95	66	530
30	4	69	0	7	82	0	10	96	0	13	111	0	16	127	0	22	140	0
40 years																		
1	60	6	994	80	4	996	100	2	998	120	1	999	140	1	999	160	0	1000
5	58	8	964	79	5	977	99	3	986	119	2	992	139	2	995	160	1	997
10	56	11	915	76	8	944	97	5	964	118	4	977	138	3	989	159	2	991
15	52	15	850	73	11	895	94	9	928	115	6	951	136	5	973	157	3	978
20	47	20	762	67	17	823	88	14	871	110	11	906	130	11	942	153	7	951
25	40	26	645	59	24	718	80	22	778	102	20	826	123	18	874	145	15	894
30	31	35	489	48	36	563	66	36	628	86	35	685	109	32	742	129	31	775
35	20	47	280	31	53	335	45	58	388	60	61	437	85	56	487	95	66	525
40	4	63	0	6	78	0	9	93	0	13	108	0	18	123	0	22	138	0

Note—All figures rounded to nearest £.

6. FARM RECORDS

The following records should be kept for management purposes:

1. *Basic Whole Farm Financial Position*

1. Cash Analysis Book, fully detailed.

2. Petty Cash Book.

3. Annual Valuation, including physical quantities of

   i. Harvested crops in store

   ii. Livestock (breeding and fattening) at (near) market value, less any variable costs yet to be borne.

   iii. Fertilisers, seeds, sprays, casual labour or contract work applied to growing crops should be recorded, but "cultivations" and manurial residues can be ignored for management purposes.

   iv. Fertiliser, seed, sprays and other sundry direct items in store,

4. Debtors and creditors at the end of the financial year.

2. *Other Financial and Physical Records*

1. Output (quantities and value) of each crop and livestock enterprise for the "harvest year" (or production cycle). It may be possible to get information of sales from a fully detailed cash analysis book (although, for crops, the financial year figures will then have to be allocated between crops from the current harvest and those from the harvest in the previous financial year, in order to check on the accuracy of the opening valuation of crops in store; this is particularly a problem with Michaelmas ending accounts). The following records of internal transfers and consumption will also be required:

   (a) Numbers and market value of livestock transferred from one livestock category to another, e.g. dairy calves to dairy followers or beef enterprise, or dairy heifers to dairy enterprise.

   (b) Quantity and market value of cereals fed on farm and used for seed.

   (c) Quantity and market value of milk and other produce consumed by the farmer or his employees, used on the farm (e.g. milk fed to calves), or sold direct.

2. A monthly record of livestock numbers; preferably reconciled with the previous month according to births, purchases, deaths, sales and transfers.

3. Costs and quantities of concentrate feed to each category of livestock, including home-grown cereals fed on the farm.

4. Allocation of costs of seed, fertiliser, sprays, casual labour and contract work specific to an enterprise. This is in order to calculate gross margins, where required.

5. Breeding record for cows, including bulling dates, date(s) served, type of bull used, pregnancy testing, estimated calving date, actual calving date, and date when dried off.

6. For each crop, total output and yield per hectare, in both quantity and value. Include each field where the crop has been grown and its approximate yield, where this can be satisfactorily obtained.

7. For each field, keep one page to cover a period of say, ten years. Record on this, each year, crop grown, variety sown, fertiliser used, sprays used, date sown, date(s) harvested, approximate yield (if obtainable), and any other special notes that you feel may have significance for the future.

8. A rotation record. On a single page, if possible, list each field down the side and say, ten years along the top. Colour each field-year space according to the crop grown, e.g. barley yellow, potatoes red, etc.

9. It is important to note that other farm records are required for legislative and cross compliance purposes such as fertiliser records within an NVZ which legally have to be kept for five years.

IX. MISCELLANEOUS DATA

1. CONSERVATION COSTS

Note: Costs can vary quite widely, depending on geographical location and the type and size of the job. Markets for such services can be highly localised, sparse in some areas, competitive in others. (N.B. Abbreviations. DEFRA: Department of Environment, Food and Rural Affairs; BTCV: British Trust for Conservation Volunteers).

Hedge Cutting. From £300 per day at an average of 3 miles per day.

Hedge Laying. Contract labour, £7.45-£10.50 per metre (excluding stakes, bindings, burning debris), or £9.50 per hour. Contractor, 15 metres/day; BTCV, 5 metres/day per person. Nov./March. Every 8 to 20 years. Lantra quotes £1.50 a metre plus 60p a metre for stakers and pleachers, 40 metres a day.

Hedge Planting. Transplants av. £43/100; netlon guards av. 65p; canes av. 10p; fencing (labour and materials): stock proof £3.50/metre, rabbit proof (dug in) up to £5.50/metre. Overall, £2.35/metre unguarded and unfenced, £9.50/metre guarded and fenced. Contract labour: planting up to £2.30/metre, fencing up to £2.60/metre. Contractor 100-150 metres/day; BTCV 20 metres/day. Pref Oct./March. Above includes repair.

Hedge Coppicing. By hand: 2 men and a chain saw, £5-6/metre plus burning debris. Contractor: tractor mounted saw, driver and 2 men, 13 metres/ hour, £34/hour.

Dry Stone Walling. Cost of stone approximately £100/tonne. Cost of building wall £70-£85 per square metre.

Amenity Tree Planting; (half acre block or less). Transplants av. 85p; shelter plus stake and tie av. £1.10; stake av. 55p; whip av. 75p. (55p-£1.10); rabbit spiral guard 33p; netlon guard av. 55p (but 20p in a 50 m roll); cane av. 12p. Trees per man day: farmer 200, contractor 400; (large-scale, 33 man days/ha). Optimal time November to April.

Shelter Belts. Per 100 metre length: 100 large species (oak, lime, etc.) £50; 66 medium species (cherry, birch, etc.) £42; 100 shrubs, £33; 166 tree stakes, shelters and ties, £260; (site preparation, weed control, labour and fencing extra). DEFRA standard costs £670/ha; windbreaks £35.50/ha.

Woodland Establishment. Conifers £200/1000. To supply and plant oak or beech transplants (2-3ft tall) in tubes £3.50-£4.00 each, dependent on shelter size. Rabbit fencing £5.50/metre (dug in). Contract labour: conifers at 2m (inc. trees) £1,500/ha; broadleaves at 3m (inc. trees) £1,000/ha; forest transplants (not inc. trees) £280/1,050. 12.5 days/ha (contractor). Optimal timing November to April. (Above not including maintenance).

Forestry, General. Contract labour: chain sawing £19/hr., brush cutting £11.00/hr, extracting timber/pulp £4.40-£10.50/tonne, chemical spot weeding 6p-8p/tree, rhododendron control £630-£840/acre.

Pond Construction. Butyl lining (0.75mm) £5.00/m^2; other linings up to £3.25/m^2. Contract labour: 150 Komatsu £27/hr.; bulldozer D6 LGP £44/hr, 13t 360° excavator £38/hr (excluding haulage), Flailmowers from £17/hr. Autumn (dry ground conditions).

Pond Maintenance. Hymac £39/hr.; Backhoe £22-24/hr. 5m^2/day (BTCV); 100 m^2/day (contractor). Timing: probably winter; time depends on ground condition and species whose life cycles may be disturbed. Every 5 to 50 years.

Ditch Maintenance. Backhoe excavator £21/hr; 13 tonne 360° excavator £31/hr.; labour £10.50/hr. preferably in winter. Every 3 to 7 years on rotation.

Pollarding and Tree Surgery. Pollard: £43-£65/stool; surgery: £163/ tree. Pollarding: 2 or 3 trees/day. Surgery: 2 days/tree. Winter. Pollard every 20-40 years.

Establishment of Wildlife Grassland Meadow. £160-255/ha for ground preparation, depending on weed burden, more for heavy land or exceptional weed burden. Seed costs very variable, but as a guide:

- Native Perennial wild flowers and grasses, £36.00/kg, 25kg/ha = £900/ha

- Nectar mix for bumble bees and butterflies £13.50/kg, 25kg/ha = £340/ha

- Bird Seed sward £4.70/kg, 10kg/ha = £47/ha for single year crop, £4.30/kg, 50kg/ha = £215 for longer sward.

- Single species native grass seeds vary from £3.00/kg (e.g. meadow fescue) to over £60/kg (Sweet Vernal).

- Single species native perennial wild flower seeds vary from £7/kg (e.g. red clover) to well over £200/kg (e.g. Birdsfoot Trefoil or Cowslip)

Permanent Grass Margins at Field Edges. To provide wildlife benefits and help control pernicious weeds, reducing herbicides at the field edge. A sterile strip provides virtually no wildlife benefit and the initial establishment costs may be offset by savings in maintenance costs in future years. Costs per 100 metres as follows. Establishment: 2m grass margins, £5.00-£6.00; 6m grass margins, £15-£19; beetle banks, £4.50-£6.00 (6m wide). Maintenance: 2m margins, 55p to 66p; 6m margins, £1.80-£2.00.

Fertiliser Losses at Field Boundaries. For a 12m spread pattern, at 150 kg/ha, loss is approx. 30p per 100m per application, or £3 for a 6ha field (450 x 150m). Loss avoided by driving further away from the field boundary/using a tilting hopper mechanism/using an appropriate border disc or deflector, costing £90.

Acknowledgement. FWAG, BTCV, local authorities, Cotswold Seeds.

2. FERTILISER PRICES 2008

A. Compounds

	Analysis			Price Per Tonne
N	P_2O_5	K_2O		£
0	24	24		560
0	18	36		605
0	20	30		584
0	30	15		595
0	30	20		634
5	24	24		614
8	24	24		629
10	24	24	(B)	640
10	10	30	(B)	550
10	15	20	(B)	509
13	13	20		530
14	14	20		530
15	19	19	(B)	630
16	16	16	(B)	538
20	4	14	(B)	420
20	10	10	(B)	457
25	5	5	(B)	402
26	0	15		397

B. Straights

Type	Price per tonne £
Ammonium Nitrate: UK (34.5% N.)	368
Ammonium Nitrate: Imported (34.5% N.) SP4/5	360
NS grade: UK (27% N, 30% SO₃)	373
Sulphate of Ammonia (21% , 60SO3.)	290
Urea (46% N.): granular/ prills	480
Liquid Nitrogen (26% N, 5% SO3)	390
Triple Superphosphate (46% P_2O_5)water soluble	690
DAP/MAP (18/46/0 and 12/52/0	800
Muriate of Potash (Granular) (60% K_2O)	580

Average price (p) per kg:	N	:	107	(UK AN)
	P_2O_5	:	150	(triple supers)
	K2 O	:	97	(muriate)

The prices above are for fertiliser delivered in 600kg bags; delivery in bulk averages £6.50/tonne less; collection of bags by farmers £8/tonne less. They are spot prices in September 2008; they vary according to area and bargaining power. (B) stands for blended; prices for granular (where available) average around £4/tonne more. They assume delivery in 25 tonne loads; add approximately £3/tonne for 10 tonne loads, £8 for 6-9 tonne loads, £15-20 for 4-5 tonne loads. Some products are also currently unavailable. Prices are likely to fluctuate greatly.

3. MANURIAL VALUE OF SLURRY AND FARMYARD MANURE

1. Composition (% by weight)

	N	P_2O_5	K_2O
Undiluted Slurry			
(faeces plus urine, or droppings):			
Cow	0.5	0.2	0.5
Pig	0.6	0.2	0.2
Poultry	1.7	1.4	0.7
Farmyard Manure:			
Cattle	0.5	0.4	0.6
Pig	0.6	0.6	0.4
Poultry	1.8	1.8	1.2

2. Available Nutrients (kg)

	N	P_2O_5	K_2O
Undiluted Slurry (per $10m^3$*):			
Cow	35	11	58
Pig	42	11	23
Poultry	118	82	82

(* = 10 tonnes; 10,000 litres)

Farmyard Manure (per 10 tonnes):	N	P_2O_5	K_2O
Cattle	17	20	46
Pig	20	31	31
Poultry	110	92	92

3. Amount per head

(faeces plus urine, or droppings)	litres per day	kg per year (1)		
		N	P_2O_5	K_2O
1 dairy cow	40	51	16	84
1 pig (dry meal fed)	4.5	6.8	1.8	3.7
100 laying hens	13	55	39	39

(1) housed all year and no losses.

Lime

The cost of lime is divided between cost of the material, cost of hauling it to the field and the cost of application. The grade and quality varies greatly, with differing contaminants, and is milled more at differing grades, some through a maximum sieve of 4mm, others farm larger. As a guide, a reasonable grade of lime, delivered 12 miles and applied at 5 tonnes per hectare (2t/acre) would currently cost in the regions of £15/tonne.

Biosolids (Sewage Sludge)

Biosolids act as good soil conditioner and fertiliser to farmers, whilst providing the most environmentally favourable method for water companies to dispose of the sludge. Biosolids vary in nutritional composition depending on processing and location, but RB209 describes its content as follows:

Biosolid Key Composition (units are kg/tonne unless otherwise stated)

	Digested Cake	Dried Pellets	Lime Stabilised
Dry Matter	25%	95%	40%
Available N	7.5	35	6
Available P_2O_5	4.5	22	4
Available K_2O	Trace	Trace	Trace
Available SO_3	6	25	8
Guideline Price £/ha applied	£16	£5	£12

Nutrient data taken from RB209

4. AGROCHEMICAL COSTS (2008)

Only the names of the active ingredients are given below, with their principal use. These materials should only be applied in accordance with the manufacturers' recommendations. Application rates can vary and there are differences between the prices of various proprietary brands. The list is not intended to be exhaustive and there is no implied criticism of materials omitted. Note, the variation in costs per hectare is primarily because of varying application rates rather than price variation between suppliers.

Crop	Function		Material	Approx. Cost £/ha per application
Cereals	Herbicides	General	MCPA	3.25-7.50
			Mecoprop-P	4.20-10.00
			Ioxynil+Bromoxynil	3.80-7.50
			Dicamba +Mecoprop-P + MCPA	15.20-19.00
			Metsulfuron-methyl	14.30
		Undersown Crops	MCPA+MCPB	46.60
		Blackgrass	Isoproturon	8.00-13.50**
			Isoproturon + Diflufenican	4.00-21.00**
			Clodinafop-propargyl + trifluralin + cloquintocet-mexyl	13.50**
			Mesosulphuron + Idosulphuron	28.40
			Florasalum + Fluroxypyr	13.25-19.30
		Cleavers	Fluroxypyr	14.25-19.00
			Amidosulfuron	11.00
		Wild Oats	Pinoxaden	14.00-37.00
		Wild Oats & Blackgrass	Clodinafop-propargyl	34.00
			Fenoxaprop-P-ethy	13.00-20.00
	Growth Regulator		Chlormequat	2.50
			Chlormequat + Choline Chloride	3.40
			2-chlorethylphosphonic acid	5.80-11.70
			2-chloroethyl phosphonic acid + Mepiquat Chloride	7.60-15.20

Crop	Function	Material	Approx. Cost £/ha per application
	Fungicides	Trinexapac-ethyl	15.75-20.00
		Azoxystrobin	29.70
		Fenpropimorph	13.00-17.50
		Epoxiconazole	25.40
		Tebuconazole	16.70
		Prothioconazole	15.50-31.00
		Chlorothalonil	4.50
	Seed Dressing	Fuberidazole + Triadimenol	5.70-9.00
		Fuberidazole + Triadimenol + Imidacloprid	12.50-20.00
		Prythoconazole + Clothianidin	11.50-18.50
		Silthiofam	21.10-33.80
		Imidacloprid + tebuconazole + triazoxide	11.90-19.00
	Aphicide	Deltamethrin	3.25-4.00
		Pirimicarb	9.10
		Chlorpyriphos	6.40-12.90
	Slug Killer	Metaldehyde	15.75
		Methiocarb	29.50
Oilseed Rape	Herbicides	Propyzamide	45.50
		Trifluralin	6.50**
		Metazachlor	32.40-54.00
	Insecticide	Deltamethrin	4.05
		Pirimicarb	9.00-13.70
		Alphacypermethrin	2.85-5.70
	Fungicide	Iprodione + thiophate-methyl	24.50-36.50
		Tebuconazole	8.35-16.70
		Flusilazde + Carbendazim	15.20-19.50
		Metconazole	21.00
	Dessicant	Glyphosate	16.50
Potatoes	Herbicides:	Metribuzin	14.75-29.50
		Linuron	12.40-23.50
		Diquat	9.50-19.00
	Blight Control	Cymoxanil + Mancozeb	9.00
		Cymoxanil + Famoxadone	14.00-20.00
		Fluazinam	10.80
		Mancozeb+Metalaxyl	23.00
	Haulm Dessicant	Diquat	37.75
Sugar Beet	Herbicides: Pre-emergence	Chloridazon:	
		overall	25.50-61.00

Crop	Function	Material	Approx. Cost £/ha per application
		band spray	8.80-20.75
	Post-emergence	Phenmedipham:	7.10-12.00
		Triflusulfron-methyl	17.50
	Insecticide	Oxamyl	34.50-51.70
		Pirimicarb	9.00
Beans	Herbicide	Bentazone	60.00
		Pendimethalin	15.00-18.00
	Fungicide	Chlorothalonil	13.50
		Tebuconazole	16.70
		Azoxystobin	29.50
Peas and Beans	Herbicide	Pendimethalin + Imazamox	37.40
	Insecticide	Pirimicarb	9.00
		Deltamethrin	4.00-4.90
Maize	Herbicide	Prosulfuron + Bromoxynil	24.75
		Nicosulfuron	22.00-32.00
Brassicas	Herbicides	Propachlor	61.00-88.00*
		Trifluralin	6.25**
Broadleaved Grass weeds and volunteer Crops			
	Cereals	Fluazifop-P-butyl	20.25-30.40
		Propaquizafop	11.00-23.50
		Cycloxydim	21.00-35.00
Grassland	Herbicides	MCPA	7.00-11.50
		MCPA + MCPB	34.00-46.75
General	Weed and Grass Killer		
	Couch Grass Control	Glyphosate	16.50-22.00
		clopyralid + fluroxypyr + fluroxypyr	24.00-48.00

Note. The above prices are based largely on retail prices paid by farmers (2008) and reflect the discounts available where there are competing products from several manufacturers. The range in prices per hectare reflects the price variation and also the varying application rates.

* This product could become delisted over the forthcoming 12 months

** All IPU's and Trifuralins come off sale at the end of September 2008 and their use become illegal after March 2009.

Acknowledgement: Particular thanks to Bartholemews 01243 784 171

5. SEED ROYALTY RATES

Farm-saved seed payment rates for autumn 2008 and spring 2009

	£/ha	£/tonne
Wheat	5.42	34.06
Winter Barley	5.55	33.06
Spring Barley	6.59	37
Oats	4.46	30.97
Peas	7.53	32.44
Beans	8.85	44.05
Oilseed Rape	8.51	1,702.35
Linseed	6.54	118.93
Triticale	6.94	39.01
Yellow Lupins	19.02	118.9
Potatoes	£18 to £272	(variety dependant)

Seed purchased from a merchant includes a component of royalty for the seed breeder. Those farmers who save seed from the previous season (farm saved seed) are legally obliged to pay the royalty. If the seed is cleaned and dressed, the royalty payment is taken at this point (per tonne), if not, the farmer is responsible for paying (per hectare). Many older varieties no longer have royalty payments payable. It is illegal to sell or buy seed unless under license.

6. FEEDINGSTUFF PRICES

£ per tonne

Cattle	Dairy:	High Energy	180 - 200
		Medium Energy	170 - 190
		Concentrate	200
	Beef	Pellets (16% CP)	215 - 230
		Concentrate	210 – 220
	Calf	Milk Substitute (bags)	1,400 - 1,600
		High Fat (bags)	1,500 - 1,600
		Calf Weaner Pellets.	230 - 245
		Calf Rearer Nuts	225 - 240
Sheep	Lamb Pellets.		225 - 240
	Medium energy sheep..		215 - 230
	Sheep/lamb cake.		230 - 240
	Ewe cake.		220 - 235
Horses	Horse and Pony Pencils.		250 - 350
Goats	Goat Nuts.		235 - 240
Pigs	Piglet Weaner		280 - 290
	Sow Nuts		195 - 215
	Early Grower Pellets		240 - 268
	Grower/Finisher Pellets.		210 - 230
	Sow Concentrate		315 - 320
	Grower Concentrate		325 - 340
Poultry	Chick and Rearer Feeds		210
	Layers Feeds.		210
	Broiler Feeds		270 - 280
	Turkey Feeds		267
Straight Feeds	Fishmeal (English; 66/70%).		640 - 675
	Soya Bean Meal (Hipro; 50% CP)		300 - 315
	Rapeseed Meal (34-36% CP)		185 - 210
	Palm Kernel Meal/Cake (17% CP)		130 - 155
	Sunflower Seed Pellets (30/33% CP)		170 - 175
	Citrus Pulp Nuts/Pellets		165 - 175
	Wheatfeed Meal (14-18% CP)		105 - 110
	Wheatfeed Pellets (14-18% CP)		110 - 150
	Maize Gluten		175 - 195
	Molasses (Cane) (5% CP)		110 - 120
	Sugar Beet Pulp (Molassed Nuts/Pellets)		110 - 130
	Brewers' Grains.		30 - 35
	Distillers Barley Grains.		185 - 220

Compound feed prices are approximate ranges in August 2008; the range incorporates differences in the ingredients

They are delivered prices for hauls more than 10 miles in 20-25 tonne loads. The additional farm delivered cost for bags ranges from £17.50 to £27.50 a tonne.

ME requirements for Friesian cows (590kg LW)

Liveweight Change (kg/day)	Maintenance	Milk yield (kg/day)			
		20	25	30	35
−0.5		147	172	196	221
0	62	161	186	210	235
+0.5		178	203	227	252

Source: Broster, W.H. and Alderman, G., Livestock Production Science, 4 (1977).

7. FEEDINGSTUFFS: NUTRITIVE VALUES

Typical Energy and Protein Contents of Some Common Feeds	Dry Matter Content	Metabolizable Energy MJ/kg	Crude Protein g/kg
Type of Feed	g/kg	DM	DM
Forages:			
Barley Straw...............................	860	7.0	10
Grass Silage (typical clamp)........................	250	10.8	150
Hay (typical meadow)...................................	850	8.8	100
Maize Silage...............................	300	11.0	90
Pasture (rotational grazed)...........................	180	11.5	160
Whole-crop Wheat (fermented)...................	400	10.5	95
Cereals:			
Barley...................................	860	13.2	120
Oats...................................	860	12.5	120
Wheat...................................	860	13.6	130
Maize...................................	880	13.8	90
Roots:			
Fodder Beet...................................	180	12.0	60
Potatoes...................................	200	13.3	100
Wet By-Products:			
Brewers Grains...................................	260	11.5	250
Pressed Sugar Beet Pulp..............................	260	12.5	100
Straights:			
Cane Molasses...............................	750	12.7	40
Distillers Barley Grains...............................	900	12.2	260
Distillers Maize Grains...............................	900	14.0	310
Distillers Wheat Grains...............................	900	13.5	340
Dried Citrus Pulp..	900	12.6	70
Dried Molassed Sugar Beet Pulp.................	900	12.5	100
Extracted Rapeseed Meal............................	900	12.0	400
Extracted Soyabean Meal.............................	900	13.4	530
Extracted Sunflower Meal............................	900	10.0	390
Field Beans...............................	880	13.3	290
Lupin Seed Meal..	900	14.2	350
Maize Gluten Feed.......................................	880	12.8	210
Palm Kernel Meal.......................................	900	11.4	200
Wheatfeed...................................	880	11.3	190

For relative values of different feeds, see previous page.

8. AGRISTATS

Some basic agricultural statistics relating to U.K. agriculture. (All figures are for the U.K. in 2007 unless otherwise stated.)

STRUCTURE

1. **Agriculture's Economic Contribution** (2007)

   Agriculture's contribution to total economy Gross   £5,753 million
   Value Added (provisional):   0.5%

2. **Agricultural Workforce** (2006)

   (a) *Agriculture's proportion of total workforce in employment:*   1.7%

   (b) *Numbers of Persons Engaged in Agriculture (June) (to nearest '00):* 526,000

A: Employed:	Male	Female	Total
Regular Full-time..............................	52,000	10,000	62,000
Regular Part-time*............................	28,000	17,000	45,000
Seasonal, Casual and Gang................	41,000	18,000	59,000
Salaried Managers			15,000
Total Employees			181,000

B: Farmers, Partners Directors and their Spouses	
Full-time..	146,000
Part-time*	199,000
Total Farmers, Partners Directors and their Spouses	344,000
Total Labour Force**	526,000

* Part-time is 39 hours or less per week in England and Wales, less than 38 in Scotland and less than 30 in Northern Ireland.

** Total labour force excludes schoolchildren but includes 'official' trainees.

3. **Livestock Numbers** (June '000 Head)

		2002	2007
Total Cattle and Calves................................		10,345	10,304
of which	Dairy Cows	2,227	1,954
	Beef Cows...............................	1,657	1,698
	Heifers in Calf...........................	728	-
Total Sheep and Lambs		35,834	33,946
of which	Female Breeding Flock...........................	17,630	16,064
Total Pigs		5,588	4,834
of which	Female Breeding Herd...........................	557	455
Poultry	Broilers...	105,137	108,753
	Laying Flock.....................................	29,778	27,321
	Growing Pullets	9,784	8,936
Farmed Deer		37	30
Goats		93	95

4. Crop Areas (June)

	Area ('000 ha) 2002	Area ('000 ha) 2007	% Total Area 2007	% Crops & Grass 2007*
Wheat	1,996	1,816	9.8	15.6
Barley (% winter in brackets)............	1,101 (50)	898 (43)	4.8	7.7
Oats	126	129	0.7	1.1
Mixed Corn, Triticale and Rye	23	27	0.1	0.2
Total Cereals (excluding maize)........	3,246	2,871	15.4	24.6
Potatoes..	158	140	0.7	1.2
Sugar Beet (England and Wales only)	169	125	0.7	1.4
Oilseed Rape (non Set-aside).............	357	613	3.3	5.1
Peas harvested dry (GB only)............	85	36	0.2	0.3
Field Beans (GB only).......................	164	125	0.7	1.0
Linseed (non Set-aside)	12	11	0.1	0.1
Vegetables & Salad grown in the open	124	121	0.7	1.0
Orchards, Small Fruit and Grapes	35	32	0.1	0.2
Other Horticulture..............................	17	15	0.1	0.1
Maize (excl. Scotland in 2002)..........	121	146	0.8	1.4
Other Crops..	85	115	0.6	1.0
Bare Fallow..	33	165	0.9	1.2
Total Tillage.......................................	4,606	4,515	24.3	38.7
Temporary Grass (under 5 years old)	1,243	1,176	6.3	10.1
Total Arable	4,848	5,691	30.6	48.8
Permanent Grass (5 years, and over) .	5,519	5,965	32.1	51.2
(Total Grass (excluding Rough Grazing))	(6,762)	(7,141)	38.4	.
Total Tillage & Grass (excl. R.G.)	11,366	11,656	62.7	100.0
Rough Grazing**..............................	5,722	5,551	29.8	
Set-aside (incl. any in non-food crops)	612	440	2.4	
Woodland...	524	663	3.6	
Other Land on agricultural holdings..	282	291	1.6	.
Total Agricultural Area***................	18,506	18,601	100.0	

*   Excluding Rough Grazing

**   Including 1,238,000 ha of common grazing.

*** Urban land and forest each approximately 2.0 million ha; other non-agricultural land approximately 1.5 million ha; total U.K. land area including inland waters: 24.1 million.

5. Size Structure

(a) *Number and Size Distribution of UK Holdings, 2005 (latest data):*

Size group (ha)	Total land area			Tillage and grass area		
	No. ('000)	%	% area	No. ('000)	%	% area
0.1 to 19.9	183.3	58.9	5.3	133.0	53.0	
20.0 to 49.9	49.3	15.8	9.4	48.6	19.3	
50.0 to 99.9	36.8	11.8	15.2	36.4	14.5	
100 and over..............	41.7	13.4	70.1	33.2	13.2	
Total..........................	311.1	100.0	100.0	251.2	100.0	100.0

Average area (ha/[acres]) per holding: 56.6 (140); tillage and grass 45.7 (113).

Size of Business (ESU)	'000 of Holdings	% of holdings	% of total ESU
Under 8......................	197.5	63.5	2.5
8 to 40........................	55.4	17.8	13.1
40 to 100	33.1	10.6	28.3
100 to 200	16.1	5.2	26.3
200 and over..............	9.0	2.9	29.8
Total..........................	311.1	100.0	100.0

Average size of holdings: 26.3 ESU. Average size over 8 ESU (which is judged to be the minimum for full-time holdings, which are 37.7% of all holdings) = 67.4 ESU, 124.6 ha (308 acres). ESU = European Size Unit (the number provides a measure of the financial potential of the holding, based on standardised gross margins).

(b) *Number and Size distribution of holdings in England and Wales, 2000 (latest data)*

Size group (ha)	By total land area				By tillage and grass area			
	Holdings		Hectares		Holdings		Hectares	
	'000	%	'0,000	%	'000	%	'0,000	%
Under 10............	62.8	36.0	212	2.0	53.2	33.6	195	2.3
10 to 30	35.2	20.2	646	6.2	33.9	21.4	628	7.3
30 to 50	19.6	11.2	771	7.4	19.9	12.6	779	9.1
50 to 100	27.0	15.5	1,937	18.6	26.6	16.8	1,900	22.2
100 to 200	19.0	10.9	2,641	25.3	17.0	10.7	2,340	27.3
200 to 300	5.5	3.2	1,342	12.9	4.4	2.8	1,056	12.3
300 to 500	3.7	2.1	1,386	13.3	2.5	1.6	916	10.7
500 to 700	1.0	0.6	592	5.7	0.6	0.4	344	4.0
700 and over.......	0.8	0.5	897	8.6	0.4	0.3	411	4.8
Total	174.6	100	10,425	100	158.5	100	8,570	100

6. Average Size of Enterprises

Hectares	2000	2005		2000	2005
			Dairy Cows	73	84
Cereals (excl. maize).....	50.7	51.7	Beef Cows......................	27	29
Oilseed Rape	25.4	35.0	Breeding Sheep.............	240	214
Potatoes	11.2	13.4	Breeding Pigs................	82	82
Sugar Beet	20.0	22.7	Fattening Pigs	480	355
			Laying Fowls	1,295	1,095
			Broilers..........................	40,834	36,141

7. **Tenure** (England and Wales, 2000 – latest data available)

Tenure	No. of Holdings	Area owned (%)	Area rented (%)
Wholly owned..................	119,254 (68.2)	4,969 (47.2)	-
Mainly owned	19,850 (11.4)	1,805 (17.1)	456 (4.3)
Wholly rented...................	22,643 (13.0)	-	1,826 (17.3)
Mainly rented...................	13,010 (7.4)	345 (3.3)	1,137 (10.8)
Total	174,757 (100)	7,119 (67.6)	3,419 (32.4)*

N.B. Mixed tenure holdings: mainly owned = over 50% owned;
mainly rented = over 50% rented.

Wholly or mainly owned, 79.6% of holdings; wholly or mainly rented, 20.4%

* N.B. As the above figures for rented land include family arrangements (e.g. farmers, or family farming companies, renting from other members of the family, or family shareholders) the percentage of 'truly' rented land is almost certainly a few percentage points less than the figures given above.

FINANCE

1. *Inputs and Outputs* (2007)

Inputs	£m	Outputs	£m	%
Animal Feed............................	2,807	Wheat.................................	1,307	8.3
Seeds	605	Barley	538	3.4
Fertilisers...............................	851	Oats and other cereals	64	0.4
Pesticides................................	547	Oilseed rape.......................	422	2.7
Hired Labour...........................	2,356	Potatoes	664	4.2
Consumption of Fixed Capital*	2,750	Sugar beet..........................	172	1.1
Maintenance: materials..........	671	Fresh vegetables................	1,062	6.8
Maintenance: buildings...........	378	Fruit	445	2.8
Fuels......................................	598	Plants and flowers	781	5.0
Electricity...............................	276	Cattle	1,657	10.6
Agricultural services..............	624	Sheep	628	4.0
Veterinary expenses................	287	Pigs	735	4.7
Net rent...................................	222	Poultry	1,215	7.7
Interest....................................	686	Milk and milk products....	2,830	18.0
Other goods and services........	2,384	Eggs...................................	410	2.6
	____	Miscellaneous....................	2,750	17.5
Total Inputs	16,042	Total Gross Output...........	15,680	100.0
Total Income From Farming...	2,538	Single Payment & subsidies	2,900	
	18,580	Total Output	18,580	
		Total Crops.......................	3,502	22.3
		Total Horticulture.............	2,289	14.6
		Total Livestock	4,419	28.2
		Total Livestock Products..	3,293	21.0
		Other.................................	2,177	13.9

* including 694 buildings and 1,199 equipment.

Note. The above layout differs substantially from that published by DEFRA.

2. Income from Farming

(a) *Index of UK Total Income from Farming* in Real Terms (av. 1974-76 = 100)*

Year	Index	Year	Index	Year	Index	Year	Index
1975	93	1984	82	1993	84	2002	39
1976	109	1985	44	1994	91	2003	49
1977	98	1986	50	1995	105	2004	43
1978	86	1987	56	1996	94	2005	35
1979	71	1988	52	1997	55	2006	36
1980	56	1989	53	1998	38	2007	38
1981	64	1990	44	1999	37		
1982	78	1991	45	2000	27		
1983	65	1992	60	2001	30		

* 'TIFF' = business profits plus income to farmers, partners and directors and others with an entrepreneurial interest in the business. It refers only to farming, i.e. diversification incomes and expenditures are excluded. There are no imputed charges (such as a rental value for owned land or value of the farmer's own labour).

(b) *Recent TIFF Values (£ million)*

	Actual	At 2007 Prices
1995 (the 1992-1997 peak)	5,061	7,012
2001	1661	1,978
2002	2,228	2,612
2003	2,839	3,235
2004	2,558	2,830
2005	2,171	2,337
2006	2,303	2,402
2007 (provisional)	2,538	2,538

(c) *Index of UK Farming Income* in Real Terms (av. 1940-69 = 100)*

Year	Index	Year	Index	Year	Index	Year	Index
1940-49	101	1978	89	1989	45	2000	26
1950-59	100	1979	73	1990	43	2001	28
1960-69	99	1980	56	1991	41	2002	37
1970	95	1981	66	1992	56	2003	46
1971	96	1982	77	1993	79	2004	40
1972	110	1983	57	1994	86	2005	33
1973	138	1984	86	1995	99	2006	34
1974	103	1985	37	1996	88	2007	36
1975	98	1986	46	1997	52		
1976	113	1987	50	1998	35		
1977	98	1988	34	1999	35		

* As this figure is no longer produced by DEFRA the figures from 1997 onwards are only approximate. Up to that year a figure for 'Labour: family, partners and director' was deducted from Total Income from Farming (TIFF) to give Farming Income.

3. UK Net Farm Income in Real Terms by Main Types of Farming
(£s, at 2005/06 prices)

Farm Type	2001/02	2002/03	2003/04	2004/05	2005/06	2006/07
Dairy..............................	31,300	15,500	22,300	24,300	24,500	19,100
Grazing Livestock (LFA)	6,400	14,200	15,100	13,400	9,300	9,000
Grazing L'stock (Lowland)	1,400	7,300	7,500	5,400	4,100	7,500
Cereals...........................	5,500	12,000	35,500	14,000	12,700	27,000
General Cropping..........	15,800	12,700	53,800	27,100	22,500	47,700
Specialist Pigs	22,200	25,600	34,000	25,800	29,000	23,700
Specialist Poultry	24,500	90,900	52,800	92,100	97,500	74,700
Mixed	5,900	11,300	23,900	15,200	15,600	20,100
ALL TYPES..................						
(inc. Horticulture)	14,400	14,900	25,300	18,400	17,100	20,600

1. In calculating net farm income various adjustments are made to the accounts, e.g. an imputed rent for owned land is deducted but interest payments are not deducted, nor is the value of unpaid labour of the farmer and spouse. Accounting years end of average in February.
2. The 2001/02 figures above exclude farms subjected to foot-and-mouth disease cull.

4. Balance Sheet of UK Agriculture (2006)

			£m	£m
Assets:	Fixed:	Land and buildings.........................	142,693	
		Plant, machinery and vehicles........	7,202	
		Breeding livestock..........................	4,222	
	Total Fixed Assets:			*154,117*
	Current	Trading livestock............................	2,537	
		Crops and stores	2,362	
		Debtors and cash deposits..............	4,828	
	Total Current Assets:			*9,727*
	Total Assets:			**163,844**
Liabilities:	Long &	Bank loans.......................................	2,467	
	Medium-term:	AMC and SASC	1,482	
		Other..	1,193	
	Total Long and Medium Term Liabilities			*5,142*
	Short-term	Bank overdrafts	3,337	
		Trade credit.....................................	1,522	
		Hire purchase and leasing	788	
		Other..	104	
	Total Short-term Liabilities:			*5,751*
	Total Liabilities:			**10,893**
Net Worth:..				**152,951**

% Equity (Net worth as a % of Total Assets): 93.35%

Total Income from Farming (TIFF) 2006 as a % of a) Net Worth: 1.668%
b) Total Assets: 1.55%
(Note: no charge has been made for farmers' own labour or management*)*

Bank Lending to Agriculture, Hunting and Forestry (2007 year avearge):...... £9,799m

MISCELLANEOUS

1. UK Crop Yields and Prices, 2003-2007 (2007 Provisional)

Average Yields (harvest years)

(tonnes per hectare)	2003	2004	2005	2006	2007	Average 2003-07
Wheat	7.8	7.8	8.0	8.0	7.2	7.8
Barley (all)	5.9	5.8	5.9	5.9	5.7	5.8
Winter Barley	6.3	6.4	6.5	6.7	6.1	6.4
Spring Barley	5.7	5.3	5.4	5.3	5.3	5.4
Oats	6.2	5.8	5.8	6.0	5.5	7.1
Oilseed Rape (excl. set-aside)	3.3	2.9	3.2	3.3	3.1	3.2
Linseed (excl. set-aside)	1.7	1.7	1.9	1.4	1.6	1.9
Field Beans (for stockfeed)	3.9	3.7	3.8	3.4	3.0	3.6
Dried Peas (for stockfeed)	3.9	3.5	3.8	3.3	3.1	3.6
Potatoes (all)	41.7	42.0	43.7	40.8	40.2	41.7
Early Potatoes	18.2	16.8	14.3	15.7	12.5	15.5
Maincrop Potatoes	44.2	44.9	46.6	43.0	43.7	44.5
Sugar Beet (adj. to 16% sugar)	56.6	58.7	58.5	56.6	60.2	58.1

Average Prices (calendar years)

(£ per tonne)		2003	2004	2005	2006	2007	Average 2003-2007
Wheat	milling	83	86	73	77	108	85
	feed	75	76	67	72	97	77
Barley	malting	82	80	77	80	122	88
	feed	71	70	65	71	103	76
Oats	milling	63	64	70	74	89	72
	feed	59	69	67	76	90	72
Oilseed Rape (excl. set-aside)		160	163	131	164	200	164
Field Beans (for stockfeed)		92	82	84	85	173	103
Dried Peas (for stockfeed)		94	85	87	80	175	104
Potatoes (all, inc seed)		102.5	123.2	100.6	128.9	143.5	120
	Earlies	133	178	141	194	154	160
	Maincrop	99	118	96	125	141	115.8
Sugar Beet (per adjusted tonne)		31	31	31	24	23	28

2. Self-sufficiency 2007 provisional, (*2002 in brackets*)

(a) *Total Food*   all food types .... 60.6% *(62.4%)*

                      indigenous type food .... 70.4% *(75.5%)*

(b) *Individual Products (production as a % of total new supply for use in the UK):*

	2002	2007		2002	2007
Wheat	102	107	Beef and Veal	71	82
Barley	117	108	Mutton and Lamb	85	82
Oats	120	103	Pork	73	69
Total Cereals	99	100	Bacon and Ham	43	42
Oilseed Rape	92	111	Poultrymeat	91	90
Potatoes	84	79	Butter	64	61
Sugar	65	63	Cheese	65	55
Fresh Vegetables	64	58	Cream	135	114
Fresh Fruit	9	11	Hen Eggs	87	81

3. Food Consumption and Expenditure, UK 2006-07

(a) *Food and Drink Consumed Within the Household*

Average quantity consumed / expenditure per person per week:

(2006-07)	2004-05 kg per week	2005-06 kg per week	2006-07 kg per week
Milk and Cream (litres)	1.984	2.027	2.022
Cheese	0.110	0.116	0.116
Meat	1.049	1.047	1.042
Fish	0.158	0.167	0.170
Eggs (number)	1.56	1.60	1.50
Fats	0.182	0.183	0.184
Sugars and Preserves	0.134	0.129	0.126
Potatoes	0.822	0.842	0.810
Other Vegetables	1.106	1.156	1.142
Fruit	1.168	1.292	1.313
Bread	0.695	0.701	0.692
All Other Cereals (inc. Pasta & Pizza) ..	0.882	0.695	0.695
Beverages (litres)	0.056	0.057	0.055
Soft Drinks (litres)	1.832	1.718	1.807
Alcoholic Drinks (litres)	0.763	0.739	0.760
Confectionery	0.131	0.123	0.123

(b) *Food and Drink Consumed Outside the Household*

	£ per week
Food and Drink excl. Alcohol	8.00
Alcoholic Drinks	3.54
Total	11.54

(c) *Total Food and Drink*

	£ per week
Food and Drink excl. Alcohol	29.55
Alcoholic Drinks	6.27
Total	35.82

Sources:　Agriculture in the UK: 2007 (DEFRA). All items except for the following:

Structure: Tables 5 and 7: Other DEFRA Statistics.

Finance: Table 4 (part), Bank Lending: Bank of England, Financial Statistics Division

Misc: Table 3: Family Food Survey, DEFRA.

9. RATE OF INFLATION; PRICE AND COST INDICES

1. Retail Price Index (all items)

Year	% increase on year earlier	Index (1970 = 100)	Index (1987 = 100)	Year	% increase on year earlier	Index (1970 = 100)	Index (1987 = 100)
1990	9.5	681	126.1	2000	3.0	919	170.3
1991	5.9	721	133.5	2001	1.8	935	173.3
1992	3.7	748	138.5	2002	1.7	951	176.2
1993	1.6	760	140.7	2003	2.9	979	181.3
1994	2.4	778	144.1	2004	3.0	1,008	186.7
1995	3.5	805	149.1	2005	2.8	1,036	192.0
1996	2.4	824	152.7	2006	3.2	1,070	198.1
1997	3.1	850	157.5	2007	4.3	1,116	206.6
1998	3.4	879	162.9	2008 (f'cast)	4.5	1,166	215.9
1999	1.5	892	165.4				

Note; Index in 1965: 80; index in 1962: 70. 1970-1994 figures available in earlier editions.

2. UK Annual Price and Cost Indicies, 2001-2005 (2000 = 100)

A. Producer Prices	2003	2004	2005	2006	2007
Feed Wheat	105.3	117.6	98.2	112.1	154.2
Feed Barley	104.3	108.3	99.1	107.9	162.1
All Cereals	105.2	114.2	99.1	110.5	163.7
Oilseed Rape	140.3	136.1	112.9	134.5	158.8
Potatoes (maincrop)	106.0	141.6	109.7	143.1	166.5
Sugar Beet	112.1	115.4	117.1	112.6	86.6
Desert Apples	124.6	120.7	116.4	122.5	140.4
All Fresh Fruit	124.2	112.4	120.1	114.6	126.7
All Fresh Vegetables	125.5	113.7	120.3	129.7	143.5
All Crop Products	110.7	115.1	108.6	118.1	143.9
Milk	106.4	109.0	109.0	106.0	122.4
Cattle	106.7	113.4	114.6	123.9	125.9
Sheep	132.5	131.4	122.9	125.5	111.7
Wool	108.4	107.3	92.3	33.6	71.7
Pigs	109.0	109.3	109.8	110.9	114.3
Poultry	99.4	101.2	100.8	99.4	108.7
Eggs	130.7	135.1	121.0	127.4	144.2
All Animal Products	*109.4*	*112.0*	*110.4*	*111.6*	*119.6*
All Products	109.9	113.3	109.7	114.2	129.4
B. Input Prices					
Seeds	116.0	110.3	108.2	104.0	153.6
Fertilisers	119.0	130.5	143.3	151.4	170.1
Plant Protection Products	95.7	100.6	102.9	103.4	104.9
Energy and Lubricants	100.5	108.8	137.4	154.8	158.0
Animal Feeding Stuffs	104.9	111.6	103.0	108.1	130.4
Maintenance and Repair of Plant	116.0	122.5	130.3	137.8	143.4
Machinery and Other Equipment	95.1	96.1	103.8	108.2	114.0
Buildings	112.1	118.1	123.7	130.9	140.0
General Expenses	105.2	114.0	114.5	115.5	119.7

10. METRIC CONVERSION FACTORS

Metric to Imperial | *Imperial to Metric*

Area

1 hectare (10,000m²)........... 2.471 acres	1 acre ....0.405 ha
	1 square mile ....259 ha
1 square km.....................0.386 sq. mile	1 square mile ....2.590 sq. km
1 square m.......................1.196 sq. yard	1 square yard ....0.836 sq. m
1 square m..................... 10.764 sq. feet	1 square foot ....0.093 sq. m

(m = metre, km = kilometre)

Length

1 mm. ....0.039 inch	1 inch...................................... 25.4 mm
1 cm...0.394 inch	1 inch.. 2.54 cm
1 m...3.281 feet	1 foot .... 0.305 m
1 m...................................... 1.094 yard	1 yard.. 0.914 m
1 km.................................... 0.6214 mile	1 mile....................................... 1.609 km

(mm = millimetre, cm = centimetre)

Volume

1 millilitre...................... 0.0352 fluid oz	1 fluid oz .... 28.413 ml
1 litre .... 35.2 fluid oz	1 fluid oz ....0.028 litre
1 litre ....1.76 pints	1 pint.......................................0.568 litre
1 litre ....0.22 gallon	1 gallon............................... 4.546 litres

[Milk: 1 litre = 1.03 kg (.971 kg/litre); 1 kg = 1.709 pints, 0.214 gal.; 1 tonne = 213.63 gal; 1 pint = 0.585 kg; 1 gallon = 4.681 kg]

1 cubic m............................35.31 cu feet	1 cubic foot.......................... 0.028 cu m
1 cubic m ....1.307 cu yard	1 cubic .... 0.765 cu m
1 cubic m............................ 220 gallons	1 gallon............................... 0.005 cu m

Weight

1 gram ....0.0353 oz	1 oz... 28.35 gm
1 kg..35.274oz	
1 kg..2.205 lb	1 lb... 0.454 kg
50 kg..0.984 cwt	
1 tonne (1,000 kg)..................19.68 cwt	1 cwt. .... 50.80 kg
1 tonne...................................... 0.984 ton	1 ton.................................... 1.016 tonne

Yields and Rates of Use

1 tonne/ha........................0.398 ton/acre	1 ton/acre......................2.511 tonnes/ha
1 tonne/ha........................ 7.95 cwt/acre	1 cwt/acre .... 0.125 tonne/ha
1 gram/ha .... 0.014 oz/acre	1 oz/acre .... 70.053 g/ha
1 kg/ha...............................0.892 lb/acre	1 lb/acre .... 1.121 g/ha
1 kg/ha.......................... 0.008 cwt/acre	1 cwt/acre .... 125.5 g/ha
1 kg/ha (fert.) ....0.797 unit/acre	1 unit/acre .... 1.255 kg/ha
1 litre/ha ....0.712 pint/acre	1 pint/acre........................1.404 litre/ha
1 litre/ha ....0.089 gal/acre	1 gal/acre .... 11.24 litres/ha

Power, Pressure, Temperature

1 Kw...1.341 hp	1 hp..0.746 kW
1 kilojoule ....0.948 Btu	1 Btu .... 1.055 kilojoule
1 therm ....10,000 Btu	1 Btu ....0.0001 therm
1 lb f ft..................................1.356 Nm	1 Nm .... 0.738 lb f ft
1 bar..............................14.705 lb/sq.in.	1 lb/sq.in................................. 0.068 bar
°C to °F .... x1.8, +32	°F to °C..................................-32, ÷1.8

11. USEFUL ADDRESSES AND TELEPHONE NUMBERS

1. General

Advisory Committee on Organic Standards (ACOS)
DEFRA, Area 5F, Ergon House, Horseferry Road, London SW1P 2AL   020 7238 5605
www.defra.gov.uk

Agricultural Central Trading Ltd. (Act)
90 The Broadway, Chesham, Bucks. HP5 lEG   01494 784 931

Agricultural Engineers' Association
Samuelson House, Paxton Road, Orton Centre, Peterborough,
Cambs. PE2 5LT
www.aea.uk.com   01733 371 381

Agricultural Law Association
6 St. Peters Close, Chislehurst, Kent BR7 6PD   020 8467 0722
www.ala.org.uk

Agricultural Industries Confederation (AIC)
Confederation House, East of England Showground, Peterborough,
PE2 6XE
www.agindustries.org.uk   01733 385 230

Agricultural Wages Board
Ergon House, Area 3A, Horseferry Road, London SW1P 2AL   020 7238 6523
http://www.defra.gov.uk/farm/working/agwages/awb/index.htm

Association of Independent Crop Consultants
Agriculture Place, Heath Farm, Heath Road East, Petersfield,
Hampshire, GU31 4HT
www.aicc.org.uk   01730 710 095

BBC Radio 4 Farming To-day
The Mail Box, Birmingham B1 1RF   0121 432 8888
http://www.bbc.co.uk/radio4/news/farmingtoday/

British Agricultural and Garden Machinery Association (BAGMA)
1st Floor, Entrance B, Salamander Quay West, Park Lane,
Harefield, Middlesex UB9 6NZ
www.bagma.com   0870 205 2834

British Association of Seed Producers
Manor House, Woodhall Spa, Lincolnshire, LN10 6PX.   01526 352 368

British Cereal Exports
HGCA, Caledonia House, 223 Pentonville Road, London N1 9HY   020 7520 3927

British Crop Protection Council (BCPC)
7 Omni Business Park, Omega Park, Alton, Hampshire GU34 2QD   01420 593 200
www.bcpc.org

British Deer Society
Burgate Manor, Fordingbridge, Hampshire SP6 1EF   01425 655 434
www.bds.org.uk

British Egg Industry Council (BEIC)
2nd Floor, 89 Charterhouse Street, London EC1M 6HR   020 7608 3760
www.britisheggindustrycouncil.com

British Grassland Society
PO Box 237, University of Reading, 1 Earley Gate, Berks. RG6 6AR   0118 931 8189
www.britishgrassland.com

British Institute of Agricultural Consultants (BIAC)
The Estate Office, Torry Hill, Milstead, Sittingbourne,
Kent ME9 0SP   01795 830 100
www.biac.co.uk

British Pig Association
Trumpington Mews, 40b High Street, Trumpington, Cambs. CB2 2LS   01223 845 100
www.britishpigs.org.uk

British Potato Council
4300 Nash Court, John Smith Drive, Oxford Business Park
South, Oxford OX4 2RT   01865 714 455
www.potato.org.uk

British Poultry Council
Europoint House, 5 Lavington Street, London SE1 0NZ   020 7202 4760
www.poultry.uk.com

British Sheep Dairying Association
The Sheep Centre, Malvern, Worcs. WR13 6PH   01684 892 661
www.sheepdairying.com

British Society of Plant Breeders
Woolpack Chambers, Market Street, Ely, Cambs. CB7 4ND   01353 653 200
www.bspb.co.uk

British Sugar
PP Box 26, Oundle Road, Peterborough, Cambs. PE2 9QU   01733 563 171
www.britishsugar.co.uk

British Veterinary Association
7 Mansfield Street, London WlG 9NQ   020 7636 6541
www.bva.co.uk

British Wool Marketing Board
Wool House, Roydsdale Way, Euroway Trading Estate,
Bradford, West Yorkshire BD4 6SE   01274 688 666
www.britishwool.org.uk

CAB International
Nosworthy Way, Wallingford, Oxon OX10 8DE   01491 832 111
www.cabi.org

Campaign to Protect Rural England (CPRE)
128 Southwark Street, London SE1 0SW   020 7981 2800
www.cpre.org.uk

Central Association of Agricultural Valuers (CAAV)
Market Chambers, 35 Market Place, Coleford, Gloucestershire
GL16 8AA
www.caav.org.uk   01594 832 979

Centre for Agricultural Strategy
University of Reading, P.O. Box 237, Whiteknights Road, Earley Gate, Reading,
Berks. RG6 6AR   01183 788 150
www.apd.reading.ac.uk

Country Land and Business Association (CLA)
16 Belgrave Square, London SWlX 8PQ   020 7235 0511
www.cla.org.uk

Crop Protection Association UK
4 Lincoln Court, Lincoln Road, Peterborough, Combs PE1 2RP   01733 349 225
www.cropprotection.org.uk

Dairy Industry Association Ltd.
93 Baker Street, London W1U 6QQ   020 7486 7244
www.dairyuk.org

Department of Agriculture and Rural Development (DARDNI)
Dundonald House, Upper Newtownards Road, Belfast BT4 3SB   028 9052 0100
www.dardni.gov.uk

Department of Environment, Food and Rural Affairs (DEFRA)
Nobel House, 17 Smith Square, London SW1P 3JR   020 7270 3000
www.defra.gov.uk

English Heritage
23 Savile Row, London W1S 2ET   020 7973 3000
www.english-heritage.org.uk

English Hops and Herbs Ltd
Hop Pocket Lane, Paddock Wood, Tonbridge, Kent TN12 6DQ   01892 833 415
www.botanix.co.uk   intray@botanix.co.uk

Environment Agency
Rio House, Waterside Drive, Aztec West, Almonsbury, Bristol
BS32 4UD   0870 850 6506
www.environment-agency.gov.uk

European Commission (London Office)
Jean Monnet House, 8 Storey's Gate, London SW1P 3AT   020 7973 1992

FACE (Farming and Countryside Education)
National Agricultural Centre, Stoneleigh Park, Warks. CV8 2LZ   024 7685 8261
www.face-online.org.uk

Family Farmers' Association
Osborne Newton, Aveton Gifford, Kingsbridge, Devon TQ7 4PE   01548 852 794

Farmers Club
3 Whitehall Court, London SW1A 2EL   020 7930 3751
www.thefarmersclub.com

Farmers Union of Wales
Llys Amaeth, Plas Gogerddon, Aberystwyth, Ceredigion SY23 3BT   01970 820 820
www.fuw.org.uk

Farming and Wildlife Advisory Group (FWAG)
National Agricultural Centre, Stoneleigh Park, Warks. CV8 2RX   024 7669 6699
www.fwag.org.uk

Food and Drink Federation
Federation House, 6 Catherine Street, London WC2B 5JJ   020 7836 2460
www.fdf.org.uk

Food from Britain
4th Floor, Manning House, 22 Carlisle Place, London SW1P 1JA   020 7233 5111
www.foodfrombritain.com

Food Standards Agency
Aviation House, 125 Kingsway, London WC2B 6NH   020 7276 8000
www.foodstandards.gov.uk

Forestry Commission
231 Corstorphine Road, Edinburgh EH12 7AT   0131 334 0303
www.forestry.gov.uk   enquiries@forestry.gsi.gov.uk

Grain and Feed Trade Association (GAFTA)
GAFTA House, 6 Chapel Place, Rivington Street, London EC2A 3SH 020 7814 9666
www.gafta.com

Guild of Agricultural Journalists
Isfield Cottage, Church Road, Crowborough, East Sussex TN6 1BN   01892 611 618
www.gaj.org.uk

Health and Safety Executive (Agriculture Sector)
National Agricultural Centre, Stoneleigh Park, Warks. CV8 2LG   024 7669 8350
www.hse.gov.uk

Home Grown Cereals Authority
Caledonia House, 223 Pentonville Road, London N1 9NG   020 7520 3926
Price Information Service   020 7520 3972
www.hgca.com

Horticultural Development Council
Bradbourne House, Tithe Barn, East Malling, Kent ME19 6DZ   01732 848 383
www.hdc.org.uk

Institution of Agricultural Engineers
West End Road, Silsoe, Bedford MK45 4DU   01525 861096

Institute of Agricultural Management
Farm Management Unit, University of Reading, PO Box 236,
Reading RG6 6AT   0118 931 6578

Institute of Agricultural Secretaries and Administrators
National Agricultural Centre, Stoneleigh Park, Warks. CV8 2LG   024 7669 6592
www.iagsa.co.uk

Institute of Chartered Foresters
7a St. Colme Street, Edinburgh EH3 6AA   0131 225 2705
www.charteredforesters.org   icf@charteredforesters.org

International Grains Council
1 Canada Square, Canary Wharf, London E14 5AE   020 7513 1122
www.igc.org.uk   igc@igc.org.uk

Land Drainage Contractors Association
National Agricultural Centre, Stoneleigh Park, Warks. CV8 2LG   01327 263 264
www.idca.org   secretary@idca.org

Land Heritage
Summerhill Farm, Hittisleigh, Devon EX6 6LP   01647 24511
www.landheritage.org.uk   enquiries@landheritage.org.uk

Lands Improvement Holdings plc
1 Buckingham Place, London SW1E 6HR   020 7222 5331
www.lih.co.uk

Lantra
Lantra House, National Agricultural Centre, Stoneleigh Park,
Warks. CV8 2LG   024 7669 6996
www.lantra.co.uk   connect@lantra.co.uk

LEAF (Linking Environment and Farming)
National Agricultural Centre, Stoneleigh Park, Warks. CV8 2LZ   024 7641 3911
www.leafuk.org   enquiries@leafuk.org

London Commodity Exchange (Euronext Liffe)
Cannon Bridge House, 1 Cousin Lane, London EC4R 3XX   020 7623 0444

Meat and Livestock Commission (MLC)
PO Box 44, Winterhill House, Snowdon Drive, Milton Keynes
MK6 1AX   01908 844 132
www.mlc.org.uk

Milk Development Council (MDC)
Stroud Road, Cirencester, Glos GL7 6JN
01285 646 500
www.mdc.org.uk
info@dairyco.org.uk

National Agricultural Centre (NAC)
Stoneleigh Park, Warks. CV8 2LZ
024 7669 6969
www.stoneleigh-park.co.uk

National Association of Agricultural Contractors (NAAC)
Samuelson House, (62) Forder Way, Hampton, Peterborough PE7 8JB   08456 448 750
www.naac.org.uk

National Association of British & Irish Millers (NABIM)
21 Arlington Street, London SW1A 1RN
020 7493 2521
www.nabim.org.uk
info@nabim.org.uk

National Beef Association
Mart Centre, Tyne Green, Hexham, NE46 3SG
01434 601 005
www.nationalbeefassociation.com
info@nationalbeefassociation.com

National Cattle Association (Dairy)
Brick House, Risbury, Leominster, Herefordshire HR6 0NQ
01568 760 632
www.nationalrural.org

National Dairy Council
164 Shaftesbury Avenue, London WC2H 8HL
020 7395 4030
www.nationaldairycouncil.org
ndc@dairyinformation.com

National Farmers' Retail and Markets Association (FARMA)
12 Southgate Street, Winchester, SO23 9EF
0845 458 8420
www.farma.org.uk

National Farmers' Union (NFU)
Agriculture House, Stoneleigh Park, Warks. CV8 2LZ
024 7685 8500
London Office, Kings Buildings, 16 Smith Square, London SW1P 3JJ   020 7808 6600
www.nfuonline.com

National Non-Food Crops Centre
Innovation Centre, York Science Park, Innovation Way, Heslington,
York YO10 5DG
01904 435 182
www.nnfcc.co.uk
enquiries@nnfcc.co.uk

NFU Scotland
Rural Centre, West Mains, Ingliston, Midlothian EH28 8LT
0131 472 4000
www.nfus.org.uk
webmaster@nfus.org.uk

National Federation of Young Farmers Clubs
YFC Centre, 10th street, National Agricultural Centre, Stoneleigh Park,
Warks. CV8 2LG
024 7685 7200
www.nfyfc.org.uk
post@nfyfc.org.uk

National Office of Animal Health (NOAH)
3 Crossfield Chambers, Gladbeck Way, Enfield, Middlesex EN2 7HF   020 8367 3131
www.noah.co.uk
noah@noah.co.uk

National Sheep Association
The Sheep Centre, Malvern, Worcs. WR13 6PH
01684 892 661
www.nationalsheep.org.uk

National Trust
32 Queen Anne's Gate, London SW1H 9AB
01793 817 400
www.nationaltrust.org.uk

Natural England
1 East Parade, Sheffield S1 2GA
01142 418 920
www.naturalengland.org.uk
web@naturalengland.org.uk

Processed Vegetable Growers' Association Limited (PGVA)
133 Eastgate, Louth, Lincolnshire LN11 9QG 01507 602427
www.pvga.co.uk postbox@pvga.co.uk

Royal Agricultural Benevolent Institution (RABI)
Shaw House, 27 West Way, Oxford OX2 0QH 01865 724 931
www.rabi.org.uk info@rabi.org.uk

Royal Agricultural Society of England (RASE)
National Agricultural Centre, Stoneleigh Park, Warks. CV8 2LZ 024 7669 6969
www.rase.org.uk info@rase.org.uk

Royal Association of British Dairy Farmers
Unit 31, Stoneleigh Deer Park, Stareton, Kenilworth, Warks CV8 2LY 0845 458 2711
www.rabdf.co.uk office@rabdf.org.uk

Royal Forestry Society of England, Wales and N.I.
102 High Street, Tring, Herts. HP23 4AF 01442 822 028
www.rfs.org.uk rfshq@rfs.org.uk

Royal Highland and Agricultural Society of Scotland
Ingliston, Edinburgh EH28 8NF 0131 335 6200
www.rhass.org.uk info@rhass.org.uk

Royal Horticultural Society
80 Vincent Square, London SW1P 2PE 08452 605 000
www.rhs.org.uk info@rhs.org.uk

Royal Institution of Chartered Surveyors (RICS)
12 Great George Street, Parliament Square, London SW1P 3AD 020 7222 7000
www.rics.org contactrics@rics.org

Royal Society for the Protection of Birds
The Lodge, Sandy, Bedfordshire SG19 2DL 01767 680 551
www.rspb.org.uk

Royal Welsh Agricultural Society
Llanelwedd, Builth Wells, Powys LD2 3SY 01982 553 683
www.rwas.co.uk

Rural, Agricultural and Allied Workers Trade Group (TGWU)
Transport House, 128 Theobalds Road, Holborn, London WC1X 8TN 020 7611 2500
www.tgwu.org.uk tgwu@tgwu.org.uk

Rural Payments Agency
Kings House, 33 Kings Road, Reading RG1 3BU 0118 958 3626
www.rpa.gov.uk

Scottish Executive Environment and Rural Affairs Department (SEERAD)
Pentland House, 47 Robb's Loan, Edinburgh EH14 1TY 0131 556 8400
www.scotland.gov.uk ceu@scotland.gsi.gov.uk

Tenant Farmers' Association
5 Brewery Court, Theale, Reading, Berks. RG7 5AJ 0118 930 6130
www.tfa.org.uk tfa@tfa.org.uk

The Stationery Office
The Publications Centre, PO Box 276, London SW8 5DT 0870 600 5522
www.tso.co.uk

Ulster Farmers Union
475 Antrim Road, Belfast BT15 3DA 028 9037 0222
www.ufuni.org

United Farmers Trading Agency (UFTA) Ltd.
Hancock House, Smallgate, Beccles, Suffolk NR34 9AE. 01502 717 877

Welsh Assembly Government, Agriculture and Rural Affairs Department
Crown Offices, Cathays Park, Cardiff, CF10 3NQ   029 2082 5111
www.countryside.wales.gov.uk   webmaster@wales.gsi.gov.uk

Women's Food and Farming Union
National Agricultural Centre, Stoneleigh Park, Warks. CV8 2LZ   024 7669 3171
www.wfu.org.uk

2. University Agricultural Economics
(Farm Business Survey work)

ENGLAND AND WALES

Northern:	School of Agriculture, Food and Rural Development, University of Newcastle, Newcastle-upon-Tyne NE1 7RU	0191 222 6902
North Eastern:	Rural Business Research Unit, Askham Bryan College, Askham Bryan, York YO23 3FR	01904 772 233
East Midlands:	Rural Business Research Unit, University of Nottingham, Sutton Bonington Campus, Loughborough, Leics. LE12 5RD	0115 951 6070
Eastern:	Rural Business Unit, Centre for Rural Economics Research, 16-21 Silver Street, Cambridge CB3 9EP	01223 337 166
South Eastern:	Farm Survey Section, Imperial College London, Wye Campus, Ashford, Kent TN25 5AH	020 7594 2925
Southern:	Department of Agriculture and Food Economics The University of Reading, 4 Earley Gate, Whiteknights, PO Box 237, Reading RG6 6AR	01189 875 123
South Western:	Centre for Rural Research, The University of Exeter, Lafrowda House, St. German's Road, Exeter EX4 6TL	01392 263 836
Wales:	Institute of Rural Studies, University of Wales, Aberystwyth, Llanbadarn Campus, Aberystwyth, Ceredigion SY23 3AL	01970 622 253

SCOTLAND (SAC Farm Business Services)

Scottish Agricultural College
Regional Offices:

North:	SAC Aberdeen, Ferguson Building, Craibstone Estate, Bucksburn, Aberdeen AB21 9YA	01224 711 000
East:	SAC Edinburgh, Bush Estate, Penecuik, Midlothian, EH26 0PH	0131 535 3430
West:	SAC Auchincruive, Ayr KA6 5HW	01292 525 252

NORTHERN IRELAND (Advisory Services also)

Economics & Statistics Division, DARDNI, Dundonald House,
Upper Newtownards Road, Belfast BT4 3SB   028 9052 0100

3. Commercial Banks: Agricultural Departments

Agricultural Mortgage Corporation (AMC)
Charlton Place, Charlton Road, Andover, Hants. SP10 lRE   01264 334 747

Bank of Scotland
Agricultural Business, Chatterhall House, City Road, Chester CH88 3AN0845 3072 852
www.bankofscotland.co.uk/corporate

Barclays Bank
24th Floor, 1 Churchill Place, London, E14 5HP   020 7166 5515
www.barclays.com

Clydesdale Bank
AgriBusiness Banking Centre, 10 Fleet Place, London EC4M 7RB   020 7395 5662

Farming and Agricultural Finance Limited (FAF)
PO Box 234, Upminster, Essex RM14 2WS   0800 225 567

HSBC Bank
Agriculture Head Office, 51 De Montford Street, Leicester LE1 7BB   0116 281 8328

Lloyds TSB Group
Business Banking Agricultural, PO Box 112, Canons House,
Canons Way, Bristol BS99 7LB   0117 943 3114

National Westminster Bank
Agricultural Services, Gogaburn Business House C, PO Box 1000
Edinburgh EH12 1HQ   0131 626 0151

The Royal Bank of Scotland
Agricultural Services, Gogaburn Business House C, PO Box 1000
Edinburgh EH12 1HQ   0131 626 0151

4. Research Organisations

Biotechnology and Biological Sciences Research Council (BBSRC)
Polaris House, North Star Avenue, Swindon, Wilts. SN2 IUH   01793 413200
www.bbsrc.ac.uk

Babraham Institute
Babraham, Cambridge CB22 3AT   01223 496 000
www.babraham.ac.uk

Broom's Barn Research Station
Higham, Bury St. Edmunds, Suffolk IP28 6NP   01284 812200
                                                     Brooms.barn@bbsrc.ac.uk

CEDAR (Centre for Dairy Research)
Arborfield Hall Farm, Reading Road, Arborfield, Reading,
RG2 9HX   0118 976 0964

East Malling Research
New Road,East Malling, Kent ME19 6BJ   01732 843 833
www.emr.ac.uk   enquiries@emr.ac.uk

Elm Farm Research Centre
Hamstead Marshall, Newbury, Berkshire RG20 0HR   01488 658 298
www.efrc.com

Hannah Research Institute
Ayr, Scotland KA6 5HL   01292 477 006
www.hannahresearch.org.uk

Institute for Animal Health
Compton, Newbury, Berks. RG20 7NN   01635 578 411
www.iah.ac.uk   iah@bbsrc.ac.uk

Institute of Food Research
Norwich Research Park, Colney, Norwich NR4 7UA   01603 255 000
www.ifr.ac.uk

Institute of Grassland and Environmental Research (IGER)
Aberystwyth Research Centre, Plas Gogerddan, Aberystwyth,
Ceredigion SY23 3EB   01970 823 000
North Wyke Research Station, Okehampton, Devon EX20 2SB   01837 883 500

Kingshay Farming Trust
Bridge Farm, West Bradley, Glastonbury, Somerset BA6 8LU   01458 851 555
www.kingshay.com   contact.us@kingshay.co.uk

Macauley Land Use Research Institute
Craigiebuckler, Aberdeen AB15 8QH   01224 318 611
www.macaulay.ac.uk   enquiries@macaulay.co.uk

Morley Research Centre
Morley St. Botolph, Wymondham, Norfolk NR18 9DB   01953 713 200

NIAB
Huntingdon Road, Cambridge CB3 0LE   01223 342 200
www.niab.com   info@niab.com

Processors and Growers Research Organisation (PGRO)
The Research Station, Great North Road, Thornhaugh,
Peterborough PE8 6HJ   01780 782 585
www.pgro.org   info@prgo.com

Roslin Institute
Roslin, Midlothian EH25 9PS   0131 527 4200
www.roslin.ac.uk

Rothamsted Research
Harpenden, Hertfordshire AL5 2JQ   01582 763 133
www.rothamsted.ac.uk

Rowett Research Institute
Greenburn Road, Bucksburn, Aberdeen AB21 9SB   01224 712 751
www.rowett.ac.uk

Scottish Crop Research Institute (SCRI)
Mylnefield, Invergowrie, Dundee DD2 5DA   01382 562 731
www.scri.ac.uk   info@scri.ac.uk

The Arable Group (TAG)
Manor Farm, Lower End, Doglingworth, Cirencester, Glos. GL7 7AH   01285 652 184
www.thearablegroup.com   tag@thearablegroup.com

5. National Agricultural Colleges

Cranfield University, Silsoe Campus
Silsoe, Bedford MK45 4DT   01525 863 000
www.cranfield.ac.uk

Harper Adams University College
Edgmond, Newport, Shropshire TF10 8NB   01952 820 280
www.harper-adams.ac.uk

Institute of Rural Sciences
Llanbadarn Campus, Aberystwyth, Ceredigion SY23 3AL   01970 624 471
www.irs.aber.ac.uk   irs-enquiries@aber.ac.uk

Royal Agricultural College
Stroud Road, Cirencester, Glos. GL7 6JS   01285 652 531
www.royagcol.ac.uk

Scottish Agricultural College (student recruitment)
Auchincruive Campus, Ayr KA6 5HW   0800 269 453
www.sac.ac.uk

Shuttleworth College
Old Warden Park, Biggleswade, Beds. SG18 9EA   01767 626 222
www.shuttleworth.ac.uk   enquiries@shuttleworth.ac.uk

Writtle College
Lordship Road, Writtle, Chelmsford, Essex CM1 3RR
.www.writtle.ac.uk.

01245 424 200
.info@writtle.ac.uk.

INDEX